Bernice M. Chappel

BITTERSWEET TRAIL

An American Saga of the 1800's

GREAT LAKES BOOKS
P.O. Box 164
Brighton, Michigan 48116
1984

Margaret D

Library of Congress Catalog Card Number 84-80978

ISBN 0-9606400-1-0 Hardcover
ISBN 0-9606400-2-9 Paperback

Second printing, 1985

Cover by Doreen Consiglio

Typesetting by
ArcheType Word Processing Services
Ann Arbor, Michigan

Published by
Great Lakes Books
P.O. Box 164, Brighton, Michigan 48116

Manufactured in the United States of America

Dedicated To The Memory Of

My Maternal Ancestors

Robert and Mary Colborn

Stephen and Lucy Bennet Avery

Amos and Hannah Colborn

Jonas and Marcia Atkins Avery

James and Lucy Colborn Avery

Come with me and we'll
peer through the dusty
windows of the past as
we experience the way of
life of Michigan's pioneers.

Bernice M. Chappel
10/2/86

ACKNOWLEDGMENTS

BITTERSWEET TRAIL became a reality because of the suggestions and cooperation of the following people:

Special thanks to my husband, Kennneth F. Chappel, who was patient with my many hours of concentration as I researched and wrote BITTERSWEET TRAIL.

Special thanks to my brother, Clayton Klein and his wife, Marjorie, for their valuable suggestions and promotion of the book.

Thanks to the following relatives for supplying information about our ancestors:

Charles W. Avery
Marvin O. Avery
Arlene and Rolland Harris

Special thanks to Helen Bridger Delay for furnishing me with genealogical records of the Avery and Atkins families.

Thanks to Ida Lowe, a descendant of the Colborn family, for names and anecdotes of the early settlers.

Thanks to Librarian Dorothy Demerest and her assistants at the Brighton, Michigan Public Library for assisting me in research.

Thanks to John C. Curry, Photo Archivist of the Michigan History Division, for assistance in the selection and reproduction of photographs, and special thanks to the State Archives for allowing me to use their illustrations in BITTERSWEET TRAIL.

Thanks to Tecla Murphy of "Poor Richard's Bookshoppe" in Brighton, Michigan, for her suggestions about the cover.

Thanks to Doreen Consiglio for the cover design.

Thanks to Tom Weber of Cushing-Malloy in Ann Arbor, Michigan, for helpful suggestions.

Thanks to Patricia Williams-Gross and John Gross of ArcheType Word Processing Services in Ann Arbor, Michigan, for their assistance in helping to produce this book.

CONTENTS

ILLUSTRATIONS

All photos not otherwise credited are reproductions from the collections of the Michigan State Archives, Department of State.

PREFACE

BITTERSWEET TRAIL is a fictionalized, historical narrative of real people and their friends who lived in the 1800's. Because of the scarcity of information about their daily lives, incidents in the book may or may not be true. Some of the anecdotes are based upon rumors which have come down through the generations. I have merely enlarged upon these incidents about my ancestors and have written what may have occurred at that time.

The historical background, I believe, is accurate. The cities, villages and institutions mentioned in the novel, and the dates of historical happenings are correct. Most of the twenty photographs used in the book were secured from the State Archives of the History Department in Lansing, Michigan.

Helen Bridger Delay, a descendant of the Atkins family, kindly furnished me with genealogical records of the Avery and Atkins families. Of the Colborn family I had little information except their names and dates of birth and death, and information gleaned from an 1880 History Of Livingston County.

So, as you read BITTERSWEET TRAIL, keep in mind that though the characters were real people of the 1800's, most of the incidents likely are fiction.

Bernice M. Chappel
1984

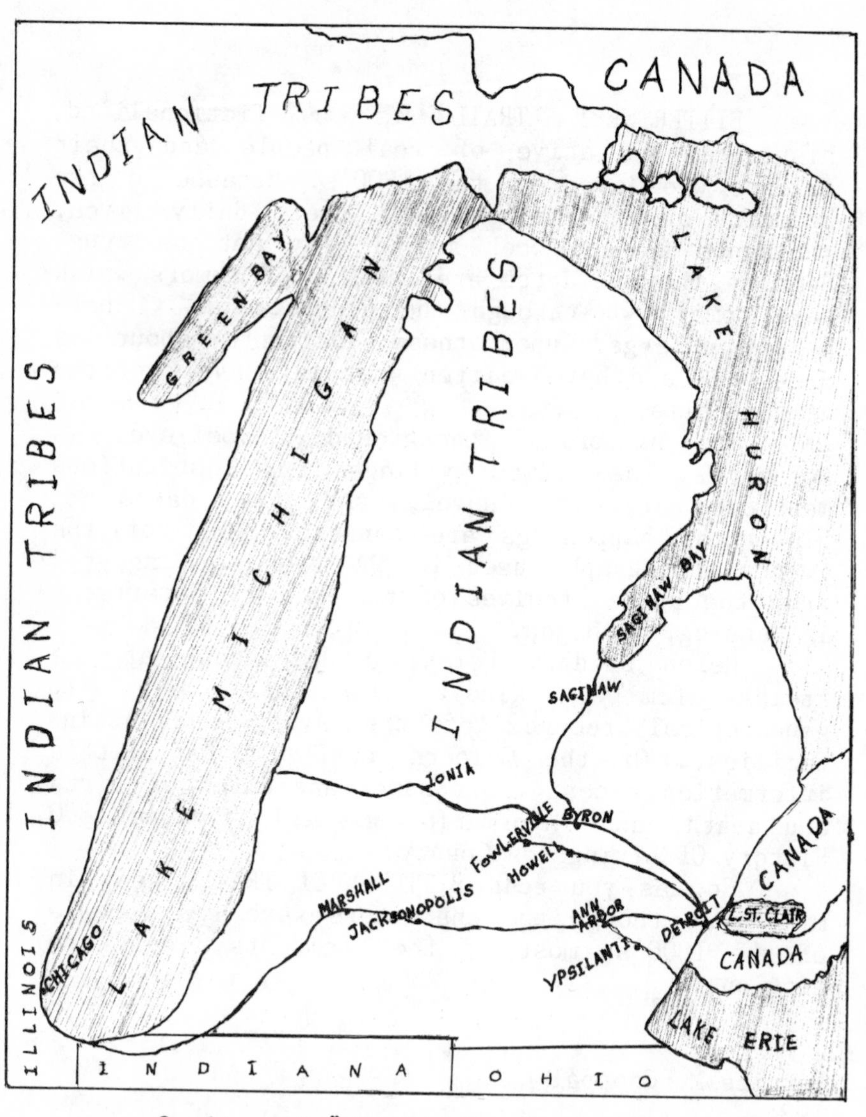

Outline of "The Tourist Pocket Map of Michigan, 1839" showing trails and settlements mentioned in BITTERSWEET TRAIL prior to 1839

Chapter I

IN SEARCH OF THE SUNRISE

(1836)

Mary Colborn parted her dark hair and plaited it into two braids which she coiled at the nape of her neck. She walked to the window of the Steamboat Hotel to stare into the half darkness of a rainy November morning. Through the mist she could see a steamboat beside the wharf at the foot of Randolph Street in the Detroit River.

Supply-filled canvas-covered wagons rolled westward through the muddy streets. Entire families bundled up against the raw wet wind huddled inside. The wide rimmed wheels cut deep tracks so that teams of horses and oxen strained to keep the wagons moving, ever fearful of a cut from the driver's whip.

Mary turned away. Tomorrow, or the day following, her family would be heading west to the government land her husband Robert had purchased July 7, 1836. Reluctantly she looked to the future which excited her husband and their elder sons, Israil and Amos. The youngest, Benjamin, who was eleven, was eager to meet Indians, but daughter Eliza at fourteen shared her mother's quiet reluctance about living in this strange wild land where bears and Indians might be unwilling to share their territory with intruders.

Mary swallowed, attempting to quiet her queasy stomach. Then, pinning a cameo brooch below the ruffle at the neck of her blue woolen dress, she gave her hair a pat as she looked around the bare one dollar per night room with its three rumpled beds and rough board floor. They'd been fortunate to find lodging. Whole families had slept on the barroom floor paying fifty cents for the space. When no other place could be found people were forced to sleep in their wagons beside the stables. She had been told there were only four small hotels in Detroit, a city with a population of five thousand.

Blowing out the candle Mary closed the door and went toward the dining room. The long table was filled with guests intent on the biscuits, johnny cake, salt pork and coffee. She wasn't hungry. The odor of salt pork made her feel nauseous.

Eliza saw her mother and motioned to an empty chair. "Where ya been, Maw?" she asked when Mary was seated. "Paw an' the boys air done eatin'. They gone to git things so we can start tomorrer."

"So soon?" There was a note of disappointment in Mary's voice. Her eyes met those of a woman across the table. The woman smiled.

"Ya've slicked up, same's me," she said touching a blonde curl that dangled below a light blue crepe turban. "Won't be any time fer fixin' ourself to look nice out there." She motioned to the west, "Or anybody to see us if'n we did." She paused. "Ya want to go?"

Mary hesitated. "My husband and boys have soft-soaped me into believin' I'll like it."

The woman nodded. "Like mine. They all got a axe to grind. They need a woman to fetch water, sew their clothes and clean and cook. Men's all alike --"

A bearded man in deerskin clothes stuffed half a biscuit into his mouth. "No use bein' ornery, ladies," he said. "Me an' my ole woman's bin in the Territory since April. She was cantankerous 'bout leavin' York state an' her kin behind. Now she's at her wits end to find time fer doin' the chores she wants. She don't say nothin' 'bout York state no more. She's took to Michigan like a duck to water. I come to Detroit to git supplies - bin gone three days. I know Sary'll be up airly to feed the baby an' milk the cow. She air a good woman, that Sary o' mine."

Eliza studied the man's clothing. "Did she make yer clothes?"

"Yep. Tanned the deerskin, and sewed it, and by gum, these clothes is better'n store bought ones. When they's too dirty, I'll thrown 'em 'way an' Sary'll sew me some more." He shoved a square of johnny cake into his mouth and got up. "Got to git a few gimcracks fer Sary and the leetle one, then I'll head west."

Mrs. Woodworth, the wife of the hotel owner, brought filled platters of the plain food and carried the empty ones to the kitchen. Refilling coffee cups, she stopped behind Mary's chair. "Ya ain't eatin', Mam." She passed the platter of salt pork to Mary. "Eat up."

"Thank ya. I'll jest have some 'a the johnny cake," Mary answered.

"How'd you ladies sleep last night?" Mrs. Woodworth asked wiping her hands on a soiled apron. "Did yer hear the ruckus in the street? Couple 'a drunk fellers got into a fight an' they was kickin' an' fightin' in the mud. Ben, my husband, said they likely roused ever'body in the hotel."

"I heerd 'em," Eliza said.

"When they's drunk some of 'em air hellers. Ben says they hesh up sooner if'n ya jest leave 'em be. Lan' sakes, I duno why most men gits mean an' noisy when they's drinkin'. Ya'd think they'd larn shootin' off their mouth jest makes a big ruckus 'cause none of 'em won't take no sass off'n a'body."

Mary shoved her chair back. "Eliza, less us go to that Disbrow's dry goods store we seen last night. If'n we don't git cloth now, Lord knows when there'll be 'nother chanct."

Mrs. Woodworth explained, "Go west on Woodbridge to Woodward. Ya'll see the market. Go 'cross Jefferson an' Disbrow's is on the corner. Ya could walk to the Capitol, too. 'Taint far. Ya might see Tom Mason - he's Governor of Michigan Territory, an' only twenty-four." She looked meaningfully at Eliza, who at fourteen appeared several years older. "He ain't married. Ya can't tell. He might take a shine to ya." The landlady and the few remaining guests smiled as the girl's attractive round face flushed blood-red. Silently she followed her mother who called to Mrs. Woodworth that they would be back for the noon meal.

Mary glanced at the clock in the lobby. "Ha'past eight," she said. "Lide, git our wraps and bonnets an' we'll see what Detroit's like. More'n likely we won't never git here ag'in."

A few minutes later they went down the rough board steps of the Steamboat Hotel to the mud-covered wooden sidewalk. The rain had stopped but a light fog hung over the city. Mary fastened her coat against the damp November air as they picked their way across muddy Randolph Street to the sidewalk on Woodbridge. Continuing west past Bates Street, they reached Woodward.

Mary stopped to inspect her muddy shoes. "This mud is turrible. We've spiled our good shoes an' we jest started."

"Ain't no use't to go back," Eliza said. "They's plumb spiled now. Maw, ya've got mud on the hem o' yer good dress."

"Law! So I have! Well, no use't to cry over spilt milk!" They turned to the right on to Detroit's main street, Woodward. Near the end of the block at the intersection of Jefferson, a fruit and vegetable market bordered the street. Potatoes, squash, pumpkins, onions, carrots, turnips, cabbage and apples were arranged in rows of crates near the edge of the muddy street. The French speaking farmers shouted out their prices in loud broken English.

"Maybe Paw'll buy some taters an' veg'tables 'fore we go," Eliza said. "Who air them people?"

Mary answered, "Them's Frenchmen. They's Catholic."

"Oh-h-h. Look, Maw, there's Disbrow's." Eliza pointed across Jefferson to the sign above the door. Disbrow's Dry Goods.

"Might's well wait 'til we come back to git cloth," Mary said as she studied a stylishly dressed couple whose horse splashed through the soft mud pulling the now familiar wide-rimmed two-wheeled cart commonly used in the muddy streets. The cart had an open box with benches set lengthwise, and a tailgate which could be opened. Some of the vehicles carried people while others transported goods. Matrons bowed to friends and acquaintances on the sidewalk. Some conducted business with the French market owners from the carts.

Mary and Eliza paused at the intersection of Woodward and Jefferson. "They's nice stores here, Maw. Here's King's Clothing Store, 'n acrost the street is Thomas Clark's Drug Store."

"We'll come back to the stores after dinner. We might's well see the town this mornin'. Fasten yer wrap, Lide. Ya'll catch yer death o' cold."

Eliza pulled her coat together. "Air we goin' to the Capitol?"

"I reckon 'tis all right. I wisht yer Paw er Amos er Israil was with us."

"They done took off airly with Ben. Mebbe we'll see 'em some'eres. Ya know where the Capitol is?"

Mary shook her head. Suddenly a dark-haired dark-skinned boy appeared at her elbow. "Ze Capitol, Meesus?" he asked.

Mary nodded. In a glance she recognized a bright energetic child beneath the ragged clothing. His bare muddy toes protruded from worn shoes.

"Me show you. Two pence?" He looked hopefully into Mary's compassionate blue eyes.

She smiled. "Show us."

The child ran a dozen steps and said something to one of the farmers at the market. He glanced toward Mary and Eliza and nodded to the boy.

"Thees way." He carried his head and shoulders proudly above the tattered clothing. They waited as several carts passed on Jefferson. At last the boy led them across the street and north along Woodward and across Larned. Here Woodward sloped downward toward a wooden bridge over a slow moving muddy stream only a few inches deep.

The boy pointed. "Savoyard Creek." He held his nose. "Smells vereey bad." They hurried over the bridge. Again the boy pointed, this time to the east. "Churches," he said.

They passed the Presbyterian and Episcopal churches on the east side of Woodward. He pointed to a building around the corner.

Eliza exclaimed, "Maw! They's a Methodist church!"

"'Tis nice," Mary said, "an' real big." She spoke to the boy. "Is yer church near here?"

"Over zere on ze nex' street. Zee Saint Anne's Catholic Church. Eet ees beeg!"

Mary nodded. "What be yer name?"

"Pierre LeBlanc. Mon père, my father, hee's Jacque LeBlanc. We leeve by zee reever," he pointed to the southeast toward the Detroit River.

They arrived at a park-like circle where streets came together at angles. "Thees ees Campus Martius." He stretched his arms, one pointing northwest, the other southeast. "Thees is Woodward Street." Turning, he stretched his arms east and west. "Meechigan Street," he said, "an' over zere ees Munro."

"Monroe," Mary repeated. "See, Lide? The streets meet in this park. It's a wheel and the park is the hub."

Pierre laughed. "A wheel! Zat ees right!"

They crossed the park. Several small groups of men stood talking. They heard Tom Mason's name mentioned as they entered the intersection of Griswold and Michigan.

Pierre pointed up Griswold to a frame two-story building. A square tower with a cupola reached high into the air. "Ees zee Capitol," he smiled.

Michigan's First Capitol at Detroit

Jefferson Avenue at Griswold in 1837

Governor Stevens T. (Tom) Mason

Detroit in 1837

"It's in the middle of the street!" Eliza exclaimed.

"Non, Mees. Griswold Street, she end by zee Capitol."

In a few minutes they stood before the well-built two-story white structure. Six columns graced the southward facing front. It was an elegant appearing building uncommon in Detroit at the time.

"Can - can we go in?" Eliza asked Pierre.

The boy flashed a smile that revealed white, even teeth. "Oui. Governor Tom Mason, he like people to veesit. Come, I show you."

"Ya think we should?" Mary asked.

Eliza opened the gate in the black iron fence that surrounded the building. "I'm goin'. Whyn't ya come, Maw?"

Somewhat reluctantly, Mary followed the two young people up the steps into the ninety by sixty foot building. The hall was rather dark, the only light coming from windows at either end, and from a few open doors. A meeting room bore the sign, "TERRITORIAL COUNCIL". A table surrounded by thirteen chairs was centered in the room.

"Zee men, zey have meeting here," Pierre explained. Soon he led them upstairs and pointed to a high door. Before he could speak the door opened and a handsome tall young man stepped into the hall. He stopped when he saw the boy.

"Mornin', Pierre. You brought us more visitors. Madam - and Miss, I'm Tom Mason." He held out his hand.

"How - de - doo," Mary bowed. "I'm Mary Colborn and this is my girl, Eliza." They shook hands.

"Do you live in the Territory?"

"Our family - my husband, three boys and Eliza, we start for our land in the mornin'."

"Where is your land?"

"Livingston County - up in the nor'west corner."

"Take you three, four days to get out there?"

"We duno. We heered the roads is bad."

Governor Mason nodded. "'Tis likely. Rain has been heavy this fall." He held out his hand. "Glad you stopped to see us. I hope the trip to Livingston is pleasant." He turned to the boy. "Show the ladies around, Pierre."

"Oui, Governor. I'll show zem zee jail."

"Ah, the jail - I think they won't want to go inside, Pierre."

"Oui, Governor. And I will take zem aside zee reever where steamboats ees."

"Perhaps they came to Detroit on a steamboat."

"No," Eliza hurried to say. "We come through Canada from York State. My paw and two big brothers druve three wagons - a team of horses and two yoke a' oxen. We jest took the ferry acrost the river from Windsor yestiddy night."

"We're keepin' ya from yer work," Mary apologized. "Come, Eliza and Pierre. We're right proud we met ya, Governor."

The young man smiled and entered an office with a sign, "TERRITORIAL SECRETARY", beside the door.

Two short blocks to the northeast they stood before the two-story jail which was nearly as large as the Capitol. A high wooden fence surrounded the building.

"Bad place," Pierre commented.

"What does people do to git put in there?" Eliza asked.

Pierre's eyes were sad, almost with a frightened look as he answered. "Zey make beeg noise in zee streets when zey ees drunk, or zey fight, or zey don't pay money zey owe. Indians, zey ees put in jail when zey ees drunk in zee town." He shook his head. "Ver-r-y bad place."

"Has ya been inside?"

"Oui. My uncle, he ees zere. I go see heem."

"What did he do?"

"He fight. He was drunk. He hurt zee man bad. Zee man, he die."

"That's turrible," Mary said. "Your uncle's in jail now?"

Pierre nodded. "Ver-r-y bad place. Zee rooms

ees leetle. He jest set an' set. Zere ees nozin' to do. Sometimes zee men ees whipped. Zee food ees bad, too."

Eliza asked, "Will your uncle get out sometime?"

Pierre shook his head. "We duno - ver-ry bad zat zee man die." They were silent. After a time Pierre went on. "My father tell me zat when I was four year old a man wass hung here."

"What had he done?"

"Zee man, he was ver-ry mad. He wass drunk, too. He hit hees wife an' he keel her. Hees name was Seemons."

"Simons?" Mary inquired.

"Yes, Seemons. Zee court say Seemons have to die, but nobody want to do eet, not even zee sheriff. Ben Woodworth, he say he do eet."

Mary gasped. "The Ben Woodworth that owns the Steamboat Hotel?"

Pierre nodded. "He ees zee one. He had board seats put over zere." He pointed to a spot in front of the jail facing Fort Gratiot Road. "My father, he say zere wass a band and peoples zey come wiz peeknik baskets, and zey push to get zee best place so zey can see zee man die. My father say some men in zee crowd wass drunk. Zee band played and Ben Woodworth wiz two of zee jail guards, zey breeng out zee man, Seemons. Zee people on zee board seats, zey cheered."

"Cheered!" Eliza exclaimed.

"Yess. Zey cheered. Seemons hands wass tied. Zey lead heem to zee high platform with a trap door in zee floor. A post had zee rope hanging down. Zey put zee rope 'round hees neck. Zey read to heem why he must die. He say he ees sorry an' zee trap door, eet opens, and Seemons, he fall through. He die. Eet break hees neck. Zee band play loud an' zee people cheer. My father, he don' like our city - Detroit, to keel people."

Mary asked, "But they don't put people to death now in Michigan Territory?"

Pierre shook his head. "Governor Mason - he not

like. My father, he say Seemon's hanging wass zee last one."

"Air ya sure Ben Woodworth was the man who done the hangin'?"

"My father say he ees. Woodworth make much money zat day at zee Steamboat Hotel. It wass not like now. Zere wass not many new people in Detroit. Woodworth's hotel was full zat day."

Eliza stared at the jail. "I don't like this place." She turned. "Less go."

Pierre led them southeast across muddy intersections until they came to Saint Anne's Catholic Church at the corner of Bates and Larned. "Thees ees my church," he said proudly.

"'Tis a beautiful church, Pierre," Mary said sincerely. "Eliza, look at them two tall towers with gold crosses on the top."

"Want to go eenside? Eet ees pretty."

"Maybe we shouldn't. We ain't Catholic."

"You could jest look een. Come."

Reluctantly Mary followed Pierre and Eliza. He held the door and they stepped over the heavy oak threshold. The church was dark and chilly. Statues in niches along the side looked almost alive. Mary and Eliza recognized one of Mary and the Baby Jesus, and another of Jesus as an adult. Candles flickered on the raised, gold-trimmed altar. No one spoke. Several women were kneeling in prayer, their lips moving silently as they fingered their rosaries. Soon they returned to the street.

"We ain't never bin in a Catholic church 'afore," Mary explained to Pierre. "We're Methodists."

The boy pointed. "Zere's zee Methodist church over zere. We wass on zee other side of eet zess mornin'."

"Yer church air prettier," Eliza remarked grudgingly.

Pierre smiled and nodded. "Does you want to see zee wharf? Zere might be a sheep in."

"A sheep?" Eliza asked.

"A boat."

Mary and Eliza smiled. "Less go, Maw. We didn't see much last night. 'Twas almost dark when we come."

They slowly picked their way through muddy intersections onto the wooden sidewalks filled with dozens of people. There were bearded men, some dressed in deerskin clothes, a few women carrying parcels or baskets of vegetables from the market, society ladies with exquisite hats and outer wraps, children following their mothers or holding to their skirts, businessmen and government officials in suits with white shirts and wide-brimmed black hats. Numerous Indians and French people mingled with the frontier men who dressed in the accepted shirt and knicker-type pantaloons above knee-high knitted socks and heavy low shoes. Though each was different in some way, they all had one trait in common - their shoes were caked with mud.

There were many carts and wagons in the streets. Eliza wondered how many of these people were going into the Michigan wilderness to make their homes.

"Zere ees zee Steamboat Hotel," Pierre announced as they crossed Jefferson. We go down Randolph to zee wharf."

As they made their way toward the river, Mary asked, "Do ya go to school?"

Pierre shook his head. "My father don' have zee money. I have seex brothers an' two seesters. You has to pay zee money to go to zee school." He paused. "But I can read some words," he said proudly.

"Yer a smart boy," Mary said. "Ya will larn."

A few minutes later they stood on the bank of the mile wide Detroit River. Across the water the buildings of Windsor, Ontario, Canada were visible.

"Windsor ees new name," Pierre pointed. "Wass Reechmond until thees year."

"Richmond?" Mary inquired.

"Yess. Zey change zee name. See! Zere ees steamboat coming. Eet ees zee Commodore Perry! She ees nice sheep!"

They watched as the ship was maneuvered near the dock and the gang plank let down. People poured off and scattered into the streets.

"Where'll they find places to sleep?" Mary wondered.

"Zey come one day an' zey go zee nex'. Zey don't stay. Like you," Pierre said.

"Do ya think they air goin' to homes in the wilderness?" Eliza asked.

"Some of zem air," Pierre replied.

Mary rummaged in her handbag. "Pierre, ya air a good guide." She pressed a shilling into his hand.

"Eet ees too much, Madam. I say two pence."

"Buy something ya ain't got." She patted his shoulder.

The boy bowed. "Zank you, Madam. I weel buy shoes." He looked down at his muddy toes protruding from the worn shoes.

Goodbyes were said and Mary and Eliza returned to the Steamboat Hotel. The men were in their room washing up for dinner. A wash stand, a large pitcher of water, a wash bowl and a bucket for the dirty water served their needs.

"Where ya bin, Maw?" Eleven-year-old Benjamin asked.

Mary removed her bonnet and smoothed her hair. "Gallivantin'."

Eliza interrupted. "We traipsed all over. We seen the market, an' the jail an' the Capitol - an' we seen Governor Tom Mason!"

"Mason?" Robert, Israil and Amos exclaimed in unison.

"He's right handsome," Eliza said softly.

Amos and Israil guffawed. "Ain't settin' yer cap fer him air ya, Lide?" Amos teased.

Eliza's face turned crimson. Mary spoke quickly. "He's a right nice gent'man, an' Lide ain't lookin' for no man yit."

"'Twon't be long 'fore Michigan's a state," Amos said. "'Tis likely Mason'll be the first state governor. He's a good territorial governor."

"Wherever we was this mornin' somebody allus had good things to say 'bout Mason," Israil remarked. "His family come here a few years back. His father, John, was Territorial Secretary. Tom was young - 'bout eighteen. He's a hot headed cuss an' he uses his fists if'n he needs to, but he has good sense."

Amos took up the story. "The blacksmith said ole man Mason didn't like Detroit - they was from Virginney and was friends of high munky-munks like Henry Clay an' Andrew Jackson. So John Mason quit an' Tom become Secretary of the Territory. He was only nineteen."

Benjamin jumped up from the bed where he'd been sitting with Amos. "Tell Maw an' Lide 'bout the cholera!"

"Yew tell 'em," Robert said as he walked to the window to look out over the misty river.

Ben stood straight. "Well - some ships come to Detroit with soldiers on 'em. They was goin' up north. 'Twas when they was fightin' some Indian war som'eers."

Amos said, "'Twas July 1832. The Black Hawk War in Illinoy an' Wisconsin."

"Ain't that far off?" Mary asked.

"Yeah, but the ships could go 'round northern Michigan from Lake Huron into Lake Michigan an' then they went south all the way to Chicago, where they landed."

Benjamin broke in. "When the ships got here some a' the soldiers was sick. They was took to a doctor and 'leven died the first night. Then more of 'em an' more of 'em got it an' they died so fast they couldn't bury 'em. Dead men was put on the ground by the dock 'til they could bury 'em." He pointed from the window. "See that buildin' there beside the dock? It was one of the hospitals. People all over Detroit was skeered an' some of 'em left t' git away from the sickness."

"The officers made the ships go 'way so more soldiers couldn't git off. They went to an island out there - Hog Island - then they went on to -"

"Port Huron," Robert volunteered. "When the ship stopped for wood at Port Huron to stoke the boilers more a' the soldiers took the chanct to run off. Some a' them had cholera an' them fellers died in the woods. Here in Detroit the sickness spread like wildfire. 'Twas worse 'n the ague, 'cause more of 'em died. Nobody knew what to do to stop it. The top floor of the Capitol was used for a hospital. A cart went up an' down the streets day an' night with a man that called, 'Bring out your dead'."

"Laws! How many died?" Mary asked.

"More'n a hunnert died in July an' August in '32."

"'N it spread all acrost the territory," Amos added. "Some towns had guards to stop stagecoaches and other travelers. Out to a place called Ypsilanti the driver wouldn't stop an' the guard shot one a' the horses. But the cholera spread jest the same. 'Way out to a leetle place called Marshall where they was seventy people, eighteen got cholera an' eight of 'em died in a week. Folk all over the territory was skeered."

Israil took up the story. "It spread fastest where the French lives along the river. That's where the poor folk air. I guess they air dirty."

Lide said, "Maw an' me got t' know a leetle French boy."

Mary nodded. "Poor leetle feller."

Amos said, "The old sick folk died first. The Mason family's cook, Granny Peg, died in the arms of Tom Mason's sister, the blacksmith said."

"Folk died so fast," Israil went on, "that they couldn't dig graves. In one big grave thirty bodies was buried."

"Mercy!" Mary exclaimed.

Ben said, "The blacksmith says all the folk on

the street wore masks over their mouth an' nose, 'cause nobody knows how ya git it."

Israil commented, "When cool weather come in the fall, the sickness stopped."

"Has it come back agin?" Eliza asked.

"Uh-uh, not 'till 1834, two year ago," Robert answered. "'Twas worse 'n the first time. In August that year three hunnert twenty people died."

"Don't forgit what the priests done," Amos said. "In '32 Father Gabriel Richard helped the poor folk. He took care o' them an' went to the dying ones. He didn't stop to eat er sleep. Then he died, too."

"Cholera?" Mary asked.

"They don't think 'twas. He was plumb wore out, an' he was old - sixty-five."

Amos continued. "The second time cholera come, Father Martin Kundig helped. He worked wherever he could, an' ag'in the cholera stopped in September."

"That was jest over a year ago," Mary said. "It might come back nex' summer."

"It might." Robert thoughtfully rubbed his hand over his bearded chin. "Tom Mason got people to clean up 'round their cabins. He tole 'em to take baths an' to keep theirselves clean. They's a creek near here, Savoyard, they calls it, that folk dump slop pails and things into. Mason had that cleaned out, but folk still dump slop pails into the creek. Nobody knows where cholera comes from."

"I'm hungry!" Ben said. "Ain't it 'bout dinner time?"

Robert took out his pocket watch. "The table likely air full now. We can go purty soon. The boys an' me fed and watered the horses an' oxen after breakfast. Them beasts put away a dollars worth o' hay since we got here."

Eliza said, "We're leavin' tomorrer, ain't we?"

"Yeah. Got the horses and oxen shod this mornin', an' we have some tools to git yit - saws, axes an' small things." Robert walked to the door. "Mebbe we better go eat."

Eliza got up. "Maw an' me air goin' to Disbrow's after dinner. We air goin' to git yards an' yards o' cloth, ain't we, Maw?"

Mary smiled. "We air goin' to git some."

In the dining room they found six empty chairs at the long table. Robert sat beside a man with fire-red hair and whiskers. Next to him was a boy who resembled the older man.

"Good afternoon," the man said. The voice was soft and calm. "I am Stephen Avery, and this is my son, Jonas." The boy nodded.

"Afternoon," Robert answered. "We air the Colborns." He pointed to each of the family as he introduced them, and in turn, each bowed slightly and muttered, "How-de-doo."

"Where be ya from?" Robert asked.

"Way back in 1823 we lived in Keene, New York. My wife Lucy and I had been married five years and we had three children, Albert, Jonas and Mary Ann. I like to go to new places. Guess it comes from reading about them. Anyway Lucy and I were ready for adventure, so we sold our farm, packed up and bought land near London, Ontario, Canada. We stayed there until 1835 when we came to Michigan. By that time we had two more little girls."

"Ya has five children?" Robert asked.

Stephen nodded, his blue eyes twinkling. "Two boys and three girls. Where are you headed?"

"Livingston County, township of Iena."

Stephen and Jonas stopped eating. "We're from Handy township in Livingston County!" Stephen exclaimed.

"Handy," Amos said, "Ain't that out beyond Livingston Centre?"

"It's west of Livingston Centre. Maybe you didn't know they've changed the name to Howell now." He laughed. "It's hard to remember, so it goes by both names."

"Ya've bin in Michigan two year. Have much land cleared?" Robert asked.

Stephen nodded. "Jonas and my other son, Albert, and I have several acres pretty well cleared. There's still a few stumps to get out, but we work around them. We had good wheat and corn crops last year. This year it was too dry in the summer. All the rain came this fall. Farming is a gamble."

"Yer wife," Mary asked, "Don't she miss York State?"

"When we first went to Canada she was lonely, but now she is as happy as I am that we are conquering the Michigan wilderness."

Jonas said, "My mother didn't like Canada. The folks there don't want Yankees living near them. They remember the War of 1812. Ma was glad to leave Canada." His blue eyes sparkled in his freckled face. "My brother Albert and I wouldn't want to go back to York State. It's hard work here, but there's hunting and fishing whenever we have time. Sometimes we get a bear, and the township pays a bounty on wolves."

"Wolves!" Eliza exclaimed. She looked at her father and brothers. "Nobody said nothin' 'bout wolves!"

Amos smiled. "Ya'll git used to 'em."

A man across the table joined in the conversation. "Oh, yeah. They's wolves galore. Some nights when they gits to howlin' all together, it sounds like a choir 'er somethin'."

Mary shuddered. "I swan, it makes chills go up my back." The men laughed.

Mary went on. "An' Injuns - air they friendly?"

Stephen Avery replied. "They're not what I'd call friendly, but I've never heard of their doing harm to settlers. They keep to themselves unless they want whiskey. We don't have any at our home, and they know it, so they don't bother us. Liquor makes them wild and crazy."

A man across the table spoke forcefully. "'Twasn't many year ago they was killin' an' scalpin' whites. I'd sooner trust bears an' wolves than them red devils!"

Stephen glanced at Mary and Eliza. Their terror-filled eyes prompted him to reassure them. "Ladies," he said, "I give you my word, I've not heard of a family in Livingston County that's been harmed by Indians." He turned to Robert. "When are you heading west?"

"Tomorrer mornin' - airly."

"We're going back then, too, if we get our supplies today. I bought a team of horses for Jonas this morning. He's been driving oxen, but he works hard, and he wants horses."

"Mebbe we can git more horses in a year er two if our crops is good," Israil said.

Stephen looked at the Colborn men. "We have been here a year and know the ropes. Would you like for us to drive west with you part way, say to Howell?"

"We'd thank ya kindly," Robert answered, "but we take the north fork o' the Grand River Trail out west o' Detroit a few miles."

Stephen nodded. "I've heard it's a better road than the south trail. We could travel together as far as Hannibal Inn. That's where the trail forks."

"Thank ya kindly," Robert replied.

Chapter II

JOURNEY THROUGH THE WILDERNESS

(1836)

Robert wakened with a start. He couldn't recall where he was. Then he remembered and springing from bed beside Benjamin he shouted, "Boys! Israil! Amos! Git up!" He pulled his trousers on and went to the window.

The young men swung their feet onto the bare floor. As they dressed Amos said, "We're well nigh ready, Paw. We'll feed the critters and milk the cow 'afore breakfast."

Ben ran to the window. "It ain't rainin'," he announced. "I can feed the hens an' Sam an' ole Squealer same's I did when we come 'cross Canada. An' I can milk Bossy, too."

As soon as the others left, Mary and Eliza got up. Mary stood a moment, then she sat down on the edge of the bed. Eliza hurriedly threw on her clothes. Turning, she spoke to her mother.

"Maw, we gotta git stuff packed 'afore they're ready fer breakfast!"

Mary rubbed her head. "I knows," she said wearily. Suddenly she rushed to the waste water pail. Bending over it, she retched and strained as beads of sweat appeared on her forehead.

"Maw! Ya air sick!"

Mary continued retching great wrenching heaves. She gasped and set the pail down. Seeing Eliza's worried look, she said softly, "I'll be all right purty soon." She got to her feet and started to dress.

"But what ails ya?"

Mary smiled. "'Tain't nothin'. Jest an upsot

stummik." She bent to fasten her heavy shoes. "Don't say nothin' to Paw er the boys."

"I don't rightly see why not!"

"Jest 'cause I don't want 'em t' know." She hesitated. "They got 'nuff on their minds gittin' us an' our stuff out to the new land."

"Feelin' better?"

Mary stuffed packages of the yard material they had purchased into a gunny sack with her blue woolen dress and Eliza's brown one. "I'll be all right." She ran the comb through her long hair.

Eliza went to the window. "The sun's gonna shine."

"Mebbe 'tis a good sign that things will be all right with us."

An hour later the loaded wagons pulled away from the stable. Stephen Avery and Jonas led the way with the new team tied to the back of the wagon. Next came Amos walking beside the yoke of oxen pulling a load of farm tools and furniture. Third in line was Israil, the wagon piled high with barrels of corn, wheat and oats. At the back of the wagon there was a crate of twenty chickens, and inside a wooden crate a red Duroc sow with drooping ears grunted and complained. Tied to the back of the wagon a red and white Ayrshire cow and heifer followed meekly. Last in line was the Colborns' only team of horses driven by Robert. Benjamin sat on the driver's seat beside his father, while Mary and Eliza found seats inside the covered wagon among barrels of cornmeal, flour, dishes, clothing and pots and pans. Sam, the mongrel dog, ran from wagon to wagon, barking sharply.

The men were jubilant. "Giddap!" Robert shouted to his matched black team. The wagon moved slowly behind the three ahead. "We'll stop at the market an' git a couple barrels a' 'taters. It's a measly shame ourn wa'nt no good back in York State." His eyes sparkled with anticipation of the adventure ahead.

"Ya might git some cabbages an' carrots an'

turnips, too," Mary added.

Other wagons were lined up ahead of them at the market on Woodward.

"Paw!" Eliza called. "The feller at the far end is Pierre's paw. Whyn't ya git the stuff frum him?" Her father nodded.

Half an hour later the little procession was on its way toward the western outskirts of Detroit. The wagons jolted over the bumpy uneven road. Pots and pans clattered, the sow squealed, the chickens cackled and the dog barked. Occasionally the cow or heifer bawled as though they objected to being led.

Now and then Amos or Israil shouted, "Gee!" or "Haw!" as they walked to the left of their oxen.

Inside Robert's wagon Mary and Eliza rocked and jolted with the motion of the springless vehicle. Eliza watched her mother anxiously. Finally she said softly, "Do yer head hurt?"

Mary brushed back a straggly lock of dark hair. She smiled weakly. "The waggin rocks sideways an' up an' down. It makes my stummik sick, but I'll be all right after a bit."

Eliza shook her head. "I wisht we was back home. I'm afeard to be goin' out in them woods with wolves an' Injuns an' - an' my maw feelin' poorly."

Mary smiled. "'Tain't nothin' much wrong with me. When we git to our place there'll be work to do. Then I'll plumb forgit all 'bout feelin' poorly."

Robert and Benjamin were discussing ways the boy could help after they arrived at the Colborn land. "They'll be work fer all of us," Robert said. "Cold weather ain't fur off. Us men'll build a shelter fer the critters while yer maw an' Lide git stuff put away in the shanty."

"Yeah, Paw. But what kin I do?"

"Ya kin water the critters. They's a nice leetle stream that runs near the shanty. 'Tis yer work to water the critters an' feed Squealer an' the chickens, an' sometimes ya'll milk Bossy - an'

Maw'll want ya to help her."

The miles passed slowly on the narrow Indian trail which was bordered by water-filled ditches. When two wagons met, one would pull to the side and stop until the other passed. Sometimes the drivers greeted one another with news about deep mud holes in the road, or of a tavern that might have lodging for the night.

Soon after the Colborns and Avery's were outside Detroit, the Michigan wilderness closed in, the leafless trees arching over the narrow trail.

At noon they stopped beside a creek for a quick lunch packed that morning by Mrs. Woodworth. Gathered about Robert's wagon they ate the bread and cold sliced ham and drank water dipped from the creek. Mary poured a container of milk. Everyone drank from the quart dipper and passed it on.

"Old Bossy's milk tastes good," Ben said. "She kicked like blazes when I milked her this mornin'."

Amos wolfed down a thick slab of ham. He wiped his mouth on the back of his hand. "It's like when Jim Smith asked his friend Pat if his cow give much milk. Pat said, 'No, ya sorta have to take it 'way frum 'er.'"

Everyone laughed. "That's like Bossy," Ben said.

"How fur is it to Hannibal's Inn?" Robert asked Stephen Avery.

The man stroked his red beard. "I reckon we'll be there by three o'clock."

"That's airly to stop fer the night," Israil said.

"Yeah," his father answered, "but after we turn on the North Grand River Trail, there ain't no more taverns."

"You might do well to stop, get a good night's sleep, and leave early in the morning," Stephen said.

"Makes me think of 'nother joke," Amos began. "Joe said to Tom, 'I ain't slept fer ten days.'

So Tom says, 'Ain't ya tired?' 'Naw,' Joe says, 'I sleep nights.'"

As the men laughed Eliza said to her mother, "Amos is happy as a lark today." Mary nodded.

Stephen asked, "Are there other settlers near your place in Iena Township?"

"Nope," Robert replied. "We air the first. Onct this summer while Israil an' me was buildin' our leetle shanty, we heerd hammerin' an' we went to find out where 'twas comin' frum. 'Twas the Parsons group. They claimed land in June this year 'afore I filed my claim. They've built a cabin, but they ain't livin' in it yit. The father, Cecil D. Parsons, an' his three sons took up more'n a thousand acres."

"How far would they be from your land?"

"I duno. Mebbe three, four miles, as the crow flies. When the boys and their wives and young'uns, an' Cecil an' Mrs. Parsons git to livin' there, they'll have a nice leetle settlement."

Stephen smiled. "You've got a couple of young men here, and a young son and daughter. When they marry, you'll have a nice little settlement too."

Israil laughed. "'Twill be slim pickin' out there in the woods, 'less we kin find a couple a squaws, an' a young brave fer Lide."

"We could do worse," Amos added. "They say squaws is hard workers. They's used to raisin' crops and cookin'. I duno about the Injun men."

Mary spoke up quickly. "We ain't marryin' Lide off to no Injun! Besides, she ain't lookin' fer no man!"

"'Specially no Injun!" Lide exclaimed. "I'd be scared to death we'd all git scalped!"

Amos picked up the stick he used to guide the oxen. "We better git goin'," he announced walking to the left of the pair.

Three hours later they crossed the Rouge River and soon the procession pulled in at Hannibal Inn on the north side of Grand River Trail. Israil, Stephen and Ben went to inquire about lodging.

They were early so there were no problems.

While the men cared for the animals at the stable, Mary and Eliza went to the bare room the family would share for the night. Mary glanced about. The complete furnishings were three quilt-covered beds, and a wash bench with a small mirror above it.

She went to the window. Dark woods crowded close to the stables behind the tavern. Chickens scratched in the manure pile in the barn yard and quacking ducks searched for food in the bottom of mud puddles. A pole-fence pen held a dozen grunting pigs wallowing in the six-inch-deep mud.

Mary turned from the window. "Ya know we might not find 'nother inn 'til we come to Byron."

Eliza gasped. "Ya mean we'll have to sleep in the woods?"

"Like they say, we'll cross that bridge when we comes to it. But when yer paw an' Israil come back frum buildin' the shanty there wasn't no inn 'tween Byron an' here."

"Mebbe somebody's built one by now."

"Mebbe. But we slept in the woods in Canada an' nothin' bothered us."

"Yeah, but I was skeered."

Before long the men came in and washed. "We're goin' down to the saloon fer a bit," Robert said. "Stephen an' Jonas will be there."

Mary frowned, but said nothing until Ben started to follow his father.

"Ya stay here with us," she called after him.

Robert turned quickly. "Let the boy alone, Mary. He belongs with men - not wimmin!"

Mary bit her lip.

Jonas and his father were waiting in the saloon, each with a mug on the table in front of him.

"'Tis good to stop early," Stephen greeted them. "We've all got two, three hard days ahead of us."

The tavern keeper took the Colborns' orders for beer. When they were served, he said, "The boy want somethin'?"

"Naw," Robert answered. "'Twill soon be time fer supper." The man spoke to the Averys. "Beer fer you?"

Stephen picked up his mug. "No, the tea is all."

Israil asked, "Ya don't like beer?"

"We don't use fermented drinks."

"What's fermented mean?" Amos asked.

"Whiskey, beer, anything with malt or grain that has worked."

"H-m-m-m," Robert said slowly. "I thought all men liked liquor. 'Course my wife is agin' it - like most wimmin."

Stephen nodded. "My family believes liquor isn't good for a person, and that we ought not to eat or drink things that are bad for us."

"Hm-m-m-m," Robert said again. Changing the subject, he asked, "How big a parcel a land did ya buy?"

"Bought an eighty. Paid three dollars an acre. In a few years, when it's cleared, we'll likely sell out and go somewhere else - maybe to Ingham County."

"We have ninety acres," Robert explained between sips of beer. "Paid two dollars an acre in July. Prices air goin' up."

Amos commented, "Me and Israil wants to buy land soon's we git some money together."

"This is a great time to be living," Stephen said. "If a man's willing to work, there's money to be made. And we are shaping the future of Michigan." He hesitated a moment. "There's something I don't like though. We're taking the land away from the Indians - just pushing them out of their hunting grounds."

"That don't bother me none," Israil said. "They's land enough fer them an' us, too. An' if they's too many a' us, they kin move north."

A man at the next table commented, "I'd ruther have Injuns than Jews. They air shysters, allus schemin' to git somethin' fer nothin'."

"They're smart," Stephen admitted, "but they've

had to be if they survived. They have always been an unwanted people - even in Bible times."

"Yeah?" Amos asked.

"That's what the Bible says."

"Us Colborn men don't know the Bible much. Maw reads it most ever' day, though."

Jonas spoke to Ben. "You won't be going to school in Michigan. Will you like that?"

Ben's smile spread wide. "Yeah. But Maw says Lide and me will have to study at home. I kin read and figger. That's all I need, ain't it, Paw?"

Robert shook his head. "Ya can't have too much larnin'. Yer Maw's right."

"In our family," Jonas said, "we have a time after supper, when the chores are done, that all of us read or study."

"What kin ya git to read so much?" Ben asked.

"Paw buys books when he goes for supplies. We read the Bible, too. And now Pa's got some good books he bought in Detroit. One's about the sun and the stars and the moon and weather. Another is about trees and wildflowers that grow here."

The Colborn men were silent. Their perplexed facial expressions revealed wonder that any family could be so deeply involved in reading.

Stephen broke in. "Our family enjoys learning new things. We've traced our ancestors back to the early 1500's in England."

"What good does it do ya?" Robert inquired.

Stephen laughed. "I guess it doesn't do any good, but we want our children to know who their ancestors were and where they came from."

The man at the next table set his mug down. "I think like you fellers," he motioned toward the Colborns. "They's work to be done in Michigan, but it ain't checkin' up to see who yer ancestors was, er where they come frum an' when they died."

Stephen laughed again. "It's everyone to his own fancy how he spends his spare time." He paused a moment, "Of course, I can't boast about some of our ancestors - you know if you climb high in a family tree, you'll usually find a worm's nest. But there's a Chinese proverb that says, 'To forget one's ancestors is to be a brook without a source, a tree without roots."

Jonas laughed. "Pa, there's another proverb, - French, I think, that says, 'He who boasts of his descent is like the potato, for the best part of him is underground.'"

The men laughed heartily in appreciation of Jonas' reply to his father.

Hannibal Inn was filling with travelers. Like the Colborns, other groups were going to new homes in the wilderness.

At supper that night Israil spoke quietly to his father. "See them folk? They're the Parsons fellers." He pointed with his knife to a family at the far end of the table.

"Yep, they be. We'll go talk to 'em when we git through eatin'."

Later the Levi Parsons group consisting of Mr. and Mrs. Parsons, their son Julius and his bride, and two other sons, Fredrick and Cecil, all came to talk with the Colborns. Three other members of the party were introduced as carpenters whose names were Wait, Strong and Waterman.

Robert asked, "Ya be goin' to yer place fer the winter?"

"Yeah. Our cabin's built," Levi said.

"But there ain't no road past Howell," Robert said.

"We kin git through. We cut brush 'fore we come out in the summer."

Israil said, "We're goin' the north trail. We'll have to cut a road south frum jest west a' Byron to our land on the county line."

Mary and Eliza were visiting with the women. "Ya'll be our closest neighbors," Mary remarked, "but I don't spoze we'll see ya. There ain't no roads."

Slender Mrs. Parsons smiled. "We'll know you're there. Jest knowin' will help." The women went to Colborn's room to visit and the men sauntered into the adjoining saloon which already was filled with boisterous drinking men.

Levi and Julius Parsons immediately recognized acquaintances. Levi said, "Want ya to meet some more 1836 Michigan settlers."

The Colborns followed the Parsons men. Levi slapped two men on the back. "Calvin Hardy and Charles Bush," he began, "I want ya to meet the Colborns. They're on the way to their land on the north Livingston line." He pointed to the Averys. "Ya know these fellers? They're old timers - been here more'n a year. Avery and Harvey Metcalf live next to each other."

Handy and Bush spoke almost together. "Yeah, we're all neighbors, along with the Fowlers."

"Must be a whole slew a' settlers west a' Howell," Amos said. "All a' ya but Averys come in '36?"

"Yeah," Calvin Hardy answered. "We're in the next township, about nine, ten miles from Howell, an' two, three miles south a' the Parsons."

Stephen Avery smiled. "There's getting to be too many people. In a year or two I'll be moving farther west."

"When'd you git to Michigan?" Israil asked Calvin Handy.

"In May. The road's was turrible. Ruts, roots 'n mud holes all the way to Howell - they called it Livingston Centre then. My wife an' three young'uns rode atop the wagon. We hit a deep hole, the wagon jolted an' my wife Patience, she was holdin' the baby, an' she fell off. The wagon wheel went over her right foot. When she started to fall she threw the baby into a mud hole. He wa'nt hurt, but Patience was turrible lame for four, five weeks."

Ben asked, "Was the bones in her foot broke?"

"Nope. She had on high shoes, an' that helped. We was close to Howell so my family stayed with the Sardis Davises fer three weeks while I built a cabin on my land."

Julius Parsons said, "My brothers Fred an' Cecil

here, an' Paw an' me come a day er two after you'd moved in to yer cabin." He laughed. "Remember Paw asked if we could sleep on yer floor that night? An' ya said, 'No!' We was s'prized that ya was so unfriendly. Paw asked, 'Why?' An' ya said, 'My cabin ain't got no floor, but ya can sleep in the cabin on the ground.' Then ya laughed."

Julius went on, "Mrs. Handy fed us good an' she took beddin' out a' boxes and made a place on the ground in the middle a' the cabin. Us men slept in a circle with our feet together, an' the young'uns was put in the half empty packin' cases fer the night."

Charles Bush took up the story. "About a week later I came, built my cabin and went back to New York. I came to live here a few weeks ago, about the same time in September that Ralph and John Fowler drove through with their families. They stayed at your place too, didn't they, Calvin?"

"Yep. Ya see my wife was the first white woman to set up housekeepin' 'round here. She likes to have company stop. It keeps her frum gettin' lonesome."

"It's November now an' the mosquitoes is gone, but in May, June an' July they was somethin' awful," Calvin went on. "The water in ponds an' creeks was full a' wigglers. You couldn't drink 'thout them slippin' down yer throat, so we spread our han'kerchef over the water an' drunk the water that soaked through the cloth."

Ben shuddered. Calvin laughed. "Think you'll like Michigan?"

"Yeah. I hope they's Indians near us. Pa an' Israil seen some last summer but they wa'nt close to our place."

Amos teased, "Ya'd be scared stiff of 'em."

Ben bristled. "I would not! I'll show ya some day!"

Everyone laughed at the boy's spunk. Stephen Avery said, "I've found if I'm friendly, but firm, I get along well with them."

When the Averys, Parsons and Colborns left at

ten o'clock, many men remained in the saloon until long past midnight. Their loud voices carried through the inn as they shouted, argued and sang.

The next morning the Colborns reluctantly parted with their new friends and headed northwest on the right fork of the Grand River Trail. Within a few minutes the little procession left civilization behind.

A morning mist was forming above the bare trees on the knolls. Mary and Eliza held their shawls close beneath their chin. The chill November air penetrated their clothing. In silence they swayed with the motion of the jolting wagon.

The two pair of oxen plodded slowly along the winding trail. Robert's horses tossed their heads. They were impatient with the slow pace of the oxen. Now and then they'd turn sensitive ears toward the underbrush on either side where wild creatures were hidden. Throughout the high hilly land of Oakland County the trail was less muddy than it had been in the flat Detroit area.

All morning things went well. The men laughed and joked as they had on the previous day. When they stopped for lunch Amos shouted to Eliza, "See that b'ar back there a spell?"

"There wa'nt no b'ar!"

"Didn't ya see how the horses kept tossin' their heads 'n flickin' their ears?"

"There wa'nt no b'ar, was there, Paw?"

"I didn't see him but there could a' been."

"Lide," Amos said, "Ya air like the feller that was learnin' his boy 'bout wild animals. He said, 'Less talk 'bout the b'ar. Do we git fur frum him?' An' the boy said, 'I'd git as fur frum him as I could.'"

Mary laughed. "Amos, how do ya think a' these things?"

"Ain't much else to think about when you're walkin' 'long side a' the oxen."

To save time they had a cold lunch of milk, johnny cake and hard boiled eggs which had been packed for them at Hannibal Inn. Mary promised,

"Tonight we'll have hot tea, 'taters an' ham."

The sunshiny November afternoon passed without problems. Occasionally oak clearings appeared along the road. About four o'clock Robert said, "Next clearing we come to, we ought a' stop fer the night." Half an hour later they pulled off the trail into a grassy patch with a small creek nearby.

Accustomed to making camp in Canada, each person went about his work. The men cared for the animals. Ben collected twigs and dry wood and made a fire. Mary and Eliza washed potatoes in the creek and hung them over the fire to boil. Then they sliced ham into a heavy iron spider and hung a kettle of water above the fire.

After the animals were cared for, the men cut four slender young elm trees to a length of about ten feet and leaned them against the covered wagon. The bottom of each pole was braced against a stick driven into the ground.

"Git the quilts and blankets, Ben," Robert ordered. "After we eat, we'll turn in."

Sitting on quilts inside the blanket-covered lean-to they ate a leisurely supper.

"This is livin'," Israil said leaning back against the wagon wheel.

"S-s-sh," Lide whispered. "I heerd somethin' walkin'." She pointed into the woods.

"They's deer out there," Israil said.

"An' b'ars," Amos added with a grin.

"An' wolves an' Injuns," Ben said.

Mary scolded, "All a' ya stop yer teasin'! I ain't right comf'trable neither. Jest stop it!"

"Ya best listen to yer Maw," Robert said with a grin. "Her an' Lide are skeered a'ready 'thout yer makin' things worse."

The men smoked their corncob pipes while Mary and Lide cleaned up after the meal. Now the woods were dark and from the clearing they seemed impenetrable. The women kept their backs toward the wagon as they worked. "Don't want nothin' sneakin' up on me," Lide whispered to her mother.

From the distance a lonesome howl drifted through the trees. Lide and her mother hurried inside the lean-to.

"They won't come near the fire," Robert said quietly.

But almost immediately, answering howls sounded from opposite directions, and then from in front of them. Sam barked wildly. Robert got up. "Amos, mebbe we'd better fetch the crate a' chickens an' put it here near the lean-to."

Israil followed his father and brother and returned leading the cow and heifer. "Don't think they'd bother them, but they might's well be closer t' the fire." He tied the cattle inside the circle of light.

"Throw more wood on the fire, Ben," Israil said as he again walked into the inky darkness to return with the team of horses.

"How 'bout Squealer?" Ben asked as Robert and Amos placed the crate of squawking chickens under the wagon.

"Might's well git all the critters here close," Robert said quietly.

The animals were uneasy, peering into the darkness, shaking their heads and stamping the ground.

Lide turned her eyes from the animals to the darkness beyond the fire. "They sees 'em!" she exclaimed. "There!" she pointed. "See them eyes?"

Mary gasped. "My laws! They's eyes all over out there!"

The wolves yipped and whined just beyond the circle of firelight. Amos threw a stick at a pair of eyes in the shadows. He was rewarded with a dog-like yip of pain followed by an angry snarl. Sam crawled under the wagon, his tail between his legs.

Ben took a slingshot from his pocket. Fitting a pebble into the strap he aimed at a pair of eyes. Almost immediately a sharp yelp came from the darkness beyond the flames.

"We'll keep the fire burnin' hard," Robert said. "They won't hurt us, they're after the chickens, I 'spect."

Ben successfully aimed at another pair of eyes. From the distance the call of a lone wolf drifted through the night air. The whispering of owls' wings in the treetops overhead had an eerie sound.

Mary looked up into the tree. "I hopes ya air right, Robert, 'bout them hurtin' us, but I ain't so sure. Now I knows how mice feel when they's hunted by them owls up there."

"The wolves didn't bother us in Canada," Lide said softly.

"They was more folk on the trail," Israil explained. "We ain't seen a body since we left Hannibal's Inn. This is the great Michigan wilderness."

"Michigan's a wild place when ya gits 'way frum Detroit," Amos said as he threw more wood on the fire and sparks shot many feet into the air.

Robert said, "All of ya go lop down an' rest. I'll keep the fire burnin'. If I gits sleepy one a' ya kin spell me."

Lide stared in terror at the eyes beyond the fire. The snarling sounds were almost constant. "I can't sleep. I'm skeered."

"Come," Mary said. "Yer Paw's right. It's no use t' set here an' stew." She went inside the lean-to and Lide followed. "Anyways, we won't see them eyes watchin' us in here," Mary whispered.

During the night Robert, Israil and Amos took turns at two hour watches. At times the wolf pack was silent. At other times a weird medley of whines, whimpers, howls and snarls reached the ears of the restless family. On several occasions a chorus of howls, yelps and barks nearly deafened the Colborns, each time causing panic in the domestic animals who pulled and jerked on the leather straps which tied them to the wagon.

As they changed shifts Robert spoke softly to Amos. "I had a mind to shoot into the pack, but the horses an' oxen air so upsot, I'm afeard they'd break loose."

"Yeah, Paw. They's rambunctious. If'n they broke loose we'd be in a peck a' trouble." He peered into the forest. "How many ya spoze air out there?"

"Can't tell. Things look as black as the inside of a hat."

"They're ornery critters, them wolves is. Ya think they're jest after the chickens an' the sow?"

"Yeah. An' they won't bother them long's we keep the fire goin'." Robert got up. "When daylight comes, they'll be gone, I 'spect."

Gradually the howling slackened and the weary family arose. While the men broke camp Mary and Eliza prepared a kettle of cornmeal mush for breakfast.

"What on airth air we gonna do if'n the wolves comes back?" Eliza asked.

"Yer Paw says they makes themselves skeerce in the daytime." Mary hurried to the front of the wagon away from the eyes of her family.

As Lide stirred the mush she heard her mother retching and coughing. Again she was gripped with a terrible thought. What was to happen to her mother in this awful wilderness with no doctor?

When Mary returned her face was pale and dark circles shone below her eyes. Eliza said softly, "I'm gonna tell Paw yer sick."

Her mother's eyes flashed. "I forbid ya! I tells ya I'll be all right! Now don't go shootin' off yer mouth!"

An hour later they were loaded and back on the trail. The men were quiet. Only Ben was talkative. "I didn't see the wolves but they was out there. Air there any near our place, Paw?"

"Yep."

Eliza said, "Did ya know, Maw?"

Mary nodded wearily.

"I'll get to see wolves, then," Ben said. "They sounded like dogs. Mebbe if'n I could ketch a leetle one, he'd git tame like a dog."

"They's wild, Ben," Robert said. "We don't want 'em nearby killin' our chickens and pigs."

"Do ya think we'll see Injuns sometimes?"

"Yep."

"Mebbe I'll have an Injun boy fer a friend some day."

"Mebbe."

The conversation was interrupted by a shout from Israil at the first wagon. "Deep mud jest ahead. Don't look good!"

The wagons stopped on a knoll that sloped down into a huge swamp. Robert, Amos and Ben went to investigate. Robert shook his head. "No place to go but through it," he said, a note of resignation in his voice.

"Mebbe the trail's hard 'nunder the water," Amos suggested.

"Nope," Robert replied. "'Twas dry most places when Israil an' me walked out the first a' August, but there was deep mud here then."

In a moment he went on. "Grab the axes. Might's well git started cuttin' trees an' throwin' 'em 'crost the trail." Five minutes later he had measured the depth of the mud. "Two feet," he said, "an' I reckon it's 'bout twenty feet 'crost to hard ground."

Israil and Amos already were dragging small logs to the crossing. As they worked wild turkeys gobbled nearby and crows and jays screamed their displeasure at the intruders. Ben started a fire and Mary and Eliza baked johnny cake in the iron kettle." Might's well cook a hot meal while we're waitin'," Mary said. "I wisht the men had time t' shoot one a' them turkeys."

Ben ran to his father and talked briefly. Soon he was back rummaging in the wagon.

"What ya lookin' fer?" Eliza asked.

"The rifle. Pa says mebbe I kin git a tom turkey."

Mary leaned against the wagon. "Be keerful," she warned, "an' don't shoot tow'rd the trail."

The sound of the three chopping axes echoed through the woods. "He won't find nothin'," Mary said. "The noise'll skeer ever'thing 'way." But even as she spoke, the rifle cracked nearby to be followed by Ben's shout.

"I got him!" A minute or two later he emerged from the trees carrying a dead rabbit by the ears.

Mary and Eliza met the excited boy. "You did right good," Mary said. "We'll skin him and make rabbit stew." She paused, "I think 'twill taste good." Ben ran to show his father and brothers.

Three hours later the mud hole was ready to be forded and the family and animals had been fed. Israil led the way. The oxen bawled as he urged them forward. The front wheels of the wagon rocked over the first log and dropped into the soft mud just as the rear wheels hit the log. Israil yelled as he struck the stolid animals with a pole and jumped from the first to the second log.

"Git goin'! Come on Ike! Come on Jack!" he shouted as he pounded them on the back. They struggled feebly once more and then stood dumbly, making no effort to move.

"Dad-ratted lazy critters!" Israil muttered as Amos and his father ran to push the wagon. Slipping and sliding from the muddy logs into the water, they grasped the spokes of the rear wheels and attempted to move them forward as Israil continued shouting and pounding the oxen on their backs. They switched their tails and flicked their ears, but refused to move.

"Unhitch 'em!" Robert yelled. "Git 'em out a' there an' we'll see if the horses can move it."

As soon as the oxen were released from the wagon they lunged over the logs and out onto solid ground where they stood calmly on the opposite side. Amos muttered again, "They're danged lazy critters."

One at a time the horses were led across the logs and hitched to the wagon. Then while Robert drove, Israil, Amos and Ben pushed. "Giddap King! Giddap Queen!" Robert shouted. The black team leaned steadily into their harnesses and slowly the rear wheels cleared the first log with a bump causing the chickens to cackle and the sow to squeal.

"Keep 'em goin'!" Israil and Amos shouted as they jumped to the next log and grabbed the wheels.

"Giddap! Giddap!" Robert yelled. Again they bumped over another log, and then another. Finally the horses struggled out onto solid ground with the first wagon.

"Two more to go," Ben said.

Robert walked to the team and unhitched them. "We'll let 'em puff a few minutes," he said patting his horses fondly. Their sides heaved and white lather crept from beneath the harness straps.

Amos made his way back across the mudholes. "I'm gonna try my pair. Mebbe they won't balk," he called.

Robert and the others followed to help push the second wagon which carried farm tools and furniture. Slowly but steadily the lunging red steers hauled the jolting wagon across to hard ground.

"Mine could a' done it, too," Israil said. "They're like people. Some tries, an' some air lazy. Mine air lazy an' ornery, too."

Fifteen minutes later all three wagons were safely across the swamp. Robert sighed. "I'm glad we're 'crost. Animals could easy break a leg on them slippery logs." He walked to Israil's oxen. "By gum, we was dang fools fer buyin' that yoke a' oxen. No wonder they was cheap. They's goin' t' give us trouble. They's nothin' more ornery 'n a stubbon ox, an' we got a pair a' 'em."

Mary called from inside the wagon. "All a' ya must be tired in yer bones. Whyn't ya put on dry clothes an' make camp?"

"Don't fidgit, Maw," Amos said. "Now we're

'crost the mash, we kin go on fer a leetle while, can't we, Paw?"

"I reckon. Ever'body's feelin' chipper now we're on hard ground."

An hour and a half later they made camp beside a small lake. After the men put on dry clothes, they built the lean-to. Ben tied Squealer by a hind leg to the wagon wheel and threw oats and corn into the crate of chickens. As he went toward the lake to get a pail of water, he stopped. Listening for a moment, he hurriedly dipped a pail of water and ran back to the camp.

"I heerd somethin' 'crost the lake," he said. "'Twas talkin', but I couldn't tell what they was sayin'."

Amos, squatting beside Bossy, got up holding a pail of warm milk. Everyone listened. From the distance there came the unmistakable sound of human voices. A horse neighed and Robert's blacks answered. The men looked at one another knowingly.

Robert took charge. "Mary, ya an' Lide git in the waggin an' keep out a' sight. Be still."

Lide's voice shook. "Injuns, Paw?"

"Duno. Could be."

Ben's eyes shone with anticipation.

Chapter III

PERIL ON THE TRAIL

(1836)

Mary and Lide crouched inside the covered wagon, a quilt over their heads. Mary whispered, "We haf t' be quiet. Stop shakin', Lide. If'n they looks in here they'll see the quilt movin'."

"I'm skeered."

"So'm I. But Stephen Avery said they won't hurt us none. Now don't talk no more."

Outside the men went about their tasks attempting to appear unafraid. The sounds of the approaching group carried through the still late afternoon air.

"Sounds like a bunch of 'em," Israil remarked.

"Think we ought t' git the guns handy?" Amos asked.

"Nope. Don't do nothin' to make 'em think we air unfriendly," Robert replied as he checked the straps that tied the animals to the wagons. Overhead, from his perch in a dead oak, a sentinel crow shrieked his anger at the intruders.

Soon the party came into sight. Suddenly they stopped, but in a moment they continued coming toward the wagons. The crow complained shrilly.

Ben counted silently - twenty-five, twenty-six, twenty-seven, twenty-eight, twenty-nine, thirty. Thirty men, women and children. Several of the Indians pulled their horses up before the Colborn men who stood with their backs to the wagon. The remainder of the group waited in the background. No one spoke as the unblinking, piercing eyes of both parties locked and they silently measured one another.

A boy about twelve years of age watched Ben. Like all the others, he rode his pony bareback. A medium-sized bow was slung from his shoulder. Ben smiled. The boy's dark face was expressionless. Ben took his slingshot and a small stone from his pocket, fitted the rock into the strap, aimed at the screaming crow and fired. The bird fell to the ground with a thud. There was dead silence.

Then the Indian who seemed to be the leader pointed to the slingshot and said gruffly, "What - it is?"

Ben walked slowly toward him. "Slingshot. Slingshot fer the boy." He pointed. "I'll give it t' him." He went to stand beside the young Indian's pony. "See?" he said fitting a stone into the strap, pulling back on the elastic, aiming at a nearby tree and releasing the elastic. A hollow ping told everyone he had made a direct hit.

Ben gave the slingshot to the Indian. "Fer ya," he said reaching into his pocket for another stone.

Slowly the boy fit the pebble into the strap, aimed at the dead oak and fired. A dull thud was evidence of his success.

"Ya did good!" Ben exclaimed.

Though his mouth was unsmiling the twinkle in the Indian boy's eyes revealed his happiness. Still he was silent, following the example set by the sober Indian men. He took the bow from his shoulder and an arrow from a small bag on his back.

A tall brave in deerskin clothing spoke to Robert. "Whiskey! Whiskey! Shemokeman whiskey! Wishicheere whiskey!"

"We don't have no whiskey," Robert replied.

The man sprang from his pony and walked to the back of the wagon where Mary and Eliza were hiding. Jumping inside, he peered in bags, boxes and barrels of clothing, cornmeal, flour and vegetables.

Robert, Israil and Amos strode to the wagon.

Robert motioned. "Git out a' there!"

"Whiskey," the brave repeated as he lifted the side of the quilt covering the women. Their pale faces and frightened eyes stared up from the bottom of the wagon. The Indian first appeared surprised, then amused. A flicker of a smile crossed his face. He dropped the quilt and jumped out beside the Colborn men.

Amos picked up the pail of Bossy's milk which he had shoved beneath the wagon. "Milk," he said. "Cow's milk." He patted Bossy. "Ya kin have it." He handed the pail to the brave who took it, turned, and walked back to the silent waiting group.

The Indians talked briefly, then one by one they sprang from their ponies. Ben still was with the young boy at one side of the party.

"What ya spoze they're gonna do?" Israil asked.

"Ain't got no idee," Robert replied. "We'll jest wait an' stand our ground."

Inside the wagon Mary and Eliza had thrown aside the quilt. Eliza, her face pale, whispered, "Air they fixin' t' scalp us?"

Mary shook her head. "I duno what they'll do, but I think that Injun was laughin' at us ahidin' there in the bottom a' the waggin."

The Colborn men still stood side by side taking in the actions of the Indian party. Ben and the young boy were working with the bow and arrows and the slingshot, oblivious to the actions of people about them. The entire group, men, women and children, were dressed in fringed buckskin, two-piece clothing consisting of trousers beneath a loose over garment. Their moccasins and leggins were fringed and decorated with bits of fur.

Five of the women chopped down three small trees, expertly cutting off the tops and branches, and after pounding two sharpened poles into the ground, they tied a third pole across the top. By this time other women had collected twigs and wood and a fire was laid beneath the top pole.

Cooking pots suspended above the fire were half filled with water into which dressed muskrats and squirrels and pieces of venison were placed to simmer along with potatoes.

The remaining women released the travois poles from their horses and untied the deerskin and bearskin robes which had been bound in bundles between the poles.

Each person silently went about his work. The men tied bells to their ponies and allowed them to roam in the woods. Soon the tinkle of bells surrounded the camp.

Taking the poles from the travois, the braves began to build their shelter. They placed stakes on each side of a large fallen oak tree and tied poles near the top of the stakes with the ends resting on the ground. More small poles were laid across the leaning ones and all were covered with a web-like blanket made from cat-tail and blue flag rushes. Inside the thirty-foot long shelter they spread their bear and deerskin blankets.

After a time Mary and Eliza came to the back of the wagon to peer fearfully at the Indians. "Maw, they don't talk to each other," Eliza whispered.

"They don't has to," Mary answered. "'Pears like they all knows what to do." She paused. "Them bells sounds kinda purty comin' through the woods."

"Ya think they'll hurt us, Maw?"

Mary looked toward the busy group across the oak clearing only two hundred feet away. "They acts like we wa'nt even here. I duno what they'll do."

"Ben an' that boy air havin' a good time," Eliza said.

"Ben allus said he wa'nt skeered a' Injuns, an' that he wanted one fer a friend."

Amos came to the back of the wagon. "Maw," he began, "Ya baked a big batch a' johnny cake today?"

"Yeah."

"'Spoze we could give it to the Injuns t' go

with their stew?" He hesitated. "It might be right smart t' stay on the good side a' 'em."

"What do yer Paw an' Israil think?"

"Same's me."

"All right. Give it to 'em."

The odor of the cooking meat drifted through the still evening air. "Their supper smells right good," Amos said. He started toward the Indian camp with the johnny cake.

"They's somebody over there that has a turrible cough," Mary said.

"I hears it," Eliza answered. "Maw, they's buildin' a fire in front a' their lean-to. Ya think it's to keep b'ars an' wolves away?"

"Mebbe. An' mebbe it's t' keep it warm inside. Look, Lide. The leader is takin' the johnny cake."

"Yeah. Now they has our johnny cake an' our milk."

"'Tis worth it if'n they leave us be. Here comes Ben."

The boy ran up to his father holding the bow and several arrows. His eyes shone with excitement. "See what my friend gived me? His bow! An' I gived him my slingshot!"

"Ya couldn't talk t' him, could ya?" Robert asked.

"No. But we understood each 'nother. I said, 'Fer ya,' an' gived him the slingshot. He said, 'Fer ya,' and gived me the bow 'n arrows. I likes him! His paw's the chief!"

"How ya know that?" Robert asked.

"I knows. I pointed to you an' said, 'My paw.' He pointed to the leader an' said, 'My paw.' I knows he's the chief 'cause he's the leader."

Israil said, "I wonder where they's goin'?"

Robert answered, "Mebbe t' Detroit t' git the fifty cents a year the guv'ment pays each Injun. The guv'ment made a treaty with the Injuns to keep th' peace - fifty cents a head each year they pays 'em."

"That's why the wimmin air 'long," Mary said,

"but there ain't no babies or leetle children."

"Mebbe a few wimmin air back at the camp takin' keer a' th' leetle ones," Amos suggested.

"They's some old folk," Ben said. "I seen one ole man with white hair an' wrinkles. He's sick an' spittin' blood an' coughin' somethin' awful. Why'd they take him?"

"To git his fifty cents," Robert answered. "They has t' be there t' git it."

Amos remarked, "I'm right glad they's goin' t' Detroit 'stead a comin' back."

"Why?" Eliza asked.

"They buys whiskey with th' money an' mebbe they'd be mean if'n they's drinkin'."

"They ain't hurted us yit," Mary said going inside the wagon.

In the distance a lone wolf howled. A moment later others joined in with long bloodcurdling howls. "They's chills goin' up an' down my back," Eliza said. "Wolves out there, an' Injuns here -"

Israil remarked, "They's goin' t' be warm tonight with a fire in front a' their lean-to. That's a good idee, Paw. Th' fire keeps 'em warm, an' the wolves won't come near it."

Amos said slowly, "Looks like they's things we kin larn from 'em."

"They's eatin' now," Ben said. "Their stew smells good."

The old Indian man continued the tortured coughing, the sound blending harshly with the almost musical chorus of the wolf pack and the tinkling of the bells on the ponies.

Mary climbed down from the wagon with a tin cup in her hand. "Spoze we dast take some honey an' vinegar over t' th' old man? It might help his cough."

Ben reached for the cup. "I'll fetch it t' him, Maw. He's settin' there by th' fire."

"Robert, ya think 'tis all right?" Mary asked.

"Yeah. Leave Ben go."

The boy walked the short distance between the two camps and slowly approached the aged sick man. Silently he held the cup out to him, and silently the scrawny hands accepted it. Another spell of coughing seized the frail old body.

Ben put his hands to his mouth, tipped his head back and pretended he was drinking. Then he pointed to the cup. Slowly the old man tipped it up and sipped the cough syrup. Though all eyes were on the boy and old man, not a word was spoken.

The aged Indian pulled a deerskin robe about his scrawny shoulders and leaned back against a pole that supported the shelter. He no longer was coughing. He took another small sip of the honey and vinegar and closed his eyes.

Ben smiled and turned to go. The young Indian boy and his father were waiting with the Colborns' pail which had contained the milk. They held it out. As Ben took it, he wondered at its weight. He glanced inside. It was half-filled with stew.

"Thank ya." He smiled and hurried back to his family. "He's stopped coughin', Maw, and look what they gived us."

"Do we dast eat it?" Eliza asked.

"Don't hurt them none, 'twon't hurt us, I reckon," Mary said. "'Twas right nice a' them t' give it t' us, an' we ain't had no supper." As she dished up the stew for her family, she said, "Don't know how long that honey an' vinegar'll help the ole man, but mebbe he kin git a leetle rest. I 'spect he's got consumption, 'specially if'n he's spittin' blood. I've heerd it spreads turrible fast 'mong the Injuns."

"Yeah. They gits white mans' diseases real bad," Israil commented.

The hoot of an owl blended with the mournful howls of the wolf pack. Bossy mooed and the black team stamped restlessly. The bells on the grazing Indian ponies tinkled softly in the wilderness. Ben sat, deep in thought, beside the fire holding his new bow while the men smoked their corncob pipes.

When they had finished eating Mary said, "Ya

think 'tis safe fer us t' git to bed?"

"They seems friendly," Robert answered. "Bein' as we don't have no whiskey, I don't b'lieve they'll bother us none."

Lide answered, "Paw, that feller that found Maw an' me in the waggin jest come in 'thout askin'. If'n I wake up an' finds an Injun standin' over me fixin' t' scalp me, I'll die 'fore he touches me."

"We'll watch fer a bit," Amos said. "The Injuns is goin' into their lean-to. When they's all inside, we might's well go t' bed, too."

"Yeah," his father agreed. "If things goes good, 'nother two, three days an' we'll be t' our land."

The night passed peacefully. The next morning the Indians were up when the Colborn men came from their lean-to. Each group went about their morning chores as though the other was invisible.

Lide and her mother cooked a kettle of cornmeal mush while the men milked the cow and fed and watered the animals. When she went to the wagon to get bowls, her mother quickly slipped into the woods behind the second wagon. Holding her hand over her mouth she tried to silently stifle her heaving stomach as waves of nausea swept over her. Finally her body triumphed and the determination not to retch was forgotten. Her straining heaves immediately brought the family.

"Mary!" Robert exclaimed. "Ya is sick!"

She wiped her mouth on the back of her hand as she straightened up to meet the inquiring faces of her family. She nodded wearily. "Must be that Injun stew. 'Tis nothin'. I'm feelin' better already." She met Lide's eyes.

"But Maw," Ben argued. "Th' stew didn't make <u>us</u> sick."

"Go on - all a' ya! Lide, dish up the mush, an' I'll make tea. There ain't no johnny cake. We gived it all away."

"I'll make tea, Maw," Lide said. "Ya lay down 'till we go."

Mary gestured impatiently. "All a' ya, let me be! I tells ya, I'm all right!"

An hour later they were ready to start another day of adventure. The Indians had rounded up and loaded their ponies and had eaten a breakfast consisting of the remainder of the stew and some cold venison and muskrat.

Ben noticed the Indian boy mounting his pony. Carrying the bow, he ran across the clearing. He held the bow up. "I likes it." He smiled and pointed to himself. "Me, Ben."

The Indian boy's face was expressionless. He held the slingshot up. "I likes," he said. "Me, Shobegun."

Ben turned. "Goodbye, Shobegun," he called. "Mebbe I'll see ya ag'in." He ran back to climb up beside his father on the driver's seat.

The November morning air was crisp and clear. Slowly the caravan made its way through the forest. Angry squalls of a pair of bluejays and a crow's shrill "Caw! Caw! Caw!" seemed to awaken the chickadees who joined in with, "Dee - dee - dee." A pair of red squirrels chattered from a branch overhead. These watchdogs of the forest warned the wild life of approaching danger. A morning mist hung above the tops of the trees which the rays of the rising sun barely penetrated. Two does and a buck cleared the trail in one leap, then disappeared into the heavy underbrush. Barking, Sam charged into the woods.

Numerous kinds of trees made up the forest. Maple, beech, oak, poplar, elm, shagbark hickory, black walnut and butternut were common, as well as wild cherry and apple. In swampy places bare willow branches drooped gracefully over cattails long since gone to seed, the silky down-like fluff sailing away on the slightest breeze. Bright orange bittersweet berries hung from vines on trees along the trail.

At noon the party stopped on a knoll beneath one hundred twenty-five foot black walnut trees. Robert and his sons gathered several bags of the pulpy hull-covered nuts while Eliza and Mary fixed a light meal.

Later that afternoon they stopped to gather hickory and butternuts. "We air more'n half way, I reckon," Robert announced as they loaded the bags of nuts on the wagons. "Mebbe we'll git t' our land day after tomorrer."

"They's a pile a' work t' do when we git there," Amos said, "if'n winter don't set in."

"Winter er not, we has t' build a shelter fer the critters," Israil said.

Two hours later Amos shouted, "They's a cabin ahead!"

"'Twan't there when Paw an' me walked out!" Israil yelled peering down the narrow trail.

The two wagons stopped before a twenty by forty foot log building bearing a crude hand-painted sign above the door.

HILLMANS
TAVERN

A whiskered man about forty-five years old appeared at the door. "Welcome to Hillman's Tavern!" he shouted. "If ya'll come in the missus'll fix supper."

"Thank ya," Robert replied. "Ya ain't been here long?"

"Nope. Ya air th' second vis'ters we've had. A man an' his son was here last week. They was goin' t' Byron." He motioned toward Mary and Eliza who stood at the back of the wagon. "Come in, ladies. I'll help th' men stable the animals."

Mrs. Hillman, tall and thin with blonde hair twisted into a knot on top of her head, smiled through colorless lips from which a short clay pipe protruded. She spoke to a girl about twelve years old who stood before the smoldering fireplace. "Patience, hang the ladies' wraps."

The woman drew on the pipe and exhaled a cloud of blue smoke. "I'm Charity Hillman," she said as her daughter hung the coats and shawls on wooden pegs beside the door.

"We air the Colborns," Mary said, wondering if her new home would be similar to this crude cabin with its hard-packed dirt floor. Ragged quilts partitioned two beds from the living quarters. Mary assumed guests must climb the stick ladder in the corner to reach the sleeping compartment above.

"Could - could we wash?" Mary asked. "We feels dirty from bein' in th' waggin all day."

The woman removed the pipe from her mouth and spit into the fireplace. The spittle hissed as it hit the coals. "Show 'em," she directed her daughter, "while I slick up." She returned the pipe to her mouth and undid her long blonde hair. "Ain't had time t' comb my hair today. Been bakin' an' cookin'."

Patience led Mary and Lide outside to an iron skillet half filled with gray water on a bench under the eaves. A grimy, once white rag lay on the bench. "Ya kin wash there," the girl said, "an' wipe yer hands on th' rag."

"Spoze we could have clean water?" Mary asked.

"Ain't none 'till Paw gits it frum the crick. Jest Maw an' me has washed in it, so 'taint very dirty." She went back into the cabin.

Mary whispered to Lide, "I'd rather have <u>our</u> dirt on me 'an theirn." They went inside without washing.

Mrs. Hillman combed and recombed her long tresses. Loose hair floated in the air and scattered on the dirt floor. She removed the hair from the comb and tossed it into the fire. Finally she completed her grooming. "Now I feels better," she said. Her grease-covered dress appeared darker in front than in the back.

"Set," she pointed to a crude stool, "an' I'll git supper. They's six a' ya?"

Mary nodded. Mrs. Hillman threw more wood into the large fireplace where an iron kettle hung from a crane above the flames. Mary's stomach lurched as the woman again spit into the fire, barely missing the kettle of food. She caught Lide's look of disapproval.

The woman kept up a running conversation. "Smoke yer pipe if'n ya'd like," she said to Mary.

"Thank ya, I don't smoke."

Mrs. Hillman shook her head. "Most ladies out here smokes," she said emphatically. "We has t' do somethin' to pleasure ourselves. Lan' knows, 'tis a hard life fer wimmin." In a moment she added, "Ya'll likely start smokin' after a time, an' chewin' snuff, too."

Mary shook her head. "I don't think I will." From her seat on the stool she observed the furnishings of the tavern. The large hearth was at the end of the room, flanked on one side by an open cupboard and on the other by the stick ladder. A narrow strip of wood nailed to the logs held a few iron spoons and the comb Mrs. Hillman had used. A tin reflector filled with bread was before the fire.

The quilt partitions to the bedroom were pinned to unhewn rafters. The quilts now were pulled aside so Mary could see a high chest. Beside it and hanging from the log wall was the family's clothing - dresses, two bonnets and two pair of a man's pantaloons.

Mrs. Hillman drew on her pipe. "Patience, set the table fer nine," she ordered.

"I kin help," Eliza offered.

"Yer a guest. Ya jest set on that trunk by yer maw 'till supper's ready."

Patience put dishes on the rough homemade table. The supports of the permanent benches were driven into the dirt floor and topped with split logs, flat side up.

"Where be ya frum?" Mrs. Hillman asked wiping her hands on her dress.

"Genesee County, York State," Mary replied. "Where be ya frum?"

"Vermont. Think ya'll like Michigan?"

"I duno. Does wolves and b'ars bother much?"

"Th' woods is full a' 'em. A b'ar killed our

dog. They'll soon be goin' t' sleep fer th' winter. We don't go outdoors much when 'tis dark." She reached for the homemade wooden splint broom and brushed pieces of bark and slivers of wood from the hearth into the fire.

"Patience," her mother directed, "light two candles and put 'em on th' table. Supper's most ready." She exhaled another cloud of smoke as she pulled the long-handled frying pan from the fire. Lifting the cover, she turned numerous slices of ham before returning the heavy pan to the hearth. "Had the ham an' taters cookin' 'afore ya come," she explained. "I cooks up a big batch an' warms up what's left fer tomorrer."

Mrs. Hillman bent above the kettle of potatoes and tried them for doneness with a fork. "Patience," she ordered, "blow the horn. Stuff is ready."

A few minutes later they sat at the rough-hewn table which was loaded with huge slabs of hot bread, bowls of milk, a dish of applesauce, boiled potatoes and ham.

Mary thought of the wash dish and wondered whether the men had all used the dirty water. She looked at Mrs. Hillman's pipe beside her plate and remembered the hissing sound as the woman spit into the fireplace. Her queasy stomach twisted. Suddenly the talking stopped. Mary glanced up to see everyone looking at her.

"Did - did ya say somethin' t' me?" she asked.

Mrs. Hillman spoke accusingly," I said ya ain't eatin' a bit - an' neither air yer daughter."

"We - we et late - 'way past noon. An' settin' in the waggin, one don't git hungry. I'll jest have bread an' milk." She broke a thick slice of bread into her bowl.

Robert laughed. "All the rest a' us has good appetites." He looked at his tall slender wife. "Mary's an easy keeper, an' specially on this trip. She ain't et enough to keep a bird alive."

Amos changed the subject. "Ya think we kin make Byron by tomorrer night?"

"Yep," the tavern keeper answered. "We air jest a day out. That's why we settled here. Should be plenty a' guests stoppin' now that more folk air comin' this fer north."

"Road purty good into Byron?" Israil asked.

"They's a beautiful bridge now 'crost the swamp 'tween the lakes," Mrs. Hillman said.

"I recalls a big swamp when Israil an' me walked out. 'Twas hard goin', even in August when 'twas dry weather."

"There won't be any trouble now," the tavern keeper replied.

Later the men sat around the table and smoked and talked. Mrs. Hillman and Patience cleared away the food and washed the dishes in a pot of gray-appearing soapsuds which stood in the corner of the chimney place, rinsed each piece in a pan of clean water and set it to "dreen" on a stool.

When they were finished, Mary said, "I'd like t' go t' bed if ya'll show me where t' sleep."

Mrs. Hillman took a candle and nimbly started up the ladder. "Foller me," she said.

The sleeping compartment consisted of one bed in the center of the room, placed there because it was the only spot with sufficient height beneath the roof. The bed was surrounded by blankets and straw ticks which were the sleeping accommodations for all guests, male and female. Old quilts fastened from the rafters served as a partial screen.

Mrs. Hillman stood beside the bed with the lighted candle. "Ya an' yer daughter want th' bed?"

Mary nodded as she glanced around the crowded sleeping quarters. In a flash of memory she saw the neat upstairs rooms of her former home in New York.

Mrs. Hillman threw back the covers to reveal wrinkled grayish-white sheets. "I ain't had time t' wash th' sheets, but the two gent'men that slept in 'em last week was nice clean peoples."

Mary sat down on the edge of the bed. "Thank

ya," she said wearily. "We'll make out." She began unlacing her sturdy shoes.

After the woman descended the ladder Mary rolled into bed fully dressed except for her shoes. "The sheets air dirty," she thought, "but tonight I won't be skeered of wolves."

The following morning they were on the trail early. The men were in high spirits. Amos was telling jokes to Ben who walked beside his older brother and the yoke of oxen. "Mis' Hillman said she'd seen some b'ar tracks up th' trail to th' north," Amos began, "an' Lide said, 'Which way's south?'" The brothers laughed loudly.

Amos and Israil carried whips made from four foot hickory sticks one and one-half inches thick at the butt and tapering to the end where a lash of braided rawhide was attached with a couple of thongs. They barely touched the necks of the oxen with the thongs to guide them. They seldom struck the animals for such treatment might cause oxen to become temperamental, or even unruly.

Ben looked out over a small marsh. "'Spoze there's rattlesnakes on our place?"

"Yeah." Amos touched the neck of the right hand ox with his whip. "Gee, Ike," he called. He chuckled, then said, "A woman frum the city was talkin' t' a country boy. She said, 'Ya had any accidents in th' fields?' 'Nope,' the boy said, 'but onct a rattlesnake bit me, an' a horse kicked me.' 'Mercy!' th' city woman said. 'Don't ya call them accidents?' 'Nope,' the boy answered. 'Them critters did it on purpose!'"

Ben whooped. "Amos, you're funnier than a crutch! Tell me some more jokes."

Amos thought a moment, then went on. "A feller was tellin' his wife 'bout a neighbor's dog that bit him on th' leg. 'Lan' sakes!' the wife said, 'Did ya put anything on it?' 'Naw,' th' feller answered, 'He liked it jest th' way it was.'"

After he stopped laughing Ben looked admiringly at his brother. "I wisht I could think up funny jokes. Israil an' Paw ain't good at it like ya air."

Amos smiled. "Paw air th' head a' th' family an' Israil air th' oldest son. They's both got a special place. Me, I air jest "Amos," nobody special, so I has larned folk pays 'tention when I tells funny jokes." He flicked the thong against the left oxen's neck. "Haw, Jack!" he shouted.

"Yeah," Ben said. "Me, too. I can't do nothin' special."

"Ya don't have to. Ya have a special place in the family. Ya air th' baby."

Ben grimaced. "Yeah, an' Paw er my brothers git t' do ever'thing 'fore me!"

"I knows how ya feels. But someday we'll show 'em. I'm gonna work like blazes on th' new land. Paw'll give me an' Israil each a fourth of what we make. Soon's I kin, I'm gonna buy my own parcel, an' it'll be bigger 'an Paw's. Ya kin do it too, when ya air older."

The Indian trail followed high ridges between several small lakes. The day was cloudy and a brisk wind blew from the northwest. The wagons jolted over roots exposed by years of Indian travel and that of the more recent Byron inhabitants. Suddenly they came to the top of a knoll below which lay a swamp with a lake on either side. Tightly laid logs provided a bridge across the half-mile of mud and water.

Amos said, "That air th' 'beautiful bridge' Mis' Hillmman talked 'bout."

"Spoze Israil's pair a' oxen will balk?" Ben asked.

"'Tis likely."

The three wagons stopped at the top of the hill. "I'll go first!" Amos called. "We gotta cross a slough t' git to th' logs," he said to Ben.

The oxen plodded down the sloping hill until they reached the deep mud. "Come on, Jack! Come on, Ike!" Amos shouted. Obediently they followed his commands. When they reached the slippery mud of the logs in the bridge, they hesitated.

Amos urged them on. "Jack! Ike!" Finally they stepped on the bridge and with a mighty heave the wagon went up and down jolting from log to log, up and down, clatter, jolt, bang, as the possessions in the wagon rattled and bounded with each jolt. Sam's sharp barks added to the racket. At last they were across the bridge and on solid ground.

Robert was already halfway across, the horses snorting nervously as their feet slid on the muddy logs. Finally, he too was across.

"Looks like Israil's havin' trouble," Amos said. "It's them ornery oxen. They're balkin' ag'in."

Robert jumped down. "We'll go help him. Mebbe if we push, they'll pull better."

Ben, Amos and their father hurried back to meet Israil. The wagon was halfway across the bridge. The oxen stood contentedly chewing their cuds oblivious to Israil's urging.

"Don't wanna fetch the horses back less'n we haf to," Robert said. "The logs is slippery and they could easy break a leg, so we'll try pushin'. Amos an' me'll be by the front wheels, an Ben, ya push at the back. Less go!"

Israil walked to the left of the oxen. He flicked the thong of the whip against the necks of the animals. "Pete! Joe! Come on!" he shouted. Contentedly chewing their cuds, they ignored him, making no effort to move.

Robert called, "Try pushin' the waggin up on their hind legs, boys, an' Israil, ya give 'em a leetle cut with the whip an' see what happens!"

Ben pushed, Robert was at the right front wheel and Amos at the left, both straining to turn the wheels forward. As Israil struck the animals with the whip they lunged forward. Amos' right foot slid under the wagon and both wheels passed over his ankle.

"My leg!" he screamed writhing in pain on the muddy bridge. Robert and Ben rushed to his side as Israil's oxen dragged the wagon bumpety, clatter, bang over the logs to the other side of the causeway.

"Amos is hurted!" Israil shouted to Mary and Eliza. "'Tis his leg!"

When they reached him Robert already had Amos' boot off. The ankle and foot were a bloody purplish red.

"Kin ya move it?" Mary asked.

Amos gripped his lower lip between his teeth and made an effort to move the ankle. His face was a sickly greenish-white color. "It's busted," he gasped. "I heerd th' bones scrunch."

"We has t' carry him," Mary said. "Don't try to stand on it," she warned her son.

Robert and Israil raised Amos so he stood on his left foot. He put an arm across his father's and brother's shoulders and hopped from log to log as they supported him.

"Jest take it slow," Robert said. "We'll git ya to Byron soon's we kin. Mebbe they's somebody there t' set it."

"Ya air green," Ben remarked. "Does it hurt ya bad?"

Amos hopped to the next log. "Yeah. Wait -" he said to his father and brother. "I gotta puke."

Supported by Robert and Israil he bent to vomit his breakfast. Lide looked at her mother. "Ya air green, too. Air ya sick agin?"

"I'm all right - jest upsot 'bout Amos."

In a few minutes they went on and finally reached the opposite side of the bridge. Mary and Eliza arranged a level place at the back of the wagon and spread a quilt for Amos to lie on.

"Ya has t' keep yer foot up," Mary warned placing a pillow under her son's head and another beneath his foot.

Amos nodded. "Ben kin drive my oxen. They's easy t' handle."

"I could drive 'em, too!" Lide exclaimed.

"Yeah," Robert said, "Ya could, but ya help Maw an' Amos fer now."

The little procession started. Ben's feelings were ambivalent. One moment he was thrilled to be doing a man's work, but shortly his thoughts turned to Amos. He recalled a neighbor back in York State who was left with a permanently stiff ankle after his team had run away, tipping the wagon over and throwing the man against a tree which resulted in mangled bones in the foot. No, he must not think such things. Amos would not be crippled.

The trail was checkered with sun, the rays slanting through the bare branches of maples, black walnut and oak. The shut-in silence of the wilderness was disturbed only by the hooves of the animals and the noisy clatter of the family's possessions when the wagons dropped into ruts in the trail to be followed by the squeals of the sow, the cackling of the chickens and the barking of the dog.

There no longer was joking and calling from wagon to wagon, but only the occasional voice of one of the drivers speaking to his animals.

The wilderness had its own sights and sounds. The chatter of a fox squirrel as he peered down from an overhanging limb before he scampered up the tree to vanish on the opposite side of the trunk. A quail boldly called, "Bob-white!" Far ahead Ben thought he saw a brown bear lumber across the trail, but almost immediately it disappeared into the thick brush. A woodchuck sat on his haunches, his front paws clasped across his fat stomach as he surveyed the passing wagons. Suddenly the heifer bawled and the little gray animal dove into his burrow.

The family paused at noon for a quick meal of bread and milk. No one voiced the fear that Amos' injury might be more serious than a broken bone. In half an hour they again were on the trail.

"Ya're doin' good, Ben," Robert said quietly as he walked past his youngest son who stood beside the oxen. Ben smiled.

The long afternoon wore on. Mary silently watched Amos. At each jolt of the wagon a grimace of pain crossed his face. Her heart ached that she could do nothing to relieve his misery. God must have meant for humans to suffer else there would be some kind of medicine to relieve bad pain.

"Lide," Mary directed, "put two pillers 'n under his foot. Got to keep it frum swellin' if'n we kin."

Gently the girl lifted the injured leg and stuffed another pillow beneath the foot. "Hurts ya bad, don't it?" she asked.

"I kin stand it," Amos murmured between clenched teeth, "'till we git t' a doctor."

Mary was silent but fearful. The foot and ankle had appeared badly mangled when she tried to clean the wounded flesh. And - what if Byron had no doctor?

Fortunately the trail was dry and the little caravan traveled steadily. No one had talked for a long time until Eliza said, "We ain't met a body, 'cept the Injuns, since we left Hannibal's Inn."

"I knows," her mother murmured. "A body alone would be in a peck a' trouble on this trail if'n things went wrong. An' Byron, yer Paw says, is the only white settlement northwest of Hannibal's Inn fer quite a spell."

A shout from Israil alerted them. "Byron jest ahead!"

Five minutes later they crossed the river and pulled into the tiny settlement which consisted of two houses and a small store with living quarters at the back.

Amos raised his head to peer from the back of the wagon. "'Tis an outpost settlement." The tone of his voice revealed his doubts about the medical knowledge of the few inhabitants.

A sign above the door read EULER'S STORE. Robert already was inside. A stout neatly dressed woman came from a back room.

"Miz Euler," Robert began, "I was here last summer."

The woman smiled. "I remember you. You're

Robert Colborn. You and Israil stopped here for supplies on your way out in August."

"Yeah, Mam." He spoke rapidly. "Do ya have a doctor here? My boy has hurted his leg bad - busted it, we thinks."

"Bring him in. My husband's not a doctor, but he's all Byron's got. Mebbe he can do something. He worked with a doctor in Detroit so he knows about setting bones." She bustled about. "Bring your boy in and put him in there on the bed." She pointed to an open door. "I'll go call Jacob - he's out back somewhere."

Five minutes later Amos lay on the quilt covered bed with his family gathered around him. Suddenly a black-bearded giant of a man strode into the already crowded room.

"I'm Jacob Euler," he announced in a deep gutteral voice. "My vife, she say your boy has mebbe a broke leg? Yah?"

"Yeah," Robert replied. "Kin ya set it?"

"Ve try." He spoke to his wife. "Get viskey an' clean rags." He looked at Amos. "Hurtin' bad?"

Amos nodded. Jacob Euler spread a white sheet beneath the injured leg. "Ve'll fill you up on viskey, den 'twon't hurt so bad, yah?"

Amos nodded silently. Mrs. Euler returned with a jug of whiskey. Her husband poured a mugful of the liquid and passed it to Amos. "Set up, son, an' drink it down." He turned to the family. "Ever'body but der fadder go out in udder room. Vife, get plaster o' paris and vater for to make cast."

Mary hesitated by the door. "Kin I stay?"

Jacob Euler shook his head. "Besser if you go, mudder." He turned to Amos. "Viskey make you feel besser? Here, drink more." He refilled the mug as he spoke to Robert. "Fadder, you strong man. You pull vile I set leg, yah?"

"Yeah. I'll do all I kin."

As Jacob closed the door he said to Amos, "Yell if you vant."

The big man cut Amos' pant leg from the knee to the bottom and folded the cloth back. The leg from mid-shin to the tip of the toes was a raw sore with scarcely any skin remaining. Silently he cleaned the skinned leg and foot. Then he grasped the toes and turned the foot slightly. Amos winced.

Euler shook his head. "Vot you do?"

"Waggin run over it. Both wheels."

"Ach." He shook his head again.

Eliza, Mary, Israil and Ben stood beside the counter in the store. No one spoke. Finally Mary and Eliza went outside to lean against the wagon.

"I wisht we'd stayed in York State," Eliza said wistfully. "Ya is sick, an' now Amos. Who will be next?"

"I knows, Lide. They says, 'Tis allus darkest 'afore th' dawn'. Mebbe when we gits to our land, things'll be better."

"Er worse!" Lide said bitterly.

Ben ran out to stand beside his mother. "He's moanin' Maw. They's hurtin' him bad 'cause Amos don't fuss easy. I can't stand it in there."

"They has t' set the bones, Ben."

Before long Israil came to join the others. "Miz Euler says we kin stay here. I'll unhook th' critters." Silently he drove the oxen and horses behind the store to the stable. Ben followed his brother.

Two women came from the cabins across the road. A brood of small children followed the younger one. A toddler, holding to his mother's skirts, shyly held a hand over his eyes.

The older woman said, "Afternoon. We seen ya come with th' hurt young man. What'd he do?"

Mary brushed back a lock of dark hair. "Broke his leg. They air settin' it now."

The brood of children stared with wide eyes at the strangers. The woman went on. "We're right sorry. A man with a busted leg can't do much - but 'twill heal. We're the Steinackers. I'm her mother-in-law." She pointed at the younger

woman. "Ya goin' far?"
"To our land in Livingston County."
"Ain't no road 'crost there."
"We knows. Reckon we'll have t' cut one." Mary hesitated. "We're the Colborns. This air Eliza, an' Ben, an Israil air puttin' the critters in th' stable. I'm Mary."
After a time Mrs. Euler came outside. "You can come in now. They are done."
"Kin ya sleep all o' 'em?" Mrs. Steinacker asked Mrs. Euler. "We has an extra bed if'n ya needs it."
"Thank you. It would be better if the young man had a bed by himself. We'll let you know after supper."
Mary's eyes filled. "Ya're all kind."
"We knows how ya feels," Mrs. Steinacker said, "Far frum home out here in th' Michigan wilderness, an' with a hurt boy - us wimmin has t' help each 'n other. The men's all alike - they has t' try somethin' new, an' we has t' go 'long with their idees."
"Come inside," Mrs. Euler said to Mary. "You look tired."
The young woman silently herded her brood back toward the cabin. Her mother-in-law called, "We'll see ya 'fore ya leave if'n ya don't sleep at our place."
Jacob Euler was packing away medical supplies in a cupboard in the corner of the store. Robert talked to him in a low tone, but Mary caught most of the conversation.
"He'll be all right?" Robert whispered.
"Yah. Ve hope. But leg is hurt bad. Many little bones in foot - some might be broke - can't tell - an' the ankle - ve hope it von't be stiff." He stopped when he noticed Mary. "Miz Colborn, go in an' see yer son."
"How be ya?" Mary asked brushing back damp hair from Amos' forehead. Ben and Eliza stood at the foot of the bed.
"All right." Amos glanced at Ben. "I'm not much

good t' th' family now, but ya got Ben."

Mary patted his shoulder. "In a few weeks ya'll be well."

"But Maw. They's work t' be done! An' I ain't no good now!" He turned his face to the wall.

"We'll git along - don't fret. We're goin' out now an' ya rest."

At supper the family evaluated the situation with the help of the Eulers. "Last August we blazed a trail out frum our land," Israil began, "but 'twill take some cuttin' t' git th' waggins through. We'd figgered three o' us could do it in a day, but now -"

"I kin help!" Ben exclaimed.

"He's right," Robert agreed.

Eliza joined in, "An' I kin help. Ben an' me together kin do as much as Amos."

"I spoze I kin help, too," Mary said slowly.

Jacob Euler watched the family as they talked. Finally he spoke to Robert. "It vould be besser for your boy if he stayed here yet. An' Miz Colborn, she looks tired. Ve vill keep your vife and boy vile you cut through trail. Dey vill be besser here."

"Yeah," Robert said thoughtfully. "We'd take the waggins an' th' critters an' git things to our place, an' then me er Israil'd come back fer Mary an' Amos. What do ya think, Mary?"

"I don't rightly know. I ought t' be helpin'."

"Maw," Eliza said, "Ya needs a rest. Ya've been poorly fer days."

Mary's eyes flashed. "Lide, I tells ya I'm all right - jest a leetle tired!"

Mrs. Euler poured more coffee. "It would be nice if you were here with your boy - and I'd like company."

"Well - 'twould be nice," Mary said slowly.

The next morning the men and Lide left Byron for the last part of the journey. Mary felt torn. Robert and the others needed her, but Amos was in no condition to be moved. He had suffered severe pain all night. Now he sat in a chair near

Euler's fireplace, his injured leg resting on a stool. Miserable and depressed, he had barely spoken all morning.

Jacob towered above him. "In little vile ve make you crutches. Den you move 'round, it be besser, yah?"

"Yeah. How long 'fore my leg'll be well?"

"Yah. Two, three month, mebbe."

"Damn! 'Twill be most spring!"

"Yah. But besser now zan spring or summer when dere's work to do outdoor."

"Them danged oxen!" Amos exclaimed. "Paw said they'd be trouble with their balkin' an' ornery ways!"

"Yah. Yah."

Amos thoughtfully stroked his brown beard as he stared into the smoldering fire.

"Vell, I be back and ve make crutches," Jacob said. Amos did not answer.

Mary carried a pan of dishwater outside. She used the task as an excuse to slip around the corner of the cabin where she vomited her breakfast. Wiping her mouth on a handkerchief from her pocket, she hurried inside with the dishpan.

Elvira Euler looked at her questioningly. "Did you sleep last night? You look pale."

She nodded. "The bed at Mrs. Steinacker's was real good - an' <u>clean</u>. We've slept in some as wasn't."

Elvira hung her dish towel. "In a few days you'll be in your home. The trip has been hard for you?"

"'Tis a long way."

"I know. I only came from Detroit."

"Was you borned there?"

"I was born in Vermont, but my father was a doctor and my parents came to Detroit when I was small. I went to a girls' school, the Detroit Female Seminary. Then Jacob came to Detroit. My father hired him to do odd jobs and sometimes to help around the office."

"An' ya married him?" Mary smiled.

Elvira nodded. "He's a good man - so kind. But like many others, he wanted to buy land in the wilderness - so here we are."

"Ya don't like livin' here?"

Elvira hesitated. "It's lonely - but I like it - if only we had children."

"Mebbe ya will."

Elvira shook her head. "We've lost three when I was about five months in the family way. Maybe God doesn't mean for us to have children - but we'll keep trying."

Mary murmured, "I don't understand. Ya wants 'em so bad - an' - an' some folks that don't want 'em - has more'n they wants." She stared from the kitchen window into the woods.

They could hear Jacob's deep gutteral voice in the next room talking to Amos who grunted occasionally. Elvira watched Mary for a time, then she brought her back to the present. "I'll tell you what I've been thinking," she began. "How would you like it if we baked things for you to take home when your man comes back?"

Mary's eyes filled. "Yer too good to us." She wiped her eyes. "I don't know what's wrong with me. I ain't never cried so easy 'till jest lately."

"Things are strange. Are you worried about Indians?"

Mary nodded as Elvira went on. "There's a camp a few miles south and west of Byron - can't be too far from your land, but they're friendly." Changing the subject she said, "Let's get busy! We have plenty of wild apples, so we'll make you a big pot of applesauce, and we'll bake a batch of bread, and -". She stopped. "I'm glad you stayed," she said warmly. "I think Jane Steinacker would like to come over too, and maybe Betsy."

"Betsy is the daughter-in-law?"

"Yes. She's quiet. You never know what she's thinking. The children could play outside, and it would be good for Betsy to get away from her house for a while."

By mid-afternoon the kitchen table was filled with dishes and pans of food for the Colborn family. Jacob was teaching Amos to walk on the new crutches. Though awkward, he soon mastered the crude, homemade supports.

Jacob laughed. "You'll be ready to run a race wid little brudder ven you gets to your place."

Amos grimaced and sat down heavily. He lifted the injured leg to a stool and leaned his head against the wall behind him.

"Hurts bad?"

"Yeah."

"Mebbe hurt two, three days. The bones is busted vich is making pain, and the skin all is off. I cleaned it good's I could. You've got 'nuff wrong to hurt bad."

Three days later, Robert arrived with the empty covered wagon.

The Seal of the Territory of Michigan

Chapter IV

ADVERSITY

(1836)

The black team plodded through the leaves on the narrow trail which the Colborns had cut to their new home. Lazy snowflakes drifted through the air. The message was clear. Winter was not far away.

The wagon jolted over exposed roots. A fox squirrel hung precariously from the tip of a swaying maple branch as he stuffed the dry wing-like seeds into his cheeks. He ignored the people below, for he was intent on adding to his den's winter food supply. Bright red and orange bittersweet berries hung from vines twenty feet long which had encircled trees along the trail.

Mary glanced at Amos who sat leaning against the side of the wagon opposite her. He hadn't spoken since they left Byron. "'Twill be good to be in our cabin tonight," she remarked. Amos didn't reply.

Robert turned. "Our Lide has done good at settlin' an' she worked right 'long with Ben when we cleared the trail. Now when we gits the barn done, an' the critters air stabled, we'll be in purty good shape fer winter. Course there's leetle jobs t' be done yet -"

"Has wolves been 'round?" Mary asked.

"Yeah. They're watchin' us most ever' night. We keeps a fire burnin' near where the critters is tied, an' they ain't got nary a chicken. When we gits ever'thin' in the barn they'll be safe frum them howlin' beasts." He turned to Amos. "Yer leg feelin' better?"

"Yeah. 'Tis all right."

"Pain ya much?"

"Some."

"We got a warm spot close by the fire. Ben put a rockin' chair there an' he said, 'This here spot's fer Amos. Don't nobody else set there when he's home'." Robert laughed, but Amos didn't respond.

Mary watched her son, a puzzled expression on her face. Why was he so quiet? Amos had always been talkative and good-natured. She wondered if he was suffering great pain but refused to complain. It would be good to get him home and into that rocking chair by the fire.

They rode in silence for a long time. Only the sound of the jolting wagon and the rustle of dry leaves broke the quiet of the wilderness.

Suddenly Robert shouted, "Thar she is!"

Through the bare branches Mary caught a glimpse of her new home, a small low sturdy-appearing log cabin. Her eyes quickly took in the building and surroundings. Tall oaks, to which rust-colored leaves still clung, towered over the cabin. Bittersweet vines twined about a young maple near the house, the orange-red berries bright against the bare trunk. A creek a few rods west of the building wound its way to the south close to the half-completed barn where Israil and Ben were working. Two nearly empty wagons to which the cattle were tied, set near the barn. The crate of chickens, half-covered with an old blanket, was at one end of the wagon on which small tools were piled.

Sam came tearing through the woods to meet them. His sharp yips alerted the family of their arrival. Bossy and the heifer bawled, the sow squealed and the chickens cackled as Lide ran to the door and Israil and Ben dropped their tools.

Everyone talked at once as they lifted Amos from the wagon and, with his crutches, he slowly made his way to the cabin.

Israil clapped his brother on the shoulder.

"How ya like it?" he asked enthusiastically.

"Looks good." Amos' voice was barely audible. He hobbled toward the cabin without a second look at the barn.

"Amos," Ben exclaimed, "jest wait 'till yer leg is well! 'Twill be a barrel a' fun clearin' an' workin' our land! I kin hardly wait fer spring!"

Israil's question-filled eyes met his father's. Robert silently shook his head.

Inside the cabin Lide showed her mother around. "Maw, ain't this a nice fireplace an' hearth that Paw an' Israil made last summer?"

Robert smiled. "We toted the clay an' stones frum way down south by the creek. 'Twas a long ways to lug 'em, but we wanted a safe chimbley. 'Twould be bad to burn out in winter."

Mary smiled. "'Tis nice. Room to cook an' we won't be cold." She went to Amos who sat in the rocker and placed a block of wood under his foot. "Let me help ya out a' yer coat."

Amos shook his head. "I'm cold."

"'Tis a cold wind today but ya'll soon warm up."

Lide exclaimed, "An' Maw, look at yer bed! Ben an' me got dry grass frum the mash an' we put it in the bed sacks, an' Paw an' Israil say 'tis a good bed! Ya an' Paw kin sleep there an' the rest a' us'll sleep in the loft!"

"Ya've all done good," Mary said approvingly. She glanced at the ladder in the corner by the fireplace which went to the loft. "Fer a time, 'till Amos is well, he'll sleep down here. I kin go to the loft well's not."

"An' Maw, we has a wood floor!" Lide went on hurriedly. "Paw says most a' the cabins jest has dirt floors."

Mary glanced at the rough split basswood logs, so different from the smooth floors of her former home. Well -- she'd get used to this way of life. She must be careful not to spoil their enthusiasm. Already Lide had been won over. She hoped she'd grow to like it too. "Ya've all done good," she said softly. "What's that I smells cookin', Lide?"

"Stew. Venison stew. Israil shot a fat deer, an' it's right good cooked with 'taters 'n onions 'n carrots 'n turnips."

Mary hung her wraps on wooden pegs beside the door. "Ya men go on with yer work. Lide an' me'll soon have dinner ready an' we'll call ya."

"Are ya warm now, Amos?" Lide asked.

He shook his head. "I'm havin' chills."

"Laws!" Mary exclaimed. "I hope ya ain't catched cold!" She pulled a quilt from the bed and covered him from head to foot. "Mebbe ya'll feel better when ya gets some hot stew into yer stummik. An' Miz Euler an' Miz Steinacker sent all that good baked stuff -"

"I ain't hungry." He leaned his head against the back of the chair and closed his eyes.

Lide went to packing boxes in the corner and took out the heavy dishes they had brought from York State. She set the crude split-log table. "Israil an' Paw made this table last summer," she explained, "an' the benches too. They'll make cupboards fer us this winter."

"We'll git 'long 'til they has time," Mary answered as she cut slabs of bread and piled them on a plate. "Where'd ya put the 'taters an' other stuff we got at the Detroit market?"

"Some's 'n under the bed an' the rest Israil an Ben buried in a hole in the ground. They covered 'em with mash grass an' dirt, an' they says when we opens it, things'll be fresh an' good."

Mary lifted the wooden covers from two barrels beneath the east window. "Our flour an' corn meal," she said softly.

Lide threw a log on the fire and it cracked and snapped as sparks flew up the chimney. With a long handled spoon, she stirred the steaming stew.

"Ya looks happy," Mary observed. "Ain't ya skeered no more?"

"They's wolves around at night sometimes - we

hears 'em howlin', but I ain't skeered in here."
"An' Injuns - ya seen any?"
"Nope."
Mary's eyes were on the sleeping Amos. "His face is so red - mebbe he's got fever," she said softly.
"He don't act like Amos," Lide whispered. "I didn't know a busted leg made a body act this way. He ain't said hardly nothin' 'bout the place - an' he was all 'cited 'afore."
Mary's eyes were troubled. "I knows."
When the men came up to wash in a pail of water outside the door, their voices wakened Amos. As they came in and took places at the table, he watched, but made no move to get up.
"Come on, Amos!" Ben called. "Lide cooks up a good stew!"
"I ain't hungry. I'd ruther lay down than eat."
"Your leg hurt?" Israil asked.
Amos nodded. "It throbs, an' the cast feels awful tight." He threw the quilt aside, picked up his crutches and hobbled to the bed.
Mary took his coat. "If 'n ya don't feel like eatin', jest swallow a leetle broth frum the stew, an' then lay down."
Silently he ate a few spoonfuls. Then, setting the dish on the floor, he rolled into bed.
At the table, conversation centered about the work at hand. "Two, three days an' the barn'll be done," Robert said. "Now that your mother's here, Lide kin help Ben cut poles to make a fence 'round the barnyard."
"They was snow in the air this mornin'," Israil said. "Any time now it'll come. Spoze we kin git up that mash grass frum down by the creek? The critters is goin' to have slim pickin' -"
"If the weather holds 'nother ten days, we'll git up what we kin. The critters is goin' to go without grain this winter. We'll turn 'em loose in the daytime to find what they kin to eat."
"When Ben an' me gits the fence done, we kin

help git the mash grass up," Lide said.

Robert smiled. "Ya is doin' good, Lide. Ya has changed frum a skeered little girl to a level-headed young lady in jest a few days."

Lide flushed at her father's praise. "We all has to help," she murmured.

The next morning while the men and Lide were at work, Mary carried numerous pails of water from the creek and poured them into a large kettle to heat over the fire. She noticed Amos watching her, but he didn't speak. Finally she said, "I'm goin' to wash clothes. Ever'thing we own is dirty." He didn't reply.

"Does ya feel any better this mornin'?"

He shook his head. "I feels cold - all but my leg - an' that's hot - an' it pains turrible."

"I wisht I knowed what to do fer ya. She thought a moment, then she said, "They's willer trees 'long the creek. I'm goin' to fix ya some tea made frum the bark. Sometimes it stops pain." Half an hour later Amos sipped a cup of willow bark tea as his mother scrubbed clothes on the wooden washboard.

All forenoon Mary scrubbed, carried water from the creek, rinsed and hand wrung the great pile of clothes. Then she carried then outside to be spread on bushes and low tree branches to dry.

As she started dinner she spoke to Amos, "Son, mebbe you'd feel better settin' in the rocker -"

His face was turned to the wall. Mary stooped to touch his forehead. It was hot. He seemed to be sleeping. Maybe the willow bark tea had quieted the pain.

Two days later Mary sat beside her ill son. He lay perfectly still, but his breathing was short and fast. His lips were drawn back and his eyes sunk into his head. "Maw," he gasped. "We gotta get this here cast off. My foot hurts turrible an' pains go shootin' up my leg - I can't stand it no more."

Mary carried a lighted candle to the bed in the corner. "Lide," she called. "Hold this so's I kin look at his toes."

Throwing back the covers she gasped as she looked at the swollen purplish-black toes below the cast on Amos right foot. Silently she covered the leg and turned to Lide. "Git yer Paw," she said tersely.

An hour later the cast had been hacked off the infected foot. In shocked silence Mary and Robert looked at the angry-looking puffed foot and ankle from which red streaks extended to the knee. Mary laid her hand on the calf of the leg. "Burnin' hot," she murmured. "He's got a turrible fever."

Amos was rolling his head from side to side. His eyes were wild as he struggled to get up. "Git the waggin off my leg! Git it off me! Them damn oxen! Help me, Paw!" he shouted.

Robert shoved him down on the bed. "Ya can't git up. Ya will hurt yer leg. Now lay down." He spoke firmly, and Amos obeyed, but he continued the restless rolling of his head on the pillow.

"'Tis the fever," Mary whispered. "He don't know what he's sayin'."

"We has to git Jacob Euler," Robert said. "I'll send Ben. He kin ride one a' the blacks, an' mebbe him an' Jacob'll be back by night."

Ten minutes later Ben was on his way to Byron. The sky was dark and snowflakes sailed through the air on a northwest wind.

"Looks like they's a storm brewin'," Robert observed as he started toward the barn to help Israil.

Mary nodded. "I'm gonna make a flaxseed poultice an' put it on his leg," she said. "Mebbe it'll draw out the pizen. 'Tis likely Jacob'll bleed him when he gits here." She closed the door.

Amos was moaning and thrashing about. When the poultice was ready Lide tried to quiet him so Mary could bind the warm mass the entire length of the swollen leg.

"He don't know what he's sayin', does he, Maw?" Lide asked after Amos murmured that he wanted to die.

Mary shook her head. "I'm gonna put bacon fat on the ankle where the skin's off," she said. "That's healin'." She spread the grease generously over the ankle and then bound it with several layers of clean cloth. "Steep up some willer bark tea," Mary ordered. "Make it strong, an' mebbe he kin sleep."

"'Tis snowin' harder," Lide observed as she hung a kettle of willow bark and water above the fire. "Does they have blizzards in Michigan?"

"I duno. I 'spect they does, but mebbe not this airly." She went on a moment later, "Paw an' Israil'll have the roof on the barn by night - an' none too soon by the looks a' the weather."

The afternoon seemed endless. Mary, sitting before the east window, worked at her mending. When Amos' ranting became unusually loud, she went to him and her voice quieted him temporarily.

Lide was baking. "We'll have johnny cake, milk an' apple sauce fer supper," she said. "But nobody ain't gonna be hungry." Her eyes rested on her brother's flushed face.

Mary turned to look outside. Silently she studied the thickening snow, then turned back to her mending.

Lide asked, "Ya think Ben's there yet?"

"'Tis likely." Mary suspected that Lide's concern for Ben was the same as her own - that the boy might become lost in the storm. For a time the only sound in the cabin was the snapping of the fire and the snoring of the dog.

Suddenly the silence was shattered by a yell from Amos as he struggled to stand. Mary and Lide rushed to grab him by the arms. He screamed incoherent phrases as they forced him back on the bed.

"We can't hold him," Mary panted. "Git Paw."

Amos still struggled. "The waggin's on me! Git me up!" he shouted. Then he again lapsed into incoherent babbling.

Robert and Israil, their beards white with snow,

burst into the cabin followed by Lide. Mary released her hold on Amos' arm as the men forced him screaming back on the bed.

"Amos!" Robert said firmly. "Ya haf to lay down. Ya'll hurt yer leg bad if ya stand on it!"

Somehow his father's voice penetrated the confused mind and Amos stopped struggling. Robert continued. "Ben'll be here purty soon with Jacob. He'll know what to do fer ya." At last Amos fell into a restless delirious sleep.

Israil said, "I'll finish puttin' the critters in the barn, Paw. Ya stay here - an' call me if ya needs me."

Robert nodded. The darkness of a stormy November afternoon descended upon the Michigan wilderness. Mary lit a candle which dimly lighted a few feet about the table. When it was time Lide served their meager supper.

Three hours later they still waited for Ben and Jacob to return. Periodically they would quiet Amos, but soon he'd again waken screaming with pain. Then there came the welcome sound of voices outside. Sam barked. They had returned.

A moment later Jacob Euler bent to enter the door. He carried a black sachel. Ben was close behind.

Mary breathed, "Thank God ya air here."

"Ve come as fast as ve could," the big man said as he tossed his coat into the corner.

Ben explained, "It took me a long time to git to Jacob's. 'Twas snowing so hard I couldn't see the trail an' I had to git down an' hunt fer the blazed trees. It took a long time but I didn't go on 'till I found a blazed tree. But comin' home was easy - King wanted to git home an Jacob's horse jest follered him."

The huge man bent over Amos as he talked in a quiet reassuring voice. "It's Jacob. Ve vant to see what ve can do fer you. Let me see the leg." He untied the poultice as Robert hurried to hold the candle.

"Yah - yah -. Hm-m-m-. Yah," he muttered. "Bad

blood in dere. Ve has to bleed him - git the bad blood out. It makes big fever."

"Kin ya see the red streaks goin' up his leg?" Robert asked.

"Yah. Yah. First ve try bleeding him." From the black sachel he took the necessary tools as Amos moaned and tossed in delirium.

"Amos," Jacob said softly, "Lay schtill vile ve help you. 'Twill hurt a little, but 'twill make you besser. Understand, yah?"

There was no response. "Vell, ve start." Jacob made a quick cut in the vein and the dark blood ran into a small pan held below the cut. "Dere," Jacob said. "Ve'll let it bleed a vile. I vish ve had leeches. Dey is goot to suck out bad blood from sore. But cutting vorks purty goot."

Amos was quiet. After a time Jacob said, "Ve stop it now and he can rest. Ve'll see in mornin' how he feels."

After the bleeding was stopped and the cut bandaged, Amos slept. Jacob insisted on sleeping on the floor before the fire. The rest of the family ascended to the loft, but there was little sleep for anyone that night for Amos muttered, shouted and screamed throughout the long hours.

Next morning at breakfast Robert said softly, "He ain't no better."

Jacob shook his head. "Dere's jest one ting ve can do. Ve haf to cut off his foot."

There was dead silence in the cabin as the family realized the implications of amputation. Amos with a peg leg - Amos a cripple.

Mary said softly, "Mebbe if we wait, he'll git better."

Jacob shook his head. "Not besser. Vorse. He vill die if ve don't cut off der foot. Der pizen vill spread. It's vorse today den it vas yestiddy. Dere's more red streaks an' dey is up above his knee now. Ve has to do it." He rummaged in the big black sachel and brought out a saw.

Mary's breath caught. She walked to the

window. Lide was crying softly. Ben sat at the table, his head on his arms.

Robert spoke to Israil. "Guess we ain't got no choice."

The young man shook his head. "If'n I know Amos, he'd 'bout soon's be dead as to have a leg off. We ought t' ask him."

Robert went to the bed. He put his hand on his son's shoulder. "Amos," he began, "yer leg ain't gettin' no better. Jacob, he says, -" he paused. "He says he has to cut it off 'er ya won't git well. Ya'll die, son. Ya want to live, don't ya?"

The only answer was incoherent babbling and the restless rocking and turning of the feverish body. Robert tried again. "Tell us, son. Jest say "yes" er "no." Do ya want to live?" There was no answer.

Israil shook his head. "He don't know what yer sayin'."

Jacob walked to Mary at the window. "Mudder, besser if you and Lide goes to barn - er outdoors somewhere vile ve do it. I bring viskey. Ve vill get it down him some vay." The big man turned to Robert. "I vill need you and Israil to hold him, an' Ben, you vill high up hold der candle. Ve vill do it on table."

Without a word Mary and Eliza put on their coats and went outside into the cold gray November morning. Sam ran to them and nuzzled their hands. Lide sobbed softly.

Mary stopped to lean against the trunk of an oak, her hand to her mouth.

"Yer sick," Lide said accusingly as her mother bent to relieve her stomach of the undigested breakfast.

Mary gasped, "I'll be alright. I'm upsot 'bout Amos. I ain't been sick fer three, four days. It's gettin' better."

Silently they scuffed through the snow toward the log barn with Sam at their heels. There was nothing to say. Inside it was warm. The horses neighed a greeting. Mary turned over two empty wooden pails and they sat down to wait.

After a long time Eliza said, "Guess I'll let 'em out. I heerd Paw say they wasn't watered."

Mary nodded silently as Lide released the cattle, pig and horses and drove them outside. They rushed to the creek for long drinks of the icy water after which they browsed on weeds and dry grass near the barn. The sow returned to her small pen in a corner of the barn and went to her empty trough.

"She wants her swill," Eliza said as she started toward the house.

A few minutes later she returned with the swill pail which contained dish water and table scraps. She didn't speak as she emptied the pail into Squealer's trough.

"Ya go in?" Mary asked.

Lide shook her head. "The swill pail was outside."

"Ya hear anythin'?"

Lide didn't answer. Mary demanded, "I said did ya hear anythin'?"

Lide's voice caught. "Yeah. They's doin' it - an' - an' - Amos is yellin' somethin' awful." She sobbed. "I wonder how long it takes?"

"Poor Amos," Mary murmured. "He wanted so bad to come to Michigan. I prayed all night he wouldn't lose his leg -"

Again there was a long silence. At last Mary said, "They'll come tell us when 'tis over." Lide nodded.

After another long wait Mary said, "I'm goin' up to the door an' see what they're doin'.

Lide jumped up. "Don't go, Maw! Ya don't want to hear that saw." She shuddered. "An' Amos yellin' -" Mary sat down again.

The chickens scratched in the barnyard outside the open barn doors. "Ain't much fer 'em to eat," Mary observed.

"I seen 'em eatin' weed seeds like birds does - an' they stays nearby. Paw says if they wanders off, foxes or wolves'll git 'em."

Mary didn't answer. Again they lapsed into a long silence. Finally Ben appeared at the door. His face was pale and his eyes looked as though he had been crying.

"Is it over?" Mary asked fearfully.

The boy nodded as he leaned against the wall of the barn. His head was down. He looked exhausted, completely spent.

"What air they doin' now?" Eliza asked.

"Puttin' him t' bed." His voice was low and expressionless.

Mary went to her son. "'Twas bad?" she inquired.

The boy burst into tears. She allowed him to cry for a time, her arm about his shoulders. When he calmed somewhat, he said dully, "The sound of that saw goin' through his leg - an' Amos screamin' - I wanted to run outside - but I had to hold the candle. Paw an' Israil couldn't hardly keep him on the table."

Mary patted him affectionately. "I knows - but ya was a brave boy t' stay an' do what ya had t' do. Now we'll go in."

Slowly they made their way to the house.

Chapter V

WILDERNESS LIFE

(1836 - 1837)

Mary stared into the kettle of simmering dried apples as she slowly stirred the fruit with a long-handled wooden spoon. Two days until Thanksgiving and there would be nothing special for dinner. Maybe they should kill a hen. Lord knows, they all needed a change - something to cheer them up. She turned to Amos.

"Spoze they'll git the mash hay up 'fore 'nother snow? Paw says we're in luck to have jest a leetle snow by Thanksgivin'."

"I duno." Amos didn't raise his eyes from his bandaged stump which rested on a big block of wood.

"'Member Thanksgivin' dinners in York State? Cranberries, pie, cake, turkey - oh, we had some good dinners, an' you boys et 'till I thought you'd bust."

Amos didn't answer. Mary wondered if he'd even heard her. She threw a small log on the fire before she sat by the east window with her mending.

"Lide's doin' good at helpin'," Mary said trying to make conversation. "She don't even say nothin' when the wolves howl at night, an' Israil says she's doin' a man's work at gettin' up the mash grass."

Amos raised his eyes. "She's doin' my work." His voice was low and expressionless. "I ain't no good t' myself er my family."

Mary held her needle up to the light as she threaded it. "Ya will be. Jacob said in a few months your stump'll heal an' he'll make ya a wooden leg. Lots a' men work with a peg leg."

"'Twon't be the same." His voice broke, "I wanted to work hard an' git my own land - 'afore Israil got hisn. Now I can't do nothin'. I wisht ya'd let me die 'stead a' draggin' me back like this." His eyes went to the guns standing in the corner.

Mary noticed and silently vowed the guns would be kept in the loft where Amos couldn't get them. She got up suddenly.

"They's somethin' ya kin do to help me. We ain't had time to shuck them nuts we picked up 'afore we got to Byron. Ya kin shuck 'em fer me." She went outside and returned with a pail of hickory nuts, a hammer and a stone the size of a small pumpkin.

"Woman's work," Amos muttered slowly making his way to the table where a batch of newly baked bread was cooling. He placed his crutches under the bench. Then holding the unshucked nuts on the stone, one at a time, he tapped them gently with the hammer. The husks fell away to reveal creamy white hickory nuts. For a time the only sounds in the cabin were the tapping of the hammer and the crackle of the fire.

Suddenly something blocked out the light from the window behind Mary. She turned to stare into the dark face of an Indian. Her heart pounded. Her thoughts raced. The guns. No. Wait and see what he wanted. She was glad Lide was with the men at the marsh.

A moment later the door opened and a tall deerskin-clad Indian stepped inside. Amos turned at the sound.

"Git out!" he shouted swinging around on the backless bench as he reached for his crutches.

The color drained from Mary's face. She was silent with terror. The Indian stepped away from the door and opened it wider to drag in a huge, dark-reddish-brown tom turkey. He held it out toward Amos.

"Fer us?" the crippled man asked.

The Indian placed the turkey on the floor beside Amos, then strode back to stand by the door. "Brade - brade -" he said in a deep gutteral voice.

Amos struggled to stand with the aid of his crutches. "Thank ya," he said softly. He turned to his mother. "He wants bread."

Mary took a large loaf of the warm bread from the table. "Fer ya," she smiled. "An' thank ya fer the turkey. 'Twill be good fer our Thanksgivin' dinner. Our men ain't had time to hunt much."

There was no expression on the Indian's dark face as he took the bread, turned and went outside.

Mary dropped weakly into her chair. "What do ya think a' that?" she gasped.

"Anyways, he's friendly," Amos said. "There must be a camp somewheres nearby. Jacob said he thought 'twasn't far frum us." He stopped, then went on. "Don't ya think he was the Injun that Ben called "the chief" when they camped by us?"

"I duno. He might be." Mary got up to lift the turkey onto the table. "I didn't know they grew so big. Amos, we'll have a good dinner day after tomorrer, thanks to that Injun." She went to the window but he had disappeared. She sighed. "He 'most scared me t' death lookin' in the winder at me that a' way." She packed the baking of bread away.

"Ain't it funny?" Mary went on, "A leetle while ago ever'thin' looked dark t' me, an' jest a leetle kindness frum that Injun changed things. Now I feels thankful - thankful yer alive - thankful our family's together - an thankful to that Injun that we'll have a real Thanksgivin' dinner."

Amos said bitterly, "'Twill take more 'n that to make me thankful to be the way I am."

"Son, 'tis allus darkest 'afore the sunrise."

Silently Amos returned to the table to shuck

hickory nuts while his mother dressed the turkey as she softly sang,

"We're marching t' Zion,
Beautiful, beautiful Zion,
We're marching upward t' Zion,
That beautiful city of God."

After a time Amos said, "That Injun acted as if he didn't know I had one leg off."

"I think he seen it, but didn't want ya t' know he'd seen. I has heerd Injuns don't talk 'bout things that makes people feel bad - not t' their face anyways."

The days passed. Thanksgiving and Christmas were over and it was 1837. The men were busy cutting wood and hunting. They built a small lean-to on the north side of the cabin where venison and other wild game was stored. Lide divided her time between working outside and helping her mother.

The family often speculated about the Indian who had brought the turkey, but he hadn't returned. Though they still were somewhat apprehensive, as the days passed their fears lessened. Perhaps Stephen Avery had been right and the Indians wouldn't harm them.

Nearly every day Ben talked of Shobegun. From his mother's and brother's description of the Indian who had come to the cabin, Ben was convinced that he must be "the chief." "Someday I'll find Shobegun," he said. "We'll hunt and fish together an' I'll have a friend again."

"Ya might," Mary said. "'Twould be nice fer ya. Ever'body needs friends."

Lide poked the fire thoughtfully. "I miss my friends, too. 'Tis lonely here."

Robert looked up from the harness he was mending at the table. "'Tis likely there'll be new people comin' to settle 'fore long. Maybe there's people nearby now that we don't know 'bout."

"Yeah, we'll have neighbors," Israil agreed.

"Come spring an' summer, they'll be movin' in." He glanced at his brother. "Ya'll be gettin' out by then to meet 'em."

Amos rocked silently before the fire. Finally he muttered, "Mebbe. But fer now I wisht this damn foot would quit hurtin'." He sighed.

Ben argued, "The foot's buried, Amos. I don't see how it kin hurt ya."

"I don't neither. But it feels like it's still there an' it hurts most as bad as 'afore Jacob cut it off - ever'day an' night the damn thing hurts bad."

Mary said softly, "Don't swear, Amos. 'Twon't help none."

Robert changed the subject. "We've been here two months an' we ain't gone hungry er cold yet. An' the weather has been good - only one leetle snow storm -"

Lide laughed. "I gits tired a' eatin' venison an' rabbit, but none a' us is gettin' skinny. An' look at Maw - she's gettin' fat. Anyways, she ain't sick no more like she was there fer a spell."

Ben exclaimed, "By crackey, yer right, Lide! Maw is gettin' fat!"

Mary flushed beet red. "'Tis none a' yer bizness if'n I gets fat - jest so long as I keeps up my work!"

The cabin suddenly was silent except for the snoring of Sam who lay beneath Amos' stump. The elder brothers stole speculative glances at their mother. Silently Robert continued his work on the harness.

In a few minutes Mary said shortly, "Lide, ya got churnin'."

"Yeah." She brought the tall wooden churn from a corner and dumped a kettle of thick sour cream into it. After putting the cover on, Lide worked the dasher up and down. It made a spatting sound as it hit the cream. Splash - splash - splash - splash -

Robert got up. "Israil, we better git the

spring boxed in so's we kin dip water. The creek's bound to freeze over soon. This weather can't hold much longer."

After the men left Ben said, "Amos, why don't ya go out with Paw an' Israil an' me? Ya ain't been outdoors in weeks. I'll help ya."

"Damn it! I ain't no damn baby! I don't need no help!" He grabbed his crutches and struggled to stand. "Where's my coat?"

Mary hurried to get his coat, cap and mittens. When Amos and Ben were gone she said, "I'm most glad t' hear him swear. He ain't showed no feelin' 'bout nothin' since we got here. He ain't acted like Amos 'afore."

Splash - splash - splash - splash - Lide didn't answer but stared glumly out of the window as she rhythmically raised and lowered the dasher of the churn.

Mary carried a pan of potatoes to the table. The cabin was quiet except for the audible hiss of the paring knife as it slid through a newly pared potato before she dropped the pieces with a splash into a kettle of water.

Splash - splash - splash - The monotonous rhythm of the churn dasher continued. At last Mary said softly, "I ought'n been sharp with ya, Lide."

The girl replied, "I didn't mean nothin' - an' neither did Ben."

Mary stood up. "I knows. I can't josh much these days."

"Yeah. 'Tis Amos, ain't it?"

Splash - splash - splash - splash - Finally Mary said, "No, 'tain't Amos." She hesitated as Lide looked at her questioningly. "It's - it's - oh, I'm 'shamed t' tell ya."

"Maw, what ails ya? Ya've never done nothin' t' be 'shamed 'bout."

"Well - well - I'm in the family way." Her face and neck flushed.

Lide stopped churning as she stared at Mary in disbelief. In a moment her expression changed. She rushed to her mother to put her arms around her. "Maw! We're really goin' t' have a baby? Oh, I'm so glad!"

Mary stepped to the window. "I'm 'shamed, Lide. I'm too old fer havin' 'nother baby."

"Ya ain't old, Maw," Lide argued. "Ya was only sixteen when Israil was borned. Ya told me that yerself."

"I'm gettin' up towards forty an' that's too old to have a baby. I'll be an old woman 'fore the baby's half growed up." She turned. "I'm shamed fer Israil an' Amos t' know."

"Does Paw know?"

Mary nodded.

"Ain't he glad?"

"Men's allus glad fer more young'uns. But they don't have t' carry 'em fer nine months, an' feel sick, an' - an' - birth 'em, an' wash fer 'em -" She wiped her eyes.

Lide returned to the churn. As the dasher splashed the cream, she said, "I'll be here t' help ya with the baby. We'll all help. When is it comin'?"

"May er June."

Suddenly the sound inside the churn changed to rapid splashing. "Butter's come," Lide said as she removed the dasher and looked inside. Firm globules of yellow butter floated on top of the buttermilk.

Mary appeared with the wooden butter bowl and ladle. "I'll do it now," she said as she gathered the pieces of floating butter into a mass with a few quick motions of the wooden butter ladle and swished the dripping yellow lump into the large wooden butter bowl. Then, adding salt, she ladled the soft butter until the buttermilk was worked out. Finally she packed it into a crock and covered it with a clean cloth.

"Less set down an' have some buttermilk," Lide suggested as she dipped two cups into the churn and carried them to the table where they silently sipped the delicious sour beverage. Small pieces of sweet unsalted butter floated in the liquid and added to their enjoyment.

The first heavy snow arrived in mid-January. It began with darkening skies and a brisk northwest wind followed by showers of snow which increased in intensity until it was impossible to see more than a few feet in any direction.

Ben stared into the storm. The snowflakes seemed to converge at a point a few inches beyond the window. He looked away to clear the momentary sensation of dizziness caused by the swirling snow.

Amos hobbled to the table and lowered himself to the bench. "Lide," he called to his sister who was washing dishes, "Where did ya put the box a' books we brung frum York State?"

"'Tis in the loft. Ben an' me kin git 'em fer ya."

Ben turned from the window and ran up the ladder. "I'll hand 'em down," he called to Lide.

A few minutes later a dozen books were piled on the table beside Amos. Mary came to glance through her hymn book. Lide and Ben were leafing through books they had had in school. Amos was reading a book on government. For an hour they forgot about the snow as they read by the light of the flickering candle.

Robert and Israil stamped the snow from their boots as they came inside. "Wind's gettin' strong," Robert said, "an' if the snow keeps comin' there'll soon be drifts."

As a blast of wind hit the side of the cabin, Mary got up. "I'm thankful us an' the beasts air in where 'tis warm, an' we has plenty t' eat."

Half an hour later with the family gathered about the table, Amos suddenly said, "What's the first number ya kin think of that's got a "a" in it?"

Lide asked, "Ya mean when ya spell 'em?"

"Yeah." Amos grinned.

Silently each one spelled the numerals. Amos watched, enjoying the puzzled faces of his family. Fifteen minutes later Israil said, "There ain't none that's got a "a" in 'em."

Amos chuckled. "Yeah, they is. Keep goin'. Don't tell how fer ya've gone, an' don't tell when ya finds it. Jest tell me."

The family cooperated, partly because they needed diversion, but mostly because they were happy to see Amos interested in something outside himself.

Finally Mary said, "I knows!" She bent to whisper to Amos. He nodded. Eventually everyone solved the problem.

"Kin ya beat that?" Israil said. "No a's in the number words 'till ya git to a thousand. How'd ya know that, Amos?"

Amos beamed. "I 'membered, an' I thought ya would, too. 'Member how Mr. Pless used t' show us tricks with numbers in school?"

"Yeah. But ya never seemed t' be listenin'. Ya was allus tryin' t' make somebody laugh."

"I heerd what he said jest the same."

"Ya'd make a good schoolmaster, Amos," Mary commented. "Why don't ya give Ben an' Lide some numbers?"

Amos flipped the pages in the worn old arithmetic book. "Did we fetch our slates?"

"They're in a box in the loft," Ben said as he raced up the ladder. For the rest of the afternoon Amos read problems from the book and the two younger children solved them on their slates.

Finally Ben said, "I'm tired a' thinkin'. Less stop."

"Jest one more," Amos said. "Here's a good one. If wilderness land is worth $3.75 per acre, how much would 90 acres cost?"

"Three hunnert thirty seven dollars an' fifty cents!" Lide shouted.

Ben jumped up. "I'm quittin'. Ya beat me all the time!"

"That's a lot of money," Amos said thoughtfully. "Two dollars an acre was what ya paid, wasn't it, Paw?"

"Yep. An' if we has good crops, 'twon't be long

'afore ya an' Israil has yer own land."

Amos didn't reply but silently stacked the books on the corner of the table.

"Will ya help us agin?" Lide asked.

"Mebbe." He hobbled to his chair near the fire.

Robert walked to the door. Wind blown snow had swept around the northeast corner of the cabin to form a two foot drift along the front of the log house. He slammed the door. "'Tis good we piled the leetle branches off the trees we cut fer the barn jest outside the barnyard. Tall hay will come in handy fer fodder fer the critters."

"We ain't got 'nuff mash grass?" Mary asked.

"Nope. Not 'nuff t' last 'till spring. They's been doin' good jest eatin' grass an' brush nearby, but with all this snow, 'twill be slim pickin'."

For two days the snow and wind continued. Daily Israil and his father broke the ice in the creek and drove the animals through three foot snowbanks for drinks of icy water. Finally the snow stopped but the wind continued its slashing onslaught.

Though Robert and Israil had thought the cabin was well-built, snow sifted in through small, almost invisible cracks between the logs on the north and west sides and lay in graceful lines along the wall. In the loft the beds were covered with fine powdery snow.

During the storm the men waterproofed their boots by rubbing them with tallow from the deer they had shot. Ben made a pair of snowshoes by bending willow boughs into long ovals. He then stretched and wove strips of deerhide across the frame.

"Shobegun would know how to do this," he muttered as he studied a way to fasten the snowshoes to his feet.

Mary occupied herself with mending the loose gray linen shirts and the below-the-knee breeches which were worn by her men. "'Spoze ya could tan deerhide?" she asked Robert. "Leather would last better an' 'twould be a lot warmer than these breeches."

"I don't know how, but next time we go t' Byron we kin ask Jacob. "'Twould be good t' make clothes of deerskins."

"Shobegun's paw would know how. All the Injuns wear deerskin clothes," Ben volunteered.

Lide and Amos sat at the table with the pile of books between them. "'Tis good t' read agin," Lide said softly.

"Yeah," Amos replied. "This book we had in school tells 'bout guv'ment. When they's more settlers, we're goin' t' need township guv'ment. I'm readin' it good so's I'll know what t' do."

They read silently for a time. Amos closed his book and stared into the fire. "I wisht I'd paid better 'tention in school," he said to Lide. "Them Avery fellers knows 'bout ever'thing. They knows 'bout guv'ment, an' the stars, an' plants, an' the Bible - they reads ever' day. That's why they is smart. An' they talks different an' we does. They talks the right way."

"Yeah. We jest talks like Paw an' Maw. Mebbe if we try we kin talk more like things is wrote in books."

Mary watched Amos and noted with satisfaction that he was coming out of his depression. He still wasn't the fun-loving, joke-telling Amos of old, but perhaps in time. There always had been rivalry between her two elder boys who were only a year apart in age. Amos seemed to be driven to outdo Israil in the physical area. Running, plowing land, cutting wood - whatever it was, he must be better than his brother. At school he had not done as well as the more serious Israil for the schoolmaster, Mr. Pless, had often punished him for inattention and for upsetting the schoolroom with his practical jokes. But Amos was different from Israil. He craved attention, and from the time he was small, he'd do anything - anything to be noticed.

Finally by the third morning the wind had died down and the sun was out. Huge mounds of snow buried farm tools. Israil, Robert and Ben shoveled a path to the barn and another to the creek. Then Ben practiced walking on his snowshoes.

When blizzards rage in the wilderness, wild animals find shelter. Deer huddle together in swamps and rabbits stay in their burrows or they hide under a snow-covered pile of brush or logs until the storm is over. When the weather is warm, deer graze and rabbits are out so that wolves easily find plenty of food. Now, however, nothing had moved for several days. Though the family occasionally heard wolves howling in the distance, none had recently come close to the cabin.

The night after the storm ended Lide and Mary were washing the supper dishes when a wolf howled nearby. Mary shivered, but didn't comment. In a minute the wolf howled again to be answered by one close to the buildings. The cry of the wolf, full-throated and vibrant, drifted through the crisp cold air. A tingle ran up Mary's back as the voices of the pack joined in to howl in chorus for three or four minutes.

Mary shuddered. "When they all howls together it makes my blood run cold."

Lide said quietly, "They can't git in here."

Robert brought the rifle from the loft and went to the door. By the light of the full moon he saw three wolves less than twenty yards away. They watched him curiously. He aimed and fired as Sam rushed from the door barking furiously.

Ben shouted, "They'll kill Sam!" He called, "Here Sam! Here Sam!"

"I missed," Robert said. "They wheeled an' run jest as I shot."

Sam sniffed the wolves' tracks, peered into the wilderness, and then trotted back to the cabin.

"They're hungry," Israil said. "They smells the venison an' rabbits in the lean-to. They'll be back."

Half an hour later the pack tuned up for an

evening chorus. Silently the family listened. They could distinguish individual voices in the chorus as the sounds rose and fell in intensity. First came a low mournful moan that stirred the emotions and lasted from ten to fifteen seconds, then another voice joined in, then another and another. The mournful howls grew in intensity until it seemed as though the whole pack had joined in an evening symphony. The harmonious blending of their voices sent tingles up Mary's back. Five minutes later the serenade ended suddenly.

The family listened. "Mebbe they is gone," Lide said hopefully. No one answered.

A few minutes later loud sniffing sounds at the door brought Sam to his feet barking furiously. Israil hurried to secure the door with a heavy board. Again it was quiet outside for a time before vigorous scratching began on the north wall.

"The lean-to," Robert said quietly. "They smells the venison an' rabbits." He picked up the gun and started toward the door.

"Wait," Israil said as he went to the loft to return with his gun. "Mebbe we kin git a couple a' the buggers." He turned to Ben. "Keep Sam in here."

The sniffing grew louder. "Must be the hull pack," Amos said as Robert and Israil closed the door behind them.

For a few seconds there was silence except for the sniffing and scratching of the wolves. Suddenly two shots rang out followed by a sharp high-pitched yelp. Another shot followed, and then silence.

Ben was out the door. "They got 'em!" he shouted to Mary and Lide at the window. "They got two!"

A few minutes later Robert said, "They won't be back tonight. They is smart. But boys, we has to keep the barn doors shut tight at night. 'Tis likely they'll try to git in."

"What did ya do with the two ya shot?" Lide asked.

"They was big buggers," Israil remarked. "We drug them into the lean-to. Tomorrer we'll skin 'em. The hides'll make warm blankets."

After the blizzard the weather settled down to below freezing temperatures with occasional light snows. Ben, on snowshoes explored the nearby wilderness with Sam. He learned to snare rabbits. Where the creek ran through the marsh he found muskrat houses and his traps yielded several animals which were skinned. The hides would be sold when they could get to Howell in the spring and the meat was cooked to provide a change of fare for the family.

Ben watched the wild creatures. Winter birds were everywhere. Chickadees chirped, "Dee - dee - dee," as they flew from tree to tree. Nuthatches crept head down as they searched tree bark for insect larvae. A flash of red became a brilliant male cardinal silhouetted against the gray of bare tree branches. Ben learned to imitate bird calls and enjoyed coaxing them to a nearby tree. The cheerful whistle of a cardinal often caused him to pause until he could locate the brilliant little singer and his drab dull-colored mate.

One bright winter day as he was removing a muskrat from a trap, he failed to look up at the whistle of a cardinal. Vaguely he was aware of the constant call, and assumed the bird was waiting for his usual answering whistle. At last he turned, and carrying the dead muskrat, he started home.

Again the whistle of the cardinal sounded nearby. Turning to search for the little singer he looked into the eyes of a deerskin-clad boy not twenty feet away.

"Shobegun!" he shouted as he dashed toward the boy. "I knowed you'd come!" He laughed. "You was the red bird that called!" He whistled and Shoebegun answered - a perfect cardinal song.

"Ben," the Indian boy said. He carried a roll

of buckskin under his arm. He held it out saying, "Fer ya."

"Fer me?" Ben took the gift and quickly unrolled two beautifully tanned deerskins. "'Tis soft," he said touching the suede-like leather. "Thank ya, Shobegun, thank ya."

The Indian boy touched his fringed two piece suit, then pointed to the deerskin which Ben held.

"Yeah," Ben said, "'Twill make a warm shirt er breeches. My maw will sew it fer me. Come with me an' we'll git somethin' t' eat."

The Indian boy looked puzzled. "Bread," Ben said. "We'll git bread."

"Brade?"

"Yeah. Maw'll give ya bread."

Together the boys made their way along the creek until they came to the cabin. At the door Shobegun hesitated. "Come," Ben motioned. "Come in."

The Indian boy stood silently just inside the door. Lide and Amos were at the table with their books and Mary was stirring a kettle of something at the fireplace.

"He come!" Ben shouted.

Suddenly all eyes were on the newcomer who stood like a statue.

"'Tis Shobegun!" Ben exclaimed. "An' see what he give me! Maw, kin ya make me breeches like hisn?"

Mary smiled at the silent young Indian. "Hello, Shobegun. We're glad you've come." She took the deerskin from Ben. "'Tis good soft leather," she said approvingly. "'Twill make a fine pair a' breeches."

"Maw," Ben said, "kin we give him some bread?"

"We'll give him rabbit stew an' johnny cake." She dished up a large portion and placed it on the table beside Amos. "Shobegun, set down an' eat." She motioned but the boy still stood beside the door.

"Fer ya," Ben said pointing to the stew.

"Come."

The boy slowly walked to the table. Ben pointed to his brother. "Amos," he said.

"Amos," the boy murmured.

"Lide," Ben said pointing to his sister.

Shobegun said slowly as he pointed to each person, "Amos, Lide, Ben."

"That's right!" Lide exclaimed.

Mary brought a bowl of stew for Ben and put it beside the one for Shobegun. "Ya set with him, Ben. He feels shy with us." Shobegun watched Mary.

"My Maw," Ben said.

Again Shobegun pointed to each one as he repeated, "Maw, Amos, Ben, Lide."

"Good!" Ben said. "Less eat." He motioned toward his mouth and pointed at the stew.

Ben chattered as they ate, explaining where and how he had met the Indian. "Paw an' Israil'll be s'prized when they gits back frum cuttin' wood," he remarked.

When they finished eating Ben said, "We'll skin the rat now. Maw, kin ya give him some bread to take home when he goes?"

"Ya come in an' I'll have some fer him."

When the muskrat was skinned and stretched to dry, Ben took his guest to the barn to show him the animals. Finally Shobegun started through the woods to the northwest.

"Wait!" Ben called. "I'll git ya some bread!"

The boy followed him back to the cabin where Mary gave him a large loaf of bread. Silently he accepted it and made his way through the woods to the northwest.

Chapter VI

INDIAN NEIGHBORS

(1837)

The early days of 1837 seemed endless to Mary. She was resentful about her pregnancy and felt trapped in the cabin with Amos who daily verbalized his bitterness about his handicap. She longed for the quiet and privacy of her former home. Though she read her Bible for inspiration, she felt sinful because she couldn't look forward with pleasure to the birth of her baby.

Lide and Ben had adjusted to the wilderness life and planned for the coming summer. Israil and his father spent part of each day cutting, piling and burning logs as they wrenched, foot by foot, fertile farm land from the grip of the wilderness.

"'Twill take a few years," Robert said, "but once ya own the land ya can clear it a leetle more every year, an' when ya're done, yer well fixed fer life."

Shobegun and Ben had become close friends as they snared rabbits, hunted with bow and arrow and the rifle, and trapped muskrats along the creek. The Indian boy often went to the cabin and sat beside the table stoically watching and listening as Amos taught Lide and Ben from the old books. He learned quickly and soon was able to speak in broken English.

Ben tired of books but Mary insisted that he spend some time each day on "figgerin' an' readin'."

Lide enjoyed studying. One day Amos said, "When they's a few more settlers near here, we'll need a school. Mebbe you can be teacher."

"Do ya think I could, Maw?" she asked, her eyes shining.

"Don't know why not," Mary replied.

From that time Lide worked every spare minute. She studied the "government book" as well as arithmetic and the tattered old geography. She practiced writing until her slate was covered with flowing handwriting decorated with swirls, flourishes and curlicues. Because there were few books, she read her mother's Bible, which pleased Mary. She made an effort to speak correctly working on changing "ya" to "you" and "yer" to "your."

Israil remarked. "Since yer gettin' yer schoolin', I hopes they's young'uns nearby someday that ya can larn. 'Course, ya could go to the Injun camp an' larn their young'uns." He laughed.

"If they're all as smart as Shobegun, they'd learn right fast," Lide answered. "Ben said he'd seen four or five childrens, -" she stopped, then continued, "children that wasn't as old as Shobegun. I'd like to help them."

"Aw, come on. Ya air gettin' t' be an Injun lover, an' ya knows well's I do 'most of 'em is ornery varmints."

Mary said, "They ain't hurted us none, an' Shobegun an' his paw air right nice t' us."

Israil shook his head. "I don't trust 'em. They's skittish wood critters that stalk up on ya like a shadder out a' nowheres. Jest yestiddy when Paw an' me was choppin' down a tree, I seen one of 'em watchin' us. He stood still's a tree, jest lookin'. A minute later I looked agin an' the varmint was gone - jest like a shadder. What's they doin' watchin' us?"

"Mebbe they's wonderin' 'bout how white folks lives," Amos answered.

Mary changed the subject. "Amos' stump is healed up good. Why don't you an' him ride over to Byron on King an' Queen an' have Jacob make a wooden leg fer him?"

"Think yer stump's healed 'nuff?" Israil asked his brother.

"Yeah. Guess I might's well see how it goes," Amos said quietly.

"Ya'll take t' walkin' 'thout them crutches like a duck t' water," Mary said encouragingly.

While Israil and Amos were gone, Robert and Ben cut and burned trees. Mary and Lide got out the yard goods they had bought in Detroit, and while Mary cut out baby clothes, Lide sewed.

"Maw, I'm glad you tole - told me 'bout the baby," Lide said as she held up a tiny garment. "Does Amos and Israil know?"

Mary bent over the table to cut another garment. "I duno. I 'spect they has an idee - I shows now. I'm gettin' big." She was silent for a time, then she said softly, "'Twill be kinda nice t' have a leetle one 'round agin."

Lide laughed. "I hope it's a girl."

"Yer Paw wants a boy. Men allus wants boys - but what would they do 'thout us womens to cook an' wash an' keep house?"

"Yeah. They don't think 'bout that."

When Ben appeared at the door Mary changed the subject. "Ya quittin' a'ready?" she asked.

Ben put his wet mittens on the hearth and selected a dry pair. "Paw's workin' yet, but he said I could go t' the camp t' see Shobegun. He ain't been here fer a while."

Mary got up slowly and went to the bread box. "Take him some bread," she said. "He allus likes it. And be back 'afore dark."

Ben headed northwest across the log bridge over the creek and through the forest to the camp two and one half miles away. A noisy blue jay shrieked, "Thief! Thief!" in a loud voice. Ben answered the call and the crest on the blue jay's head stood straight up in anger. The call seemed to waken the chickadees who flew about twittering, "Dee, dee, dee." Even a pair of red squirrels began chattering at him from the branch overhead.

Through the oak, maple, beech and poplar forest, Ben made his way along a trail six inches deep and three feet wide which had resulted from years of trips by the Indians to the creek near the Colborn farm. The trail skirted swamps, sinkholes and marshy places, eventually coming out at the Indian camp.

Ben had visited the camp before. Always the activity had interested him. Outdoor cooking, women skinning animals, children playing and men coming in with game, all had given him an idea of the home life of the Indians.

The half dozen shacks seemed deserted. Four mangy dogs came barking to greet him and to coax for the bread. A feeling of fear gripped Ben. Something was wrong.

Puzzled, he stood staring at Shobegun's home. The shack was a squat log hut with a flat roof and no windows except for a pane of glass nailed over a square hole in the rough door. He looked at the other hovels. They seemed deserted except for thin spirals of smoke ascending from rusty pipes through the roofs. All of the huts were ancient and tumble-down in appearance with only one window, their low bark shed roofs nearly touching the ground in the rear. Ben wondered how anyone could live in these places in cold weather.

Holding the bread above the heads of the barking dogs, he went to the door of his friend's home. He called, "Shobegun! 'Tis Ben!"

The door opened and the Chief, thin, haggard and with sores covering his face, stared at Ben who held out the bread in greeting. "Fer ya," the boy said.

Silently the tall man accepted the gift. Shobegun's voice came from the interior of the dark hut. "Stay out. Sick here. All sick peoples."

"But I kin help ya!" Ben called. Standing in the doorway, his eyes became accustomed to the darkness. Like their father, Shobegun's and his elder sister's faces were covered with huge sores. Their mother murmured from her pole bunk along the wall.

Ben knew. They had smallpox. He remembered when his family had it in York State five years before. The same sores. He called, "Is ever'body in the camp sick?"

"Yeah," the Indian boy said quietly. "Bad sick."

"Tell yer Paw I'll be back. I'm goin' home fer help."

Shobegun interpreted for the Chief whose stoic, haggard eyes did not change in expression as he closed the door.

Ben ran the two and one half miles to the cabin. Bursting in the door he shouted, "Maw! The Injuns has got smallpox! They's all sick! All of 'em!"

Mary said, "Mebbe 'taint smallpox. Mebbe 'tis somethin' else."

"No! 'Tis smallpox! Big sores, an' Shobegun's maw don't know what she's sayin' - she jest talks an' talks - Maw, 'tis smallpox. We gotta help 'em!"

Mary got up. "Yeah. We gotta. Go call yer Paw, an' Lide, bring in a big piece a' venison an' three, four muskrats. We'll cook up some soup fer 'em. Poor Injuns - somebody has t' help 'em. I hope yer Paw will take things to the camp an' do fer 'em 'till they're better."

Lide mixed a huge johnny cake as Mary prepared the soup. Thoughtfully, she said, "Paw an' Ben won't get it again, will they?"

"Folks don't hardly ever git it two times," Mary answered.

The sound of coughing outside told them that Robert was returning from the woods. Inside the door he wiped his mouth as he watched the bustling women. Mary explained the conditions at the camp.

"Ya're fixin' a powerful lot a' food. Ya plannin' to feed the hull camp?" he asked.

"They's all sick. We has t' help 'em," Mary

answered as she tossed a pan of vegetables into the simmering kettle.

"Tis a long time till we grows more. They won't be no wheat this summer, an' them 'taters an' carrots'll soon be gone. Ya can't give 'em too many." He suffered another coughing spell.

"'Tis only Christian t' help 'em," Mary said. "Ben says the hull camp is sick. We can't set here so close an' do nothin'." After a moment she said, "Ya'll help Ben tote the soup, won't ya?"

"I spoze I'll have to, but the critters has t' be watered an' the cow milked first. 'Twill be dark by then. We'll take the rifle, an' while I'm at the barn, Ben, ya make a torch t' keep the wolves away."

Mary shivered, but said nothing as Ben set the gun beside the door. An hour later father and son loaded with pails of soup and johnny cake, and with the rifle slung over Robert's shoulder and the flaming torch carried by Ben, they set off for the camp.

They talked very little, though Ben muttered, "I wisht Israil was here 'stead a' bein' in Byron with Amos. 'Twould a' been better if we'd had King and Queen to ride."

Only the whispering of owls' wings in the treetops overhead and the cry of a wolf in the distance broke the stillness of the winter forest. The grease-soaked rag torch burned slowly in Ben's hand. Finally the boy asked, "How we gonna see in their shacks?"

"Maw stuck candles in my pocket," Robert answered. "We'll get 'em fed, an' then go home. This soup was boilin' hot when we left. Mebbe 'twill still be warm."

At last they reached the edge of the camp. Ben stuck his torch into a snowbank to extinguish the flame. Barking dogs descended on them, and just outside the camp ponies neighed.

Ben went to Shobegun's hut and shouted, "Paw an' me brung ya some soup!"

The Indian boy opened the door. "Bad sick," he

said. "Stay out."

"We'll help you," Ben said pushing past Shobegun. "We'll not get sick."

Robert set the pail of soup on the dirt floor and lighted a candle from his pipe. "Eat," he said opening one pail.

Shobegun's father crawled from his pole bunk to get wooden bowls from the rough table. He dipped dishes of soup and carried them to his sick squaw and daughter before he and Shobegun ate.

The squaw muttered to herself, but did not eat. The daughter appeared to be grown - perhaps seventeen or eighteen years old. The family's swollen red-blotched faces were definite evidence of the dread disease of smallpox.

Ben motioned to the remainder of the soup and johnny cake. "For people," he said as he pointed outside to the other shacks.

Shobegun interpreted for his father who immediately pulled another deerskin tunic over his head and weakly tottered toward the door.

They went from shack to shack delivering warm soup. Everywhere it was the same. Indians with feverish, flushed faces in various stages of the disease were shaking with chills and vomiting while their voices rambled in delirium.

Some, like Shobegun, were past the early stages of the disease but remained weak and with little appetite. All who were conscious made an attempt to swallow a little of the soup and to eat a few bites of the johnny cake. In the dim light of the candle, Robert and Ben were aware that several of the Indians lay motionless in their bunks. Ben wondered if they were dead. Finally the Chief led the way back to his shack. "Thank ya," he said in a gutteral voice. The dogs still barked furiously as they had since Ben and his father arrived.

Shobegun came to the door as Robert covered the remaining soup and set it inside. "Mebbe there's 'nuff fer tomorrer mornin'," he said.

The boy leaned against the wall for support. "Thank ya," he said softly as the Chief closed the door.

When the torch was burning again they started toward home. Not until they were a quarter mile down the trail did the dogs become quiet.

"They're turrible sick, ain't they?" Ben asked.

"Yeah. I' spect some a' them bunks had dead Injuns in 'em," Robert replied.

"It smelt bad in them shacks," Ben said. "It made me sick. Bad smells an' puke - I've been in Shobegun's shack 'afore, but 'twasn't like now."

"They must 'ave been sick a week an' mebbe longer. Nobody was able t' hunt, so there wasn't no food."

A wolf howled nearby. In a moment an answer came from the right.

"They're follerin' us, Paw, an' the torch ain't burnin' good."

"If they gits too close I'll shoot one. That'll skeer 'em off."

They walked without talking, listening. Robert had the rifle in his hands. Suddenly he whirled to face a pack of ten or twelve stalking animals not twenty feet behind. Instinctively he fired into the middle of the pack. The vicious animals ran snarling into the woods leaving one of the pack dead beside the trail.

"Damn critters," Robert said. "That'll keep 'em 'way fer a while."

Ben asked, "Ya think they was fixin' t' jump on us?"

"I duno. Ya hears stories 'bout 'em doin' it, but I never heerd anybody say it happened t' them - still, if they was hungry 'nuff, I 'spect they'd jump on a person."

A few minutes later Sam came tearing down the trail to meet them as they crossed the log bridge near the cabin, while to the north the wolf pack howled their nightly symphony.

The following day Mary and Lide prepared more food for the sick Indians, and again Robert and his son went to the camp in near zero weather.

Three disease-ravaged men, one of them the Chief, were attempting to drag a fat deer to the camp. Ben ran to the edge of the woods to meet them.

"Wait!" he shouted. "Paw an' me'll help!"

Robert set the food beside the Chief's shack. Then, together they dragged the deer into camp. Shobegun, his face swollen, appeared at the door and carried the food inside.

"Tell 'em I'll skin an' cut the deer up," Robert said. "They haf t' git out a' the cold."

An hour later he and Ben helped the Chief distribute the meat to the shacks. Back at Shobegun's home Ben asked, "Air ya better?" He could see the boy's mother and sister still in their bunks.

"Better. Soup good."

Robert motioned toward the other shacks. "Others air better?"

Shobegun didn't answer for a moment. Then he said, "Dead." He held up two fingers. "Dead," he repeated.

"Two air dead?" Robert asked.

"Yeah. My Paw's Paw, an' girl - leetle girl."

"Ask yer Paw what we kin do t' help."

Shobegun talked rapidly to his father who answered briefly. The boy turned to Robert. "He say you help us. You good man. Now we kin do."

"But ya can't put dead people in ground." Robert motioned. "Ground hard. Kin we help?"

Shobegun repeated, "We kin do."

Ben picked up their empty pails. "I'll come back," he said to his friend as he and Robert passed the dogs who were fighting over deer entrails.

Back at the cabin Mary insisted they take baths and that they scrub with soft soap. "They's no tellin' what diseases the Injuns has besides smallpox," she said as Ben grumbled about having to take a bath in winter.

Lide asked, "You think Shobegun's grandfather was the ole - old man that died?"

"Yeah. An' I thinks he's the ole man yer Maw

sent the honey an' vinegar cough syrup when they camped by us," Robert answered. "I seen him last night. He was real sick."

"Pore ole man," Mary said. "He was haf dead two, three months ago. You 'spoze some a' them got smallpox in Detroit an' it's been goin' through the camp ever since?"

"Mebbe. I duno how they's goin' t' bury them dead Injuns with the ground froze three feet deep an' none of 'em strong 'nuff to work."

Sam's bark brought Lide to the window. "'Tis Amos an' Israil! An' Amos is wearin' his wooden leg!" She rushed to the door. Israil helped his brother from the horse and he walked slowly toward the house.

"Look at ya!" Robert roared. "No more crutches! How's it go?"

Amos' face was drawn. "Guess I'll git used to it."

"'Tain't like yer own," Mary agreed, "but 'tis better 'n crutches."

Amos dropped into his chair. "Jacob said 'twould take a while fer my stump t' git tough. I can't wear the peg leg too long 'cause the stump gits sore, but I'll walk on it a leetle more ever' day." That afternoon he went to the barn to help with the chores.

Ben went to the Indian camp each day for the next week. The sick gradually were recovering and Shobegun said they had food. Ben wondered about the dead Indians and how they had been buried, but he respected the Indians' right to privacy and didn't ask. Then one day he was astonished when he discovered how burial in winter was solved by his new friends.

Two scaffolds about ten feet high had been erected by cutting the tops from eight small adjoining trees. Four trees provided the support for each scaffold. A pole platform about four by eight feet was fastened to the four leg-like supports. On top of each scaffold lay a deerskin-covered corpse with only the face exposed.

Ben tried to conceal his astonishment by appearing to watch the dogs and the people about camp, but when he stole glances at the platforms from a distance of fifteen or twenty feet he could see the wrinkled, scarred face of the old man who had coughed so violently the night the group had camped near his family. The second corpse was small. Surely this was the little girl who had died with smallpox.

Walking home along the snowy trail, Ben's mind was filled with questions about these strange primitive people. That night at supper he told the family about his discovery. "Do you spoze they put the dead ones out on the platforms 'cause they couldn't dig graves?" he asked.

Amos' face was intense. "They was all sick. They couldn't keep the dead ones inside long, an' if they put 'em outside, dogs er wolves would eat 'em. On them platforms they'll freeze an' be safe 'till spring when they kin bury 'em. What else could they do?"

Robert said, "I'd have buried 'em, but Shobegun's paw tole him, 'We kin do.'"

Israil exclaimed, "They's heathens! An' I heerd some men talkin' in Detroit 'bout how settlers was marryin' up with squaws."

Amos said quietly, "I hears squaws is good workers. Jacob said some man near Byron married up with a squaw an' she works in the garden an' fields an' takes care a' the baby an' house real good."

Israil snorted. "Squawmen! Any white man that marries up with a squaw is a damned squawman! An' what man wants half-breed young'uns?"

Mary said, "Their ways is not our ways, but that don't mean our ways is best fer ever'body. God made us all, an' He must a' knowed what He was doin'."

The winter months passed and the days began to lengthen. Robert, Israil and Ben spent many hours each week clearing their land. Amos gradually took on more of the barn work for he now was able to wear his wooden leg all day.

In late March the weather moderated. Warm sunny days and cold nights indicated that it was time to tap the sugar maples. The men drove the team hitched to a stoneboat through the woods where they threw off sap buckets beside each maple tree. Then they returned to bore three inch holes in the tree trunks about three and one-half feet from the ground. Sap buckets were hung on wooden spouts driven into the holes.

Morning and afternoon of each day the sap was collected in barrels and taken on the stoneboat to the backyard where Amos stoked the fire under a large iron kettle. There the sap simmered until much of the water was boiled off and the thick molasses-like maple syrup remained.

Mary and Lide strained the golden liquid through a woolen cloth when sufficient water had evaporated. The resulting product was a pure rich syrup. Some of the sap was boiled until all of the water had evaporated when hard maple sugar was formed. Then, when Mary wanted sugar, she cracked off a piece. Heating the sugar softened it so it could be measured.

One day early in April, Lide went with Ben to the Indian camp. As usual the scrawny dogs announced the arrival of strangers. There was an unusual amount of activity in camp with all of the people gathered near the scaffolds where the wrapped corpses lay. Shobegun ran to meet them. "We bury them," he said pointing to the scaffolds.

"Kin we stay?" Ben asked.

"Ya're friends. Ya an' Lide stay. I go with Paw." He walked to his father who was leading the procession. Beside the Chief a wrinkled old squaw was followed by Shobegun, his sister and mother, and behind them the remaining families walked. All filed slowly toward the scaffolds to the slow beat of drum rhythm provided by three men who stood below the scaffold. The moccasined feet made no sound. Silently they shuffled toward two open graves at the edge of the clearing where they formed a circle around them.

Lide and Ben stood beside the Chief's shack and watched as two tall Indian men ascended ladders and gently lifted the wrapped body from the scaffold and handed it down to waiting hands below. The rhythmic drum beat continued. The dogs howled mournfully as the body was gently lowered into the three-foot-deep grave where it was wrapped in a clean white blanket.

As the people silently waited, the ladders were placed beside the second scaffold and the child's body was removed and carried to a small grave near that of the old man.

The bodies were covered with leaf mold from the forest and over that the soil which had been removed from the grave was placed in a mound. A pile of six inch poles lay nearby. The poles, neatly notched at the corners, were placed over the graves.

A pole three feet high and three inches thick was set at the head of each grave. Ben and Lide could see that something was painted on each pole, but from a distance they could not determine what it was.

When burial was complete, the rhythm of the drums accelerated to be joined by two flute-like instruments made from hollowed-out red cedar poles with curves cut out around and between the finger holes. The music made a fearful noise as blankets were brought from a pile nearby and hung on poles about the graves to partition them off from the camp.

Silently the people returned to their shacks - all except the wrinkled old squaw beside Shobegun's father and a young woman who went inside the blanket enclosure.

Lide whispered, "Ya think that's the old man's squaw and the little girl's mother?" Ben nodded.

A pony neighed. The dogs sat, their noses held high, as they howled mournfully in unison with the monotonous, weird music.

Shobegun's family returned to their shack, and except for the young Indian boy, they ignored Ben and Lide. As he paused Ben asked, pointing toward the grave, "Your grandpaw?"

"Yeah. Big Chief 'afore my Paw." He went inside with his family.

As Ben and Lide returned home the sound of the beating drums, squealing flutes and howling dogs followed them. "That music makes shivers go up my back," Lide said. In a moment she continued. "Shobegun's sister is right purty, isn't she?"

"Yeah. But she didn't have them scars 'afore the smallpox."

"Ya - you know her name?"

"They calls her Mequa."

"Mequa," Lide repeated. "It's kinda purty. I'd like to git t' know her like you knows Shobegun. Mebbe I can go with you again to see them."

All night the weird Indian music continued. Early the next morning at sunrise the Michigan wilderness again was silent.

Chapter VII

FROM DARKNESS TO DAWN

(1837)

Through the cold damp spring of 1837 the Colborn men continued the tiresome work of clearing their land. Great piles of logs lay waiting to be burned. On the few dry days a thick haze of blue smoke hung over the area from many fires of smoldering logs and brush.

So, though April was a cold rainy month, the men worked on at clearing the land. Robert had acquired a cough, so deep and ugly that Mary was concerned. "Ya ought'n be out in the cold rain," she often said as Robert gasped for breath after a coughing spell.

"'Tain't nothin'," he'd reply. "When we gits some warm weather, 'twill be better."

The first summer the men planned to plant as much corn and oats as possible on the cleared land. They would work around stumps which would be removed the following fall and spring to be used for fences. There would be no wheat, which would necessitate their buying grain at Howell to be made into flour.

"By the summer of 1838, if crops air good, we'll be out a' the woods," Robert said.

Mary and Lide continued sewing for the baby. "You knowed - knew about the baby when we bought store cloth in Detroit, didn't you, Maw?" Lide asked as she hemmed a diaper.

Mary smiled and nodded. "'Twill be nice havin' a leetle one around ag'in," she murmured.

Sam barked and Lide opened the door. Shobegun and Mequa were standing outside. "Come in," she said holding the door open wide. "Ben's helpin' the men clear the land." She paused. "Mequa," she went on, "I'm Lide, an' this is my Maw."

The Indian girl did not reply but stood quietly, her dark eyes expressionless. Lide noticed the fringed deerskin dress and moccasins. "They're her best clothes," she thought. She turned to Shobegun. "I'm glad you brought Mequa."

"Kin ya larn her talk?" the boy asked.

"I'd like to help her." Lide went to the bench beside the table. "We'll sit here." She motioned to Mequa who shyly sat beside her.

Mary made tea and brought it to the table. Lide put the cup before the dark-eyed girl. "Tea," she said. "This is tea." She sipped from the cup. "I am drinking tea. You drink tea."

Mequa picked up the cup. "Drink tea," she said in a soft musical voice.

"That's good." Lide pointed to Shobegun. She spoke slowly. "He - is - a - boy. Shobegun - is - a - boy."

"Boy," the girl repeated. "Shobegun - boy."

Lide pointed to herself and then to Mequa. "I - am - a- girl. Mequa - is - a - girl."

"Girl. Mequa - girl. Lide - girl."

"You do good," Lide beamed as she and Mequa sipped their tea.

Shobegun opened the door. "Me go see Ben."

Mary nodded and returned to her sewing, but from the corner of her eye she observed the visitor. Mequa's dark hair was parted in the center and braided so that two heavy braids hung over her shoulders. A beaded band circled her head. Her dress and moccasins were made from the same soft deerskin as that which Shobegun had brought to Ben. Scars from the smallpox still marred the dark face, but they would gradually become less noticeable.

The voices of the girls droned on at the table. Mary hoped they would be friends. This Michigan wilderness was no place for a girl like Lide. No young people - no parties - no good times. All

Lide had to look forward to was work. And when the baby came, there'd be more work.

Mary roused herself when she heard voices outside. A moment later Amos, Ben and Shobegun came inside. Their clothing carried the strong odor of wood smoke.

Lide said, "Mequa, this is Amos."

He smiled and took two halting steps forward, his wooden leg clattering on the floor. "How'd do," he said staring at the Indian girl. Her eyes dropped.

"We are gettin' to know each n'other," Lide explained, "and Mequa is larnin' - learning to talk English."

"That's right nice," Amos said.

Lide turned to Shobegun. "Will you bring Mequa to see us ag'in."

The girl got up as her brother said, "We come ag'in."

Mary, Amos, Ben and Lide called "Goodbye" as the brother and sister went out and closed the door without a reply. Amos tapped his way to the bench. "Don't talk much, do they?"

"Injuns is quiet folk," Ben said. "'Member when they camped by us an' they didn't talk to one 'nother hardly a'tall, an' when I'm to their camp, they don' talk much neither."

Lide said, "Mequa's real purty, ain't she? Amos, you think she's purty?"

"Yeah." He stirred uneasily.

"Maw," Lide asked. "How old you think she is?"

"Mebbe seventeen er eighteen."

"If she comes back a few times I'll have her talkin' English. She's like Shobegun. She learns easy."

That night at supper Lide still talked of Mequa. At last Israil said, "Ya ought'n git thick with them Injuns. 'Tis bad 'nuff that Ben has the boy here - we don't need no squaws 'round here too."

Lide turned to Mary. "Maw, you don't care if Mequa comes to see me, do you?"

"'Tis all right with me."

"How 'bout you, Paw? You've seen her 'afore."

"Jest when she was sick. I don't see it does no hurt if'n she comes sometimes."

"Amos, how 'bout you?"

"I thinks we ought t' be friends with the Injuns. I say let 'em come when they wants." He stroked his beard thoughtfully.

Israil snorted, "They's dirty and lazy, good-fer-nothin' varmints! I don't know what ails all a' ya. As fer me, I don't want nothin' t' do with them. Ya knows them as plays with cats kin 'spect to git scratched."

"Not if'n you're good to 'em," Lide argued.

Israil got up from the table. "I'm goin' t' the barn," he said slamming the door as he went out.

As the wet weather continued, no work on the land could be done so hardwood logs were snaked up from the forest to be piled east of the house. After the logs seasoned for a few months they would be cut up with a bucksaw and the family would have dry wood for the following winter.

While Israil and Amos harnessed the team, Robert returned to the cabin for another swig of Mary's vinegar and maple syrup cough remedy. "Damn cough," he muttered. "Can't work good 'cause a' these coughin' spells." He wiped his beard. "Gonna cut a big oak this mornin'. 'Twill burn good next winter."

When the men were gone, Mary finished skimming the milk pans. Expertly she ran a knife around the edge of the pans, clearing the cream away as she folded it up like a leathery blanket on the flat tin skimmer and slipped it into the cream crock. Another two, three days and there'd be enough cream to churn.

The men would be cutting the big oak now. She wished the rain would stop so they could work on the land. She put her hand on her stomach as the baby kicked violently. Lide was washing the breakfast dishes. They hadn't talked for a long time. Suddenly she was gripped with a feeling of impending disaster. What was it? 'Twasn't time for the baby.

A short time later the sound of Israil's sharp "Whoa!" to the horses carried into the cabin.

"They back a'ready?" Lide said as she dried a milk pan.

Mary was sure something was wrong. They had been gone only a short time. They couldn't cut and trim a tree so soon. She went slowly to the door. Her hand shook. Her feet were like lead. She stumbled and threw the door open. "What's happened?" she heard herself screaming. A shiver went through her. The horses stood, their heads down. Amos stepped off the back of the stoneboat. Ben stood staring at something - someone lying on the stoneboat. Robert - it was Robert!

Lide came running. There was confusion - a mingling of voices. Ben sobbed, "The tree! We was choppin' - it was ready to fall. He had a coughin' spell an' didn't see it was goin' the other way. We all yelled, 'She's goin' the other way!'" His voice caught, "But it fell an' he was n'under it." The boy leaned against the cabin and sobbed.

Israil said, "We got him out but 'twas too late. He never knowed what hit him."

They stood silently about the stoneboat with tear-filled eyes. Finally Ben said, "The horses knowed. They didn't tear home like they allus do. They walked slow. Look at 'em." King and Queen stood, their heads low.

Mary drew a long quivering breath. There were things to be done. She now was head of the family. She must be strong. Poor little Ben - an' Lide. Like her, they were trapped in the Michigan wilderness. And Amos, with his peg leg. She brushed back a lock of gray-streaked hair from her forehead. If only they had stayed in York State, Robert would be alive. But they must not leave him lying there in the rain. They must fetch him inside.

"Lide, turn down the bed," she ordered. "Boys,

carry yer father in an' put him on the bed."

The boys, their eyes agonized and wet, tenderly lifted Robert and carried him inside. His chest was blood-stained and blood trickled from his nose and mouth.

"It stove in his whole chest," Israil said softly.

There was no time for grief. That would come later. "We has to have a coffin," Mary said. "Them nice walnut boards yer father fetched frum York State - where air they?"

"Overhead in the barn, Maw," Israil said. "Amos an' me kin make a coffin." They went outside.

"Lide, git the store cloth out a' the trunk in the loft. See if there's 'nuff brown cambric to line the coffin."

Ben stood uncertainly beside the door. "Go help yer brothers," his mother ordered.

Mary went to the bed. She bit her lip. She wouldn't give way to grief. Awkwardly she made her way to the kitchen and returned with a pan of water and a cloth. Tenderly she wiped the blood from Robert's face. He looked uncomfortable with his head twisted to one side. He wouldn't know, but she must straighten his head on the pillow. She took the damp cloth and carefully cleaned his beard and brushed his hair back. Then she pulled a quilt over him and stood back. He looked as though he was sleeping. He'd have to be dressed in his good suit. The boys would do it before his body stiffened.

Lide came down from the loft carrying the roll of brown cambric. She'd been crying. "I think they's 'nuff," she said. "I'll sew it. 'Tis the last thing I kin do fer him." She glanced at her mother. Her eyes were too bright. Such control wasn't natural. 'Twould be better if she cried. She unfolded the cambric and spread it on the table.

Mary leafed through her Bible. "We has to plan fer the funeral."

"I wish we had neighbors," Lide said softly.

Mary didn't answer. The cabin was silent except for the soft patter of spring rain on the split-basswood log roof. All night she sat beside Robert's body, refusing to lie down.

The family feared for their mother. She was too composed, too much in control. But still she remained in the chair beside the bed oblivious of her promise to help Lide with lining the coffin. At last it was finished. Israil remained with Mary and Lide but Amos and Ben went to the loft for a few hours of rest.

Next morning Mary yielded to pressure and went to sit in the rocking chair while Israil and Amos carried their father to the coffin. They gathered about for a last look at the body of the big man they had all loved so deeply. Lide gently stroked the heavy brown beard and Mary clumsily stooped to kiss the cold brow of her husband. Straightening, she went to stand at the window looking at the open grave at the edge of the yard.

While Amos and Israil put the cover on the coffin, Lide placed her mother's shawl about her shoulders. "Be ya all right?" she whispered.

Mary nodded, dry-eyed and silent, her open Bible in her hands. Finally she asked, "Will ya read the 23rd Psalm?"

"Yes, Maw."

At last everything was done and they were ready to carry Robert to his final resting place. The door stood open. Israil said, "Amos an' me'll carry the front an' Ben an' Lide'll take the back. We'll try to git it on our shoulders."

Lide passed the open Bible to her mother and stood at the back of the coffin with Ben.

"'Twill be heavy," Amos said. "When we gits it up onto our shoulders, walk slow so's nobody stumbles." He hesitated. "Let's all lift together. Ready - heave-oh-hee."

The front end lifted a foot off the floor but, though Ben and Lide tugged and strained at the back, the heavy walnut box refused to budge.

Mary moved clumsily between Lide and Ben. "I kin

help," she said quietly.

Four "No's" sounded as one loud voice. Israil and Amos set the front end down.

"We kin git the team an' stoneboat," Amos said.

"Yeah. We kin slide it onto the stoneboat," Israil added.

And still the steady rain continued to add to the gloom of the day. As the elder sons stepped outside they were startled to see the Chief, another Indian man and Shobegun standing at the corner of the cabin.

Israil muttered, "We ain't got time fer ya now. Go 'way."

Shobegun stepped forward. "We help carry Paw," he said in a halting voice.

Amos answered, "Thank ya. That's right nice of ya."

The four men took their positions at the corners of the coffin with Ben and Shobegun in the center on each side. A mighty coordinated tug and the heavy box was on the shoulders of the pallbearers. Stepping in unison, they slowly started across the muddy yard to the open grave beneath a huge oak.

Mary and Lide walked behind the coffin oblivious to the cold rain. Amos was at the front right corner and each time he stepped on his peg leg the front right corner of the coffin dipped a few inches as the end of the wooden leg sank into the soft soil. With this rocking motion they continued to the grave where the coffin was carefully lowered into the ground.

Silently Mary and Lide went to the head of the grave. The sons and the Indians stood at the sides. The Indians stared stoically into the forest as though they were purposely avoiding the possibility of observing the family in their grief.

Lide's eyes were on the open Bible. The pages were covered with rain spots. Her voice began:

"The Lord is my shepherd; I shall not want.

He maketh me to lie down in green pastures; he

leadeth me beside the still waters.

He restoreth my soul ...."

Dry-eyed Mary stared at the coffin. Robert would never see the child she carried. He had been happy here in the wilderness. But he was gone - forever.

Lide was finishing the Psalm. "Surely goodness and mercy shall follow me all the days of my life, and I will dwell in the house of the Lord forever."

Lide closed the Bible. Suddenly the rain stopped and a glimmer of April sun lit up the bare trees of the rain-soaked forest.

"Sing with me," Mary said softly to Lide. She began the old hymn, "Rock of Ages." Her voice quivered but grew stronger as Lide's voice blended with hers.

"Rock of ages, cleft for me,
Let me hide myself in thee
In the waters and the flood
From thy wounded side which flowed
Be for sin a double cure.
Wash me now and make me pure."

Mary gathered up a clod of wet earth in her hand. Holding it over the coffin, she crumbled it, allowing it to fall on the coffin. "Goodbye, Robert," she whispered.

The wilderness seemed suddenly intensely quiet. No bird called, no wind stirred as the somber little group stood about the open grave.

Finally Amos moved. "Lide, take Maw to the cabin. We'll finish up here."

As they closed the door, Mary saw the Indians helping to fill the grave. Later when the sons came inside Lide said, "Air the Injuns gone?"

"They went soon's the grave was filled," Amos answered. "'Twas right nice of 'em to help."

Ben said, "Wonder how they knowed 'bout Paw?"

"Humph," Israil growled. "They's allus watchin' frum the woods. They prob'ly seen the tree fall on him." He turned to Amos and Ben. "Ya knows how often we sees 'em standin' like shadders, jest watchin'. They knows ever'thing we does." No one answered and the subject was dropped.

The Colborns soon settled into a daily work schedule. Mary, as head of the family, made final decisions about the farm. She steeled herself to be firm and unemotional. Not once had she cried or complained. Lide now worked in the fields with the men. While Israil plowed around the stumps with the four oxen hitched to the breaking plow, Amos drove the horses on the homemade spiked-tooth harrow to level the rough ground. Ben and Lide dug out and piled tree roots loosened by the plow and harrow.

Amos was constantly annoyed when his wooden leg sank deep into the soft ground, often causing him to fall. The frequent wrench of the peg leg rubbed his stump until it was raw. Mary formed a pad of soft deerhide which he inserted between the stump and the wooden leg. While this relieved the soreness of the stump he still was frustrated with having to pull the peg leg from the earth.

One day Mequa arrived with a curved piece of a large buck's antler. "Fer Amos," she said to Lide. "Make foot fer Amos."

"Mequa!" Lide exclaimed. "It might be jest what he needs. Let's show him."

Amos was unhitching the team near the barn. Lide called, "Mequa brought you somethin'!" She held up the curved piece of antler. "She thinks you can make a foot of this. Can you fasten it on the end of the leg?"

He studied the antler. "H-m-m-m. It might work." As the girls watched, he secured it to the end of the peg leg, strapped the crude prosthesis to the stump, stood up and stomped backward and forward without sinking into the soil of the barnyard. He smiled for the first time in many months.

"By golly, it works!" Back and forth he stomped. "Thank ya, Mequa. Now why didn't I think a' that? Thank ya!"

The Indian girl shyly looked at the ground without answering.

When the supply of meat was low, Ben was given the day off to hunt or to fish in a lake near the Indian camp. Together, he and Shobegun roamed the woods with rifle and bow and arrow. Deer had deserted the area near the farm so the boys must go farther into the forest to find game. Then they'd skin it, wrap the choice parts of the carcass in the deerhide and, together, they'd carry it home.

On rainy days Shobegun and his sister usually arrived to sit at the table with Lide for two or three hours while they were taught English. Soon Mequa was speaking as well as Shobegun. Lide often told them of her old home and of her special friend, Hannah, in York State.

One day Mequa said, "Name Hannah. Me like. Me will be Hannah now."

Lide argued, "But your name Mequa, 'tis a good name."

"No. Me Hannah, your friend." And from that time she no longer answered unless addressed as Hannah.

By early June the corn and potatoes were planted as well as a large garden of vegetables. Amos and Israil decided to cut a trail to the Parsons settlement.

"'Twill be good to visit them," Israil said. "We ain't seen 'nother white man, but Jacob, since last November. I think we kin make a trail in five, six days."

Mary had talked little and made few demands since Robert's death, but on a bright morning after Ben, Amos and Israil left to work on the trail, she mentioned to Lide that "something fresh" would taste good. "I seen dandelions an' they makes good greens."

"Yeah, Maw," Lide replied, "An' there's wild strawberries ripenin' now too." She thought a moment. "Will you be all right if I go and find some?"

"I'm good. Stay's long as ya want," Mary said confidently. "If'n ya're not back fer dinner, 'tis all right. The men won't be home 'fore 'most night 'cause they took lunches."

When she was alone Mary dropped her shapeless figure into the rocking chair. This was the first time she'd been by herself since Robert's death in April. For many minutes she gave way to her pent-up grief in long wrenching sobs. She missed him. And she was resentful that he had been taken from them.

The baby kicked restlessly, bringing her back to the present. There wasn't any woman to help her with the birth when the time came. Lide wouldn't know what to do. She drew a long quivering breath. Well - she could do it by herself, if she had to.

She leaned her head back and tried to recall beautiful times with Robert. There was the day they were married in her parents' home back in 1813. She'd been only sixteen years old, and nine months later Israil was born. Then, a year later, Amos came, then Lide and finally Ben.

She shifted her position, vaguely aware of an occasional dull ache in her lower back. Now she was remembering last September when Robert had returned from Michigan. They had been apart all summer and were like young lovers. She leaned ahead to relieve the recurring backache. Suddenly she knew. She was in labor!

She undressed, got the bed ready and put water on to heat. She laid out clothing for the baby. The pains were coming fast it seemed. She knew what to expect. She hoped it wouldn't be long.

Suddenly the door opened and Hannah stood before her. "Lide's gone," Mary gasped, her hands clenched. "I'm sick."

Without a word the Indian girl was gone. Mary was glad. Like an animal in the forest, she'd rather be alone at this time. An hour passed. Just as she had staggered to the bed and could neither lie down nor stand for the grind of pains, the door opened and with moccasined feet as soft as snow, a squaw was inside. She stalked in silently like a shadow out of nowhere.

The squaw's dress was a sort of long red flannel shirt fringed with deerhide and with many animals' teeth sewed on. Vaguely Mary realized it likely was the woman's best dress and that wearing it had been to honor the white people. Really, it looked heathenish, and so did the long black braids and the dull staring eyes.

Later, however, as the squaw bent over the bed, the face changed. Kindness and sympathy shone from the wide face and dark eyes. A strong dark hand stroked her forehead. "Me help," the squaw said. And suddenly Mary trusted herself and her baby to this understanding woman.

At last it was over. Through tired eyes, Mary saw the Indian woman washing her howling daughter and wrapping her before the fire. She could sleep. Everything was all right. But before she dropped off the squaw carried the baby to her and placed it beside her. A lovely little girl. She cradled her in her arms.

The squaw was back at the bed with a warm brew she had brought. It tasted like venison broth. She drank deeply. Then she and the baby slept.

When she opened her eyes, the woman was gone. From the afternoon shadows she thought it must be about three o'clock. Lide would soon be home, and after a time, the men too. She was content. She had Robert's beautiful baby and all was well.

Chapter VIII

WIDENING HORIZONS

(1837)

Since the Colborn men had opened a trail east on the Shiawassee, Livingston County line, then south to the Parsons settlement, the family had a window on the world. They now had an outlet to the village of Howell for the Parons group had cleared a road from their settlement to Howell in 1836.

The brothers enjoyed contact with other men so Amos and Israil frequently visited the Parsons group consisting of Levi and Triphena Parsons, son Cecil D. and his wife, Elizabeth, and sons Frederick and Julius and their wives. Samuel, the youngest was unmarried.

Other families at the settlement were Lorenzo Strang, a carpenter and his family, Waterman Fay, whose wife, Ruth, was a daughter of Levi Parsons, and Timothy Wait, also a carpenter, who was the father-in-law of Julius Parsons. This large group had settled in Iena Township, later renamed Conway, in 1836.

At the Colborn home there was conversation about the convenience of having a blacksmith, carpenters and a small general store nearby. Because of the number of people in the settlement, Levi Parsons' store carried a small stock of necessities.

One afternoon after a visit to the settlement, Amos talked with his mother. "'Member Paw said settlers would be movin' in soon? He was right. Benjamin Sherman an' Gaius Fuller air buildin' cabins east a' here 'bout two miles. 'Fore many years this land'll all be bought up. I wants to git a parcel 'fore it's gone."

Mary rocked Baby Lucretia. "You an' Israil got 'nuff to do. They's more land t' clear 'fore ya're ready t' buy a parcel."

"Yeah, but I wants my own land. This is yourn. I wants my own farm so I don't have t' ask you er Israil 'bout ever' move I makes." He hesitated. "Israil's jest like he was when we was leetle - he thinks I don't know nothin'. Someday I'll show him I'm jest as smart as he is - an' mebbe smarter."

Mary shifted the sleeping Lucretia to her other arm. "I knows. But 'twould be better fer ya if'n ya didn't work ever' day frum 'fore sunrise 'till after sunset. What ya tryin' t' do, show ya kin do more work than Israil?"

"I kin - an' with a peg leg, too."

Mary shook her head. "I hopes ya gits yer land. I kin tell ya won't be happy 'till ya does. This fall there won't be wheat t' sell, but mebbe next year we'll have a good crop. There's some gold coins left frum our sale in York State."

"I knows. Maw - kin - kin I borry 'nuff frum ya t' buy a hunnert acres west a' your land? I'll pay interest an' I'll pay ya back ever' cent. An' I'll help with the work here, too."

Mary rocked silently for a moment. "Ya would pay the money back, if'n ya could. But ya knows how farmin' is - bad years an' good years. We wouldn't have nothin' t' trade, an' no money t' buy with - if'n they was bad years."

Amos silently studied the floor. His dejected appearance touched Mary. At last she said, "How much would a hunnert acres cost?"

"I duno. Prob'ly two dollars an acre. That'd be two hundred dollars." He got up. "I ought'n ask ya. Mebbe ya ain't got that much t' spare."

"Set down!" Mary ordered. "I ain't through talkin' t' ya." He sat down. "I'll let ya have it. Ya better git t' the land office in Detroit soon's ya kin."

"Maw! Ya won't be sorry, an' I'll pay ya back!"

Mary seemed to be thinking aloud. "'Tis good

the oats is cut an' flailed. Ben an' Israil kin keep things goin' while yer gone. The crops air growin' an' ya'll be back in six, seven days - an mebbe 'afore that."

Jubilant with anticipation and happiness, Amos left the house. Mary still held her baby. She could see clouds on the horizon. Israil would be angry that she had loaned the money to Amos, and maybe Ben and Lide, too. But her mind was made up. Amos would leave tomorrow. She'd have to tell them.

Lucretia opened her eyes and yawned. Mary bent to brush a kiss on the baby's forehead. "Yer Maw is stirrin' up a hornet's nest, I'm 'fraid, Cretia." The baby smiled.

Lide came in with beets and carrots from the garden. She washed her hands and paused to tickle the baby under the chin. "Ain't she beautiful Maw?"

"'Most as purty as you was," her mother answered.

"Beets are ready to make into pickles, and the cucumbers has to be picked again." Lide smiled at her baby sister.

"Tomorrer we'll git at 'em." Mary brushed a fly from the baby's face and carried her to the bed where she stooped to change a wet diaper.

"Squealer's pigs are growing fast," Lide said. "We'll have plenty of pork this winter."

"Mebbe even some t' sell," her mother added. She went on, "An' the heifer's calf is growin' too. When Bossy freshens we'll have plenty of milk and cream. Mebbe we kin sell a leetle butter in Byron er to the Parsons store. The hens air moltin' now, but purty soon they'll be layin' ag'in, an' the leetle chicks air half growed. Looks like we'll have somethin' to eat this winter 'sides venison an' muskrats an' rabbits. We ought a' be livin' high off the hawg."

Lide started to set the table. "We can't count our chickens 'afore they're hatched, Maw. Hawks and weasels and foxes has got some - they'll get more. They's no telling how many will be left by fall."

Mary was scraping a pan of new potatoes. "Yeah. You're right. Anyway we ain't heerd wolves much lately. Mebbe there is gettin' to be too many peoples 'round here an' they've gone 'way."

"Remember Israil said he'd seen a bear back in the woods? I'm scared when I'm alone away from the buildings."

"I knows. But Israil an' Amos says bears air more skeered a' us than we air a' them."

That night at supper Mary said, "I've been thinkin'. 'Tis August, an' there's a leetle let-up in the work. Amos talked t' me 'bout goin' to Detroit. He'd be gone mebbe six er seven days."

The cabin suddenly was silent except for the cooing of the baby on her mother's bed. Finally Israil said to his brother, "Yer a queer coot. Ya ain't said nothin' t' me 'bout goin' nowhere."

"I jest talked to Maw 'bout it today."

"Why ya need t' go down there? We kin git anythin' we need at Byron er Parsons."

Mary cleared her throat. "I might's well tell ya. Amos is goin' t' the land office to buy him a hunnert acres. I'll lend him most a' the money we got left frum the York State sale."

Israil jumped up so suddenly he upset the bench, dumping Ben on the floor. "What! Maw, air ya losin' yer mind? Ya think ya're doin' right by me - an' Lide an' Ben?"

Amos said, "She ain't givin' the money t' me. I'll pay it back, with interest."

Israil paced back and forth. "That ain't the 'greement we had with Paw."

Mary said quietly, "I knows, son. But Paw's gone an' now I has t' decide things. Amos has allus had second best 'cause he's younger 'n you. You allus got to do everythin' first. Now, 'tis Amos' turn. An' - an' Amos has had a bad time - losing his foot an' all. Yer time, an' Ben's too, will come when ya buys yer land. An' if we has the money, I'll help both a' ya jest like I'm helpin' Amos."

Israil stopped pacing and glared at his mother and Amos. "So I has t' be my brother's keeper 'cause he lost a foot - is that it?"

Amos got up and limped toward the door. "I'm sorry ya feels this way. I'll do my share a' the work here, same's 'afore. Nothin'll be different fer ya. I won't ask ya t' do anythin' on my land."

Israil stopped beside his mother. "I won't forgit this. Ya might see the day ya'll be sorry ya give our money t' Amos! Have ya forgot paper money's no good? They's hard times ahead. Ya'll see the day ya'll wish ya hadn't give yer hard cash t' Amos - but by then it'll be too late!" He stamped outside.

For a minute no one spoke. Then Amos said, "How does ya feel, Lide?"

"I'm glad for you."

"An' you, Ben?"

"I figger Maw did right. An' I'll help ya clear yer land when I don't have t' work here."

Mary went to get the baby. "I has good children - even Israil - though I 'low I'm sorry we got in a squabble with him. I hopes he won't hold a grudge 'bout it."

Though no one said anything, they all knew Israil was not one to forgive and forget.

A week later Amos returned. His business transaction at the land office in Detroit was completed. He brought items which the family had requested, among them, two books for Lide, several pieces of cloth for his mother and candy for Ben. Israil had said there was nothing he wanted but Amos brought him a gallon of whiskey which he grudgingly accepted. Amos also brought a small supply of expensive Peruvian bark in the event ague should strike the family.

He was excited and filled with news. "I don't like the city," Amos said. "Nothin' but peoples an' dirty streets an' that leetle creek -

Savoyard, they calls it, stinks to high heaven. Peoples dump their slop pails in it, an' skeeters! If'n ya're anywheres near Savoyard, ya'll git bit wherever yer skin's bare. In August we don't have as many skeeters, but near that creek they's swarms of 'em."

Ben asked, "Did the cholera come back?"

"Didn't hear nothin' 'bout cholera, but most ever'body has the ager. That's why I bought the Peruvian bark. They says sooner er later ever'body in Michigan has ager."

Following the trip to Detroit the men and Lide cut, raked and stacked the winter feed into haycocks to be pitched onto wagons and hauled to the barn. Amos worked at top speed for he was eager to finish storing the marsh hay so he could start clearing his land. Each night he was exhausted.

Several times during haying, Shobegun and Hannah came to help. They talked little but their help lightened the work for Lide and Ben. One day Amos remarked to Hannah, "Ya works good fer a girl. Ya works faster 'n Lide."

The Indian girl heard but continued pitching hay without an answer. She talked with Lide and she seemed comfortable with Mary, but when Israil or Amos were present, she was silent.

At the end of haying, Lide gave Hannah a length of cloth which Amos had brought from Detroit. "You can make something," Lide said. "'Twould make a nice dress."

Silently Hannah fingered the pink cambric material. Then she said haltingly, "You help Hannah?"

Lide laughed. "I'll help. You're about my size, only taller. Come tomorrow and we'll sew."

Lucretia wakened from her afternoon nap with a lusty cry. Mary brushed an annoying fly from the baby's face before she sat in the rocker to nurse the child. She was glad Lide and Hannah enjoyed being together. She was growing fond of the quiet Indian girl who was so eager to learn the white mans' ways - and Shobegun, too. He was a nice boy.

That night at supper Amos was too exhausted to eat. He left the table, yawned and dropped into the rocker. "I don't see why I'm so tired," he complained.

"Ya've been workin' too hard," Mary said.

Soon he limped outside. "I'll get the chores done an' then I'm goin' t' bed."

When he was gone Mary said, "He'll work himself t' death."

Israil grunted, "That's what he bargained fer. I ain't sorry fer him. An' he softsoaps them Injuns so they'll work fer us. I heerd him talkin' t' the girl, tellin' her what a fast worker she is - I'd ruther do it all myself than t' have 'em hangin' 'round. Ya can't trust any a' them varmints."

"They been right nice t' us," Mary commented, "'specially their helpin' when yer Paw died. An' Hannah an' Shobegun air polite young'uns. An' their mother helped me when Cretia was borned."

"Hannah! Her name ain't Hannah! Jest shows she's 'shamed a' her Injun name."

Lide joined in. "It don't matter what her name is, I like her! If she wants to be called Hannah, that's what I'll call her!"

As soon as the milking was done and the animals were penned in the barnyard, Amos climbed the ladder to his bed in the loft. "I'll be all right in the mornin' after a good night's sleep," he said. But a short time later he shook with fierce chills which lasted for two or three hours.

Lide piled quilts and blankets on him, but still he shook. Later he complained of back pain and a raging headache. At last Mary climbed the ladder. She put her hand on his head. "He's got a ragin' fever," she said softly.

"'Tis the ager," Israil said. "He catched it in Detroit. If'n he'd stayed home, he wouldn't a' catched it."

Amos moaned, "Git me some a' that Peruvian

bark. I feels turrible."

The next morning he seemed to have recovered, though he still was tired. He forced himself to help with the chores and to eat a light breakfast. Then taking his axe and bucksaw, he set out for his land across the creek. Ben went with him and together they explored the forest which one day would be fertile fields.

Suddenly Shobegun appeared as Ben and Amos were standing near a dozen eight-foot-long and three-foot-wide mounds.

Ben asked, "What makes them humps?"

Amos shook his head. "I duno. We ain't got none on Maw's land." He looked at Shobegun. "Ya know what they air?"

"Injuns. Dead Injuns," the boy replied.

"Ya mean 'tis an Injun buryin' ground?"

"Long time Injuns dead here."

Ben picked up the axe. "Let's put a leetle pole fence around it so nobody won't dig 'em up er walk on the graves." He paused, then spoke to the Indian boy. "We've wondered - do ya always put yer dead ones up on them scaffolds?"

Shobegun shook his head. "Jest once. My Paw talked with Injuns from that way - long ways." He pointed west.

"When?" Amos asked.

"Last time in Detroit after we see you."

Ben continued. "They tole yer Paw that's how they buries people when the ground's froze up?"

"Yeah."

"'Tis a good way," Ben said. "Let's start the fence."

Amos leaned against an oak. "'Nother time. I feels turrible ag'in. I'm goin' t' the house."

"Shobegun an' me'll put a fence 'round the graves. Ya go back 'till ya're better."

Mary insisted that Amos lie on her bed for at midday in August the loft was unbearably hot. After taking more of the Peruvian bark medication, he lay down, his head throbbing and his whole body shaking with chills.

"I'll be better soon," he said. "They says nobody ever dies from ager. They jest wishes they could."

Lide and Hannah were sewing on the pink cambric dress patterned from an old one that Mary had worn. The bodice was fitted and attached to a full flowing skirt. By mid-afternoon Lide suggested that Hannah go to the loft to try it on.

Ten minutes later the girls came down the ladder. Mary glanced up. "Hannah, ya air beautiful!" she exclaimed. "As purty as a pitcher."

Hannah's usually expressionless eyes sparkled at the compliment. A faint smile lingered about her lips.

"Turn 'round so Maw can see the back," Lide said. "Here, Hannah. See yourself in the lookin' glass."

The girl went to the mirror beside the door. Though she said nothing, her expression showed her pleasure. Then, taking her dark braids she twisted them about her head, and still holding them up, she turned her face from side to side.

"I like it up," Lide said. "Let me do it."

As Hannah sat on the bench, Lide arranged the dark hair in the same style as her own with a coil at the nape of the neck. When she finished she said, "Now look at yourself."

"Yer a right purty girl," Mary said again.

Lide went to the bed. "You 'wake, Amos?" she asked.

"Yeah."

"Raise up and look at Hannah."

He slowly sat up. Then as he caught sight of the Indian girl he sat bolt upright. "Damn!" he exclaimed. "You looks right nice, Hannah." The girl's dark face flushed and she stared at the floor.

Mary took charge. "Lay back down, Amos, an' quit starin'. An' Lide, we has t' git things started fer supper."

When Hannah and Shobegun left for the Indian camp the girl proudly carried the folded dress over her arm.

Lide called, "I hope your Paw and Maw likes it." Hannah turned and a faint smile flickered across her face, but she was silent.

Amos' first attack of ague lasted for several days. Morning and early afternoon found him feeling able to work but about every second day he'd have another attack of chills, fever and head and body aches followed by copious sweating. Then he'd feel as well as ever until the next attack. Gradually the attacks came less frequently but the family knew they might occur at any time.

The last Sunday in August the Colborns went on the wagon to the Parsons settlement. Mary and Lide were excited for they hadn't been away from the farm since they had arrived the previous November. The event to which they were going was a Methodist Episcopal meeting at the home of Levi Parsons. The Reverend Washington Jackson, a circuit rider for the church, was to hold the meeting. The entire settlement crowded into the house together with Mr. and Mrs. Levi Bigelow and Mrs. Amasa House.

The Reverend Jackson was welcomed into Conway Township for he brought spiritual consolation, news from the outside world and books and guidance in manners and morals. He also held religious meetings, performed marriage ceremonies, baptized the young and buried the dead. He rode horseback from Ann Arbor through miles of wilderness so that he might provide religious services for frontier people.

After hymn singing and a lengthy prayer, a shrieking Lucretia was baptized before her embarrassed family and several amused neighbors. Scripture reading and a sermon an hour and a half in length was followed by another prayer and hymn, and the service was over.

The congregation poured into the Parsons' yard where rough tables held a potluck meal to which each woman had contributed. The men gathered to discuss the possible results of Michigan's statehood which had occurred on January 26, 1837.

"We're the twenty-sixth state," Amos said as he hobbled over to lean against a giant beech tree. "We oughta have a town meetin' an' elect some officers. We needs a town supervisor, a clerk, assessor an' a highway commissioner. Soon we'll want schools an' we'll need a school inspector."

The men nodded in agreement. "'Course town meetin' is allus in April," Levi Parsons said. "We kin have it here at my place next April. Anyone opposed?" No one spoke, and he continued. "There'll be new settlers. They's comin' in fast now. Ever'body should tell any new peoples that moves in 'bout the spring meetin'."

Lide searched without success for young people in the group. All of them were either younger or older. She was glad Hannah was her friend.

Israil stood watching the crowd. Amos was bobbing around from group to group. Damn him, he'd always found it easy to talk to folk, and he knew how to soft-soap them, too - just like he had their mother so that she gave him all that money. And Ben, he made friends easy. There he was gabbing with some boy like he'd known him all his life. Their Maw was having a good time visiting with the women about babies and cooking and housework. Suddenly Israil felt lonely. Somehow people didn't take to him like they did to Amos and Ben. He missed his father for they'd always been able to talk. On the way home he was silent as he drove the team while the family chattered about the happenings of the day.

In September the men prepared the ground to plant wheat and rye which would mature the following summer. Working around stumps was slow frustrating business. As usual, Pete and Joe, the temperamental oxen team, lived up to their reputation. Often they would balk and nothing Amos did would cause them to budge. Then, when they were ready they'd take off and refuse to stop at the end of the field, but would stubbornly plod forward dragging the harrow into the middle of a swamp where they would pasture on green marsh grass. Meanwhile Amos yelled and swore and stamped about while Ben and Israil chuckled. But Amos refused to be beaten. It was as though there was a battle of wills between him and the oxen. Somehow, they were less troublesome with Israil and Ben, but each third day, Amos again battled the stubborn animals.

By late September the winter wheat was planted on Mary's land. Ben and Amos then used the breaking plow and harrow and when the ground was roughly dug up they scattered wheat in four good sized oak clearings on Amos' land. "If our wheat does good next year we ought t' have a good bit t' sell. 'Twas a fair price when I was in Detroit," Amos said.

A frost came by mid-October changing the corn leaves from green to a grayish-tan. With a curved-bladed hand corn cutter the stalks were cut, bound and set in shocks.

After the potatoes were dug and stored in a pit with cabbage, turnips, carrots and onions, the men returned to the field to husk the corn crop. Kneeling, they pulled the cut corn stalks to them, quickly husking each ear and snapping it from the stalk before they tossed it onto a pile of golden ears waiting to be hauled to the lean-to granary which they'd built behind the barn.

The corn stalks also were drawn to the barn where they were stacked to be used for fodder for the cattle during winter. This year the animals would have grain and hay. There would be no need for them to eat "tall hay" as they had the previous winter.

Squealer's litter of ten pigs which had been born in mid-January were eight months old. Two would be saved for breeding purposes, four would be sold and four would provide an abundance of smoked hams, shoulders, roasts, bacon and soup. There also would be plenty of lard. The heifer had freshened in July, about the time Bossy became dry. Both the sows and cows were taken to the Parsons settlement to be serviced for breeding for Levi Parsons owned an Ayrshire bull and Lorenzo Strong had a Duroc boar.

"We're in purty good shape fer winter," Mary remarked one evening. "Only one thing we ain't got - 'nuff flour. We'll eat more johnny cake, an' some day 'afore winter Israil an' Ben kin go t' Howell an' buy a barrel a' flour an' git some corn ground into meal." She smiled. "Yer Paw would be right proud a' us."

Suddenly a terrible commotion came from the barnyard. Pigs squealing, chickens squawking, Sam barking, horses neighing and cattle bawling. Something was wrong out there.

Israil and Ben led the way to be followed by Amos hobbling at top speed with Mary and Lide following. The animals in the barnyard were crowded together, their voices raised in terror at something that was happening on the opposite side of the barnyard.

Ben yelled, "A b'ar! He's got a pig!"

Israil raced back to the house to get a rifle. Amos seized a stout stick and charged after Ben who was frantically pulling the gate open. "Go back to the house!" Amos shouted to his mother and Lide.

In the half darkness and shadows from the surrounding wilderness they could see a big black shape walking upright like a man and hugging one of Squealer's pigs to his bosom. Sam streaked past them baying as he raced through the gate to savagely nab the bear's hind legs. The big animal dropped the bleeding pig and grabbed Sam who set up an awful yelping.

Amos and Ben brandished clubs and yelled. The animals crowded in terror against the pole fence until it snapped and they spilled out into the surrounding forest.

Together Amos and Ben approached the big beast, their clubs swinging. Suddenly the bear released

Sam and lumbered off at a surprising speed into the darkening wilderness.

"Where'd she go?" Israil yelled rushing up to the fence with the rifle.

"Into the woods," Amos replied.

Ben yelled, "Squealer's hurt bad, an' some a' the pigs is bleedin'."

The sow, half of her left ham torn away, squealed in agony. Two of the pigs were badly torn and bleeding. Sam crawled into the barn, his chest cut by the claws of the bear.

The men bent over the injured pigs. "We'll have to kill 'em," Israil said as Mary and Lide came up with the baby.

"They're sufferin'," Mary said. "Lide git the butcher knife. They'll be good fer meat if they bleeds out."

"Ben!" his mother shouted. "Git a fire started an' some scaldin' water heatin'. We've got work t' do! 'Twill be moonlight soon an' we kin see t' work outside."

Lide carried the baby to the house and returned with the knife. Israil with the long pointed butcher knife jumped astride the squealing sow's back and quickly plunged the knife into the juglar vein. As her life blood gushed out, the squeals became weaker until finally the sow was silent. As she lay bleeding, Israil proceeded to kill the two injured pigs.

Ben appeared from inside the barn. "Ya won't kill Sam, will ya?" he asked fearfully. "I think he'll git better."

"We'll see how he is tomorrer," Amos said. "Maw told ya t' git the fire goin' an' the water heatin'. Git goin'!"

When things quieted down the oxen and horses returned from the woods. As the hogs lay bleeding the horses were harnessed and hitched to the stoneboat, the pigs were rolled onto the flat low tool and pulled near the fire where flames raced skyward against the background of the dark wilderness. From the cabin the mens' figures were silhouetted between firelight and darkness. Amos, his limp evident, hobbled about poking the fire and rearranging each stick of wood to the best advantage beneath the kettle of water. Ben carried more wood to stoke the fire. Israil rolled the hogs from the stoneboat and drove the team back to the barn. After an hour the water in the kettle was boiling. In the meantime a wooden barrel was placed below a pulley which was fastened to a sturdy branch of an oak tree. A rope was passed through the pulley and an end was tied to the back legs of one of the hogs. The boiling water was transferred to the barrel. The pig then was pulled up by the free end of the rope and guided into the scalding water. After a few minutes the steaming carcass was raised from the water and tested with a sharp round metal scraper to determine whether the bristles had been loosened. When the men were satisfied, the water was returned to the kettle to be reheated in preparation for scalding the next carcass.

The first pig, still suspended from the pulley, was scraped until the bristles were removed and the pink skin shone. As they worked, Amos said, "'Tis lucky there's moonlight."

Israil slit the belly of the pig while Ben held a large pan to catch the "inwards." The intestines, heart, liver and lungs were taken into the house and emptied on the well-covered table.

"Whew!" Lide exclaimed. "I'd forgot how bad the inwards smells."

The reddish-brown of the heart and liver stood out against the red and pinkish-white of the capillary-streaked intestines and the pale red of the lungs. Lide and Mary trimmed the fat from the internal organs and placed it in a pail. The liver and heart were cut away, placed in a pan and stored on a shelf in the outside shed.

By the time Lide and Mary had finished and the intestines were set aside, Ben appeared with a second pan of warm smelly inwards. By midnight all three pork carcasses hung from the oak tree about ten feet above the ground. By morning they would be cold and could be cut up.

The barn was checked to make certain the bear couldn't get inside if she should return. "We gotta git her," Israil said. "None a' the critters is safe 'long's she's 'round."

"I got an idee," Amos volunteered. "Mebbe if we put the in'ards in the barnyard tomorrer night she'll come back an' we kin shoot 'er."

"Might work," Israil answered. "We'll see tomorrer night."

Ben checked to see how Sam was doing. The dog licked the boy's hand and appeared alert. "He'll git better," Ben prophesied confidently.

Shortly after the family had gone to bed a wolf howled nearby. In a moment the lone cry was answered by a chorus of voices which came closer until five minutes later the entire pack was gathered below the three suspended pork carcasses.

Mary went to the window. In the moonlight she could see ten snarling animals fighting among themselves as they licked the blood-stained grass where the butchering had occurred. Part of the pack jumped toward the hanging pigs in a vain effort to reach them. Others sat with noses in the air uttering blood-curdling howls. "They're callin' every wolf in the woods," she said softly.

An animal approached the cabin and a moment later the familiar sniffing began at the door. Chills ran up Mary's spine as another wolf came and both animals sniffed at the threshold while others went to the shed where the internal organs were stored. Finally, her heart pounding, Mary went to the ladder and called, "Will one a' ya come down an' drive these critters 'way? They makes my blood run cold."

Israil pulled on his breeches and descended the ladder. Picking up the rifle, he yanked open the door. The two wolves ran but he fired and one fell beneath the suspended pigs. The others melted into the wilderness.

Israil returned and set the rifle in the corner. "Go to bed, Maw. They won't be back tonight," he said softly.

But there was little sleep for Mary that night. Bears and wolves were driving her crazy with fear. At least, she no longer was scared of the Indians. Maybe someday she'd get used to this wilderness life. But tonight she was lonely and so tired of having to be strong. If only Robert had lived. She cried silently as she cuddled Lucretia. Finally, just before dawn she fell into a restless sleep.

Shortly after breakfast Shobegun and four Indians appeared at the door. Mary recognized the Chief. "Come in," she said holding the door wide.

The Chief and one of the other men carried rifles. Lide descended the ladder as Shobegun said, "Amos - Israil?"

Mary motioned. "They're out t' the barn." Silently they stalked toward the log building. She closed the door and turned to Lide. "What do ya make a' that? They're carryin' guns."

"Mebbe they're hunting."

"They've never had no guns when they was here 'afore."

"I'll empty the dish water and maybe I can see what they are doing," Lide said. In a moment she was back. "They're standing by the fence and Shobegun's talking to Israil and Amos."

Soon the brothers came to the house. "We're loanin' 'em our rifles," Amos said. "They wants t' hunt the bear an' they only has two rifles."

Israil hesitated by the door. "Spoze they keeps our guns?"

"I trusts 'em. They ain't been dishonest yet, an' if they kin ketch that bear, 'twill be safer fer them an' us." After a few seconds Amos added, "Wonder how they knowed 'bout the bear?"

Israil retorted, "They's allus watchin'. Them woods is full a' eyes - Injun eyes."

Amos explained to his mother and Lide. "Shobegun

says they wants t' help, an' they knows how t' git the bear, but they needs more guns."

Mary nodded. "I trusts 'em."

The men took the rifles to the waiting Indians who silently disappeared into the forest. When they were gone, Israil, Amos and Ben lowered the hogs and, one at a time, they carried them to the cabin to be cut into hams, shoulders, roasts and side pork. The excess fat was trimmed from each piece of meat and would be used later to make lard.

As the women worked Mary asked, "Could ya boys make a smokehouse? We has t' git the meat curin' er it will spoil."

Three hours later a crude log smokehouse four feet square and five feet high stood a short distance from the cabin door. The hams, shoulders and side pork were rubbed with salt and hung above a smoldering fire of green hickory wood. It would be Ben's job to keep the fire smoking steadily during the day, and each night to carry the meat into the shed where it was safe from animals. After four or five days of steady smoking, the meat would be cured and it would keep for long periods of time.

Mary and Lide cut the fat into half-inch squares in preparation for "trying out." This work was accomplished by hanging iron kettles of the fat above the fire and heating it until the grease was fried out. When only a handful or two of crisp brown cracklings remained, the lard was strained through a cloth into five-gallon crocks. When the melted fat cooled and hardened it was creamy-white in color. The lard was stored in the shed and would provide shortening for baking until the next butchering. The leftover cracklings were added to feed for the chickens.

When hogs were butchered, all parts were used either for food for the family, the chickens, the pigs or old Sam who, by the next day, was mending nicely after his one-sided battle with the bear.

Amos sawed the heads of the pigs in half, then

chopped them into smaller pieces which would be simmered for several hours. Then the cooked meat was left to cool when it was removed from the bones, chopped, seasoned and stored in the cool shed. The result was a coarse headcheese which was served hot with pancakes and maple syrup.

About three in the afternoon the Indians appeared. Two of them were carrying a large bear suspended from a pole over their shoulders.

"Ya did good!" Amos exclaimed. "Where was she?"

"In woods, long way," Shobegun said. He motioned toward the somber Indian men. "They say, 'good guns. Shoot good'."

The rifles were returned to the Colborns.

"Thank ya fer killin' the bear," Amos said. He spoke quietly to Mary. "Kin we give 'em a couple a' pork shoulders?"

Israil frowned but didn't speak. Mary nodded. "Shobegun, tell 'em the meat needs more smokin' an' 'twill be better." She selected two pork shoulders from the smokehouse and gave them to the men.

"Thank ya," the Chief said gruffly.

The next day Hannah and Shobegun came carrying a large piece of bear steak which they presented to Mary. "Ya're good neighbors," she said. "Yer Maw helped me with birthin' Lucretia, an' yer Paw give us a turkey an' bear meat. I'm glad ya lives near us."

A faint smile flickered across the Indian girl's face.

Chapter IX

AN IMPROBABLE MARRIAGE

(1838)

The winter of 1837 - 1838 in Michigan was a cruel one for first year settlers, many of whom came unprepared for wilderness life. Those in remote areas were close to starvation, often resorting to boiled acorns for food when wild game was scarce. Tree tops called "tall hay" kept cattle and horses alive.

But for the Colborns, their second winter was a calm, pleasant time. Food grown the previous summer was plentiful. On stormy days, Israil and Amos repaired old farm tools and constructed new ones. Lide and Ben resumed their school work. Often Hannah and Shobegun sat with them absorbing knowledge and learning the English language.

In October Israil and Ben went to Howell to have corn ground into meal and to buy flour. They also purchased another "government book" for Amos who wished to study so that he would be knowledgeable when town meeting day arrived in April.

If the weather was pleasant the men cleared more land so that additional acres could be cultivated in the spring. Stumps from the previous cutting were chopped and dug out. Then the oxen were hitched to the partially loosened stumps and they were yanked from the ground. Whenever there was extra time, Amos and Ben worked at clearing the one hundred acres which Amos had acquired the previous summer. Israil showed no interest in the project. Shobegun and Hannah, however, often appeared, and together with Ben and Lide, they speeded up the work. They got along well and enjoyed one another's company.

Amos no longer brooded about his handicap. He had accepted the physical problem and he'd learned to cope. The antler of the buck which had been attached to the end of the peg leg to serve as a foot had broken, but Amos whittled a curved piece of hickory wood into the proper shape and attached it to the wooden leg. The family now were accustomed to the clumping sound of the peg leg on the cabin floor, and to Amos' permanent limp.

Mary's work at the cabin was endless. When Lide was outside with Amos and the young Indians she was constantly caring for Baby Lucretia or cooking, washing and mending. There was water to be carried from the spring for laundry, for drinking and for cooking. In winter, wet, newly-washed clothes were frozen stiff within a few minutes after they were hung outside. Upon bringing the frozen clothing in, they were thrown over a line at the south end of the cabin to finish drying.

One night at supper Mary said, "Ya think we could dig a well 'fore long? 'Twould be nice t' have water nearby."

"We kin try soon's the frost's out," Israil replied. "I'll find a good forked maple stick an' do some water witchin'."

"Think ya kin do it?" Ben asked.

"I've seen Paw find water in York State. I kin do it."

Amos said, "Talkin' 'bout wells makes me think a' somethin'. A doctor was walkin' 'long in the dark an' he fell in a farmer's well. He yelled an' the farmer come out, lit a torch an' looked down the well at the doctor. He yelled, 'Doc, what ya doin' down there? Ya ought a' take care a' the sick an' leave the well alone!'"

Everyone laughed. "By gum!" Ben exclaimed. "I likes yer jokes, Amos. Ya ain't telled any 'afore fer a long spell."

That spring soon after maple syrup and sugar making were completed, the Colborn men set about locating an underground vein of water so they could dig a well. Israil cut a crotch from a maple branch about the thickness of his little finger with prongs two inches long. He turned his palms up and took the end of a prong in each hand with the point of the crotch straight up. Then he walked around. Finally the point of the stick dipped sharply toward the ground.

"Right here!" Israil exclaimed. "If'n we dig we'll find water here!" The spot was about twenty feet east of the kitchen door.

Digging started immediately. A hole ten or twelve feet across was made. When it got down to where it was hard to throw the dirt out, they started another hole in the center, a smaller size, and dug down again. They then threw the dirt onto the shelf and another man would relay it up with a long-handled spade.

Finally at a depth of eighteen feet, they hit water. Ben rushed inside to tell his mother who came to look down into the hole where Israil and Amos were watching as sand caved into the water from the sides.

"Ben!" Amos called. "Git us some boards frum overhead in the barn. We haf t' hold the sand back until we kin lay up the bottom an' sides with stones."

Next the horses were hitched to the stoneboat and stones, uniform in size and tapering at one end, were brought from stonepiles in the fields. The pointed ends were placed toward the center of the well making a circular form. Dirt was pressed against them from behind so they would not fall in.

"That looks right nice if'n I do say it myself," Amos said admiringly.

"Does look purty good," Israil agreed. "Now we needs a windlass."

Two ten-foot long twelve-inch logs were anchored in the stones on either side of the smaller hole so that about five feet of the logs protruded above ground level. Another short log was fitted securely between the hollowed out ends of the upright logs so that it could be turned by a crank on one end. A rope with a bucket fastened to it was wound around the short log and tied securely. The bucket was lowered into the well and raised, filled with water, by turning the crank.

Several times that spring the men reported that new people were settling nearby. The Martin brothers, Tom and John, and their families were a short distance south of Amos' land. Benjamin Sherman and Gaius Fuller now were living east of the Colborns. Amos contacted the new people in the area to tell them of the April 2nd town meeting at the Parsons settlement.

Seventeen electors from Conway Township were present at the meeting. Levi Parsons was chosen as moderator and Lorenzo Strang as clerk. A committee of five was picked to nominate officers. Many of the settlers were strangers to Israil and Amos though they all lived within the township. Among them, in addition to the Parsons group, were John Coughran, Henry Hoyt, Stephen Dailey and Joseph Alexander.

Amos was chosen as one of three school inspectors and as a highway commissioner. Because of the problems the settlers were having with wolves it was agreed that a four dollar bounty would be paid on each wolf killed in the township for one year.

Israil, less civic-minded than Amos, voted at the town meeting but declined an office. When the brothers were home, Amos suggested that Lide might be interested in teaching the children of nearby settlers.

"We don't have a school," she worried.

"'Twouldn't be 'till next fall," Amos said. "Mebbe I kin git a leetle cabin up on my land by then. Ya could teach the Martin an' Fuller an' Sherman young'uns. Mebbe there'll be more here by fall."

Lide's eyes sparkled. "How'll we get money for a school?"

"'Twon't cost nothin' but our work to make a leetle cabin on my land. An' if crops is good, folks likely would be willin' t' give a couple a' shillin' a week to pay ya so's their young'uns could git a leetle schoolin'." He paused. "What do ya think, Maw?"

"We needs a school, but I can't see how ya air gonna work with Israil here, clear an' work yer own land, an' build a cabin too."

"Yeah," Israil added. "Looks t' me like yer bitin' off more'n ya kin chew. Air ya forgittin' ya got two hunnert dollars, an' interest, t' pay Maw? An' it better be in silver an' gold. She don't want none a' that good-fer-nothin' paper."

Amos stamped across the floor, his wooden leg beating an irregular tattoo on the rough wood. "No, dammit! I ain't forgot! The wheat looks good this spring, an' if the crop turns out an' the price stays up, I'll make Maw a payment. An' with that four dollars a head wolf bounty an' the furs I trapped this winter - I ain't worried! Air ya worried, Maw?"

Lucretia, crawling about on a quilt on the floor, sat up to stare at Amos. His angry tone was frightening. Suddenly she began screaming. Lide picked her up.

Mary ignored the crying baby. "I ain't worried, Amos. I knows ya'll pay." She slapped a mosquito on her forehead. "The skeeters air thick as a cloud outside. They is such a pesteration. The baby's got bites all over her."

Amos resumed his tirade. "Israil, I ain't askin' fer no help frum ya, but ya let me alone, do ya hear? I'll clear my land, raise my crops an' pay my debts - an' I'll do it even if'n ya don't think I'm as smart as ya air!"

Mary went to the door, picked up the smudge pan and carried it to the fireplace where she placed a few coals in the pan. Going outside she covered them with green grass. Then, placing the smoking pan near the front door, she came inside. "I declare," she said to Amos and Israil, "Ya two fights as bad as ya did when ya was leetle. Ain't ya ever goin' t' grow up?"

The brothers silently glared at one another. Then Israil stormed outside to nurse his jealousy of Amos.

By early June oats and corn were planted, the garden was growing and Amos was clearing more land so that in September he would have additional acres to plant to winter wheat. Nearly every day now Hannah and Shobegun spent several hours working with him.

Suddenly one day as he watched the Indian girl swing an axe and chop down a tree almost as rapidly and expertly as he could do it, he was struck with her beauty. She moved gracefully, her tall figure gliding through the forest on moccasined feet, her dark face serene and expressionless. Feeling his eyes on her, Hannah looked up. He smiled across the stump of the tree she had just cut. Her eyes dropped and she turned to begin chopping the branches from the fallen tree.

"We air killin' two birds with one stone," Amos remarked.

"Birds?" Hannah glanced up, puzzled.

He laughed. "We air clearin' the land an' cuttin' logs fer the cabin - we're doin' two things at onct. 'Tis like ya throws one stone an' kills two birds at onct."

She didn't answer, but from that day Amos watched Hannah and speculated. She was beautiful, she was strong and a good worker. And he liked her. In short, she would make a good wife who would produce healthy children, and she'd work in the fields with him. Together they'd pay off his mother, then they'd buy more land - and more land - He'd show Israil.

Three weeks later they were ready to build the cabin. Ben, Shobegun, Hannah, Lide and Amos scouted the land for the best location. It must be close to the creek, and not too distant from Mary's cabin. Several suitable sites were

An Indian Girl of the 1800s

A Stump Fence

considered, but Amos was unable to decide. Finally he turned to Hannah. "Ya've lived in the wilderness all yer life. Which spot do ya like?"

Silently she led him to a place about one hundred feet from the creek among a stand of tall sturdy oaks. "Here, I like," she said simply.

"Here it will be. 'Twill be a nice spot fer a home."

"Home?" Lide exclaimed. "I thought 'twas going to be my school!"

"Yeah, Lide. But someday I'll marry up with a woman, an' then 'twill be my home." He looked at Hannah. She stared at the ground, her face expressionless.

Ben and Shobegun were listening. Ben said, "Ain't none but married womens 'round here. Where ya goin' t' find anybody to marry up with?"

"Gimme time - gimme time," Amos laughed.

The next two weeks were spent in building a twenty by twenty-four foot cabin. Ben and Shobegun helped Amos with the heavy work while Lide and Hannah carried clay and stones for the chimney, cleared the underbrush from the front of the cabin and ran errands to Mary's home.

At last, except for glass for windows, the building was complete. Finally Ben and Shobegun left to shoot crows in Amos' cornfield with their slingshots and Lide went home to help prepare supper.

Hannah started to leave when Amos said, "Wait up, Hannah. I wants to talk with ya."

She stopped and turned back. He was intensely aware of her dusky beauty. He remembered how she had looked in the pink "civilized" dress with her hair up. Why, dressed that way, she didn't look like an Indian.

"I - I - ," he stammered. "I wants t' thank ya fer helpin'," he began. She was silent. "Does ya like the cabin?"

She raised her eyes. "I like," she said softly.

"Would - would ya marry up with me an' we'd live

here?"

Her face flushed a dusky red. She looked puzzled as her glance met his.

"I wants ya t' be my wife," Amos said slowly. "Will ya?"

"Yeah." Her voice was so low he barely heard.

He took her hand but she pulled away, her eyes staring out into the wilderness. "Ya'll be close t' yer Maw an' Paw an' friends at the camp. Ya kin go see 'em any time ya wants. An' they kin come here. We'll git married next month."

"Git married? How?"

"Levi Parsons. He'll marry us. 'Twill be after the wheat an' oats is cut. Then we'll git married 'fore the fall work begins." He hesitated. "Yer Paw an' Maw - will they feel bad if ya marry up with me 'stead a' an Injun feller?"

She didn't answer. Her eyes had a distant far away look. Amos wondered what she was thinking.

Suddenly he said, "I'm going home with ya. I'll ask the Chief myself."

"Yeah," she whispered.

They walked northwest to the trail which led to the Indian camp. Hannah was silent but Amos rambled on with plans for their future. "We're gonna have a good wheat crop. I'll sell all I kin - we'll eat stuff made out a' cornmeal. I wants to pay Maw the money I owes her soon's I kin. We'll work together - we works good together - ." He stopped. "There's Ben jest startin' home."

"Ben!" Amos shouted. "I'm goin' t' the Injun camp with Hannah. Tell Maw I'll be home t' help Israil with the chores."

The boy ran up to his brother. "Why air ya goin' t' the camp?" he asked.

"I ain't tellin'. Mebbe I'll tell ya when I gits home."

An hour and a half later Amos came into the cabin as the family were finishing supper.

"Ya made quite a stay," Israil remarked. "We oughtn't git thick with them varmints. That girl an' boy hangin' 'round is bad 'nuff 'thout our traipsin' t' their camp all the time. Ben, I means ya, too. Ya're allus runnin' over there with that boy."

Amos sat down at the end of the bench and filled his plate with potatoes, boiled smoked ham and carrots. "Brother Israil," he began, "an' the rest a' the family, too. We're gonna be seein' a heap more a' them Injuns." He stopped. All eyes were on him, waiting. "I'm marryin' up with Hannah in August."

There was dead silence in the cabin. Israil's mouth stood open. Ben and Lide stared at Amos. Mary reached down to pick up Lucretia who broke the silence with, "Maw - maw - maw."

"I'm glad fer ya, son," Mary said sincerely. "Hannah is a nice girl an' she'll make ya a good wife."

Israil jumped up. "Maw! What air ya sayin'? My brother a - a - squawman!"

Amos jumped up to face his brother, his eyes flashing. "Less git it straight - I'm marryin' up with Hannah. Don't ya never let me hear ya sayin' things t' her 'bout her relations - er mean things 'bout her!"

"Squawman! Squawman!" Israil taunted.

Amos' right fist lashed out catching Israil full on the chin. Unprepared, he was knocked off balance and fell backward striking his head on a block of wood beside the fireplace. He didn't stir.

"Stop it!" Mary shouted as she sat the baby on the bench and went toward Israil. "Amos, what has ya done? Ya has killed yer brother!"

Lucretia screamed and outside the door Sam barked furiously. Amos snorted as he picked up the pail of drinking water and dashed it into Israil's face. "Git up an' fight like a man!" he taunted.

Israil opened his eyes and sat up, water dripping from his hair and beard. He struggled unsteadily to his feet as he watchfully eyed Amos.

Mary stepped between them. "Stop it, ya two!

Ain't no sense in this! Now, stop it!"

Amos shoved Mary aside. "Maw, we has t' settle this. I ain't takin' no more frum his mean mouth. I'm goin' t' shut it once an' fer all!" He shoved Israil toward the door. "Git outside!"

Mary dropped into the rocking chair. "Dear God," she prayed, "don't let 'em kill each 'nother."

The sound of fists striking flesh carried into the cabin. Ben and Lide stood silently in the door while the baby, wide-eyed, climbed into her mother's lap. Sam, his nose pointed skyward, howled mournfully. Flies buzzed about the uncleared supper table. "I oughta put the food away," Mary thought. But she didn't stir.

Finally Lide said, "Guess it's over. Amos is lettin' Israil get up."

"Is he hurted bad?" Mary asked.

"I don't know. He's bleeding some."

Ben exclaimed, "By gum! I never knowed Amos could fight like a' that!"

Amos' voice carried into the cabin. "That's jest a taste a' what ya'll be gittin' if ya don't watch yer mouth 'bout Hannah!" He turned toward Lide and Ben in the doorway. "Our big brother don't look so big no more, does he?"

The days settled back into a regular schedule, and the fight was not mentioned again. Lide, Mary and Hannah planned for the wedding. The Indian girl wished to wear the pink cambric dress. Lide showed her how to put her hair up, and though they were a little small, she managed to squeeze her feet into a pair of Lide's shoes.

"Ya looks beautiful," Mary whispered as the girl stood before them in all her finery. "Amos will be right proud a' ya." She listened. "He's outside! Quick, up in the loft! 'Tis bad luck if'n he sees ya in yer weddin' clothes 'afore the weddin'."

Hannah scurried up the ladder just before Amos came in. "The wheat's cut an' shocked, Maw. We'll draw it up an' stack it when 'tis dry. It kin be flailed after the weddin'. Now I'm goin' t' git my wheat cut. Looks like it'll turn out good."

"I'm glad, son." He turned toward the door. "Jest a minute." She called to the loft. "Lide! Hannah! Kin ya come down so's we kin talk?"

Lide came first and Hannah followed, again dressed in her deerskin clothes.

"Amos," Mary began. "In 'nother week ya'll have yer grain cut. Does ya have a date in mind fer yer weddin'?"

Amos scratched his head. He looked at Hannah. "Kin we figger on August 19th?" he asked.

"Yeah," she answered softly.

"Now, 'nother thing," Mary went on. "Air we askin' folk frum the Parsons group, an' other neighbors t' come fer a leetle party after?"

"'Twould be nice, Maw," Amos said, "but 'tis hard work fer ya t' do all the cookin'."

"Lide an' Hannah'll help me, won't ya girls?"

They nodded. "'Course," Lide said.

Amos studied the floor. Finally he said, "We'll ask the Chief an' the rest a' the people at the camp." He paused. "Only - if'n we asks the Injuns, we can't have any whiskey fer the men. I don't know what t' think."

"'A course we'll ask the Injuns. They're Hannah's family an' friends. We kin do 'thout whiskey," Mary said. Silently she wondered how Israil would react. "An' mebbe Ben kin ride over t' Byron an' ask Jacob an' Elvira an' the Steinackers."

"'Twill be a big party, Maw," Amos said slowly. "Sure ya wants t' do it?"

"I wants t' do it. Ya're the first a' my young'uns t' marry up."

"Thank ya, Maw. Now I gotta git t' cuttin' my wheat. Kin I take some bread an' cold ham so's I won't need t' come back 'till night?"

Lide went tc the kitchen area. "Hannah an' I'll get enough ready for all of us. Five of us can make it go fast if we work until night."

They worked silently, Amos and Ben cutting the

wheat with scythes while Shobegun, Lide and Hannah followed as they bound the loose grain into bundles which were held together with a band of twisted wheat straw. After five or six bundles were formed, they were shocked by setting them upright with the grain heads up. Last of all, two bundles were laid overall to cap the shock.

The small grain field sloped to the creek. It was a warm day and each time they worked their way across the field and back, they stopped for a drink. As Amos was straightening and wiping his mouth, he was aware of a shrill harsh buzzing, like a locust, only louder. A huge rattlesnake squirmed and twisted under his peg leg, thrashing about as it struck at his left boot. Quickly Amos got its head under his heel and ground it off.

"Ya put an end to the varmint," Ben said.

"They is bad," Shobegun said. "Our cousin, he die frum rattlesnake bite."

"Yeah," Amos agreed. "But if'n ya cut a bite open, ya kin suck out most a' the pizen. Only ya has t' do it quick 'afore it gits in the blood."

Lide declared, "I'm not drinking here again. I'll go thirsty 'till I get home." She turned to Hannah. "Are you afraid of rattlesnakes?"

"Not when I sees 'em first. I git 'way fast."

"That's smart," Amos agreed.

Ben announced, "This one had sixteen rattles."

"We needs to watch," Amos warned. "When ya gathers the wheat off the ground, be keerful ya don't git a rattler, too. There's leetle ones 'round, 'most likely."

He tossed the dead snake into the woods. "Last spring me an' Israil was out early down by the stone pile. We was gettin' stones fer the well. 'Twas April, an' the night had been cold. The sun was comin' up an' we seen a funny lookin' ball 'most as big's a bushel basket in 'tween a couple a' big rocks. 'Twas heavin' an' twistin' an' squirmin'. Then we seen 'twas a tangle a' rattlesnakes, big an' leetle, all twisted together in a ball. An' a big blacksnake was twined in with the rattlers."

"Ya never telled us," Ben said.

"No use t' scare the wimmin."

Lide asked, "Where did the snakes go?"

"As the sun got warmer, the snakes got livelier, an' finally they went off in all directions up an' down the stones. I seen one that had twenty rattles. We've been in luck that none a' us has been bit, 'cause they's thicker'n spatters 'round here. When I was in Detroit I got some spirits a' Hartshorn fer snake bite. They tells me 'tis good t' put on the bite an' t' take fer medicine too."

Lide shuddered. "I hope we don't need to use it. Now I'm scared to bind up the wheat."

Hannah said, "We look good fer rattlers."

The others started back to work but Amos lingered to walk with Hannah. "I likes t' hear ya talk," he said softly. "Ya talks good."

"Lide, she helps me. An' Shobegun, too."

"When we air married, I'll larn ya, too. An' if Lide has a school in our cabin, ya kin git schoolin' 'long with the others."

The Indian girl nodded soberly. Amos wondered what she was thinking. He hoped she'd grow more comfortable with him, and that she would like the white man's way of life.

On August 17 Amos rode one of the horses to the Parsons settlement to secure the marriage license and to invite the people to the party. Two days later all the family except Israil rode on the farm wagon to the home of Levi Parsons.

Hannah, shy and uncomfortable in her new clothes, hardly spoke on the drive through the forest. With the Colborns and Mrs. Parsons looking on, Levi Parsons performed the marriage ceremony at 11 a.m. Then amid light chatter from Lide, Ben, Mary and Mrs. Parsons, the newly married couple turned to go outside. They were greeted by twenty-five laughing, cheering, rice-throwing settlers. Amos laughed and shielded his eyes but Hannah covered her face in terror. She could only believe that these people disliked her, else why were they throwing rice at her?

Seeing her fear Amos whispered, "White folks throw rice at weddings. Smile. Look happy." He took her arm and hobbling beside her they went to the wagon. He turned to the crowd. "Come soon's ya kin to our party." Then amid cheers and cries of "Congratulations," they started home.

"You is a beautiful bride," Mary whispered.

"Why they throw rice?" Hannah asked.

"It means they hopes ya'll be happy an' that ya has many young'uns."

The rest of the way home Hannah silently pondered the strange ways of the white man.

Ten minutes after they arrived, five Indian men and Shobegun dashed up to the cabin on their ponies. "Ain't yer Maw comin'?" Mary asked her new daughter-in-law.

"Womens don't come," Hannah replied.

Amos, with Shobegun acting as interpreter, tried to talk with the men as his mother and Lide hurried to carry pans of food to the crude table in the yard. By this time wagons from the Parsons settlement and the Byron people were arriving. There was great commotion as children and men shouted greetings and women carried the food they had brought to the table.

Amos and Hannah stood together receiving congratulations and accepting gifts brought by the guests. A length of muslin, several cooking pots and kettles, a few fancy dishes, a small mirror and a Bible were among the gifts.

Hannah, uncomfortable and shy, stood beside Amos, an unnatural smile frozen on her face. Lide's shoes hurt her feet. She wished they'd all go home, but the guests were eating and talking. Her father and the men from the camp stood together a little apart from the others. Shobegun and Ben were racing around with two boys from the settlement. Suddenly she was homesick for the camp.

"Smile," Amos whispered.

Her eyes were expressionless, but the stiff,

unnatural smile returned to her face. Jacob Euler came to shake hands. Amos said, "Hannah, this is Jacob Euler, the man that sawed my foot off."

"Yah. He says it so it sounds bad."

"'Twas bad," Amos said quietly.

"Yah. You has purty vife, Amos," he said. "An' you has goot husband, Miz. Colborn."

Hannah nodded silently.

"Vere you live?" Jacob asked. "You build cabin?"

"Yeah. An' I bought land. Got a good crop a' wheat."

Jacob shook his head. "Dey tells me veat prices is going down."

Amos' smile disappeared. "I ain't heerd. What else do they say? Why's wheat prices goin' down?"

"Dere's too much veat. Nobody vants to buy, an' nobody's got gold er silver to pay vith."

"Mebbe in Detroit 'tis better."

Jacob shook his head. "Ve hope. Farmers crops is goot. I hope you gets goot price. Vere is Israil?"

"I duno," Amos replied. "He don't like parties much."

People filled their plates and gathered in groups to visit. The new settlers were glad to meet their closest neighbors who lived from two to six miles away.

Amos, guiding Hannah from group to group, was a congenial host. He attempted to introduce the Indian men, and with Shobegun's help, to explain where each family lived. He felt the explanations were unnecessary since, as Israil said, "The woods round here is full a' Injun eyes."

The women gossiped about new neighbors. Often when Amos and Hannah approached a group, they suddenly became silent. Nevertheless, he introduced Hannah and hoped that gradually she would be accepted.

Mary and Elvira Euler were catching up on the news. Elvira again was pregnant. Perhaps this time things would go well and she would deliver a healthy baby. As she talked her eyes followed Lucretia who toddled happily from group to group.

"She's a lovely child," Elvira said softly. "It's a shame her father never got to see her." She paused. "You're a brave woman, Mary, carrying on as head of the family and having Lucretia by yourself."

Mary hastened to explain. "I wasn't alone. Hannah's mother helped me. She was real good, but I ain't seen her since that day Lucretia was borned."

"A squaw? Was she clean?"

Mary laughed. "I didn't look close, but I kin tell ya, she looked good t' me." In a moment she asked, "Do ya know who the young feller is that's talkin' t' Lide?"

"H-m-m-m. I think his name is Martin."

Mary nodded. "They's two Martin families. The men is brothers. I met the men an' their wives, but I ain't met the young'uns."

"They seem to be having a good time - the boy and Lide," Elvira said.

Mary didn't reply. In a few minutes she and Elvira drifted over to visit with Mrs. Levi Parsons and Mrs. Wait. Amos and Hannah stopped to talk with Benjamin Sherman and Gaius Fuller. After introductions Amos asked, "How's yer crops?"

"Wheat an' oats turned out good," Gaius said, "but I spoze ya've heerd prices is way down - if ya kin sell yer grain a'tall."

"What they payin'?"

"'Twas two dollars a bushel. Now it's about three shillin'."

"Damn! A man can't make no money at them prices!" Amos exclaimed. "An' ever'thin' ya has t' buy is sky high!"

Benjamin Sherman said, "Ya come in 1836?"

"Yeah. November."

"Was the first winter purty hard? I've heerd tell a' people gol-darn-near starvin' - boilin' up acorns t' eat, an' no salt er lard er butter. A feller told me in Howell that if it wasn't fer the Injuns, his family would a' starved. Beef an' pork was so high he couldn't buy it, but the Injuns sold venison cheap - an' fish too. He was sick that first winter an' couldn't hunt."

Amos answered, "We brought as much food as we could, an' we allus was able t' shoot a buck er rabbits - an' there was muskrats, too. Course, we got tired a' wild game, but with our vegetables an' game, we wasn't hungry." He hesitated and glanced at Hannah. "My wife's family brought us a turkey onct. They've been right nice t' us."

Moving on Amos and Hannah stopped to talk with Levi Parsons and his eldest son, Julius. After conversation about the ruinous farm prices, Levi said, "Remember Stephen and Jonas Avery that was with you at Hannibal's Inn?"

"Yeah. Seen 'em?"

"They was in Howell last week when I was there. They ask 'bout yer family. 'Course they didn't know 'bout you havin' yer foot off, er yer Paw's gettin' killed, 'er 'bout yer leetle sister."

"Wisht I could see 'em. They's nice people - an' they's got a pile a' book larnin'."

Julius said, "They've moved two times. First Stephen had land in Handy Township, but he sold it an' moved to Eaton County, an' now he's talkin' 'bout buyin' over southwest a' here in Ingham County, Locke Township, he said."

"How far'd that be frum us?"

"I duno. Four, five miles as the crow flies. But there ain't no trail."

Levi said, "Guess Stephen must have itchy feet. He lived in Canada fer a while 'fore he come t' Michigan, an' 'fore that, he lived some'ere in York State. Now he's bought an' sold Michigan land onct and is talkin' 'bout sellin' ag'in."

Julius laughed. "Some folks likes movin'. Well, 'tis ever'body t' his own fancy like the ole woman said when she kissed her cow."

The men laughed heartily. Amos knew Hannah didn't understand the joke. He'd explain it to her later. Damn that Israil. It wouldn't have hurt him to have put in an appearance at the party, even if he wouldn't go to the wedding.

About two o'clock the Indians left. When they were gone Amos brought out a jug of whiskey and passed it around. By three-thirty, the men were "feelin' good," but most people had several miles to travel, so they prepared to leave. While Mary, Lide and Hannah bid their guests good-bye, the men hitched their horses or oxen to the wagons. At last they were gone.

"'Twas a good party," Mary said with satisfaction.

"'Twas nice being with people again," Lide said.

"We seen ya makin' eyes at Jack Martin," Amos teased. "'Peared like ya was gonna talk to him all afternoon."

Lide blushed. "Well - I hadn't talked to a young man in so long I had to learn how again."

"Yeah. That's a good 'scuse." He turned to Hannah. "I'm gonna do the chores an' then we'll go home."

"I has some things t' send with ya," Mary said. "An' I'm gonna give ya a weddin' ring quilt. That'll be my present."

"Thank ya, Maw," Amos said. "We 'preciates all ya've done, don't we, Hannah?"

She nodded silently.

An hour and a half later they started for their home carrying their gifts and enough food for supper and breakfast.

PREJUDICE

(1839)

Amos, Hannah and their sleeping two month old baby, Betsy, rode atop a load of wheat through the Michigan wilderness. This was Hannah's first trip outside her home since their marriage. Silently she cuddled Betsy. In her stoic way, she adored the baby. She knew Amos was disappointed that his first born had not been a boy, but there would be other babies. There would be boys for Amos.

The late September sun slanted through the colorful orange, gold and red leaves of the woods. Squirrels darted up trees, their cheeks stuffed with nuts which they would add to their winter storehouse. A crow cawed shrilly as he flew from tree to tree suspiciously watching the progress of the intruders.

Amos clucked to the horses. "Get up, King! Get up, Queen!" He slapped the reins against the black teams' sides and their speed increased slightly. The wagon jolted over roots in the narrow road.

"I could walk faster on my peg leg," Amos muttered.

Hannah didn't reply. Accustomed to her silence, he went on. It was as though he was talking aloud to himself. "When we gits to Howell, we'll take some wheat and corn to the mill so's we'll have flour and corn meal this winter. Then I'll sell my wheat. The price ain't good, they says, but 'tis better'n last year. I ain't paid Maw much in two years. Israil's layin' up money. I ain't payin' off my debt fast 'nuff. But he ain't got no family - yet. He's gonna marry up with that Sarah

Grant that he met last summer at Parsons. I 'spect she's a high toned one. She'll spend his money. They won't have nothin' to do with us. Well - he deserves 'er - I guess they deserves each other."

As the wagon jolted over a rut Betsy wakened with a cry, her black eyes wide. Silently Hannah opened the front of her red cotton dress to nurse the baby.

"After we sell the wheat we'll git ya a new dress an' shoes. Like that?" Amos asked.

"Yeah." Betsy nursed ravenously.

Amos joked, "She eats like a leetle pig." He was silent for a long time. Finally he said, "I've been wonderin'. We've been married more'n a year, an' Lide had her leetle school at our place 'till last May, an' you knows English now. Why don't ya talk t' me? Ya don't say hardly nothin'."

Hannah didn't answer. Amos continued. "I gits lonesome fer somebody t' talk t' me. Why don't ya try?"

"Injuns don't talk 'less 'n they has somethin' t' say," she said softly.

"Ya likes t' have me talk, don't ya?"

"Yeah."

"Can't ya try a leetle? Tell me 'bout things ya like, an' 'bout people. Tell me how ya feels 'bout things."

"I'll try."

"Ya think Lide will marry up with Jack Martin? Has she said anythin'?"

"She likes him."

"He'd make her a good man. He's hard workin' an' he's got a good head on his shoulders. Course if Lide leaves, 'twill be hard fer Maw. Cretia's jest a baby, an' Ben's only a boy, though he's becomin' a man fast. When Israil an' Lide marry up 'twill be hard fer Maw - less'n one of 'em lives with her. But that high-toned Susan Grant wouldn't live with her mother-in-law, an' I 'spect Jack Martin would want a home near his father's. Well - we'll cross that bridge when we comes to

An Indian Papoose

The State Seal

it."

"Bridge? Where?"

Amos laughed. "We'll do somethin' 'bout Maw when Lide an' Israil air gone - that's what I means."

"I'll help Maw."

"Ya air a good woman, Hannah," Amos said softly. Her dusky face flushed, but she didn't reply. "An' yer real purty." He looked at her as he appraised her appearance. Dark hair parted in the middle with two braids worn Indian fashion over her shoulders - her red dress was becoming but she still wore deerskin moccasins. "Like I said," he went on, "we'll buy you some white woman's shoes an' a new dress."

"I'll have three dresses - my pink wedding dress, this red one, an' a new one."

"An' don't forget, you'll have shoes 'stead a' moccasins."

Hannah didn't answer. Her eyes rested on Betsy's face. The baby yawned, stirred slightly and again fell asleep.

Amos lightly touched one of Hannah's braids. "'Spoze ya could put yer hair up 'fore we git t' Howell? Ya looks nice with it up."

She didn't answer for a time, then she said softly,"I ain't got no hairpins."

"Why didn't ya ask Maw er Lide fer some?"

"I duno. I likes my hair this a'way."

"When we kin git hairpins, will ya wear it up while we're in Howell?"

"Yeah." Her mask-like expression revealed none of the hurt she felt. Amos didn't like her Indian hair style. She had discarded her head band because he disliked it, and she'd put away her deerskin clothing. Now he wanted her to put her hair up and wear white woman's shoes. If he wanted a white woman, why did he marry her? He was ashamed to be the husband of a squaw! She withdrew into her shell and rode silently the rest of the way to the village of Howell.

Amos, accustomed to his wife's silent ways, was

unaware of her hurt feelings. He talked of his plans. "We'll be in Howell by two o'clock. Then we'll leave the corn and wheat at the mill an' go sell the rest a' the wheat. Ya be thinkin' what color dress ya want, an' after we gits yer things, we'll git a hotel room an' stay overnight. We'll eat at the hotel. Won't ya like that?"

"Yeah."

"Less have our ham an' bread now so's we won't waste time eatin' when we gits there."

Hannah bent to get a towel-wrapped package from the bottom of the wagon. As the horses plodded eastward, Amos and Hannah slowly munched their sandwiches.

"I wants t' tell ya," Amos began. "Howell is a place where jokes is played on 'most ever'body. They don't hurt nobody, but they likes to do things fer a laugh. They might do somethin' to us."

"I'll be 'fraid." Her voice was low.

"Nothin' to be 'fraid 'bout. If they does somethin' to us, jest laugh. The fellers don't hurt nobody. 'Course they gits purty drunk an' loud, sometimes."

Soon they pulled into the western edge of the village. "There's William McPherson's blacksmith shop," Amos said. "I have to git a plow point tomorrer."

A few minutes later they passed Mills' Dry Goods Store and Elisha Hazard's grocery. "Guess we'll git a room out east at Shuabel Sliter's place. 'Tis a leetle cheaper than the other hotels that's right in town. They's three others now. The Old Stage House, the Eagle Hotel an' the Temperance Hotel."

Two hours later when their business at the mill and the sale of the wheat were completed, Amos tied his team at the hitching post before Mills' Dry Goods Store. Suddenly a huge drunken man lunged from the door of the Old Stage House. Across the street, a carpenter, Elijah Coffern, was working on a roof. Alexander McPherson, the fifteen-year-old son of the blacksmith, carried a loaded water squirt gun. When he was within range of the carpenter the boy let fly with a stream of water which hit Coffern in the face. The man muttered, wiped his face on his sleeve and rapidly descended the ladder in pursuit of young McPherson who dashed across the street and past Amos' and Hannah's wagon.

Both Coffern and McPherson were laughing as they rushed past the huge drunken man who leaned against the front of the Old Stage House. People on the street stopped to watch the excitement. Everyone was laughing and two merchants were placing bets on the winner.

"I got two shillin' that says young Alex will win!" Tom Turner said.

"Nope," Frances Monroe replied. "Elijah'll outrun Alex. He's had 'nuff a' this water gun business. Just as he gets to work somebody comes 'long an' shoots him. Seems like every man an' boy in town's got a squirt gun. I bets my money on Elijah."

The pair dashed behind the dry goods store with Alex well in the lead. The drunken man staggered into the middle of Grand River Street. "Now all you squirters, hear this!" he shouted. "Ya all knows me, Levi Bristol. Ya knows I can break anybody in two with one punch. Ya knows I'm ugly when I'm drunk - an' I'm drunk now!" He struggled to stay on his feet. Regaining his balance he shouted, "I dare anybody to come out here in the street an' squirt me. The first one that dares to squirt me will git his head knocked off!" He waited, but no one challenged Levi Bristol. For two or three minutes he ranted and roared. "Come on, ya cowards! Don't any a' ya squirters dare tackle a real he-man?"

Suddenly a young boy carrying a quart squirt gun stepped into the street and slowly advanced toward Bristol.

"'Tis Leander Smith!" Tom Turner said. "Bristol will kill the boy!"

Slowly the child came on toward the roaring mountain of a man. "Like David and Goliath," someone near Amos muttered. Hannah stood close to her husband, her dark eyes taking in the strange encounter.

"Leander!" Tom Turner shouted. "Back off! He'll kill ya!"

But the boy who appeared to be about eleven years old, continued advancing toward Bristol. He brought his squirt gun up and aimed at the face of the staggering, cursing giant. A stream struck Bristol square in the eyes. Suddenly he straightened, then he lunged and plunged and whirled himself along in spirals through the dusty street while he uttered yells of rage and pain which resulted in dead silence among the onlookers. He didn't seem to know or care where he was going. Roaring like a bull he burst through the door of Elijah Hazard's grocery where he stamped and whirled into the counter which overturned, spilling cheese, candy, sugar and coffee onto the floor.

Elisha Hazard rushed to confront the bellowing Bristol. "Get out a' here, ya drunken bum!" he shouted.

Bristol, his fists in his eyes, brushed Hazard aside as he spun his huge body back into the street. "Help me!" he screamed. "My eyes is afire! I'm goin' blind!"

Leander Smith stood beside Amos' wagon, a wide smile on his face. Hannah, frightened, hugged Betsy and clung to her husband. The boy shouted, "Got 'nuff, Levi?"

"Somebody help me!" the big man pleaded.

"Jest wash yer eyes out with water!" Leander shouted. "I squirted you with whiskey and pepper."

Alexander McPherson suddenly appeared with a pail of water and a crowd gathered round as the huge man squatted to dash handsful of water into his burning eyes. A few minutes later, red-eyed, he searched the crowd for his tormenter, but

Leander had disappeared.

Bristol now was calm and dead sober. Elisha Hazard called, "What ya gonna do 'bout the mess in my store?"

"I'll pay fer the damage I done," he said meekly.

The crowd broke up and business again proceeded as usual. A short time later Amos and Hannah returned from Mills' Dry Goods Store with several packages. They climbed into the wagon and drove three-fourths of a mile east on Grand River to Shuabel Sliter's log tavern where they planned to rent a room for the night.

Hannah, holding Betsy, stood just inside the door as Amos went to make the arrangements. Shuabel Sliter, a small fair-skinned man with pale blue eyes and blonde hair and beard, chewed slowly on a huge quid of tobacco. "Ya want a room an' t' put yer team up fer the night?"

"How much will it be?" Amos asked.

Sliter studied Hannah. "Yer wife?" he asked.

"Yeah. My wife an' baby. How much fer the room an' t' put up an' feed my team?"

"We don't gen'rally rent to Injuns. But - gimme a dollar an' ya kin stay."

Amos spun around, his peg leg clattering on the wooden floor. "Keep yer room!" he said. "I wouldn't stay here if ya give it t' me free!"

"Come, Hannah," he said as he clumped out the door.

"I didn't mean nothin'," Sliter called. "Ya kin stay!"

Amos didn't answer. Fifteen minutes later he made arrangements to stay at the Eagle Hotel.

Hannah cared for Betsy before putting her on the bed for a nap. Then she opened her packages to inspect her dress and shoes.

Amos, sitting by the window, eagerly read the Detroit Free Press which he had purchased in the lobby. From his intense expression, Hannah knew he was disturbed by something in the newspaper. Silently she put on the new brown paisley dress and sturdy black shoes. The shoes felt stiff and strange on her feet. She glanced at Amos. She had never seen him so deeply engrossed in reading.

Going to the mirror, Hannah twisted her long black braids into a knot on top of her head where she pinned them securely with the new hairpins. She hoped Amos would be proud of her when they went to the dining room for supper. When she was finished she sat on the bed beside Betsy and waited.

Finally Amos folded the newspaper and laid it aside. For a long time he stared out of the window into the barnyard where ducks quacked and Plymouth Rock hens cackled. Now and then the rooster crowded lustily.

At last Amos got up, washed his hands and face in the wash basin and combed his hair and beard. "'Tis time t' go t' supper," he said shortly.

Hannah gathered up her sleeping baby and silently followed Amos to the dining room. Several guests already were eating when they sat down at the long family-style table.

"Evenin'," the man across the table said. "I'm Warren Grant. I live a few miles north of the Fowlerville settlement."

"I'm Amos Colborn, an' this is my wife Hannah an' our baby."

"How-dee-doo. I've heard of the Colborns from Stephen Avery. You're on the county line, ain't ya?"

"Yeah. The Avery's live in the same place yet?"

"They sold their land and bought in Locke Township over in Ingham County. They moved last February. Ain't seen 'em since. Nice folk, they be, but they're turrible religious. I have a license to sell liquor, an Stephen talked to me 'bout it. Said I was harmin' peoples' bodies an' minds by sellin' liquor."

Amos nodded. "Ever'body has a right to make up his mind as seems fittin' t' him. Me, I don't see no harm in a nip now an' then." He hesitated a moment, then went on. "I wisht I had book larnin' like them Averys."

For a few minutes the conversation stopped as everyone ate stewed chicken, dumplings and mashed potatoes together with thick slabs of homemade bread and butter and cooked cabbage.

Though there were two other ladies at the table, Hannah noticed they did not join in the conversation.

"Seen the Free Press?" The question was asked by a middle-aged man at the end of the table. "That's quite a story."

Amos remained silent but two or three of the men said they'd read it. Glancing sidewise at Hannah, they dropped the subject.

Later Amos explained to his wife that he was going to spend an hour or two in the hotel saloon. He removed most of the wheat money from his wallet. "Keep this fer me," he said. "Don't want to lose my payment fer Maw. I'm lucky. I got paid in silver. 'Nother couple years an' we'll own our land free an' clear. We're gonna own a big farm someday."

Silently Hannah took the money and placed it in her bosom. Three hours later, Amos returned to their room, roaring drunk. She could make no sense of his ramblings about treaties with hundreds of Indians, and United States troops who were driving them beyond something called the Mississippi. At last she got Amos into bed where he fell into a deep sleep until eight o'clock the next morning when he was wakened by Betsy's crying.

Sitting on the edge of the bed, his head in his hands, Amos asked, "You got the money?"

Hannah removed it from her bosom and he replaced it in his wallet. She sat beside the window to nurse Betsy. Amos lay back on the bed. "When ya air done feedin' her, we'll git some breakfast. I need coffee."

Hannah had on her new dress and shoes, and her hair was up. Amos hadn't noticed the evening before, and he was in no condition to observe his wife's appearance this morning.

Because they were late in appearing for breakfast, the other guests had finished and gone. By ten o'clock Amos had the team and wagon at the front door. A few minutes later he stopped to tie the horses before the blacksmith shop.

"You wait here," he said to Hannah. "William might have to make the plow point."

The Indian woman watched people on the street. She was puzzled for they seemed to be gathering along both sides of the dusty road. Some shaded their eyes against the eastern sun to peer down Grand River Street.

"They're comin'!" someone shouted. "They're comin' 'round the bend!"

In the distance Hannah saw a great crowd of people entering the eastern edge of Howell. Along each side of the crowd many mounted United States soldiers kept the people in line. Her heart lurched. Those walking people were Indians! What were they doing? Would they take her and Betsy and drive them along with the others like cattle?

Now they were close enough so she could see their faces. Sad - sad - mournful faces. Old wrinkled faces and frail faltering bodies, young men, women and even children. Several women carried babies. All were silent and wore mournful, sad, desperate expressions on their faces.

Amos hurried to the wagon. "I'm sorry ya seen this," he said softly.

People along the street were talking in low voices. "'Tain't right," one woman said to another. "They're human too."

Hannah hugged Betsy. "What - what they doin' with 'em?"

"The soldiers air takin' 'em out West - out 'cross the Mississippi to a reservation - a place where they kin live together."

"Air they makin' 'em go?" Her voice trembled.

"Yeah."

Joseph Skilbeck, a Howell resident, stood beside

Amos. "Wish we could stop this thing some way, but we're helpless against the government. The Indians signed treaties. They didn't know they were signing away their rights."

While Skilbeck and Amos talked, Hannah studied the unhappy faces of the Indians. She was one of them. She might have been in that crowd being driven along by soldiers on horseback. When one of them got out of line he was herded back just like Sam herded the cows. She reached up to remove the hairpins from her braids which tumbled down over her shoulders. She was proud to be an Indian. She wanted these people to know she was one of them.

"Halt!" The order came from an officer at the front of the procession and was passed on from mounted soldier to mounted soldier.

The tired Indians stopped. They looked like whipped dogs, Hannah thought. Where was the proud Indian spirit? What had the white man done to them?

The officer at the front shouted, "Take 'em for a rest off to the right on the village square!" Again the order was passed down the line.

Silently the exiles made their way toward the shaded grassy square. They quietly followed the crowd, some bent and limping with age, all with downcast eyes and stoic expressions on their dark faces.

Suddenly a girl of about fifteen lifted her eyes to meet Hannah's. She carried her head proudly. She was the first one Hannah had seen who still showed a spark of spirit. The girl halted momentarily. Quickly Hannah pulled her to the back of the wagon and pushed her down on the floor beside the barrels of flour and cornmeal. With one motion she threw a blanket over the girl.

Turning back to face the crowd she was aware that several of the Indians had seen, but they continued their slow shuffle to the village square. Amos and Joseph Skilbeck still were talking. Betsy cried and Hannah quieted her.

What would Amos do when he discovered the girl in the wagon? Would he be angry? Would he send her back to be driven along for days and days to some place she'd never heard of? Hannah's heart pounded. She wished they'd start home. She climbed into the wagon and sat waiting on the seat.

Amos, oblivious to her, was in the center of a crowd of whites, all watching the miserable exiles as they lounged, dejected, on the grass. Finally he returned to the wagon. "Might's well go. I've seen 'nuff a' this thing."

He untied the horses and climbed up beside her. From the corner of her eye Hannah could see the motionless blanket at the back.

Betsy immediately fell asleep. For half an hour no one spoke, then Amos said cheerfully, "'Twill be good to get home. Things is nice there. Our land, Maw, Lide an' Ben - yeah, an' even Israil - a feller knows what to 'spect there."

"Yeah."

"An' with the wheat money an' the bounty from the wolves I've shot, an' from the trappin' I did last winter, I kin pay Maw half a' what I owe her." He looked at Hannah. "Ain't that great?"

"Yeah."

"Ya got yer hair down agin," Amos said accusingly.

"I likes it this way. I'm Injun."

For the next two hours they talked very little. Amos silently planned for the future and Hannah worried about his reaction when he discovered the stowaway.

At one o'clock they stopped for the box lunch prepared for them at the Eagle Hotel. As Hannah opened the box, Amos said, "Jest a minute. I wants to count how much money we has fer Maw." He reached for his wallet. Excitedly he jumped from the wagon and frantically searched his pockets.

"It's gone! My wallet's gone!" His voice was low - unbelieving. Again he searched every pocket. Hannah stared at her husband, a sandwich held in mid-air.

He jumped into the wagon. "Maybe it fell out in here." He snatched up the blanket. "What - what?" he exclaimed.

The Indian girl sat up. Her eyes were wide but they showed no fear. Amos turned to Hannah. "What - who - where did she come frum?"

"I not know her."

Amos leaned against a barrel of flour. "This is a purty kittle a' fish. Our money gone an' another mouth t' feed."

Hannah passed a sandwich to the girl who accepted it silently. Amos searched the bottom of the wagon box.

"It's gone - a whole year's work - gone. I had the money when we left the hotel. Ya give it t' me." Hannah nodded. "There must a' been a pickpocket in that crowd that was watchin' the Injuns." He tossed his head in the stowaway's direction. "An' what air we gonna do with her?"

"We'll keep her." Hannah paused before she said softly, "I could a' been one a' them Injuns."

Amos patted her arm. "I understands. I wisht we could a' helped all of 'em. We'll find a way. But Maw - I hate t' tell 'er I can't pay nothin'."

"Yeah."

"Might's well git goin' an' git it over with." As Hannah passed him a sandwich, he motioned. "I don't want nothin' t' eat."

Hannah, with Betsy, went to sit with the girl. Through a mixture of the Potawatomi language and English, Hannah haltingly conversed with her. After a time she returned to the wagon seat.

"What did ya find out?" he asked.

"Her name White Fawn. Her tribe frum place called Sag-in-ah."

"Saginaw. Yeah, what else?"

"She is glad to stay in Michigan. She will work."

By four o'clock the black team pulled into Mary's place. Sam had announced their arrival by running and barking to meet them and jumping at King's and Queen's noses. Israil and Ben stood beside the well. "How'd it go?" Israil asked.

Amos shook his head without answering. Lucretia ran to meet them. "Amos! Hannah!" she called. She stared at White Fawn. "Who that is?"

"A friend," Amos answered climbing down from the wagon. "We all needs t' talk," he said to Lide and Mary who stood in the doorway.

Their mother was aging, Amos thought. Her gray streaked hair and the missing teeth made her look older than her years. And now he was going to add to her burden.

A few minutes later they gathered about Mary's table. Amos began by telling them about White Fawn and their reason for keeping her. "She don't understand much English," he said.

Lide answered, "We'll teach her."

Amos continued, "'Twon't be easy, but some way we'll manage t' feed 'nother mouth."

Israil smirked, "Yer gittin' quite a harem, Brother."

Amos glared at Israil. "Shut yer mouth 'fore I shut it fer ya!"

The cabin became quiet. At last Amos got up and limped to the window. After a moment, he turned abruptly. "I might's well tell ya. I lost all my money. My pockets was picked. I can't pay ya anythin' this year, Maw."

For a moment no one spoke. Mary got up slowly. "I'm sorry." Her voice faltered. "I wanted t' help Israil buy some land, but 'twill have t' wait. 'Tis no use to cry over spilt milk."

"Gol. That's turrible," Ben said.

"How much did you have?" Lide asked.

"I reckon 'bout a hunnert an' twenty-five dollars - an' all in silver. But Maw, I'll pay you ever' cent I owes. I will!"

Israil picked up his hat. "Promises - last year promises, this year promises - but no money. Promises don't pay debts er buy land!" He stalked outside.

Chapter XI

RELIGION, POLITICS AND DEATH

(1843)

The cold, gray, half-light of a March dawn gave promise of a dark, gloomy day. By the light of a flickering candle on the rough board table, Stephen Avery and his wife conducted daily devotions.

Selecting a passage from his well-worn Bible, Stephen slowly glanced around the table at his family. His wife, Lucy, rather stout and two years older than he, brushed bread crumbs from the table onto her plate. At fifty-two she was an old woman.

Albert, twenty-four years old and the eldest child, planned to buy land when he had sufficient money. Stephen hoped he'd find a wife who would be a helpmate. That young woman, Rebecca Macomber, that the family met at camp meeting would be a fine choice.

Twenty-two year old Jonas, everyone said, was "a chip off the old block." Stephen was especially fond of Jonas for he saw himself in the young man as he'd been at the same age. They were similar in appearance and temperament. Fair-skinned with red hair and flashing blue eyes, Jonas was quick to lose patience and given to temper outbursts.

Then, there were Stephen's three daughters, Mary Ann, going on twenty-one, already was considered an "old maid" by the younger girls. Melissa at seventeen was frail and subject to severe problems with her lungs. And the youngest in the family, Harriet, who at age sixteen promised to be the most intellectual of the girls, also was the most beautiful.

The farm Stephen had bought from Almon Whipple in February of 1839 produced bountiful crops. Most of the land was cleared and the log house was comfortable. At the Locke Township meeting in April of 1839 he was elected to the offices of Justice of the Peace, Assessor and School Inspector. He also was Overseer of the Poor, an office which sometimes demanded that he take over the nursing duty of ill patients. But he was thankful for good health, and for some medical knowledge which caused him to be in demand in times of illness.

"Paw," Jonas said. "We're waiting for you."

Stephen smiled and stroked his red beard. "I was wool gathering, thinking about how fast my family's growing up." He placed the Bible on the table and pulled the candle close. "The 67th Psalm, which I have chosen today, set me thinking about how good God has been to us. Listen.

> God be merciful to us and bless us;
> And cause his face to shine upon us; Selah.
> That thy way may be known upon the earth,
> thy saving health among all nations.
> Let the people praise thee, O God; let all
> the people praise thee.
> O let the nations be glad and sing for joy;
> for thou shalt judge the people righteously,
> and govern the nations upon the earth. Selah.
> Let the people praise thee, O God; let all the
> people praise thee.
> Then shall the earth yield her increase; and
> God, even our own God, shall bless us.
> God shall bless us; and all the ends of the
> earth shall fear him."

Stephen closed the Bible. For a moment there was silence, then Lucy said softly, "That was nice, Stephen. We don't give thanks as we ought for our blessings."

The family, as they had been taught since

infancy, sat respectfully waiting for morning devotions to end.

"Mother," Stephen said to Lucy, "Would you pray?"

She folded her hands and waited until every head was bowed. "Dear Lord, we come to thee with thankful hearts for our many blessings. We pray for strength that we may be better pilgrims and that we may be living examples to friends and neighbors of a family who lives to glorify God.

"We pray thou will forgive us our sins. Help the girls to think less of their appearance and more of serving thee. Help Stephen and Jonas to control their tempers, and Albert to not become greedy for land before it is thy will he should have it.

"And dear Lord, help me to be an example to my family and neighbors so that they will see the happiness and joy one can have in serving thee.

"All this I ask in thy name. Amen."

After morning devotions the family went to their daily activities. Albert and Jonas took their rifles and went into the forest behind the barn.

"Let's try to get a young buck," Albert suggested. "They are better eating."

Jonas had a coughing spell. Wiping his mouth on his glove, he said, "Guess I'm always going to have these spells. I thought when I was out of the hay and grain, I'd be better. Dust always has made it worse, but this year it doesn't get better."

"You're just like Paw. He's had it as long as I can remember, and he said his father, Grandpa Simeon Avery, had it too."

Jonas cleared his throat. "Guess it's the Avery curse." He grinned.

"Maw and Paw'd say you should pray about it," Albert laughed. Suddenly he stopped walking. "Sh-h-h," he whispered. Stepping behind trees, they waited several minutes. Finally a spikehorn buck walked from behind a small pine. Jonas aimed, fired and the young deer dropped.

The brothers suspended the carcass from a pole and started toward the house to dress it out. As they worked, they talked. Albert said, "Pa's gone to help the poor folks again. Seems like he spends too many hours taking care of them."

Jonas set the pan of deer entrails on the ground, then he returned to the carcass which was suspended from a branch eight feet above the ground. "That's the way Paw is. If anybody needs help he feels that as Overseer of the Poor it's his duty to do what he can. He's a good man. We were small, but do you remember how he changed after he got religion?"

Albert laughed. "It was like a change from darkness to daylight."

Jonas wiped his hands on a rag and stepped back from the swaying carcass. "After it cools we'll cut it up for Maw. The girls don't like to do it."

The brothers started toward the barn. "Speaking of the girls, have you noticed Melissa lately?" Albert asked.

"Why?"

"She looks mighty puny. She's so thin, and she coughs something awful."

"It's the Avery curse, I guess."

"Could be more than that."

"What do you mean?"

"After some of her coughing spells she's spitting up blood. She tries to hide it, but I've seen it two times."

Jonas was silent for a time, then he said, "I don't suppose Paw's noticed. He's too busy helping other sick folks."

"What could he do if he knew - besides to pray?"

"Prayer wouldn't hurt, and maybe it'd help," Jonas answered. "When we have warm weather and sunshine, they say that's good for - lung problems."

"Consumption, you mean," Albert said softly.

Jonas picked up a rock and fired it with all his

might at the side of the barn. The report sounded like a rifle shot. He leaned against the barnyard fence. "Damn!" he exclaimed, "Don't say that! It's not right that a seventeen year old girl should die! Sometimes I wonder why God lets such things happen!"

"Well - maybe she'll get better, like you said."

"People don't get over consumption," Jonas replied. "I don't want to talk about it anymore."

Albert looked toward the house as he closed the barnyard gate. "We've got a visitor," he said.

"Clarissa Lighthall!" Jonas exclaimed as he disappeared into the barn. "I don't want to see her!"

Albert called, "Good morning, Mrs. Lighthall."

"'Morning, Albert. Is your family home, or are you alone?"

"Maw and the girls are inside," Albert shouted beating a hasty retreat into the barn.

The woman was dressed all in black. Her long skirt swept the ground and her straggly gray hair hung across her face at the sides of her bonnet. Over her shoulder she carried a four foot long stick to which a bundle was attached. She knocked at the door which Lucy opened.

"Good morning, Clarissa," she said. "Won't you come in?"

The woman brushed back a lock of gray hair. "Good day, good day. Not long I'll stay."

"Well, come in. The air is chilly." Lucy closed the door behind her.

"Mam, you're kind to your guest. I'm here on a quest." Clarissa leaned her stick against the wall.

"Well - sit down." Lucy motioned toward the table. "There's coffee left. It'll warm you."

"Thank you. 'Twould be nice. Truly, I'm cold as ice." She glanced at the girls who stood in the door to the kitchen.

"Good morning," each girl murmured. They had

been in awe since childhood of this strange woman who spoke only in rhyme.

"You'll each make a good wife in this world filled with strife." Clarissa sat at the table and Lucy returned with two cups of steaming coffee.

"We haven't seen you all winter. Have you been well?" Lucy asked.

"I've worked to the west. People say I'm obsessed. But I'm doing my best to help the unblest find God, peace and rest." She sipped her coffee.

Melissa coughed violently, her handkerchief to her mouth. Clarissa watched. Finally the girl sighed and wiped her mouth.

"Dear, something's wrong with your chest. God can heal. He'll hear your request."

Melissa smiled. "It's nothing. Pa and Jonas and I all cough."

The old woman clasped her hands about the coffee cup. "Now the reason I'm here really is to bring cheer, to teach folk to revere their God, and to fear his judgment severe."

"Yes." Lucy looked puzzled. "We revere God."

"I know you're devout, it's known round about. Of that there's no doubt. But would you consent to meet and augment a Christian event?" Clarissa took another sip of coffee.

"Are you asking us to a meeting?"

Clarissa nodded. "At the Atkins' home. Fanny is so alone, but she'll further God's work. She is not one to shirk."

"We'll come, Clarissa. When is it to be?"

"On March 6, weather permitting. An all day's meeting's most fitting." The old woman got to her feet, picked up her stick and bundle and opened the door. "Thank you, Lucy, you're kind. 'Tis not ever thus, I find."

As she went out Lucy said, "We'll see you at the Atkins' on the 6th."

The girls came giggling from the kitchen. "She is the strangest woman I've ever seen," Harriet gasped. "Does she ever say anything that doesn't rhyme?"

Lucy carried the coffee cups to the kitchen. "I've never heard her."

"But how does she do it?" Melissa asked.

"She's educated."

"So are our family, but none of us talk in rhyme," Melissa argued. She went on, "I wonder if she's a little crazy? When we were younger, I was scared of her."

Mary Ann commented, "She's enough to scare anyone. She looks - well - wild. I wonder what happened to make her so strange?"

"Your father heard in Leroy that she had a tragedy in her life when she was back east, and it left her mind clouded."

"What kind of tragedy?" Harriet asked.

"Something about her young husband and baby dying in a fire. He was thought to be drunk, and he and the baby burned to death while Clarissa was in the barn milking."

"That's terrible," Mary Ann said.

"After that," Lucy went on, "she came to Locke Township with her brother and she took to talking in rhyme and wandering about with a few clothes tied to a stick over her shoulder. Wherever she went she spread the word of God. Some people call her the "traveling angel." She preaches the word of God but she always mentions temperance. In her clouded mind she probably thinks whiskey was the cause of all her sorrows - and maybe she's right."

Melissa was unable to attend the religious meeting at the Atkins home. Every afternoon, now, she was feverish, and she spent much of the time in bed. The family were concerned, but she insisted that her problem was an ordinary cold and that she'd recover in a few days. So the morning of March 6 all of the Averys, except Melissa, piled into the wagon to ride the short distance to the Atkins farm.

"It's nice that Clarissa planned to have the

meeting at Fanny's place," Lucy said. "It must be hard for a woman with no husband in this wilderness."

Stephen clucked to the team. "They say her husband, Israel, died in London, Ontario when they were on the way to Michigan."

"She has a family of children," Mary Ann added. "That should help. It's eight, isn't it, Ma?"

"That's right. I've only talked with her once. Her oldest boy, Harmon, is twenty-two, and there are two other boys, Wesley and Samuel. I can't remember the girls' names but three of them are married."

Stephen guided the team around a mud hole in the road. "The oldest boy, if he's twenty-two, should be able to keep things going." He was quiet a moment before he went on. "Jonas," he said, "do you remember the Colborns that we met in Detroit in 1836?"

Jonas nodded. "I wonder how they're getting along?"

"When I was in Howell last week I ran across Levi and Julius Parsons - they live a few miles from the Colborns. They said Robert, the father, was killed in the woods, so Mrs. Colborn, like Mrs. Atkins, is the head of the family."

"She has two grown sons," Jonas said. "I expect they'll manage."

"One of the boys, Amos, is married and has a baby. Julius said he married an Indian girl."

Albert said, "Wonder how it's working out?"

"Julius says she's a hard worker. Takes the baby to the fields in one of those Indian cradles and hangs it on a tree branch while she works with Amos." Stephen continued. "I guess this isn't gossip - Julius seemed certain it was true. He said Amos and his wife have another Indian girl living with them. She hid under a blanket when they were in Howell that time the government troops were driving all those Indians west to the reservation."

Harriet asked, "They didn't know she was in the

wagon?"

"Guess not. Anyway, Amos didn't. The girl's so glad to be left in Michigan that she works hard in the fields, too. Amos will do all right, though he had his pockets picked in Howell - lost all last year's wheat money."

"That's too bad," Mary Ann said. "Wonder how the family feels about the son marrying a squaw?"

"Julius said they all like her except the oldest boy, Israil. He's furious about it."

"I hope it works out for them," Lucy said. "I feel bad when I think about all those Indians being driven from their homes to new places out west. They say many of them died on the way. They're probably so unhappy they don't want to live."

When they pulled into the Atkins' yard they saw three families already had arrived. While the men unhitched the team, the Avery girls and their mother carried in food they had prepared for the noon meal. Mrs. Atkins and her daughters, Louisa and Marcia met them at the door and carried the food to the kitchen.

Clarissa Lighthall was circulating through the crowd of people who were gathered in the house. A short service followed by personal testimonials would make up the morning session. Then the group would break for the noonday meal, after which a longer afternoon service would be conducted.

The neighbors enjoyed exchanging news. Lucy heard Stephen and several of the men discussing the need for a community church. Clarissa, replying in rhyme, agreed to help "to the extent of her ability."

Jonas and Albert talked with Harmon Atkins about farm work. "We're tapping the maples next week," Albert said.

"How's your wheat look?" Jonas asked.

"Fair," Harmon replied, "though it's most too early to tell."

Jonas' eyes followed the trim figure of fourteen year old Marcia Atkins as she helped her mother in the kitchen. Fair, blue-eyed and shy, she was an attractive girl. Sensing his attention, she looked up to meet his gaze. Her face colored. He smiled and she dropped her eyes and turned away.

Suddenly Jonas was seized with the desire to own land and to build for the future. He would have to spend less money on books and non-essentials and to save so he could purchase land. He was twenty-two years old. Albert had been saving to buy land for several years.

As the meeting came to order with hymn singing and prayer, Jonas daydreamed. He would be a fine farmer. He would keep records of his expenses and crops. He would buy only the best cows and he'd sell the ones that didn't produce. And some day he would find a good wife - then life would be complete.

Jonas forced his thoughts to return to the present. They were having testimony meeting during which people described ways that God had helped them. Most of the young people did not participate.

Mrs. Fanny Atkins testified. "We have been here about a year. Without God's help I could not have survived. When my husband, Israel, died at London, Ontario in June of 1842, I felt there was nothing to live for. I didn't want to go on to the Michigan wilderness, but could only think of our old home at Elba in Genesse County, New York State.

"My children were set on going to the land their father had bought. Our daughter, Louisa, had married Stephen Scofield before we left York State, and Stephen and our sons Harmon, Wesley and Samuel were dead set on taking the younger children and going on.

"Our daughters, Lute and Anna, had married in York State. Lute's husband is William Denio and Anna's is Thomas Laurie. They hadn't wanted to leave their home so after my husband died, there were six in the group who decided to go on.

"I mourned over Israel's death until I was very

sick. I couldn't eat and hoped I would die. I couldn't face coming to Michigan's wild country with Indians, wolves, and a rough log cabin for a house. I'd have felt more able to face the hardships if Israel had been with me. I took to bed at the inn and expected to die there.

"If it hadn't been for Mattie Wheatley, the innkeeper's wife, I likely would have died. She visited me in my room, brought food and made me feel she cared about me. My family had gone on to Michigan and I had promised to follow when I was better, though I didn't expect to ever go on.

"Five weeks after my family left, Mrs. Wheatley brought a traveling Methodist minister to visit me. He read the Bible, talked to me about my duty to God and my family, and he prayed with me. Suddenly as we were praying, I saw a golden cross with a blinding light shining on it. It seemed as though God said, 'Take up your cross and follow me.' I promised God I would do my best. From that moment I began to feel better, and two months later I rode with a family who were coming to Livingston County. In Howell I hired a man to bring me here. Thank God I came. There still are things I can do to glorify God and to help my family."

There was a chorus of "Hallelujiahs" as she sat down. Clarissa murmured, "The Lord had power to transform grief, and bring your sad heart sweet relief." The testimonials continued until noon when the meeting broke for dinner.

The young people gathered in the kitchen, and with plates loaded with food, they sat on a bench along the wall to eat. There was much laughter and joking.

Jonas sat beside Marcia. "What do you think of Locke's wandering poet, Clarissa?" he asked as he balanced a plate on his knee.

Marcia's blue eyes twinkled. "We laugh at her, and I'm a little afraid of her, but Ma says she means well."

Jonas nodded and stuffed a chunk of ham into his

mouth. "Do you like Michigan?"

"It's exciting, and you never know what's going to happen. Last week Harmon shot a bear that was after our pigs. I keep a diary and every day there's something new to write."

"I keep a daily record, too. And I always tell what the weather is each day." He stopped, then added, "Look at Harmon over there with my sister, Harriet. She's all taken up with what he's saying."

Marcia laughed, a musical, happy tinkle of sound. "He's probably telling her about a new kind of bird or plant he's found. He keeps records of things, too. Right now he's worried about the passenger pigeons."

"Why?"

"He says people slaughter them by the thousands, and that some day there may not be any left - they'll become extinct."

"He may be right," Jonas said thoughtfully. "Every spring and fall when they're migrating Pa and Albert and I kill a bunch of them. Have you seen them when they're migrating?"

"No, but Harmon says John Audubon watched a flock once that passed in a stream that lasted three days. The flock was so thick it darkened the sun."

"Audubon's the artist that wanders through the woods and paints pictures of American birds. I've read about him."

"Harmon reads everything he can find about Audubon. I don't know which is most interesting to him, nature or doctoring. It surely isn't farming he's interested in."

"I didn't know he is a doctor!"

"He isn't really, but he reads everything he can find about medicine and diseases."

"Does he know anything about consumption?"

"I don't know. 'Course, he's my brother and I think he's the smartest person I've ever known."

When people began getting settled for the afternoon session Jonas said, "It's been nice talking with you, Marcia. If we get the church built soon, maybe I'll see you there on Sundays."

Marcia's face flushed. "Maybe," she said, her eyes downcast.

On the way home in the late afternoon, Stephen and Lucy planned for the new church. "It would be nice if we could build it in April," Stephen said. "Jim Bell will donate the land, and if everyone turns out to help, we can hold services by the middle of May."

The moment they entered the house the women sensed something was wrong. Melissa, her face flushed, lay curled into a ball on her bed with a towel to her mouth. She was coughing, a tearing dry, harsh racking cough.

"Your cold is worse," Lucy said softly. She placed her hand on Melissa's head. "You have a high fever. This thing is lasting too long." Her voice was low, almost as though she was thinking aloud.

"I'll be all right," Melissa said quickly as she slid the rolled towel under the covers.

"I'll take that," Mary Ann said, "and get you a clean one." As she carried the soiled towel to the kitchen, she stopped. Blood! The towel was covered with bright red blood. She knew what it meant. She'd heard her father describe the progress of the disease in two of the poor who had died. Consumption! Melissa had consumption! She leaned against the wall in the kitchen, her knees trembling. There had been a little blood on the towels, sometimes, but this - this was a hemorrhage!

Reluctantly she returned to her sister's side with a clean towel. The coughing spell was over and Melissa lay quietly resting. Harriet was chattering about the day at the Atkins.

"I talked with Harmon," she confided. "He's not going to be a farmer."

Lucy commented, "There's not much else for young men to do in the wilderness."

"He's going to be a doctor," Harriet said.

"Right now he's helping Wesley with the farm work, but he studies medical books when he has time."

Lucy hung her bonnet and shawl beside the door. "Goodness knows we need a doctor around here. Your father knows some about medicine, and there's that Jacob Euler over at Byron, but he's not a real doctor either. The nearest doctor would be at Howell or Lansing Township. But Lansing Township is a small settlement - maybe they don't have a doctor. I think 'tis only a clearing in the forest with a few settlers along the banks of the Grand River."

The Avery family was saddened by Melissa's illness. Every day they earnestly prayed for her recovery, and they stubbornly clung to the adage that "Where there's life, there's hope."

Stephen discussed the illness with Harmon Atkins. They decided that as consumption was a disease of the lungs, pure fresh air was a reasonable treatment. As a result, Melissa was encouraged to sit outside in a rocking chair when the days were warm.

In addition to the rest and fresh air treatment, Lucy tried old folk remedies - onion poultices and cough syrup made from wild cherry bark and another of honey, vinegar and alum. Melissa was fed chicken soup at least once each day. Another remedy was apple cider vinegar added to a glass of warm water to be taken several times daily.

Lucy recalled another old remedy for respiratory problems. Short, bud-bearing twigs from the pine trees, together with the needles, were covered with water and simmered slowly for three days. The solution was strained and thickened with wild honey and given by the teaspoonful several times each day.

However, in spite of the many home remedies, the girl's frail body grew thinner. She tired easily and after a severe coughing spell, she was exhausted. As the summer progressed the lung hemorrhages occurred almost daily.

The family members reacted in different ways to

Melissa's illness. Lucy, Mary Ann and Harriet were saddened and depressed as the disease steadily progressed. Albert became silent and withdrawn while Stephen and Jonas were given to outbursts of anger over minor incidents. A broken strap on a harness, or a cow that kicked during milking was enough to throw them into a tirade. Still, as Lucy often reminded the family, "Life must go on."

And so routine tasks occupied their days. Albert and Jonas were planting the crops, splitting rails for fences and picking up and hauling stones from the fields. Stephen spent much time helping to build the church on the Bell farm in an oak clearing. The neighbors called it the "Bell Oak Church." Within a short time a small settlement grew up nearby which was known as Bell Oak.

Stephen's many township duties required a considerable amount of time, and when poor families needed special care, he willingly assumed the duty. He also was interested in politics. He believed Governor Tom Mason was a fine young man and he was enthusiastic about the governor's plans for Michigan's future. Railroads which would criss-cross the state were planned, and some were already operating. The Central Line out of Detroit in 1838 and 1839 opened the railroad era in Michigan, and unlike some of the others, was profitable from the beginning. Gradually the line was extended to Jackson and on across the state from the original line which ran only to Ypsilanti.

Economic problems had been building for several years. The flow of new settlers into Michigan had slowed. Vast loans had been made by state banks and their branches to land speculators without security in gold or silver. President Andrew Jackson issued his Specie Circular in July, 1836, directing government agents to accept only gold or silver in payment for public lands. This decision caused inflation to skyrocket. Though the order had helped to end speculation in land prices, interest rates and wages continued to rise. These conditions resulted in the Panic of 1837 which struck the country shortly before Jackson left office. His successor, Martin Van Buren, faced a depression about two months after he became president.

Stephen had closely followed events leading to the Panic of 1837. When he sold land or grain he had accepted only gold or silver in payment. Though the panic and resulting depression were discouraging, he believed Governor Tom Mason eventually would lead the state out of the bad times if people would be patient and confident. Some of the plans for railroads, canals and roads were delayed until the economic conditions stabilized.

But there was much unrest and uncertainty. Mason's Democratic party was in disarray. The Whigs were gaining ground in a campaign charging the Democrats with mismanagement of state affairs. Banks in Michigan, as elsewhere in the country, were failing.

Stephen agreed wholeheartedly with Governor Mason and others who argued the necessity of a canal around the rapids in the St. Mary's River. Access by water to Lake Superior and to Michigan's upper peninsula was dependent upon a way to bypass the rapids. The project would be costly and the Federal government was asked to provide the needed funds. But Congress was uninterested, and even some people in the state felt the project was too costly for possible benefits.

By following the news in the Detroit Free Press, which he purchased on infrequent trips to Howell, Stephen learned that Governor Mason had persuaded the state legislature to appropriate funds for initial surveys, and then in 1839, for a beginning of construction. The canal was to be just short of a mile long with locks to lift ships up or down eighteen feet between the level of Lake Superior and that of the lower river.

But a controversy with the War Department about the construction of the canal through the grounds of Fort Brady at the falls stopped the work and the project was discontinued with little accomplished except the surveying of the route.

Stephen worried about Melissa, but he found he could temporarily put her illness from his mind if he worked himself into a state of exhaustion. He sympathized with Lucy, Mary Ann and Harriet who were with the ill girl every hour of the day.

By June the crops were planted. Weekly services were being held at the Bell Oak Church and Stephen acted as lay leader until a minister could be located. On Sunday, family members took turns staying with Melissa while others attended the service.

After church one Sunday, Stephen and Lucy walked through the woods. Stephen commented, "Jonas always manages to talk with Marcia Atkins after church. Have you noticed?"

Lucy smiled. "She's young, but she's a fine Christian girl, and maybe in a year or two -"

"Yes, Mother. Our children are grown. 'Tis time they're thinking of marriage. I've noticed Harmon Atkins often talks with Harriet, but he's so busy studying birds and his medical books, I don't know that he'd be intersted in marriage."

Lucy smiled. "I think Harmon's brother Wesley is sweet on Harriet. I've seen him making eyes at her."

"They're both fine young men," Stephen said, "but Harmon is the thinker." He paused. "Mary Ann's almost twenty. You think she'll marry Jim Nichols?"

"They pair off at socials, but she doesn't say much. 'Course Harriet and Melissa keep telling her she's an old maid, but at twenty it's time she was married. Albert is the one I worry about. He doesn't show much interest in any of the girls around here."

Stephen stroked his beard thoughtfully. "We're avoiding talking about Melissa."

Lucy stared into the forest. A wild turkey gobbled nearby. Finally she said, "What is there to say? We know it's only a matter of time. That cough is wearing her out, and the bleeding gets worse every week. I keep hoping for a miracle but –"

Stephen kicked a log so hard he nearly lost his balance. "The days of miracles are over, Mother," he said bitterly.

At Sunday dinner Albert and Jonas discussed information they had heard at church. Jonas began the conversation. "Jim Nichols says the Red Cedar and the Grand River flooded in Lansing township a few weeks ago."

"I understand it floods there 'most every year," Stephen said.

"But this time the water took out a dam on the Red Cedar that supplied power for a mill. John Burchard and James Seymour built the dam a year or two ago."

Stephen nodded. "I've heard their names. Guess they had a good thing going in that mill with people settling near there."

"They say Burchard drowned."

"He did?"

"Back in 1841 Burchard and Seymour saw the possibilities of a dam on the Red Cedar. So when the dam was finished Burchard built his cabin not far from the camp of Chief Okemos and his tribe. This spring when the floods came and the dam gave 'way, Burchard and his wife just stood and watched. Finally two other men volunteered to go with him in a canoe to see if they could make repairs to stop the damage. It was too late. The water was so swift it pulled them through the break in the dam and Burchard drowned."

"That's terrible!" Mary Ann exclaimed.

Albert took up the story. "Seymour, Burchard's partner, has decided to rebuild the dam. He needs workmen and he'll pay fifty cents per day, and room and board is included."

"Hard cash is scarce," Jonas said. "Wish it was

so I could work a few weeks. Jim said a man named Page is doing the hiring."

Stephen mused, "The crops are in and other things are not urgent. Why don't both you and Albert go and work during the summer? You could lay up some hard cash to put toward the farms you both want."

Jonas asked, "Could you manage alone, Paw?"

"I'll get along fine. Go, if you'd like."

The following day Stephen took Albert and Jonas to Leroy. Then with their clothes in a bundle that was carried over their shoulders, they walked westward toward Lansing following an old Indian trail which ran along the banks of the river until they arrived at the campsite of Chief Okemos.

Barking dogs and dirty children rushed to meet the brothers, to be followed by the wrinkled old Chief, a short, heavy-set Indian who, even in summer, always wore a bright blanket about his shoulders.

"Good-day, Chief," Jonas said. "Can you tell us where to go to get work on the dam?"

The poker-faced old man stared at the brothers with shrewd, dark eyes. Finally he said, "Need tobac."

"We don't have tobacco. Where can we find Jacob Page?"

The old Indian stared at them solemnly. "Need whiskey."

Albert said, "Chief Okemos, we don't have any whiskey or tobacco."

The dogs continued barking as the children stared with solemn faces at the brothers. Adults, listening, watched from the doorways of their shacks.

"Need flour," the Chief said gruffly.

"We're sorry, but we don't have flour. We came to work for Jacob Page."

The stoic old face stared up at the tall young men. "Need clothes," he said.

Jonas demanded, "Do you know where we can find Jacob Page?"

"Chief Okemos know. Need clothes."

The brothers each removed a shirt from their pack. "Tell us where to find Jacob Page and we'll give you these shirts," Jonas said.

The short, blanketed old man turned toward the Red Cedar. "Follow river. You find." The Chief accepted the shirts and stood without moving until Jonas and Albert were around the bend in the river.

A short time later at about six in the afternoon they came upon a sprawling log cabin on the banks of the Grand River. The building appeared to have been recently enlarged. A man washed his hands and face from a pan on a bench near the door.

"Does Jacob Page live here?" Jonas called.

The man turned, smiling. "He does. He's my Paw. I'm Isaac Page. What kin we do fer ya?"

"We're looking for work."

"Come in. Paw's inside. Ya've come t' the right place."

Fifteen minutes later the brothers were hired. They would board and sleep in the sprawling cabin which accommodated twenty men. As they sat about the supper table, the men discussed the need for a dam.

Jacob Page and his son, Isaac, were the millwrights in charge of the project. "Ya likely wondered why I asked if ya drink," Jacob said. "I ask that of ever'body I hire. Can't no man carouse all night an' do a day's work the next day. I've sacked three fellers that come home drunk. We pay good wages, an' we 'spect ten hours a' work for fifty cents."

Benjamin Rolfe stuffed a piece of bread into his mouth. "I thinks most a' us needs the money so we won't take no chance on gettin' sacked. I know my Alvin an' me needs hard cash t' pay our taxes. Hard cash is as scarce as hen's teeth these days."

"Yeah, we was lucky," Alvin Rolfe said. "My Maw an' my wife, Annie, got work here cookin' an' cleanin', so they's four a' us workin' now. We

Chief Okemos

Early Train and Wagon Scene

jest closed things up at our place over near Mason."

At night the men slept on the floor. No one complained for after ten hours of heavy work they joked that they could have slept standing up. The Rolfe women in addition to cooking and scrubbing also did the laundry and mending for the twenty workmen.

Jonas and Albert grew accustomed to seeing blanket-wrapped old Chief Okemos and some of his tribe sitting on the river bank watching the progress of the dam building. Often they begged for food, clothing or whiskey. Jacob Page was annoyed by their insistence but he held his tongue. Stories still were told of acts committed by the Chief when he was in his prime and Page thought it wise to "let sleeping dogs lie." Jonas, personally, thought the old man was more to be pitied than feared.

On Sunday Jacob Page held a church service at his inn. Twice during the summer a Methodist Circuit Rider conducted the meeting. A few other settlers from the area also attended church at the inn for the only other religious meeting place was at Mason about ten miles to the southeast. The few nearby settlers had originally migrated from New York, and Lansing was named for the village from which they came.

By August the dam was completed and Jonas and Albert returned home to help their father with harvesting the wheat, rye and oats.

While they were in Lansing the brothers often had talked of Melissa. Albert seemed accepting of her approaching death, but Jonas continued to hope that she would be spared. But when he saw her, he knew. Melissa was going to die. A wave of anger swept over him as he looked at his young sister, once so beautiful, but now a fatigued, thin shadow of her former self. The incessant racking cough that ravaged her frail body and left her gasping for breath was tearing her life away and propelling her ever closer to death.

An air of sadness pervaded the family, though each one attempted to appear cheerful before Melissa who now rarely left her bed. They performed daily tasks mechanically because life must go on.

The day after Albert and Jonas returned, Lucy made soft soap. In keeping with the idea that nothing should be wasted, she saved used fat from frying doughnuts, and from bacon and side pork. Once each year, when sufficient grease had accumulated, a wooden barrel with holes bored in the bottom, was filled with ashes from the fireplace and placed on a wooden frame about six inches from the ground. Boiling water was poured over the ashes and it was left to "leach" for two days. A container below the barrel caught the liquid as it dripped through the bottom. This residue was lye. The waste fats which had been saved for the past year were added to the lye and the two were placed in a kettle and hung above the fire where they boiled until the liquid jelled. The result was soft soap, a thick, yellow, slimy, strong-smelling substance which was used for laundry, washing dishes and baths.

Lucy sighed as she dipped the soft soap into two-gallon crocks. "I'm glad that job's done," she said to Mary Ann who was slicing smoked ham for dinner.

"This knife's as dull as a hoe," the young woman muttered. "Maybe one of the men will sharpen it for us."

Harriet finished setting the table. She had recently changed from a light-hearted, chattering girl to a silent young woman. She went to Melissa's bedside. The girl turned restlessly. Harriet raised her sister's head and plumped the pillow. "I'll get some dry sheets," she said quietly, "and a dry nightgown. You've sweat until everything is wet."

"I know. I'm sorry to make so much washing for Maw and you girls. I'm nothing but trouble for all of you." She turned her face to the wall.

"Melissa, we're glad to do things for you. You rest and I'll be back in a minute with dry things."

While she was gone, Melissa coughed violently resulting in a hemorrhage which soaked her towel. Harriet returned to find her sister holding her chest and panting for breath.

"Is the pain bad?" she said softly.

"It's bad."

"Do you think you can sit in the chair while I change the bed?"

"Yes."

With Harriet's help, Melissa walked a few steps to the chair. Before she sat down Harriet helped change the damp nightgown. Melissa dropped into the rocker, completely exhausted from the exertion.

The first Sunday in October Jonas volunteered to sit with Melissa while the family went to church. When they were gone, he said, "We'll have a good talk while they're away." Melissa did not reply. "I'll be right back," he said. "Mary Ann asked me to do something."

A moment later he dropped into a chair near the bed holding a whetstone and the butcher knife in his hand. "I promised to sharpen this," he grinned. "Mary Ann says it's dull as a hoe." He drew the alternate edges of the long knife along the abrasive stone. Over and over he honed the knife, occasionally testing it gingerly with his right thumb.

Melissa watched. Finally she said, "It must be nice to do something useful."

"I never thought about it, but I guess it is." The knife hissed as he drew it across the whetstone. Concentrating on the rhythmic sound of the honing, Jonas didn't realize there had been several minutes of silence.

Finally Melissa said softly, "You know I'm not going to get better."

He slowly put the knife and whetstone down on the table beside the bed. "Do you want to talk about it?" His voice was gentle.

She swallowed and nodded. "I'm so tired," she sighed. "I'm a burden to all of you. Maw and the girls do for me, and do for me - and what's the use of it all? It won't make any difference. Nothing can stop this." She motioned toward her chest.

Jonas sat on the bed and took her hand in his. "Little sister," he choked back a sob, "You are not a burden to us. We'd do anything to keep you comfortable." He got up and went to the west bedroom window to wipe away a tear. He stood there a time to regain composure. Suddenly he turned. "The cows are in the cornfield! Will you be all right while I get them into the barnyard?"

"I'll be all right. You don't need to hurry."

"Be back soon's I can!" he called as he ran to the field closely followed by the dog.

Half an hour later, Jonas, perspiring and angry, still had three stubborn cows to chase from the near-ripe corn. Swearing softly under his breath, he and the dog again took up the chase. Finally, more than an hour after he had left Melissa, the cattle again were penned in the barnyard.

Stopping at the well, Jonas drew a bucket of cool water. After a drink from the rusty tin dipper, he dashed water over his sweaty hands and face. "I'll be in in a minute!" he shouted through the open door. There was no answer. Perhaps Melissa was sleeping.

Going inside he tossed his hat onto a hook and strode toward the bedroom. "Sorry it took so long but -" It was quiet. She must be sleeping. He tiptoed to the door.

"My God!" he uttered. "She's had a hemorrhage and fainted!" Her face was as white as the pillow but both arms and hands lay in puddles of congealed blood on the wedding band quilt. Frantically he seized the bloody left arm to feel for the pulse. "Melissa!" he shouted. "Mel -" His voice ended in a croak. The razor sharp butcher knife lay in a pool of blood beneath her right hand.

"No! No!" he shouted and again he seized the left arm to search for a pulse near the gaping wound on the inside of the wrist. At last he knew. Melissa was dead. Dead by her own hand.

He paced the floor, his head throbbing. Why? Why? Why had he left that damn knife near the bed? Why had he left her alone? She had hinted that she didn't want to live. Suddenly he was filled with boiling anger about the injustice of life. Why did God allow such things to happen? She was not yet eighteen years old. Was she born for this? His mind was confused. He'd been taught that God answers prayer. They'd prayed - and prayed - and God had turned a deaf ear.

The family was returning. Bracing himself, he met them at the door. "Maw - and Mary Ann and Harriet - don't come in," he said. "Something's happened to Melissa." He hesitated. "She's dead." His voice was low and unemotional.

Then everything was confusion. Bedlam. Disbelief. Shocked questions. Drawn faces. Tears.

Albert and Stephen removed the soiled bedding and gently washed the blood from Melissa's hands, while outside in the early October sunshine Jonas explained as best he could what had happened. Finally Albert called them in.

Lucy repeated again and again, "I don't understand. I don't understand how she could take her own life."

No one expressed the thought that was in every mind. The Bible said it is a sin to commit suicide. Did this mean Melissa was in Hell - to burn and suffer forever?

But there were things to be done. The men must make a coffin. The day and time for the funeral had to be decided and someone must inform the neighbors. Since it was known that Melissa had consumption, if nothing was said about the conditions of her death, people would believe she died a natural death from the ravages of the disease. The family justified their decision by saying nothing would be gained in giving the neighbors a topic for gossip.

For two nights before the funeral, Harmon and Wesley Atkins sat with Stephen and Albert beside Melissa's body. By the light of the flickering candle, in her soft pink dress the young woman looked like a sleeping child.

By half-past one the following day the Avery yard was filled with sympathetic neighbors. The Atkins, Fuller, McKee and Cole families were there as were two or three of the poor families whom Stephen had helped. The log cabin was overflowing with standing people for the brief service.

Since no minister was available, Stephen, with tear-filled eyes, read scripture, prayed and spoke of Melissa. He began by saying, "We're gathered in the presence of God to give thanks for the life of our daughter, Melissa. We give thanks for the joy of having her in our family for eighteen years, for it was eighteen years ago today that she entered our family. Yes, today would have been her birthday." He paused and swallowed. Lucy, Mary Ann and Harriet were sobbing. Albert and Jonas stared at the floor.

Stephen drew a breath and continued. "We cannot deny the question that is in all our minds. Why should a young woman, barely out of childhood, not have been allowed to live? Everything in our minds argues that Melissa should have lived!" Again he paused.

Finally he continued. "But we have to accept God's ways without understanding. And for us - that's nearly impossible. But - we must trust in God that his ordering of life is right, though it sometimes may look wrong to us. If we were wiser with more understanding, we wouldn't measure Melissa's life by its length but by the great love which she gave so beautifully and which touched all who knew her."

When the service was concluded, the coffin was carried to a pleasant oak clearing on a hill near the house. The pallbearers were Stephen, Albert, Jonas and the Atkins men, Harmon and Wesley, and Jim Nichols. Behind the coffin came Lucy and the girls, followed by the neighbors and friends.

The sun shone through the red, gold and orange of the October wilderness. Wild turkeys gobbled and a doe watched from behind a growth of Michigan holly entwined with the orange-red of the bittersweet vine.

When the graveside service was concluded, the pall-bearers remained to fill the grave while the rest of the group returned to the house. Finally the family was alone.

Later, they silently went about their routine work. The men, who were milking, were deep in thought. Suddenly Jonas jumped up, seized his milking stool and slammed it against the wall of the log barn. It fell, shattered, on the dirt floor.

Two quick steps took him to Stephen's elbow. "You say 'Trust in God!'" he shouted. "What kind of a God would cause a girl to suffer as Melissa did? Why was she born? Just to suffer and die?" His voice lowered. Calmly he said, "I don't believe there is a God."

Striding from the barn he dashed into the darkening wilderness. A wolf howled mournfully in the still evening air.

Chapter XII

DETROIT EXPERIENCES

(1844)

Jonas slapped the reins against his horses' slick sides. "Giddap!" he shouted. Reluctantly the team ventured into the melee of horses and oxen, all pulling huge loads of grain topped by farmers who hoped to sell their bountiful harvest for a good price in Detroit.

But Jonas was not hopeful. The market would be flooded, the price would be low, and even more serious was the value of the paper money. As his eyes took in the city sights, he brooded. He was impatient. He wanted his own land for he had decided he couldn't speak to Marcia Atkins of marriage until his goal of land ownership was in sight. He had hoped it would be this year, but now -

Shouting and commotion on the wooden sidewalk at the edge of the city caused the drivers to halt their teams to watch a policeman who was confronting two people. A well dressed man and a woman who carried a baby argued loudly with the city official.

The blonde, whiskered man shouted, "I demand an explanation! Why are you annoying us?"

The officer's handcuffs dangled from his belt. "You're both under arrest. You, John Randall, for harboring and aiding a fugitive slave to escape, and you, Liz Andrews, for running from your master, Sam Andrews."

The woman, who could have passed for white, cried silently, her tears dripping on the blanket which covered her sleeping baby. John Randall shouted, "Show me proof that I'm an Abolitionist who's helping runaway slaves! And show me proof that my wife is Negro! Look at her! She's as white as you are!"

The officer nodded. "And look at her baby!" He roughly pulled the blanket from the baby's face. "Black as the ace of spades," he muttered. He snapped handcuffs on the protesting man. "John Randall, you've helped the last nigger escape to Canada. The Underground Railway has just lost an agent. Both of you are going to the station house. It will be jail for you, Randall, and you Liz, will be returned to your master. He don't take kindly to losing a purty gal like you."

The wagons began moving slowly as the officer and his prisoners started toward the station house. A phrase flashed through Jonas' mind. "Man's inhumanity to man." His father had said for years that someday there would be trouble over the negro issue. That woman didn't appear black - she probably had a white father - but she surely had a black baby. But, what if she did have negro blood? She was a human and had as much right to freedom as - as he did. And the Indians - they weren't slaves but they were persecuted by the government. Being driven like cattle to the reservations when they didn't want to go - was that freedom? If there was a just God he wouldn't permit such unfair treatment of helpless people.

Jonas was amazed at the growth of Detroit since he'd last been there. He'd read that the population was close to 10,000. It had doubled since he was there with his father in 1836. The streets were filled with wagons and two-wheeled carts. Humans of all descriptions strolled along the board walks. Fashionable ladies, well dressed businessmen, unkempt housewives with a line of tousled children in tow, farmers in gray shirts and breeches, a few Indians, a priest - all were intent on their personal business.

After waiting in line for an hour at the grain storage elevator, Jonas sold the Avery wheat for forty-four cents per bushel, receiving his pay in bills of the St. Clair Bank. Hesitating before the cashier, he said, "I'd rather be paid in hard cash."

"Wouldn't everybody?" the sallow young man replied. "The St. Clair bills are all we've got. Take it or leave it." He glanced at the man behind Jonas. "Next?"

Jonas pocketed the money and returned to his team and wagon. Half an hour later the horses were stabled, fed and watered and he had a room at the Steamboat Hotel near the Detroit River.

Strolling outside he walked up Randolph to Jefferson where he turned left to Woodward Avenue. Stopping at King's clothing store, Jonas purchased gifts for his family. Shawls for his mother and for Mary Ann and Harriet and shirts for his father and Albert. He thought of Marcia, but it wouldn't be proper to buy wearing apparel for a lady friend. A book - he'd buy her a book.

A short walk took him to a small book store where he browsed. So many volumes tempted him that for a time he forgot to look for a book for Marcia. Reluctantly replacing the volumes on the shelves, he approached the storekeeper. He could afford only one book and that must be for Marcia.

"Any particular book you're looking for?" the man asked.

"I saw a book back there about Stevens T. Mason. I've always admired him. I believe he was a good governor."

The storekeeper nodded. "He did his best for Michigan, but he wasn't appreciated. The Masons were a right nice family. 'Twas a shame he died so young. We need politicians like Stevens Mason."

"I read in the Free Press that he died early in 1843. About thirty, wasn't he?"

"Thirty-one. Died of lung fever in New York. Left a nice wife and three little ones." The man shook his head. "He was twice the man we've got for governor now. John Barry can't hold a candle to Mason."

Jonas glanced at the big clock on the wall. "Can you recommend a book for an educated young lady?"

"About how old?"

"Fifteen. She's a neighbor of ours out in Ingham County." Jonas looked at the floor.

The man smiled knowingly. "But you hope someday she'll be more than a neighbor, huh?"

"Well - maybe."

"There's a new book on Michigan life written by a former Detroit woman by the name of Caroline Kirtland."

Jonas took the book, "A New Home." He thumbed through the pages, chuckling now and then. "Marcia'd like this. It's about life in Livingston County at the time my family and hers settled a few miles away from where Mrs. Kirtland and her husband lived. I'll take it."

As Jonas paid for the book he asked, "Is there a bath house nearby?"

The storekeeper stepped to the door. "David McKinstry has a bath house next to his restaurant." He motioned. "Go back to Randolph and follow it to Monroe. It's not far."

Jonas picked up his bundles. "Thank you," he said. "See you next time I'm in the city."

Fifteen minutes later he entered the bath house which consisted of many stalls in each of which stood a wooden tub filled with warm water. Nails in the wall were used to hold clothing while the men patrons bathed. After a leisurely bath and a shampoo of his flaming red hair and beard, Jonas dressed, paid the cashier and returned to the Steamboat Hotel.

The door to his room stood open. Glancing inside he saw a young woman filling the water pitcher on the wash bench. "Afternoon," he greeted her.

She turned to face him, a buxom, dark, smiling young woman with dangling gold earrings. "Sir, I'm Anna, the maid. You must be Mr. Avery."

"That's right." Jonas put his packages on the bed."

"Ya been shoppin'?"

"For my family."

"Ya married?"

"No. Are you married?"

She shook her head and smiled coquettishly. "No, but I'm lookin'."

"You ought not have any trouble, a pretty lady like you."

"Thank ya. 'Tis nice t' be called a lady." She picked up the pail of water. "I has t' go now, but if ya ain't busy, I kin come back after supper when my work's done. After nine o'clock, my time's my own."

Jonas hesitated. "Well -"

She flashed a smile over her shoulder. "I'll be back."

He closed the door and walked to the window. His temples were pounding. Dammit. He hadn't planned for things to go this far - or had he? She had charms that would tempt any man. Luxurious dark hair, sparkling black eyes, luscious red lips, and a full round bosom. For a moment he imagined her in his arms.

"Dammit!" he said aloud. "I've got to get out of this room!" Locking the door he went to the hotel saloon and ordered whiskey. "If Paw and Maw could see me now -" he thought as he downed part of his first glass of the unfamiliar liquor. "But they'll never know, and what they don't know won't hurt them." Thoughts of Anna returned to torture him. He'd better go easy on the whiskey or he'd be in no shape to -

"Evenin'," someone drawled.

Jonas glanced up to see a flashily dressed man standing at his side.

"Evening," he replied.

"Ya a stranger here?"

Jonas nodded. "Just got in this afternoon."

"Mind if I set with ya?"

Jonas pulled out a chair. "Sit down." He toyed

with his half-filled glass. Unaccustomed to alcohol, his head was spinning.

"I'm buyin'." The man got up.

"No more for me," Jonas said, "but I will have one of those ham sandwiches there on the counter." He got up.

"Sit down! The sandwiches goes with the drinks."

In a moment the man was back. Jonas ate half a sandwich, hoping the food would clear his light-headed feeling. He didn't like the looks of his companion. There was something strange about his eyes - he had shifty eyes. He was up to something. But what was it?

The saloon was rapidly filling with men of all descriptions. Jonas recognized two who had been in line to sell their wheat. In the corner four men were singing a raucous tune. The noise level was rising rapidly.

"Ya ain't drinkin' much," Jonas' companion remarked.

"I said I didn't want any more." Jonas shoved the second drink across the table. "It's yours."

"Don't drink much, do ya?"

"Much's I want." He took another bite of his sandwich. His head was clearing.

"Ya busy tonight?" The shifty eyes slid to Jonas' face.

"Yeah. I'm busy."

"I kin take ya to some good lookin' wimmin - if ya've got a few dollars. Bet ya don't git t' the city much. Ya ought a' do the town."

Jonas got up. "Thanks, but I'm busy." He walked unsteadily into the dining room. Perhaps some coffee and a light meal would make him feel better.

Mrs. Woodworth was serving the guests at the long table just as she had when he was there in 1836. She was heavier and there was more gray in her hair. Silently he slid into an empty chair. He hoped he wouldn't have to talk to anyone.

The chicken and biscuits and gravy were good.

Suddenly he caught snatches of conversation between two men across the table. "There's two or three of 'em workin' the hotels," one man said.

"How'd they know which ones?"

"Reckon they watch when the fellers get their wheat money an' then foller 'em to see where they stay. I heerd of two that lost the whole thing last night. One a' the crooks bought drinks 'till the farmers was half drunk, then they got 'em outside an' robbed 'em. Happens all the time."

Jonas felt for his wallet. It was safe. Finishing his supper, he returned to the room. He'd heard of the robbery of farmers before. That fellow in the saloon was one of them. He removed a dollar from his wallet before he slipped it under the straw tick mattress. He lighted the candle on the rough table as he wondered if Anna would return. His feelings were ambivalent. Strong physical desire battled with his wish to wait for Marcia.

He thought of his parents and Albert. Never before had he been by himself to make moral decisions. His father or Albert had always been with him in Lansing, Fowlerville or Howell. But now he was on his own - and he might have lost their wheat money -.

There was a soft knock at the door. His heart lurched. She'd come back! As he opened the door, Anna flashed a seductive smile. God, she was beautiful. She stepped inside and threw off her lacy white shawl. Her dress was low cut and revealed smooth olive shoulders and a hint of the full bosom below. Speechless, he stared at her in the dim light.

She looked at him, puzzled. Finally she said, "You wanted I should come?"

"Er - yes." He stood as though rooted to the spot.

She stared at him. "Somethin' is wrong? Ya don't like me?"

"No - yes - I like you."

She laughed softly. "You bin with a woman

before?"

"Er - er - no."

She went to the table and blew out the candle. Then her soft body was pressed tightly against his as she reached up for a lingering kiss. His arms held her to him in a vice-like grip. They stood locked in passionate embrace as desire swept through him. He led her to the bed.

Several hours later he wakened. Anna was gone. He lay for a long time living over again the hours they had spent together. Suddenly he thought of his wallet. Jumping from bed he ran his hand under the mattress. It was still there. He went to the table and lit the candle. The dollar bill was gone. He sighed. She was a whore, but a very beautiful one.

The next day when he again was outside the city, he pondered his experience. Since he no longer believed in God, he could not be punished for his transgressions. But Bible verses kept coming to his mind. "To be carnally minded is death." He had been consumed with carnal desire last night and it had been good.

He thought of Marcia. Dear, innocent little Marcia. She would be a fine wife - if she'd have him. He hadn't discussed with her the fact that he was an atheist. He'd have to tell her. Another Bible verse came to him. "Who can find a virtuous woman? for her price is far above rubies." If ever a woman was virtuous, the description fit Marcia.

Jonas mentally figured the amount of money he had saved toward the purchase of a farm. "Not enough," he said aloud. "I'll have to wait 'till next year. The second night of the homeward journey Jonas stayed at the Independence Hall in the village of Fowlerville. He arrived in the rain at half past three and decided to stay that night for former friends might be gathered in the saloon.

Several men greeted him enthusiastically. There was talk of a plank road to some day be built from

Detroit to Lansing.

"'Twill be a time yet," Ralph Fowler said to Jonas over drinks. "Stock has to be sold, $125,000 worth, before they start buildin' the road. And with money as tight as 'tis now, it likely will be years 'afore 'tis done."

William Sherwood, the village blacksmith, said, "I seen O. B. Williams from Williamston a few days ago. He says we ought a' try to get a road through to Lansing an' forgit 'bout Detroit. They're nothin' but a bunch a' shysters down there with their robbin' a' decent folk." He spoke to Jonas. "Have any trouble?"

Jonas fingered his whiskey glass. "The crooks are working the saloons, but I was lucky." After a moment he went on. "I'd like to see that plank road built to Lansing. It would be nearer for us, and like you say, the people are more like us."

Lorenzo Palmerton joined in the conversation. "I heerd that C. P. Bush and Eli Barnard from Livingston County, and four men from Wayne County are commissioners that will take money subscriptions on the plank road. But I figger 'twill be years 'afore she's built. Money's so damn scarce."

"Yeah," Fowler agreed. "Ya can't sell the best fat cow for five dollars in hard cash." He turned to Jonas. "I'm takin' my wheat to Detroit next week. What they payin'?"

"Forty-four cents - and in bills of the St. Clair Bank. The market's flooded with wheat."

Harvey Metcalf said, "I got cows - three of 'em to sell. But with the price so low, mebbe I'll keep 'em." He ordered another drink.

"How's your father?" Ralph Fowler asked Jonas.

"Busy, as usual. Spends some time every week working with the poor. He's township overseer, you know."

Several of the men nodded. "We was sorry when your family left Handy Township," Calvin Handy replied.

Jonas smiled. "Paw has itchy feet. He likes to

move on when there's too many people. He hasn't mentioned moving again, but we're getting new neighbors every month."

Phineas Silsby said, "We must have close to 9,000 people in Handy, Cohoctah and Conway. They keep comin', an' ya wonder why. The way prices is now they can't make no money. I'll warrant if these hard times keeps on some of 'em will sell their land an' go back east."

Several of the men nodded. After a time Tom Dailey said, "The thing I don't like is the way the banks is goin' busted. Ya don't know from one day to the next if yer money's any good - 'less you've got it in hard cash."

"I hear the St. Clair Bank's purty shaky," Harvey Metcalf said.

Jonas' heart lurched. "I hadn't heard that."

"Lost any more sheep, Fowler?" Ruel Randall asked.

Ralph Fowler nodded. "This wilderness ain't no place fer sheep. 'Tween the wolves an' bears, they ain't got a chanct. I bought thirteen in '39 from Losson Gordon. I've got three of them ewes left. 'Course I've raised lambs, an' I've sold some, but 'tis uphill business tryin' to raise sheep here."

Suddenly Jonas' thoughts wandered. This pleasant friendly atmosphere was a contrast to the noisy raucous confusion of saloons in Detroit. Here, you could trust people. He finished his drink. The saloon was blue with smoke from the pipes of the local men.

Henry Metcalf packed tobacco into his corncob pipe. "Ya smoke, Jonas?"

"No, but I'm thinking of starting."

"Yer Paw wouldn't like it."

"I guess not, but I'm grown now and I can make decisions for myself."

The men nodded. "Yer Paw's a good man, Jonas, but he's so religious, don't seem's though he'd have many good times."

Jonas shrugged. "'Tis his way, and he's happy,

and so's my mother. I'm not sure about my sisters and Albert. None of us have had much chance to –" he paused, then laughed, "as Paw says, 'to be polluted by worldly things.'"

Calvin Handy said, "Ya knowed the Colborns, didn't ya? I seen Amos last week. He was goin' t' Detroit t' sell his wheat. Thought the price might be better than in Howell."

"How's he doing?" Jonas asked. "I understand he married a squaw."

"Yeah," Handy answered. "He's a worker, an' with a peg leg, too. He bought 'nother forty acres. Guess that squaw a' hisn makes him a good wife. They've got two little girls. I could tell he felt bad he didn't have boys."

"Did he say anything about Israil?"

"Yeah. He married Susan Grant an' he bought land near his mother and Amos. The girl, Eliza, or Lide they calls her, she has married a neighbor, Jack Martin."

Jonas nodded. "Then the boy, Ben, must live with his mother."

"Yeah," Handy answered. "Amos says Ben is nineteen, an' he works the farm fer his mother. She's gettin' old, but there's that little girl that was born after Robert was killed. She's seven, an' goin' t' school."

Several of the men got up to leave. "Looks as though the rain's stopped," Jonas said.

Ruel Randall remained seated. "I ain't in no hurry," he said. "My boy'll git the night chores started."

"Are you the only doctor in Fowlerville?" Jonas asked.

"I ain't really a doctor, but people come to me when they're sick 'cause I know a few yarbs an' things that helps sometimes."

"You knew my sister, Melissa, died a year ago?"

"I heerd it. Consumption. I'm sorry. Must 'ave hit your family hard."

Jonas nodded. "Don't seem to be much that can be done, once you get it. It's not like the ague that we all have and we feel miserable, but no one dies from it."

"I hear there's typhoid up near Lansing," Ruel said. "'Tis a bad sickness. Hope it don't spread."

"I don't know much about it."

"You have an awful fever an' ya can't eat. After two, three weeks of it, some people die. From what I've read, nobody knows what to do, but we know it's catchin'." Ruel got up. "You play cards?"

"Never have. Paw and Maw won't allow cards in our house."

Ruel nodded. "We have a card game here most nights after supper. If you'd like t' learn, set in with us."

"Maybe I will. I'd like to see how it goes. Do you gamble?"

"Not for money. Most a' the time 'tis just a game. We bet with kernels a' corn." He laughed. "It's somethin' to do in the evenin'."

Later as Jonas sat with his friends, a drink and twenty kernels of corn at his elbow, he mastered the game of poker. After two hours of play, Lorenzo Palmerton remarked, "Ya catch on fast, Jonas. Ya've a sharp mind." He laughed. "If ya ever git short a' money, ya could pick up a bundle playin' cards."

The next morning before he left Fowlerville, Jonas purchased a pipe, some smoking tobacco and a deck of cards.

Smoking his pipe as the team plodded along over the old Indian trail toward home, Jonas argued with his conscience. His parents would be hurt if they knew the sins he had committed on this trip to Detroit. Liquor, a woman, cards, smoking - all the worldly things they were opposed to. But he wouldn't tell them. They'd smell tobacco smoke on his clothes, but they'd believe it was from being with companions who smoked. His atheist attitude was a comfortable one. No more fear of God's punishment for minor sins. He'd live an honest, upright life, for that was his nature, but when you're dead, you're dead. There was no hereafter. All the Hell you get is here on earth. His thoughts went to Melissa. Poor girl, it was unthinkable that she was burning in Hell because she had been unable to tolerate more suffering and so had ended her life. Melissa was at rest. He admired her courage.

"Little sister," he said aloud. "We're two of a kind. You gave me the courage to break away from the narrow, religious teaching of our parents. We're both free - free at last!"

Chapter XIII

LIFE MUST GO ON

(1844-1845)

Lucy Avery blinked and rubbed her eyes, then made another attempt to thread her needle. She sighed. "Mary Ann, will you do this for me? I declare, it's getting so I can't see to sew."

Quickly her eldest daughter threaded her mother's needle. "Your eyes are getting worse?" she asked quietly.

"I'm getting old," Lucy said softly. It's hard to be going blind." She held Stephen's hand-knitted sock to the window as she darned a hole in the heel.

"After Jim and I are married next March we'll be near enough so I still can help you, and Harriet will be here."

"I shouldn't complain," Lucy said. "Everyone has a cross to bear and mine will be blindness. I have much to be thankful for - a good husband and four grown children." In a moment she continued. "It's just that I remember how my mother was - she was blind. And it's getting so I can hardly read the Bible. That's the way life is - everybody gets old. Have you noticed your Paw? He's not feeling good. He's been helping all the folks that's been sick 'till he's tired out. Today he's at Clarissa Lighthall's place. She's got the fever now."

"So many folks have it," Mary Ann answered. "It's real bad, Paw says. But nobody has died near here. Do you think 'tis typhoid? They have typhoid fever in Lansing, Harmon Atkins says."

"It started around here about a month ago when that Morris family west of us got it," Lucy said.

"Your Paw and Harmon wonder if maybe it comes from the water. Jed Morris built his barn and outhouse on the creek above the house so they get their water after it has passed the outbuildings. Harmon and Paw say they can't understand why Jed built that way."

"You know the Morrises, Maw. I shouldn't say it, but they are trash. Mrs. Morris is always smoking that filthy corn cob pipe and Jed's drunk every week, and their clothes are so dirty they'll most stand alone."

Lucy nodded as she started work on another sock. "Clarissa and your Paw took care of them when they were down with the fever. Then Clarissa got it." She continued. "She's real sick. She has the fever and bad headaches and she can't eat."

Harriet came in with a basket of laundry. "I got the clothes off the line just in time. It's starting to rain."

Mary Ann taunted, "If you hadn't talked so long with Harmon you would have had the clothes down in plenty of time."

Harriet flushed. "He's usually so busy he doesn't have time to talk," she answered. "He was coming from Clarissa's place. Paw sent word he can't leave her alone. She's awful sick. He'll stay until Harmon can come back and take over."

"Poor Clarissa," Lucy said. "She's a good woman - but strange."

Mary Ann laughed. "I wonder if she's still talking in rhyme?"

Harriet smiled. "Harmon says she is. Seems as though that's the only way she knows how to speak."

Lucy folded the darned socks. "Someday Harmon will be a fine doctor. Your Paw says he does real good with sick folk."

"He studies enough, he should know what he's doing." Harriet tossed her head. "He doesn't have even an hour or two to go to socials like most young folks."

Mary Ann joined in. "Wesley never misses a social. Everybody likes him." She glanced at Harriet from the corner of her eye. "I've seen him watching you. I think he's stuck on you."

"Stop it, Mary Ann! Just because you and Jim are making plans don't mean I want to get married. Besides, Wesley's just a boy - compared to Harmon."

"He's nine months older than you! And he's level headed. He'll be a fine farmer. Harmon will be a good doctor, but he won't have time for a wife and children. Between doctoring and traipsing through the woods studying birds, there won't be much time for a family. If you ask me, you'd do better to set your sights on Wesley."

"Well, I didn't ask you!" Harriet flounced from the room.

Lucy said softly, "You shouldn't tease her. What will be, will be. She's almost seventeen, but she's got time. And Harmon is the brother that will make a mark in the world."

Late that night after the rest of the Averys were asleep, Stephen returned home. Undressing quickly he crawled into bed beside Lucy.

"How's Clarissa?" she whispered.

Stephen drew a deep breath. "She's a mighty sick woman. Harmon will stay with her tonight. She vomits every few minutes - hasn't kept anything down for two, three days."

"She's going to get better, isn't she?"

Stephen hesitated. "I have my doubts. She's delirious with the high fever and the only way I've been able to keep her quiet was to read Scripture to her. She talks in rhyme, just as she always has. When I left she said, 'Soon I'm going to my heavenly home, and there I'll never be alone.'"

"Poor Clarissa," Lucy murmured.

Next morning Stephen was ill. He was feverish, with headache and pain in his back, arms and legs. The family was alarmed but Stephen insisted he had an attack of ague and that he'd soon be better. "A few doses of Peruvian bark will fix me up as good as new," he joked.

"But it sounds like the fever that folks around here are having," Harriet said.

Her father replied, "I'm tough as a pine knot. I've never caught any of the diseases from people I've helped, and I'm not going to start now."

When it was time for morning devotions, Lucy asked Mary Ann to read the Scripture. When she prayed Lucy asked that Clarissa might be healed and that Stephen soon would be well. The fact that he remained in bed during the morning devotions did not go unnoticed by the family.

About eight o'clock Harmon came to the door. "Clarissa's dead," he announced. "I did all I could. She died about six this morning."

No one spoke for several seconds. Then Lucy said softly, "Stephen can't help you over there today. He's sick. Some of the other neighbors will see she gets a decent burial, won't they?"

"We'll take care of things," the young doctor promised. "Let me take a look at Stephen." He went to the bedroom. A few minutes later he came out. His facial expression was solemn. "Would you step outside a minute?" he whispered to Lucy.

The August morning sunshine slanted through the branches of the maple tree in the front yard casting shadows across the door of the log cabin.

"What - what is it?" Lucy asked fearfully.

"Typhoid. He has all the symptoms."

Lucy gasped. "But - but - he's had several ague attacks. Maybe it's ague."

Harmon stared at the ground. "There's a chance, but I doubt it."

"Should he take the Peruvian bark?"

"It won't do any harm. But give him cold sponge baths to keep the fever down and get him to drink plenty of water and milk. You might steep up some willow bark, and make it strong. Get him to drink a half cup every hour. It should help the head and back pain."

Harmon stared into the wilderness. "This fever

is going through the whole township. It's bad in Lansing, too - and nobody knows what causes it - though I wonder about the water. I got Jed Morris to move his outhouse away from the creek, but you have a well and you don't drink the creek water. It's catching. Stephen has cared for four people that had it."

"Clarissa is the only one that has died," Lucy said hopefully. "We'll do whatever you tell us, Harmon, and we'll pray."

He turned suddenly. "I'll be back later today."

The family was stunned by Stephen's illness. For the first time in their memory he was so ill he was unable to leave his bed. When attacks of ague had struck he felt "droopy" but he had refused to stay in bed. This disease was different.

For days the fever raged in Stephen's body. Constant vomiting and the high temperature and dysentery caused severe dehydration. Finally the deadly bacteria resulted in intestinal ulceration accompanied by bowel hemorrhages.

The family was frantic with worry. Mary Ann sobbed, "He's always been so strong. Surely he'll get better."

Harriet pleaded with Harmon. "Please, please, do something to help him. I can't stand seeing him like this. Harmon, he doesn't know any of us!"

The young doctor shook his head. "I wish I could help. I don't know what to do." There was quiet desperation in his voice.

Lucy came from the bedroom with soiled sheets. Harmon inquired, "You're boiling the sheets and anything he uses, aren't you?" She nodded. He continued, "Since we don't know how the disease spreads, we can't take chances."

"There's only one thing we can do," Lucy said. "Pray. We must pray as we've never prayed before that if it is God's will, he will get better."

Jonas motioned to Albert and they went outside. "I can't stay in there and watch him die," Jonas said as they walked toward the barn. "He's not going to get better."

Albert replied dully, "While there's life, there's hope. You know what Disraeli said, 'What we anticipate seldom occurs; what we least expect generally happens."

Jonas threw the harnesses on his team. "I'm going to work on the wheat ground. You going back to the house?"

"I might's well work too. There's no sense of staying in there. Paw'd say, 'life must go on,' if he knew. I'll tell Maw where we are."

Two hours later Harriet came running to the field, her long skirt whipping about her ankles and her dark hair flying in the stiff September wind. Her eyes were red and tears coursed down her cheeks.

"He's gone," she sobbed against Jonas' shoulder."

Silently the brothers unhitched the teams and started toward the barn. It was hard to realize their father never again would walk his land, plant his crops or help his neighbors. It was as if a light had gone out leaving the family groping in darkness.

Inside the house Mary Ann sobbed softly as she helped her mother wash her father's body in preparation for burial. "The boys will dress him in his good suit," Lucy said softly. "And they'll make the coffin."

Mary Ann wondered how her mother could be so composed, so accepting. Such stoic resignation was unnatural. Her parents had been married for twenty-six years, yet her mother was calmly placing coins on her father's eyes as though he were a stranger lying there in death.

Finally Lucy said, "He's at peace. We had a good life together. I thank God I was allowed to have him for twenty-six years. God needed him more than we did."

Mary Ann wiped her eyes. "I don't know how we'll get along without him. It won't ever be the same."

"It's darkest before dawn, but the sun always rises in the wilderness of life," Lucy answered.

That night while Jonas and Albert made the coffin, Jim Nichols and Wesley Atkins sat beside Stephen's body. The next morning Albert, Jonas, Jim and the three Atkins boys, Harmon, Wesley and Samuel carried the body to the oak clearing where Melissa was buried. Neighbors and friends filed in a solemn procession behind Lucy, Mary Ann and Harriet.

Jim Bell from Bell Oak eulogized his friend, Stephen, at the graveside. He mentioned the man's strong religious faith and his charity to the unfortunate. He concluded with the words, "Stephen Avery's death is deeply mourned by his family and by everyone who knew him. He gave his life serving God and people who were in need. He has gone to his reward."

Marcia Atkins sang the hymn, "Jesus Lover of My Soul." Her clear strong soprano voice reverberated through the wilderness as she sang the old hymn which had been composed by Charles Wesley many years before.

Lucy, her face calm, stared at the pine coffin. Harriet and Mary Ann sobbed softly. Albert and Jonas, their hands behind their backs in the stance so often assumed by their father, gazed with unseeing eyes into the woods beyond the oak clearing.

Lucy concentrated on the words of the old song:

> Jesus, lover of my soul
> Let me to thy bosom fly
> While the nearer waters roll,
> While the tempest still is high.
> Hide me, O my Savior, hide,
> Till the storm of life is past,
> Safe into the haven guide,
> O, receive my soul at last.

Jonas' eyes briefly met Marcia's as she ended

the hymn. She was so beautiful. He wondered what life held for her. Would he be a part of her future? Jim Bell scattered a handful of sand over the coffin as his deep voice intoned the words, "For dust thou art, and unto dust shalt thou return." Less than a year before on October 4th they had stood here at Melissa's funeral. Who would be next? And what was the goal in life? Melissa - why had she been born only to die at age eighteen? His father had left his children, but what was his reward for years of service to his family and neighbors? Death. Death in the prime of life. Maybe his reward had been the pleasure he received from helping the unfortunate. Heaven? All the Heaven or Hell there was was here on earth.

Jim Bell offered a short prayer and the service was over. People turned and silently started back toward the house.

Albert touched Jonas' arm. "When they're gone we'll help fill the grave."

The typhoid illness gradually ended with no more deaths in Locke Township. Harmon continued to wonder about the cause of the disease. As he retraced the course of the illness his thoughts traveled in a circle. It seemed that in many families visited by Clarissa Lighthall, one or more members had been smitten. And Clarissa had spent several weeks in Lansing early in the spring where the fever was prevalent. But she hadn't been ill until a short time ago. It seemed impossible that she could have carried the disease in a dormant stage in her body, and that she could have spread it even before she, herself, was ill. Still, in every family where typhoid had struck, Clarissa had recently spent from one to three days.

A few weeks after Stephen's death, life in the Avery household went on much the same as before. Albert and Jonas carried on the farm work. Mary Ann sewed and planned for a March wedding. Harriet, though strongly attracted to Harmon

Atkins, allowed his brother Wesley to call on her. She enjoyed Wesley's company, but secretly she compared him unfavorably with the learned and studious Harmon. Lucy, though her eyesight was failing, continued with her daily household chores. The sewing and mending she gradually turned over to her daughters.

Each year in the fall the Avery women, like all other frontier ladies, made candles. Tallow was saved from the deer and cattle which provided part of the family's meat. When a large quantity of the fat had accumulated, it was melted in a huge kettle over the open fire. Six wicks were evenly spaced and fastened on numerous sticks which were dipped repeatedly, one at a time, into the melted tallow until the candles were large enough to be placed in a candle holder.

When the fall farm work was done, Albert and Jonas decided they would each go to Lansing to work in a mill for a few weeks. Jonas would go in December and January, and when he returned, Albert would replace him in February and March.

Jonas planned to speak to Marcia when she reached her sixteenth birthday in March of 1845. She would make a fine wife and mother - if she would have him. In other than the area of religion, they thought alike. Both had voracious appetites for learning and when they were together their discussions were stimulating. Jonas, however, was sure Marcia had no idea of his atheistic beliefs. He knew she was as attracted to him as he was to her, but in fairness, he must tell her before they talked of marriage. He was secretive about his changed ideas relating to his earlier faith for his mother would be hurt if she knew. Harriet and Mary Ann were not especially religious, though they attended church regularly, as did Albert. But he also went to church, though the sole reason was to see and talk with Marcia.

Early in November with a few possessions packed in a bundle carried over his shoulder, Jonas walked the old Indian trail to the sawmill in

Lansing. Someday in the near future this trail would be a plank road connecting Lansing and Detroit, but the completion of the project was still some time away.

Jonas decided that if he found work he would not board at the sprawling house where he and Albert had stayed while they worked on the dam since a second hotel had opened downstream near the sawmill on the Grand River. He arrived late in the afternoon at Carley House where he secured meals and a room.

Caroline Carley, an attractive woman in her early twenties, showed him to his room. "Supper is served at half past six," she said, "and breakfast is any time after six." She opened the door.

"Mam," Jonas began, "do you know if they're hiring at the mill?"

Caroline brushed back a stray lock of auburn hair. "They may not need men at the mill, but they always seem to hire lumbermen."

Jonas tossed his bundle onto the bed. "I need work for a couple of months. I'll see them tomorrow."

She nodded. "Several men who live here work in the woods." Turning, she said, "The saloon is adjacent to the dining room."

Jonas closed the door. Caroline Carley seemed pleasant - and from her speech, he gathered she was educated. He wondered if she had a husband, and if she was unmarried, what was a beautiful young woman doing alone in this wilderness outpost?

After dinner most of the men gathered in the saloon. They were a rough, unkempt appearing lot with straggly, unwashed hair and beards. A giant of a man approached Jonas, a large drink in his hand. "My name's Tom Fyfe," he said.

Jonas set his mug on the table and extended his hand. "Jonas Avery," he said.

Fyfe dropped his huge body onto the bench. "Gonna be round long?"

"If I can get work at the mill."

"Where ya frum?"

"Near Leroy, east of here. Locke Township."

"I've heerd of it. I'm frum down Jacksonburgh way. My wife an' boys'll keep things goin' while I earn a few dollars in the woods."

Jonas sipped his beer. "Who do I see about getting work?"

"Eric Arnold's in charge a' ever'thin'. He's at the mill."

"What are they paying?"

"Fifty cents a' day fer ten hours work."

"Same as a year ago when I worked on the dam."

"Lansing's growin'. Miz Carley's place here is new. It got so there wasn't no place t' stay." He motioned. "The other boardin' house couldn't keep all the men so Miz Carley had this place built."

"Is she married?"

Tom Fyfe laughed. "Hell, no. She ain't got time fer no man. She's a worker, she is. She'll make a pile a' money in this place. She's smart, an' she knows how to handle business." After a moment he asked," You play cards?"

Jonas tapped his pipe ashes into the tin cup that served as an ash tray. "Not much."

"We has a little game 'most ever' night," Fyfe said. "I'll see if there's two others that wants to play." He hoisted his huge body to a standing position, then lumbered over to a table where three men were drinking. In a moment he shouted, "Come on over!"

Jonas sauntered across the saloon, his beer in his hand. Fyfe quickly made the introductions. "Fellers," he began, "this here's Jonas Avery. He might be livin' here if he gits work. Jonas, this here's Pete Payne." He pointed to a small blonde bearded man, "an' Will an' Bob Barnes. They's twins. We're all farmers tryin' to make a leetle extry cash."

The Barnes brothers looked exactly alike, Jonas thought. And Pete Payne was so small that heavy work in the woods must be difficult. He held out his hand to each man.

"Set," Tom Fyfe said. "We'll play a few hands 'afore turnin' in." He pulled a soiled deck of cards from his pocket.

Jonas took a sip of beer. "If you don't mind I'll watch for a while. I don't play much."

"Them's the fellers ya has t' keep an eye on," Bob Barnes joked. "Them as don't know how t' play takes ya ever' time."

The men put five pennies on the table before them. Tom dealt each man five cards, and bets were placed. Jonas watched as cards were discarded and more were drawn from the deck in an attempt to improve hands. As play proceeded he became confident of his ability to play as well as any of the four. Finally he took Tom Fyfe's place at the table.

An hour later when the game broke up Jonas had won five cents. As he pocketed the pennies, Bob Barnes said, "I tole ya. Them as don't know how t' play allus wins."

"Beginner's luck," Jonas laughed.

The next morning he left for the mill with the other men. Eric Arnold hired him as a woodcutter. All day, from early morning to dark, they sawed and chopped as trees were cleared on land adjacent to the mill. Teams of horses and oxen pulled the logs to the mill. The men were allowed half an hour to eat the cold lunch packed for them by the cook at Carley House, then it was back to work until nearly dark.

At any time of day Old Chief Okemos and several of his tribe might appear. The old man, with his blanket about his shoulders, was a pitiful sight. Small and stooped, his face wrinkled with age, he begged for food or pennies. Usually the men gave him sandwiches or cake from their lunches. The younger Indian men were aware that the chief was more successful at begging, so they stood back and watched, knowing that eventually the old man would share with them.

Jonas liked the woodcutters. As with him, farming was their life, and their ambition was to pay for a farm and to make a decent living. Each evening, over a mug of beer, they talked or played cards. He enjoyed the sociality. With practice he became more experienced at cards and soon his winnings were averaging fifty cents a week.

Jonas thought often of Marcia and his mother. They would disapprove of his drinking, smoking and gambling, but what they didn't know wouldn't worry them, and he was gaining the equivalent of one day's pay each week by gambling.

He wondered about Caroline Carley. She was cool, polite and business-like in their contacts. Then one night as he entered Carley House he noticed an open copy of Nathaniel Hawthorne's "Twice Told Tales" on the desk at Caroline's elbow.

"Mam," he began. "I notice you're reading Hawthorne. How do you like his writing?"

She smiled. A dimple showed in each cheek. "Have you read this book?" she asked.

"Yes, mam."

"Do you read much?"

His blue eyes met her brown ones. "My family are readers. I've read from the time I was small. My problem is to get books, but we have the 1837 edition of "Twice Told Tales."

She slowly and thoughtfully placed a book mark between the pages before she closed the volume. Somewhat reluctantly she said, "I'd - I'd like to invite you to visit me after supper. It's not often I have the opportunity to talk with someone who enjoys reading as I do."

"Thank you, Miss Carley. I'm looking forward to visiting with you."

"I should be free by half past eight," she said. "My living quarters are the third door to the right." She motioned.

Jonas bowed. "I'll be there."

He hadn't realized how much he missed intelligent conversation. Over coffee, they talked. Caroline said, "I like Hawthorne's way of showing the make-up of human nature. He paints word pictures of his characters' personalities. He's especially good, I think, at showing the darker side of our personality."

"I agree," Jonas replied. "I've read that he wants to 'probe the depts of our common nature.' Those are his words."

"It seems that his stories deal with our sins and with morality. I wonder if he is a religious person."

"I don't know, but he says he doesn't avoid reality, but rather that he deals with it as he sees it in life. His ancestors, like mine, were very religious. He's older than we are, so he probably recalls hearing of the days of witchcraft."

Caroline replaced her coffee cup on the table. "We've come a long way since the days of witchcraft." She hesitated, then continued. "I don't know your religious beliefs, but from my own experience, and from those of my family, I've decided that if there is a God, he's not a loving God." She stopped suddenly. "I've said too much."

Jonas looked at her questioningly. "You have doubts? You are an atheist?"

She nodded. "I've seen too much suffering and injustice. A just God wouldn't permit wars, persecution and personal suffering. Death, yes, but merciful, quick death, not long tortured months and years of suffering. I hope you're not offended by my outburst."

Jonas stared outside into the darkness. "I'm not offended. I completely agree with your views. I'm also an atheist."

They sat in silence, each one deep in thought for several minutes. Finally Jonas got up. "I've enjoyed talking with you, Miss Carley. It's nice to speak with someone whose views are the same as mine. There are not many that I can speak with about my atheistic beliefs."

She nodded and walked with him to the door. "I

know. One can be ostracized for expressing such ideas in public." She laughed. "They won't burn us at the stake these days, but with some groups it might be more kind if they did."

Jonas was content at Carley House. Work in the woods was tiring, but each day brought him closer to his goal of owning a farm and marriage to Marcia. Sunday afternoons were spent with Caroline in her quarters where they held long discussions about literature and the evils of slavery.

Caroline had read of a negro woman Abolitionist who called herself Sojourner Truth. "We'll be hearing more about that woman," Caroline said. "She was born a slave in New York around 1790 but was freed under state law in 1827. She moved to New York City and became very religious. She says God has told her to work for the abolition of slavery. She is traveling and preaching across Ohio and Indiana. If she comes to Michigan, I'd like to hear her."

Jonas related his observation of the arrest of the Abolitionist man and the slave woman and baby in Detroit. "Sooner or later, there'll be trouble," he said. "It will be the northern states, who dislike slavery, against the southern ones who can't grow their cotton without slaves to work in the fields."

Caroline changed the subject. "Do you get to Detroit often?"

"I've been there twice. With my father in 1836, and I went alone last summer. Have you been there?"

"Once." She paused a moment. "Want to hear about it?"

"Sure."

"My story isn't a pretty one, but it accounts for the way I am. Ambitious, secretive - not the typical woman who is satisfied with a husband and children. That's not for me. I want money and possessions so that my physical wants will be satisfied. That's why I work this boarding house for every dollar I can get out of it."

"Your goals are different from most women's," Jonas agreed. "You don't ever plan to marry?"

She shook her head. "Why should I? I like things as they are. Why bring children into the world to suffer and struggle and die? I'm responsible only for myself. That's the way I like it."

"Don't you like children?"

She hesitated toying with an auburn curl beside her ear. "Yes. I like them so much I don't want them to live the kind of life I've been forced to live. I couldn't bear to see them cold, hungry and destitute."

"That would be hard. My family never have much money, but we haven't wanted for food. And there always has been a strong feeling for the family." He stopped, deep in thought. "My parents brought us up by the Bible. It was 'love one another and love your neighbor.' My father was a better man than I'll ever be. And my mother is a fine woman. Someday I hope to marry a woman like her." He stopped, then went on. "My mother would be terribly hurt if she knew my atheistic ideas."

"You've had a life quite different from mine. I know I'm bitter and selfish in thinking only of myself."

"What will happen in later years? Don't you think you'll miss the companionship of a husband and children?"

Caroline shrugged. "Perhaps. But marriage leads to responsibility for a husband, and probably children as well. I have lived without marriage this far in my life quite well. I think - I can manage without a man in my life."

"You were going to tell me about your childhood."

She sighed. "It's not a pretty story. My mother was the daughter of a merchant in New York City. She went to a female seminary and was educated to live the life of a lady. Then she met my father, Albert Carley, the son of a city official. He had romantic dreams of going west and of making a fortune by buying and selling government land.

"Though her parents objected, Mother married Albert Carley. He worked as a tailor for several years until he accumulated enough money to buy land near Eaton Rapids. When I was fourteen years old my father left New York in April to buy land and to make a home for Mother and me. We lived with my grandparents in New York and I remember the angry arguments about our going to that 'God-forsaken place called Michigan.' But Mother was determined."

"How did you feel about it?"

Caroline laughed. "I thought it would be a great adventure. My grandparents asked me to stay with them, but I wanted to travel, so Mother and I left the following spring.

"We arrived at Detroit with no problems. Mother hired a man with a team to take us to Jackson - Jacksonburgh, they called it then. The driver was a shifty-eyed fellow, and before we'd gone many miles, we were suspicious of him. Still, there was nothing to do but to go on. We couldn't walk in the mud and carry our boxes and grips, so we kept quiet and hoped for the best.

"The second day out of Detroit we noticed a cart behind us. The driver didn't seem to want to pass, for he followed us closely for two or three hours. On the narrow wilderness trail the sun was warm by noontime, and as I looked back the man on the cart took off his jacket. A sheriff's badge glistened on his vest.

"Without considering my words, I said, 'That's the sheriff back there!' Our driver took a quick look, bolted from the wagon and raced into the wilderness with the sheriff running and shouting behind him.

"We stopped the team and waited for the sheriff to return with his prisoner. Finally he came back, but the man had escaped."

"What was he wanted for?" Jonas asked.

"Robbery. In Detroit. He had robbed his

employer, the man who owned the team we were driving. The sheriff was kind enough to allow us to finish the journey to Jackson. He left us there and drove the team and wagon back to Detroit, leading his horse and cart behind.

"We were on our own and still a long way from Eaton Rapids. A man at the hotel told us to follow the trail along the river. So we put our grips in storage at the hotel together with a few boxes we had brought on the wagon. My father could pick them up by boat, for there wasn't a road to Eaton Rapids.

"The cook packed a bundle of sandwiches for us and we started the next morning. I'll say one thing for Mother. She never complained though the trail was rough and by noon we both were exhausted. As we rested and ate our lunch, a settler came walking down the trail toward Jackson. When he learned where we were going, he said, 'Ya kin cut off ten miles by takin' a short cut up thar a ways.' He pointed to the northwest. 'Ya watch sharp up about half an hour frum here, an' you'll see a big rock on the right. They's a leetle trail there. Foller it, an' it'll bring ya out in Eaton Rapids.'

"Well - we got lost. After a few hours that little trail just seemed to disappear. We decided to follow it back to the river where we'd pick up the main trail, but we couldn't find it. We were in a predicament. We wandered about until dark. I was half scared to death at the thought of sleeping in the wilderness, for my grandparents had painted frightening pictures of things that might happen in the night in Michigan woods. Wolves, bears and Indians were very real in my imagination that evening.

"Mother had matches, so we gathered wood and made a fire which we would keep burning all night. We ate our last sandwich and sat facing the fire with our backs against a big tree. We didn't sleep much for wolves howled in the distance and we could hear something walking through the brush."

Jonas scratched a match on his boot sole and lit his pipe. "Must have been pretty scary for a couple of women." He blew a smoke ring.

Caroline laughed. "Oh - that was the good part of our life in Michigan. Well - finally the sky began to lighten in the east and suddenly we heard a rooster crow. A rooster! Out there in the wilderness! Mother said, 'If we can follow the sound of his crowing, we'll find people.' We jumped up and waited. He crowed again.

"'It's this way,' I said as we started southeast. Every two or three minutes, the rooster crowed, and each time he sounded closer. At last we saw log buildings.

"A man, Jack Turner, opened the door. We explained that we were trying to get to Eaton Rapids. 'You're 'bout five miles frum there,' he said. 'Come in an' have breakfast, then I'll take ya to the river. Ya'll be there by noon.'"

Jonas puffed on his pipe. "Did he live there alone?"

"Yes. Said his wife was coming before winter. We had a good breakfast, and then he guided us to the river. We were in Eaton Rapids by half-past twelve. My father's land was a short distance away.

"He was happy to see us, but we were shocked at his appearance. Thin, and with ragged, dirty clothes, he didn't look at all like the dapper tailor who once had made suits for wealthy New York men."

"What was the matter with him?"

"Ague. He'd been having attacks for several weeks and there wasn't any quinine in the settlement."

"Quinine," Jonas said. "We call it Peruvian bark. Ague is one of the curses of the Michigan wilderness."

Caroline nodded. "My father had been able to build a rough shelter for us between the attacks. Dirt floor, cracks where we could see light between the logs, a makeshift fireplace - I wondered how we could spend a winter in the shack. But Mother and I went to work, filling the cracks with clay and cleaning up the place. Most of the time my father lay on his bed which was a pile of quilts in the corner. We all slept on the floor.

"Our food was muskrats, wild turkey and venison, and the woods were filled with wild berries. Father said over and over, 'When I feel better, I'll walk into Jackson, build a boat and get your things at the hotel. I'll buy flour, cornmeal and other things we'll need for the winter. Then, I'll pole the boat downstream to Eaton Rapids.'

"An Indian camp of three or four families was about a mile from our place. We often saw them watching, but they didn't bother us. Soon we decided they were curious, that's all."

"When did your father go to Jackson?"

"Not until the end of October. By that time Mother and I had learned to use the rifle and to skin a deer. There were two other white families at Eaton Rapids, the Eatons and the Algers. Like us, they were barely surviving. Father had money to buy supplies, but they were destitute.

"Mother and I had tried to prepare for winter. The one small window let in so little light that the shack was shadowy and dark, except near the fireplace. We didn't have candles so we stayed in bed during the dark hours, but during the day we cut and piled wood near the cabin, and we smoked and salted venison for food in bad winter weather. I complained about the hard work and repeated often that I wished we'd stayed in New York City. But Mother never uttered a word of regret for our coming, or any criticism of my father. Only once, I recall her saying simply, 'We've made our bed and we'll lie in it.'

"The night after Father left for Jackson, the weather turned cold. We hurried to bring up more wood before winter set in. Freezing nighttime temperatures together with a cold, sleet-like rain continued for two days. Then, in mid-morning of the third day, Father appeared at the door and staggered inside to drop on his bed.

"'Albert!' Mother exclaimed. 'What on earth has happened? You're soaking wet!'

"Father covered his face with his hands. 'I lost everything in the river. It was before dark last night and I thought I could make it home. But there was a rock that I didn't see and I hit it. There was a big hole in the old boat. The water poured in soaking the salt, flour, sugar and cornmeal. Then the boat went to the bottom of the river. I managed to save a box or two of your things, and your grips, but everything is wet. It's on the riverbank near the Indian camp.' He pulled a quilt over himself and turned his face to the wall.

"Mother said, 'Where were you all night?'

"He answered, 'The Indians were watching. They helped pull things out of the river and took me to their camp. This morning I went to look at our things. Only a few clothes are any good - everything else is spoiled.'

"'Well, you're safe,' Mother said. 'That's what matters. Get out of your wet things and I'll dry them before the fire.' By this time his teeth were chattering. 'I'm so cold,' he kept saying."

Caroline stopped. Jonas waited, then said gently. "Don't go on if you don't want to think about it."

She sighed. "I want to. I've never talked to anyone about it before. It just seems as though you understand and it's a relief to talk to someone about those awful days." After several moments she said, "To make a long story short, my father died with lung fever. He'd been wet and cold in the rain for two days before he wrecked the boat. It was too much for him to fight off after those attacks of ague. The Eatons and Algers, and the Indians too, they all tried to help. We buried him a little way from the cabin."

Outside Jonas could see the snow drifting lazily through the late December air. His time at the mill was up. Tomorrow he'd pack and go back home. Caroline was speaking.

"That winter seems like a horrible nightmare." She shuddered. "We were always cold and hungry. When I went to the river for water, I'd watch for game. We still had some ammunition for the rifle, but game was scarce. Sometimes the Indians would bring meat, and the white families shared with us, but everyone was suffering. We dug under the snow for acorns from oak trees, and we boiled the acorns. Sometimes that was our only food for days at a time.

"For several years Mother and I struggled to survive in that awful little shack. During the summer we dried berries and tried to grow a little corn. The Indians gave us the seed. Wolves didn't bother us much, perhaps because with the Indians and Eatons and Algers, there were about twenty-five people in the area. Mother and I kept our sanity by talking about the books we had read. We discussed the writers' ideas and talked of our own thoughts on the subjects. Mother talked about God and the Bible, too.

"And always I dreamed of the day when I could escape from the Michigan wilderness, when I'd no longer be cold and hungry."

Jonas asked, "Why didn't you go back to New York City and your grandparents?"

Caroline shook her head. "Mother wouldn't go. She was too proud to admit defeat. But silently, I vowed I'd go, by hook or by crook, when I could." She sighed. "Then Mother began to be sick. She couldn't keep food down and everything she ate hurt her stomach. I was trapped. I couldn't leave her. I was trapped in this hellish wilderness with a sick mother.

"Then, last spring, a man from Vermont came downriver from Jackson. He was looking for land and wanted to buy our hundred acres. We told him we hadn't paid the taxes, but he allowed for that and made us an offer we couldn't refuse. And Jonas, he paid us in hard cash!"

"Your luck had turned. At last you had a way out."

"A way out, yes. But Mother was thin and white as a ghost, and she had that gnawing pain in her stomach. I didn't know how to help her. Then Mr. Eaton said he was going downriver to Lansing, and we could go if we wanted to. He suggested that we use the farm money to build a boarding house in Lansing, and he advised us about the business arrangements. We opened here the last of August, and all ten of my rooms are rented."

"I'd say you're doing fine," Jonas said. "At last you're out of the woods in more ways than one. But what of your mother? Where is she?"

There was a long pause. Finally she said softly, "Dead. She died a month after we opened Carley House. But she died happy that I had a business, and that I no longer would be cold and hungry."

For many minutes neither of them spoke. Then Caroline said, "Now do you understand why I'm bitter, self-centered and why I don't believe there's a God? Would a just God allow suffering such as we knew? We prayed every day for strength and help. God, how we prayed. Mother kept saying, 'The Bible says, 'Ask and ye shall receive.' Finally I became angry. I'm still angry. From now on Caroline Carley will take care of herself without any help from anyone - or from God!" Her brown eyes flashed defiantly.

"Your life has been hard," Jonas agreed. "You're made of good stuff to have survived."

"Thanks, Jonas. Thanks for listening. I needed to share my misery with an understanding person."

He stood up. "You're strong, and you have things coming your way now." He paused. "I'm leaving in the morning, you know. My brother will come to take my place in the woods, and he'll rent the room I have here. I want you to know I've enjoyed our visits together."

Caroline gasped. "You're leaving so soon?" She got up quickly and came to him, taking his hand in hers. "I'll miss you. You're the only person I've ever been able to talk to and to tell my innermost thoughts." Tears welled up in her dark eyes, spilled over and made tiny rivulets down her cheeks.

He took her in his arms to comfort her. He caressed her forehead tenderly. She put her lips up to be kissed. Suddenly they were consumed with burning passion that would not be denied.

Two hours later when Jonas returned to his room, the snow had stopped and it was pitch dark outside.

Chapter XIV

THE EXPANDING FAMILY

(1850)

Lucy Avery sat in the rocking chair before the east window of her old home. On her lap she held a pan of peas which her gnarled hands shelled as her near sightless eyes stared in the direction of her four year old grandson.

"Jimmy," she said. "Is Charles Wesley awake?"

The little red-haired boy ran to the bedroom. "He's crawling on the bed, Grandma."

"Can you lift him down on the floor? He fell off the bed yesterday."

A moment later the baby was scooting along the worn board floor of the old cabin as he explored under the tables and chairs.

"I'm going to the garden with Ma and Alice," Jimmy announced going toward the door.

Lucy brushed a hand across her eyes. "Don't go until your Maw is back," she said. "Somebody has to watch Charley. He's putting everything into his mouth these days."

Suddenly Jimmy yelled. "No! No, Charley!" He ran to the baby to remove a fuzzy caterpillar from the baby's wet mouth. "Grandma! He had my caterpillar in his mouth!" He inspected the damp, wriggling creature. "Charley 'most ate you," he said to the strange little pet.

"You'd better put your caterpillar outside," Lucy said laughing. "Charley eats anything he finds on the floor."

Jimmy cradled the wet, wormlike larvae in his hands. "I'm going to keep him, Grandma. Uncle Harmon says he'll be a pretty butterfly someday -

if something don't eat him first."

Lucy laughed again. "Something like Charley?"

Marcia and Alice came in loaded with produce from the garden. As they piled vegetables on the kitchen table, Alice said, "Grandma, Ma and I seen bear tracks in the garden!"

Marcia, her fourth pregnancy showing, removed her sunbonnet and hung it beside the door. She brushed back a lock of perspiration-drenched blonde hair. "We aren't sure, Mother Avery." She turned to the children. "But Jimmy and Alice, look at me." She waited until she had their attention. "I don't want you going alone to the woods."

Both children objected. "We want to find caterpillars," Alice whined.

Jimmy joined in, "Uncle Harmon said if we'd find caterpillars he'd tell us what kind of butterflies they'd be!"

Marcia washed her hands and picked up the baby. "Do as I say," she said. "Unless your father is with you, you're not to go into the woods alone until we know what's out there. You play near the house."

Nero barked a low half-growl. Then as the two older children went outside the big black dog ran to meet them as they skipped toward the barn.

Marcia sat down holding the baby. "I thought all the bears had left since Locke Township has so many settlers," she mused. "We haven't heard wolves in three, four years because most of the deer are gone. There's not much for bears to eat here, now. I'm worried about the children and our farm animals."

"If a bear's out there, Jonas and the neighbors can get him," Lucy said confidently.

Marcia sighed. "Seems like I tire out fast. Here it's only the middle of the afternoon and I'm tired."

"Taking care of three small children, and with another coming in a few months, 'tis no wonder you're tired. And I'm no help. You even wait on me."

"Mother, don't talk that way. You know we like having you here. It's not you - it's me. Seems like all I really want to do is to write poetry, or in my diary about things that happen to us."

"You do beautiful poems, Marcia. And keeping a family record is nice. Some day your children and grandchildren will know how we lived in the Michigan wilderness."

Marcia mused. "While I was at the garden I noticed how the bittersweet is climbing up the trees along the path. This fall it will be beautiful. I love bittersweet when it's all orange and red. When we go to the garden we'll walk along a bittersweet trail." She paused. "Life is kind of a bittersweet trail. Some good, some bad. We have to take the bitter with the sweet."

"You have a way with words, Marcia," Lucy said. "I like that - life is a bittersweet trail."

Marcia sighed as she put the baby on the floor. "I thank God every day for my children - only, I wish He didn't send them so fast. I'll have four by the time I'm twenty."

"They're lovely children, Marcia. And their baby days pass fast and they're grown before you know it."

She shrugged. "Jonas doesn't have much patience with them. He has such a temper. He spanks them for no reason - such little things."

Lucy nodded. "Jonas was always the hot-headed one of my boys. He's just like Stephen was before he was saved."

"Father Stephen Avery had a bad temper? I never knew that."

"When the children were small in York State, he was like Jonas is now. No patience. Then he found the Lord and he became a changed man."

"I pray for Jonas," Marcia said softly, "but he doesn't like me to mention it."

"He goes to church with you," Lucy said.

"That's because you want to go as much as I do,

and I can't handle the team and the children, too, so he drives us. He'd never go if he didn't feel responsibility for us getting there."

Lucy smiled. "Jimmy is going to be another hot-headed Avery. It seems there's one in every generation. Charley, well, he's too young to tell, but he seems easier to handle than Jimmy, don't you think so?"

"Yes." Marcia paused. "It's strange, but Alice is different too. She never is unhappy. And she follows Jimmy's lead."

"My girls were the same way. Of course Albert was no trouble, either. It always was Jonas. But when he was growing up, in fact until after Melissa's death, he was religious. He took part in family devotions, though he often had temper outbursts over small things. After Melissa died, he changed."

Marcia got up. "He's a good husband even though he's impatient and cross sometimes. I'll keep on praying for him."

As she prepared supper, Marcia continued the conversation with her mother-in-law. "Have you noticed that Jimmy and Alice follow Harmon everywhere when he's here?"

"He's good with children. Maybe it comes from being a doctor." Lucy paused, then continued. "I'm glad Harrriet married him, even though Wesley hadn't been dead quite a year. Harmon always was the one of the Atkins brothers she wanted for a husband."

"Yes, poor Wesley. He was a plodder - but a good man. I agree that Harmon is more the kind of man Harriet should have. They've been married since New Year's Day. Do you think she's in the family way yet?"

"I don't know. Harmon is a good father to little Israel. The boy won't remember Wesley as his father. Let's see - Israel's a few months older than Jimmy. He's four years old."

Marcia hung a kettle of potatoes over the fire. "When we were children, Wesley always was healthy. It's hard to realize he could be taken sick with lung fever and that he was dead a few days later."

"The years take their toll," Lucy said as though she were thinking aloud. "Melissa, Stephen, Wesley and little Alfred - all buried out there in the oak clearing. Now Mary Ann, she and Jim are doing all right. Albert and Rebecca have been married two years, but - their first baby, little Alfred, only lived a few months. The oak clearing holds many of our loved ones." Lucy rubbed her forehead. "I'm sorry, Marcia. I don't mean to complain, but it's hard to see famiy taken from you."

Suddenly Marcia said, "I haven't heard Jimmy or Alice for a long time." She went to the door and called. There was no answer.

"It's almost suppertime," Lucy said. "Maybe they're with Jonas at the barn."

"I'll go find them." Marcia was outside the door when she called back, "Charley's on the floor. He'll be all right."

As she called the childrens' names, she hurried toward the barn. Jonas appeared in the horsebarn door. "What's wrong?" he asked.

"Have you seen the children?"

"Not since noon. How long have they been gone?"

"I don't know. They went out about three, but I thought they were playing near the house with Nero." She stopped as though dreading to continue. "I saw bear tracks in the garden this afternoon," she said softly.

"Is Nero gone?"

Marcia wrung her hands. "I think he's with them."

"He's some protection. Do you have any idea where they might be?"

"Jimmy wanted to find caterpillars. I told them not to go to the woods or garden unless you were with them."

Jonas' eyes flashed. "Then they disobeyed." He

looked toward the woods which surrounded the farm buildings on three sides. "I don't know where to start looking," he said.

"Try the garden." She brushed her hair back impatiently. "Oh - I don't know. Maybe they wouldn't go there. Alice saw the bear tracks. Goodness knows where they went."

"Damned young'uns," Jonas muttered. "I'll tan their breeches when I find them." He started toward the dense forest to the south.

Marcia shouted, "Should I get Harmon and Samuel?"

"If I'm not back in half an hour, I guess you should." He began calling the childrens' names. The echo reverberated between forest and buildings. "*Jimmy*! Jimmy! *Alice*! Alice!"

Marcia returned to the house as she silently prayed, "Please God, help him find them." She fed Charley, listening all the while for the return of Jonas and the children. Jonas' voice gradually grew more faint, and soon there was silence. He must be far away.

"I'm going to get Harmon and Samuel," she announced. "I'll be back as soon's I can."

"Don't run," Lucy warned. "You don't want to lose the baby you're carrying."

"Yes, Mother." She was out the door and headed north to her old home a mile away. As she hurried along the narrow trail she repeatedly shouted the childrens' names. She mused, "Trying to find two little children in this wilderness is like hunting for a needle in a haystack."

Breathless, she arrived at the Atkins home as they were finishing supper. "Marcia!" her mother said, alarm showing in her voice. "What's happened?"

"Jimmy and Alice are lost! Harmon, will you and Samuel come to help Jonas search?"

The men hurried to the barn to hitch up the team. Five minutes later they were on the way. Harriet and Marcia talked in low voices as the men shouted the childrens' names.

Marcia nervously twisted her handkerchief. Harriet patted her sister-in-law's arm. "They'll find them. There's still two hours of daylight. And Harmon knows these woods like a book."

"But the bear! I saw bear tracks in the garden!"

"The bear is probably more scared of us than we are of her - or him."

"I hope it's a male. If the children got between a mother and her cubs -" Marcia shuddered. "Harriet, I'm scared." She trembled.

Harriet spoke firmly. "Get hold of yourself. Getting upset won't help anything. Remember your baby. And who knows? When we get back Jonas likely will have found them."

But the moment they turned into the yard they knew from the silence surrounding the house that Jonas and the children hadn't returned. Lucy came to the door. Charley stood beside her clinging to her long skirt.

Harmon said, "Did Jonas take a rifle?"

"No," Marcia answered.

"Samuel and I have ours. Don't look for us until you see us at the door. If you hear three shots, one after the other, you'll know we've found them. Samuel's going north and I'll go west. You said Jonas went south?"

Marcia nodded. Samuel already had stalked into the shadowy wilderness with a steady stride. A minute later Harmon disappeared in a westerly direction.

Charley, by holding on, walked unsteadily along the edge of the table. When he loosened his grip he sat down hard on the floor. "Bump!" he said, getting up to try again.

"He won't be crawling much longer," Harriet said brightly. No one answered.

After several minutes of silence, Harriet said, "Marcia, you should eat something."

"I'm not hungry. Fix a plate for Mother Avery. Charley had his supper." She stood at the door looking to the southeast. Above the trees faint, flickering flashes pierced the dark blue evening sky. "It's lightning," she said dully.

"'Tis so hot it's likely heat lightning," Lucy said.

Harriet set a pitcher of milk and a plate of johnny cake on the table. "Come, Marcia," she said. "You'll feel better if you eat."

Dully Marcia dropped into a chair beside the table. She broke a square of johnny cake into a bowl and poured milk over it. After eating a few spoonfuls, she choked. "I can't eat when my children are out there scared and hungry and in danger." She returned to the door. With tears in her eyes, she prayed silently, "Please, God, return them safely."

The minutes dragged into hours. Harriet lighted a candle and placed it on the table. Marcia roused herself to get Charley's nightgown and a dry diaper. As the baby objected loudly to bedtime preparations, Marcia proceeded as though oblivious to his protests. Carrying him to the bedroom she pulled the trundle bed from beneath the full sized one and placed the screaming child on the tiny straw-filled tick.

"There, there," she said soothingly. "Let's say our prayers." Clumsily she knelt beside the trundle bed. "Dear God, be with Charles Wesley this night. Keep him safe." Her voice caught as she tried to swallow the lump in her throat. "And dear God," she whispered, "protect Jimmy and Alice, and keep them from harm - and - and - send them back to us. We ask it in thy name. Amen." Bending to kiss the baby who now was quiet, she whispered, "Goodnight, little Charley."

"'Nite, Ma-ma-ma," he babbled.

As Marcia left the bedroom Harriet remarked, "Charley's talking young. He won't be a baby much longer."

"He learns from Jimmy and Alice," his grandmother replied when Marcia didn't answer.

A flash followed by a low rumble warned of the approaching storm. Harriet glanced at Marcia's drawn, white face. "Maybe it won't amount to much. Maybe it will just be a shower."

A sudden blast of wind hit the cabin followed by almost constant sharp zigzag lightning and crashing thunder. Then the rain came - a downpour beating and pounding on roof and windows.

Marcia moaned. "My poor babies. Alice is so afraid of storms. Why don't the men come home? They can't see out there. I can't think." She paced from window to window. "The children are wet and cold and hungry and scared." She stopped beside Lucy's chair. "Was it only this afternoon that I complained about my children coming so close together?"

Lucy reached for Marcia's hand. "Sit down, dear. Take your Bible and read. You will feel better. Just remember two things. The Bible says, 'Ask and it shall be given you,' and 'With God all things are possible.'"

Silently Marcia pondered the words while outside the storm raged. "Thank you, Mother," she said making her way to the table where she read uninterrupted for half an hour.

Suddenly the door burst open and Jonas stood before them, water dripping from his beard and clothing. He shook his head in answer to their questioning looks. "They must have gone in another direction," he said hoarsely.

"Harmon and Samuel are searching," Harriet said.

"It's pitch dark out there. They might's well come in." Jonas' voice was almost a whisper. "We can't do anything until morning."

Marcia took a cup from the cupboard and filled it with coffee from the large coffeepot which steamed near the fire. "Drink this and then change into dry clothes," she said calmly.

A short time later, one at a time, Samuel and Harmon returned. "The rain's about stopped," Samuel said as he hung his shirt over the back of a chair to dry.

"We'll find them in the morning," Harmon

promised as he sipped coffee before the fire.

Jonas scratched his head. "I can't understand where Nero is. Surely he would have heard us calling."

The night seemed endless. Though they tried to rest, no one slept. Before four o'clock the women were preparing breakfast and Jonas was milking his cows. Samuel returned home to report to his mother and to do the chores at the Atkins farm. By six o'clock Harmon and Jonas were ready. The signal remained the same. Three quick shots meant the children were found.

"I'm going east," Jonas said. "The children never have gone on the land across the road, but I don't know where else to look."

Harmon answered. "You go southeast, and I'll go northeast." They soon disappeared into the wet forest, again calling the childrens' names.

Raccoons and rabbits were out searching for food. A sentinel crow shrieked his anger at intruders in the lonely forest. A fox peered from behind a bush. Gray squirrels raced up trees to jump from one swaying branch to another. As the sun rose above the treetops a hawk, silhouetted against the blue sky, screamed, "Fierce! Fierce! Fierce!"

Slowly Jonas went on, his eyes scanning the forest floor. Suddenly his heart jumped. In the distance something black - an animal - lay underneath a huge beech tree beside an uprooted oak. He grasped his rifle. Was it the bear?

He stalked the black animal cautiously. It didn't move. Could it be sleeping? Somehow, it didn't look big enough to be a bear, unless it was a young one. Then, when he was twenty-five feet away, he knew. It was Nero.

He bent over the quiet unmoving dog and touched him. He was dead, his throat torn and covered with dried blood. Wide gashes were ripped in the fur of his back and sides. "Poor Nero," Jonas said softly. Suddenly an awful fear seized him. If the bear did this to strong, powerful Nero, what had it done to Alice and Jimmy? He was almost afraid to find the children for they, too, might be dead.

He turned away from the dog and started around the fallen oak. Its soil-covered roots extended ten feet into the air forming a secluded shelter far back under the root system. He'd better check it out. That would be a perfect hiding place for the bear.

Peering into the semi-darkness, with his rifle ready, he jumped in surprise as Jimmy shouted, "Pa! Pa!" The little boy rushed into his father's arms closely followed by Alice, her face tear-streaked and dirty. For a moment he knelt with his arms about the children.

Getting up, he said, "I have to signal Uncle Harmon that I've found you." Pointing his rifle skyward, he fired three shots.

"I'm hungry," Alice whined.

"So'm I," Jimmy added. "We had berries to eat yesterday but that's all we had."

"We'll go home so you can show Ma and Grandma you're all right, and you'll have a good breakfast. Let's go!"

They detoured around the spot where Nero lay so the children didn't see the dead dog. As they made their way toward home, they talked. "You're not wet," Jonas observed. "Were you under the roots of the tree when it rained?"

"Uh-huh," Jimmy said. "Nero was with us and just when it started to get dark we seen a bear. Nero ran at the bear. He growled and growled."

Alice grabbed her father's hand and began to cry. He patted her head. "Nero fighted with the bear," she sobbed.

"We was scared," Jimmy went on. "The bear picked Nero up and started carrying him. The bear walked on his back legs. Nero fighted and bit so hard the bear dropped him. Then they had an awful fight. The bear roared and Nero growled. They fighted and fighted. We was so scared we run way back under the roots and hid. We couldn't see them anymore, but we kept still so the bear wouldn't find us."

"The bear went away?" Jonas asked.

"We didn't see him after we went under the roots. But it was quiet. We waited and waited for Nero to come back but he didn't find us. We was scared to call him or look for him 'cause the bear was out there. Did Nero come home?"

"No."

Alice said, "Then it rained and the storm scared me. And I was cold."

Jimmy continued, "We was cold all night. Then we went to sleep and we didn't wake up 'till I seen you looking at us."

"You didn't hear me calling you?"

"No." Alice said softly. "You're nice to us, Pa. We thought you'd be grumpy."

Jonas ignored the statement. "Let's hurry along. Everyone is worried about you. We hunted for you half the night. Uncle Samuel and Uncle Harmon helped me."

"We didn't get any caterpillars," Jimmy said softly.

"Yes - caterpillars," Jonas replied. "What did your mother tell you about going in the woods alone?"

The children hung their heads. "What did she say?" Jonas repeated.

Jimmy stared at his feet. "She said not to go."

"And you went. The whole family has been worried, and your mother and Grandma Avery and Grandma Atkins are about sick with worry. Did you think about that?"

"Uh-uh."

"You disobeyed. You did wrong," Jonas said sternly. The children trudged silently beside their father, their heads down. "And you know what might have happened. You know now why Ma said you shouldn't go into the woods, don't you?"

"The bear's out there," Jimmy replied. He hesitated. "Are you going to spank us?"

"You did wrong. Anyone who does wrong has to be punished. But we'll take care of that later."

The children didn't reply. After a time Jimmy said, "We prayed. We asked God to keep the bear away and He did."

Jonas was silent. Finally he said, "You know why the bear went away?"

"Why?" Alice asked.

"Because Nero fought so hard to protect you. I found Nero. He's dead. The bear killed him."

The children cried. As Jimmy wiped his eyes on his shirt sleeve Alice sobbed, "Poor Nero."

"Nero gave his life for you, and if you had obeyed Ma, Nero would be alive now."

They walked in silence for several minutes. Then Jimmy said, "We prayed like Ma says we should, and God sent Nero to fight the bear, and the bear went away 'cause Nero hurted him so bad."

"Yes. Nero saved your lives. But after this I hope you'll think before you disobey your Ma and Pa."

"You won't spank us?" Alice said fearfully.

"Look!" Jonas said. "What do you see there through the trees?"

The children shouted, "Our house!" They raced across the narrow trail into the welcoming arms of their family.

For the next two days the neighborhood men hunted the bear. Finally an old male was killed. Though people were cautious about allowing children to go in the woods alone, no more bears were seen in Locke that summer.

In spite of the last days of her fourth pregnancy, the fall days passed rapidly for Marcia. Preparations for winter and for the coming of the baby together with her daily work of cooking, washing and caring for her family, occupied every waking hour. Many nights she was too exhausted to write in her diary, but she fell into bed the minute the children were asleep.

Each night Jonas sat at the table writing daily

reports about crops, weather, family and political affairs. Early in their marriage Marcia and Jonas had agreed that though they recorded thoughts and feelings along with accounts of their life, their journals were private affairs not to be read by the other.

Baby Mary was born in November on a cold, desolate, rainy day. The birth was easy, the baby healthy, and Marcia was happy to relax in bed for nine days while Harriet took over the care and management of her family. She reveled in the luxury of having time to write and to read books which Jonas had purchased.

She chuckled as she reread Charlotte Kirtland's "A New Home," the story of the Michigan frontier in Livingston County less than twenty miles southeast of their home in Locke Township. Marcia and Harriet had a good laugh about the slovenly woman who wanted to borrow her meticulous neighbor's baby. It seems the slovenly, pipe-smoking woman's baby was unable to nurse because he had a sore mouth. As a result the mother's breasts were painfully full and she wanted to borrow a hungry baby to relieve her.

"Well," Marcia laughed, "that would be painful. Mrs. Kirtland says the woman, a Mrs. Doubleday, shrieked that she'd not lend her baby, but she came to Mrs. Kirtland who had a glass tube with a rubber bulb which drew the milk from the breast. This was loaned to the unhappy mother, and for months afterward it was borrowed by women for miles around when there was a need."

Harriet smiled. "I've heard of those glass tubes. I guess you'd have to get them in Detroit."

Marcia flipped the pages of the book. "This same meticulous Mrs. Doubleday also had a sharp tongue and she often lashed out at her awkward, meek, good-natured husband. He didn't say much but to get even with her, he wrote little rhymes which he called "poetical justice." Here's one:

'Bolt and bar hold gate of wood,
Gate of iron springs make good,
Bolt nor spring can bind the flame,
Woman's tongue can no man tame.'"

Harriet laughed. "That sounds like a good book."

"It's the one Jonas bought for me in Detroit before we were married," Marcia replied. "There's another part here I'd like to read you about the neighborhood gossip. It seems Mrs. Nipper was a thirty-five year old widow who lived alone in the village. Listen: 'No man sneezes at opening his front door, no woman sweeps her steps after breakfast, no child goes late to school, no damsel slips into the store and no bottle comes out of it, no family has fried onions, no cow is missing at milking time, but Mrs. Nipper knows all about it and will tell anybody who will listen. She whispers with mysterious meaning while her light eyes dilate with enjoyment.' Isn't that good writing, Harriet? I wish I could write like that."

"Does this Mrs. Kirtland still live in Livingston County?" Harriet inquired.

"No. I understand she and her family went back to Detroit. They were not very well liked by their neighbors after this book about them was published, so the Kirtlands finally left and went back to the city." Marcia stretched. "It's nice when Jonas takes the children to the barn. The rest in bed and the quiet house, and your help, make me feel like a new woman." She peeped at the tiny sleeping baby beside her.

Harriet got up. "You deserve some rest. Enjoy it while you can."

"You don't mind being away from Israel?" Marcia asked.

"Harmon takes him along on some of his calls, and the rest of the time he stays with Mother Atkins. He likes being with her. She spoils him."

"You know, Harriet, we both have nice mothers-in-law."

"The best! And just see what nice daughters they have! Where would you find nicer daughters than you and I?"

Marcia laughed so heartily that Mary wakened with a cry. "Dinner time, Baby," she said as she prepared to nurse Mary.

After supper that night when the dishes were washed and the children in bed, Jonas, Marcia, Lucy and Harriet talked of recent happenings in the United States. Jonas opened the discussion. "I hope our government did the right thing in taking the land that had belonged to Mexico. I can't forget that that land was Mexico's until we took it by force."

Lucy said, "Seems as though I remember the people in Texas wanted to belong to the United States."

"Yes, Maw. Texas joined the Union in 1845, but Mexico still claimed the land. All the trouble came to a head when General Zachary Taylor fought Santa Anna. Both sides claimed they'd won. Then more battles were fought and we took Mexico City. What could the Mexicans do? They were beaten."

Marcia sighed. "War is so useless. All that fighting and killing for a piece of land."

"It made Zachary Taylor a hero in the United States," Harriet said. "He was elected President after it was over."

Jonas concluded, "We paid Mexico $15 million for the land but I'm sure they don't feel we should have it. In fact, they're still arguing about where the western part of the boundary should be between Mexico and the United States."

Harriet said, "Part of that land is where the Donner Party was headed in eastern California. Maybe Mexico feels that tragedy partly evens the score."

Jonas stroked his beard. "I can understand people looking for adventure and a better place to live," he began. "Michigan settlers, all of us, did that. But those people in the Donner party set out on a twenty-four hundred mile trip with wagons pulled mostly by oxen, and with no trail through the country of savage Indians. From the start it was doomed to failure."

Lucy said, "They were expecting to find gold in California. Men will sacrifice their families - even their lives for gold."

Marcia mused, "The love of money is the root of evil."

"How far could they travel in a day over the prairie?" Harriet asked.

"If there was no trouble with the wagons, or Indians, about fifteen miles," Jonas answered. "At best, that would have been over four months of steady traveling. But more people joined the party until there were eighty-seven. The bickering began about what route to take over the mountains and about who was to make final decisions."

"When did they start the trip?" Marcia asked.

"The middle of April in 1846."

"Then they should have been there by early fall."

Jonas explained. "They had constant trouble. Bad weather, broken wagons, sickness, death and Indians. Wolves molested their animals and howled outside the camp at night. They were far behind schedule when they reached Salt Lake Valley at the end of August. Because of the desert and the lack of water, they had made only thirty-six miles in twenty-one days."

"That must have been a terrible trip for the women and children," Harriet said. "And they'd gone too far to turn back."

Jonas nodded. "I've read that they reached Donner Lake by the end of October, but they had to go over the mountains with their ox wagons, and they couldn't do it. They were trapped. Then several heavy snow storms came, starting in early November."

"Why didn't someone try to walk out to get

help?" Marcia asked.

"They did. Two groups tried, but failed because of the snow. Then seventeen people started out in the middle of December on homemade snowshoes. Several of them died on the trail, but the rest reached California in the middle of January. After getting supplies together, the relief party started. Not until about the first of March did they get back. By that time half of the eighty-seven people had died of starvation and disease. They ate mice, their animals and even their shoes."

"That's awful," Marcia said. "I'd heard a little about it but I didn't know so many died."

Jonas shook his head. "That's bad enough, but they say the starving people became cannibals and that many of the bodies were eaten by the survivors."

Harriet asked in a shocked voice, "Do they know that story is true?"

"A member of the Donner Party named Patrick Breen kept a diary. What was left of the group finally reached Sutter's Fort in April of 1847, a year after they started west."

"Cannibals!" Lucy exclaimed. "They were people like us and they became cannibals!"

"Well, Maw," Jonas replied. "The paper I read when I was in Lansing in 1847 said they ate animal hides that they had cooked and cooked until they were soft. Finally there were no more hides and then they cooked up their shoes. I don't know what people would do if they were starving."

Lucy nodded. "Yes. We shouldn't judge them."

"The cannibal story was known by the Indians," Jonas said. "It said in the newspaper that when Indian children didn't behave, their parents told them if they weren't good the white men would eat them."

Marcia shuddered. "Let's not talk about it anymore. I'm sure I'll have nightmares. How did it happen you didn't tell us about it after you read the newspaper?"

"You were in the family way. I didn't want to mark the baby," Jonas answered.

Harriet said, "Harmon says he's not sure babies can be marked that way before they're born."

"Well," Marcia said, "I'd rather be safe than sorry."

Soon the cabin was quiet as Jonas busily wrote in his journal. The candle flickered as he turned a page. After he had made the entry for the day, he flipped back to previous pages, reading sketches here and there.

His eyes fell on the April 3, 1845 entry. In part he had written: "Brother Albert returned this afternoon from his two month stay at Carley House while he worked in the woods. We both are nearer by several dollars to having enough to buy land. I have decided to ask Maw if she will sell me the old place since Albert has his eye on a 90 acre piece two miles west of here that he thinks will be cheaper since it's not cleared.

Albert told me Caroline Carley was married less than a week ago to a drummer named Ezra Albert who sells supplies to rooming houses and hotels. He travels from New York City to Buffalo, Detroit, Lansing, Jackson and Chicago. He makes his rounds twice a year. Caroline had seen him only once before when he was at Carley House at the opening in September.

I'll admit I was surprised since she was so positive she never would marry only two months ago. What kind of marriage can she have with a man she sees only twice a year? Anyway, I wish her well."

Jonas closed the journal. He had stayed at Carley House the previous August when he sold his wheat in Lansing. Caroline was as beautiful as she had been when he'd stayed there in 1845. She had a little auburn-haired daughter, Jennifer, who now was five years old. Carley House was prospering and Caroline seemed content.

He looked away, thinking. Perhaps her strange marriage was her way of having her cake and eating it, too. She was practically a single woman except for two visits of her husband each year. And marriage allowed her to have children. But she had said very positively that she didn't want children.

He shook his head. He'd never understand women, and especially Caroline. She was a conundrum.

Log Cabin

Chapter XV

CHANGES IN PIONEER LIFE

(1855)

"Grandma Atkins," Jimmy began, "Uncle Harmon said if you'd put up a lunch for us, he'd take us to the woods to learn 'bout birds 'n trees."

As Fanny dried her hands on the corner of her apron Mary ran to her grandmother. "Can I go to the woods, too?" she asked.

Fanny smiled at her little five year old granddaughter. "Of course you can go. You're not the baby anymore. Lilla Dale is the baby in your family now."

"I like living in your house, Grandma," Alice said as she watched Fanny put a kettle of eggs on to boil. "Ma is so busy she don't have time to tell us stories like you do."

"Yeah! Stories!" Six year old Charley exclaimed. "'Member you said you'd tell us 'bout Grandpa Atkins sometime?"

Fanny spread butter on thick slabs of homemade bread. "I will, Charley. Maybe after supper tonight before you go to bed." She wrapped the bread in a clean towel and placed it in a bucket.

"We won't let you forget," Jimmy said, "'cause we're going home tomorrow."

Fanny sighed. "Poor Marcia. I hope she can handle everything. A new baby makes work, and your Grandma Avery can't help her."

Eight year old Alice said, "I'll help. I'll do dishes and set the table."

"And I'll take care of the baby when I'm not in school," Jimmy volunteered.

"I can carry in water," Charley said.

Mary said softly, "I'm too little. I can't do anything to help."

Fanny patted the little girl's head. "You can keep things picked up around the house. There's plenty for all of you to do to help your Maw."

"Yeah," Jimmy said. "But we have to help Pa, too. We have to pick up stones in the fields and hoe in the garden. I don't like to pick up stones 'cause Pa gets grumpy and hollers at us if we don't work fast enough."

"Yeah," Charley added. "I don't like it neither."

"Me, neither," Alice said.

Mary said, "Pa scares me. He spanks hard."

Fanny changed the subject. "Now, let's see. Bread, hard-boiled eggs, radishes and cake. That should fill up six hungry explorers."

"What's 'splorers?" Charley asked.

"People who are looking for new interesting things. Isn't that what you'll be doing in the woods?"

"Yeah!" Jimmy laughed, "We're 'splorers."

A short time later Harmon and his nine year old stepson, Israel, came in from the barn. "Who's going for a tramp in the woods?" Harmon asked.

"Me!" came from the children as one voice.

"Israel, you and Jimmy take turns carrying the lunch." Harmon turned to his mother as the children dashed outside. "Don't look for us until you see us, Maw."

Fanny said softly, "I'm glad you're taking them. Jonas is hard on them."

He nodded. Outside, he talked to the five children. "We are going to learn to see things today." They laughed loudly. "You think that's funny? I don't believe any of you see very well."

"I do," several of them shouted.

"All right. How many kinds of birds have you seen since we stood here?" They were silent. "You haven't seen any, have you? I've seen four kinds just since we came outside." No one spoke, but they began looking closely at the trees.

"There's one!" Mary shouted. "A black one! He says, 'Caw! Caw!'"

Jimmy said, "That's a crow. He pulls our corn up when it's small."

"I see a blue one on the hollow post," Charley said. "What kind is that?"

"That's a hard one to remember. It's a bluebird," Harmon answered with a straight face.

The children shouted with laughter. "You make funny jokes Uncle Harmon," Alice giggled.

Jimmy pointed to a branch overhead. "There's one I know. It's a robin and she has a nest up there."

"That's right. What do you see sitting on the barn roof?" Harmon asked.

"Sparrows!" Jimmy said. "Pa don't like sparrows. He says they eat too much grain."

"He's right," Harmon replied, "but they do some good, too. Let's start walking and watch. We'll see how many kinds of birds we can see when we look carefully."

"I know the four kinds we saw," Israel said. "Crow, bluebird, robin and sparrow."

"You ought to know," Charley retorted. "Uncle Harmon tells you all them things!"

"All birds do some good," Harmon said, "They catch flies and mosquitoes and other insects and worms. Without birds, insects would eat our crops. And birds eat weed seeds, too."

"Yeah, but the chicken hawks steal our little chickens," Jimmy said.

"That's right. But they catch mice and rats."

"Guess we'd better keep chicken hawks in our barn," Charley said. "It's full of rats and mice."

"There's a red bird!" Mary said as a flash of red disappeared into a five foot high evergreen. "He's pretty!"

"That's a cardinal. Maybe he has a nest in that evergreen. Be very quiet and I'll look." Slowly Harmon went to the little tree and peered between the branches. In a moment he came back. "There's a nest. I'll lift you up, one at a time, to see it. Be quiet and don't touch the eggs."

After each child had seen the four white speckled eggs in the nest made from weed stems and dead leaves and grass, they moved on.

Harmon explained, "Cardinals, robins and bluebirds are song birds. We like to hear them sing. Crows don't have a pretty voice. They're not songbirds."

"Look, Pa," Israel said. "There's a Baltimore Oriole's nest." He pointed to a six inch nest hanging from the tip of an elm branch."

"So it is." Harmon asked, "Do you remember seeing a bird about the size of a robin, only he's bright orange and black? And he sings a pretty song."

"I've seen them," Alice said.

"That is a Baltimore Oriole's nest. What kind of tree is it in?"

"It's - it's an elm." Jimmy said.

"Good. Watch for trees you know as well as for birds."

The nature study lesson continued until past noon when they came to a small creek where they had lunch. As they ate, Harmon questioned the children about birds and trees they had identified.

"How do you know so much about birds, Uncle Harmon?" Jimmy asked.

"If I wasn't a doctor, I'd be a naturalist. When I get tired of being with sick people that I don't know how to help, I go to the woods for an hour or two. It rests me. I've studied John Audubon's bird books, too. He's painted many bird pictures."

Charley asked, "Don't you ever get grumpy with Israel?"

"Ask Israel."

"Does he?"

"Sometimes. Like the time I chopped the little lilac bush that Grandma had planted. He spanked me that time."

Harmon laughed. "You were about four then. Israel's a pretty good boy most of the time." He patted his stepson's shoulder.

"I wish you was my Pa," Charley said. "Pa spanks some of us most every day." He hesitated and then went on. "And sometimes he says things that makes Ma cry. I don't like that - it makes me feel like - like hitting him! Only I don't, 'cause then he'd spank me somethin' awful!"

Harmon interrupted. "See those birds in the top of that tall oak tree over there?"

"There's 'bout a hundred," Jimmy answered. "What are they?"

"Passenger pigeons. Someday there won't be any left."

"Why?" Alice asked.

"There's plenty of them up there now," Israel said.

"When we first came to Michigan they were thicker than spatters. But now we only see a few flocks. People have killed them to eat. Once the trees were so full of passenger pigeons they'd break down the branches. Then at night men came with lights and sticks and knocked them out of the trees with their long poles. I read that John Audubon once saw a flock pass in a steady stream for three days."

"You're joking!" Jimmy exclaimed. "That couldn't be!"

Harmon nodded emphatically. "It's true. Audubon said there were so many they darkened the sun and their wings sounded like thunder. But there never will be that many again, and someday, they'll all be gone. There's less every year."

Alice said, "I don't see why people would want to kill so many birds."

"They sell them in New York City and Chicago for two cents apiece." Harmon went on, "There's not much meat on one. It's not worth the trouble to dress them."

After an hour or two, the group returned to the

house for a snack of cookies and milk.

That evening when the work was done, the children with Fanny and Harmon, sat on the porch. A smoldering smudge pot kept the mosquitoes at a distance.

Israel shouted, "Here comes Uncle Samuel and Aunt Mary!"

The children ran to meet their relatives. Samuel, Harmon's younger brother, carried one year old Ada, and Mary, his wife, cradled month old Wesley in her arms.

Alice stood beside her aunt watching the baby. "He's so little," she said. "He's like Lilla Dale. They're new little babies."

Israel announced, "His name's Wesley. He was named for my father."

"That's right," Samuel said. "Wesley, my brother, died when you were a baby. Then your mother, Harriet, married Uncle Harmon. Mary and I wanted to name the baby after your father, so now we have another Wesley Atkins."

"I don't 'member Uncle Wesley," Mary said.

Alice said, "I do. And I remember when Uncle Samuel and Aunt Mary were married. They had a shivaree at their new house that night and we all went."

"Yeah," Jimmy laughed. "Pa and Uncle Harmon pounded on the house and the other men had pans they hit together. And everybody yelled and hollered until you and Aunt Mary got up."

"I 'member," Charley said. "Aunt Mary had cider and fried cakes for us. I never been up so late again."

"I wish I 'membered all them things," Mary said to her grandmother.

"Grandma," Jimmy said, "You promised to tell us about Grandpa Atkins."

"So I did. Well - three years before Israel and I were married, he fought in the War of 1812."

"Israel?" Several children questioned.

"Grandpa Atkins' name was Israel, and you," she patted Israel, "are named for him. We were living in York State when Congress declared war on Great Britain. Israel thought it was his duty to fight for his county. There was fighting in many places on land and also on the water. There was a big battle on Lake Erie that was won by Oliver Perry."

"Was Grandpa in it?" Charley asked.

"No. He was in the land army. Grandpa was a big man, six feet two in his stocking feet. One day he came upon an Indian who had caught a British officer and was just about to scalp him. Grandpa struck the Indian over the head with the butt of his rifle. The Indian said, 'Ugh,' and fell over the cliff where they were standing."

The childrens' eyes were wide with surprise and fright. Finally Jimmy said, "I thought Grandpa's side was fighting the British."

"They were. And the officer said to your Grandpa, 'You have saved my life in order to take it yourself.' But Grandpa said, 'I'm not a murderer. I only kill a man in a fair fight.'"

Alice sighed. "I'm glad he didn't kill the officer."

"Me, too," the other children murmured.

Fanny continued. "The officer said that someday he would repay Grandpa for saving his life and he went on his way."

Israel asked, "Was this in a battle?"

"No, it was between battles. They were very near to my parents' home. Your great-grandparents were my parents. Their names were Charles and Mary Knight, so my name was Fanny Knight before I was married.

"Soon your grandfather came to our house and asked for a drink of water. He was a handsome man, so tall and nice-looking. I got him a cup of water and we talked. I had never seen him before that day. Three years later we were married."

Little Wesley fretted and his mother put him over her shoulder as she said, "That was interesting, Mother Atkins."

"Yeah," Jimmy said, "but tell us more about the war. What happened to Grandpa after he left your house?"

"Several months later he and some other American soldiers were captured and accused of being spies. They were sentenced to be shot. Then the British officer, whose life Grandpa had saved from the Indian, came along. He noticed Grandpa and remembered him. Because he was a high-up officer he had the authority to order Grandpa freed. When Grandpa thanked him, the officer said, 'I hope I have in a measure repaid my debt to you.'"

"Paw was quite a man," Harmon mused. "We've always felt bad that he didn't get to clear his land here in Michigan. He thrived on excitement and adventure."

Israel asked, "What happened?"

Fanny rubbed her head. "I don't like to think of that time." She paused, then went on. "On the way to Michigan we came through Canada. Grandpa was taken sick and he died in London, Ontario. That's where he's buried."

Harmon murmured, "Likely was a heart attack."

"The Indians in Michigan don't scalp people," Jimmy said.

"Many years ago they did," Harmon answered.

"Why don't Indians live near us?" Alice asked.

"There are Indian camps not far away," Samuel said. "A few miles north, there's a small camp. One of their girls married Amos Colborn."

"Indians marry white people?" Jimmy asked in surprise.

"Sometimes. There's a big Indian camp near Lansing. It's what's left of old Chief Okemos' tribe. They don't hurt anyone now, but back when Okemos was young, he was a powerful man. President George Washington was troubled by the skirmishes led by Chief Okemos in 1791 in northern Ohio down near Lake Erie," Samuel said.

"How old is he?" Jimmy asked. "I've heard Pa talk about him."

"Do you know, Harmon?"

"I don't think anyone knows. But if he was leading braves against Americans in 1791, that was seventy-five years ago. He must be close to a hundred. I understand he led battles in Indiana, Ohio, Michigan and Ontario. He fought against the whites because the land was being taken from the Indians by the pioneers. I've read that he finally admitted defeat and that many years ago he went to a Colonel in Ft. Wayne, Detroit, and said, 'Now I make peace and fight no more. White man too much for Indians. Me fight plenty enough.' Now he's a beggar, a broken old man."

"It's sad," Fanny said softly.

"There's another small tribe a few miles south and east of Leroy," Samuel said. "Most of the Indians that still live around here are to be pitied. They're poor, the game is leaving, and they are in bad shape. I talked with a man named Richard Jacobs in Leroy. The Indians helped him and his neighbors hunt a bear that was killing their animals. The settlers had been worried about their children."

Jimmy said, "I remember when Alice and me got lost and a bear killed Nero."

Alice nodded. "And Pa spanked us 'cause Ma said not to go in the woods."

"Yeah," Jimmy said. "He hit us hard that time." In a second he said, "There aren't any bears in the woods now, are there?"

"There might still be a few. It's best not to take chances," Harmon said.

Alice led year old Ada, who was beginning to walk, back and forth in front of the house. "In a year Lilla Dale will be walking," she said to Fanny. "Tomorrow we'll go home and Aunt Harriet will come back here."

"We'll tell Ma we was 'splorers with Uncle Harmon," Charley said. "I liked that."

"Mother Atkins," Mary asked, "have you finished reading "Uncle Tom's Cabin?"

"Not yet. It makes me sick to think what is happening to the slaves in the South. Beatings and all kinds of evil things. No wonder the Abolitionists help the Negroes escape whenever they can. I'd help too, if it was so I could."

"Maw, you'd be breaking the law," Samuel teased.

"Any law that allows one man to own another like a cow or horse is evil! It should be broken. I don't believe God will long tolerate this - this evil thing in our country!"

"The South is angry because the fugitives seldom are caught in the North. That's because most people here feel like you do, Maw, and they help them escape to Canada."

Harmon said, "Feelings are running high down there against the North, I hear. Do you think it will come to Civil War?"

Samuel shook his head. "I hope not - because I would have to go."

"Have to?"

"I'd volunteer. I feel like Maw. Sooner or later slavery has to be stopped and it will take more than a few slaves escaping through the Underground Railroad to stop it. It will take force - brute force!" He banged his fists together so violently that Ada stared at her father, her eyes wide.

Harmon said, "I read in the Detroit Free Press that this fellow, Abraham Lincoln, opposes all the things Senator Stephen Douglas stands for. He believes slavery must not spread to new states because it is evil. But Douglas refuses to admit slavery is wrong. I understand from the newspaper that Lincoln opposes Douglas wherever he can."

"Who is Abraham Lincoln?" Fanny asked.

"I gather he's a lawyer from Springfield, Illinois, but I guess he's pretty much unknown outside his state," Harmon replied. "He ran for the Illinois legislature and was elected."

Samuel said, "I figure the Whig party is finished. This new Republican Party looks like the one to watch. It was formed at a little place in Wisconsin last year, and according to the Free Press, at a meeting in Jackson last summer, they adopted the name, "Republican."

Harmon said, "The Detroit Free Press supports the Democratic Party and the Advertiser and Tribune favor the Republicans, I've noticed."

"They're all Detroit papers, but their viewpoints are different."

"Remember, Maw," Harmon said, "when we settled here in 1842 we didn't see a newspaper for months. Then, when the State Capitol was moved from Detroit to Lansing in 1847, they got busy on the old Grand River Trail and built the Plank Road."

Jimmy said, "I've never seen the Plank Road."

"I went to Lansing once with Pa," Israel bragged.

"Tell us about it, Uncle Harmon," Jimmy begged. "Pa says it's real nice and that it's made from thick planks."

"That's right. And it's wide. Eighteen feet wide so that wagons or stagecoaches can pass. The plank road runs between Lansing and Detroit. People have to pay at toll gates to drive on it."

"How much does it cost?" Jimmy asked.

"The toll from Lansing to Detroit is three dollars. That's expensive. But if you go from Leroy or Williamston to Lansing, it is one cent a mile per horse. There are several toll gates before you get to Lansing."

Charley said, "Then it costs more for a wagon and team of horses than it does for one horse on a buggy."

"That's right. Anyone who rides the stagecoach to Detroit plans on a twenty-four hour trip with an overnight stop in Howell. It takes twelve hours of steady travel."

"Pa and me rode on the stagecoach," Israel said. "How much does it cost to ride on the stagecoach, Pa?"

"Seven cents a mile per person. So, son, don't expect to go often by stagecoach."

Israel rambled on, "And they change horses about every twelve miles. We changed in Williamston. There were six horses on our stage, but some have four."

Alice asked, "Do the horses go fast?"

"Yes," Israel answered. "It felt like we were flying. That's why they need fresh horses so often. The stagecoach makes a rumbling noise when it goes over the planks."

Harmon said, "People come with their children for miles around to see the stage rumble past. The coaches are painted bright colors - yellow, or red or green - and they have pictures of famous people painted on the sides. The stage also carries mail and newspapers. It's twenty-five cents to send a letter."

"I wish I could ride on the stagecoach sometime," Charley said enviously. "All I get to do is pick up stones!"

"Your time will come," Fanny promised. "I've never ridden on it, and neither has anyone else here but Harmon, Samuel and Israel."

Jimmy declared, "Someday Charley and Alice and me might walk to Leroy to see the stagecoaches on the Plank Road."

"Someday your Paw or maybe Uncle Harmon will take you," Fanny said. "You musn't go by yourselves. It's too far."

"I know something we haven't talked about," Israel announced. "The name of Leroy has been changed to Webberville. It's named for a Mr. Webber, one of the first men to settle there."

Alice said, "Then there's no more Leroy?"

Harmon replied, "Webberville is a settlement in Leroy Township. They've only changed the name of the settlement."

A strong breeze from the south ruffled the leaves of the maples in the yard. Samuel looked at the evening sky. "We need rain," he said. Suddenly he jumped up. "There's a fire! It's close! Might be at Jonas' place!"

He rushed to untie his horse. By the time he was in the buggy Harmon was there. "Giddap!" Samuel shouted. The horse raced toward the south kicking up a cloud of dust.

Mary cried, "Our house! Our house is burning down!"

"We don't know," Fanny said. "Maybe it's only a big brush fire. Your Paw has been clearing that marsh land."

For two or three minutes they watched as the black smoke rose high above the tree tops. Mary got up. "Mother Atkins, I'm going. Will you keep Ada and Wesley? Maybe I can help."

The older children clamored, "We want to go! We can help! Please, Grandma!"

Fanny held the baby, her eyes on the towering smoke. "All right. Go with Aunt Mary." They all started running except little Mary.

"I'm scared, Grandma," she said. "I'll stay with you."

The south wind was growing stronger. Long before they were at the Avery farm, smoke filled the air so that breathing was difficult. Mary knew the burning building could not be saved. Still she ran. The children had disappeared in the cloud of smoke. Towering flames licked below the black smoke. She could hear the crackle of the fire. Poor Marcia and Jonas. Breathing great heaving breaths, she broke into the clearing about the house. Then she saw it - the barn roof fell in and showers of sparks and pieces of burning timber sailed through the air on the strong south wind.

Breathless, she hesitated. Marcia, holding her baby, leaned against a wagon beside blind Lucy. Harriet turned and screamed, "The house! The roof's on fire!"

Frantically the men drew buckets of water from the open well. By the time Jonas got a ladder up and climbed to the roof, flames were racing to the peak of the wood-shingled house. It was useless to try saving the tinder dry building.

"Let er go!" he shouted. "Get everything outside!" In a frantic flurry of confusion and screaming voices, Jonas, Samuel, Harmon, Harriet, Mary and the four children rushed to carry out furniture and other belongings.

Marcia pushed the baby into Lucy's arms. "Hold her. I have to help!" she shouted.

Ten minutes later Jonas yelled, "The roof's going! Everybody get back!"

Retreating behind the wagon piled high with household articles, clothing and bedding, they watched as the roof collapsed with a roar in an inferno of spurting flames and showers of sparks. Silently they shielded their faces from the intense heat.

Harriet stood with an arm about her mother's shoulders. "I'll take the baby," she said.

"Our old home, the house Stephen bought for us," Lucy said in a monotone. Her sightless eyes saw in imagination the death of her home.

Neighbors were pouring into the yard. The Fullers, McKees, Coles, Bells and Morris families came to offer help.

"Thank you kindly," Jonas repeated over and over. "There's nothing you can do right now." The men stood together in a group between the burning remains of the barn and house.

"It's tough," Levi Cole said. "Did you save all the stock?"

"All but three calves. The horses and cows were in the pasture."

"How about your household goods?" Jim Bell asked.

"We got the beds, bureaus, tables and chairs. So many people were running outside with things I don't rightly know what they saved." He stared into the darkness. "It's the middle of July. I've got until winter to harvest my crops and build a house and barn."

"Ya know how it started?" Jed Morris asked.

Jonas shook his head. "I'd turned the horses and cows out for the night and I was writing at the table. Marcia said she smelled smoke. I thought it was from the fireplace, and didn't get up. A few minutes later she screamed that the barn was on fire."

"It's tough luck," Jim Bell said softly.

Frank McKee volunteered, "Ya kin store yer things in my shed 'till yer house is built."

"Thanks, Frank. We'll bring a load of them over tomorrow."

Tom Fuller asked, "Where'll ya stay?"

Harmon and Samuel spoke together. "At our place."

"My wife has a nice family," Jonas said. "And Albert and Mary Ann, my brother and sister," he explained, "they'll put up some of the children. We'll manage."

"And my sister and her husband," Samuel said, "the Stephen Scofields, they'll help."

Later that night at the Atkins home when Jonas and Marcia were alone, she said, "It's a terrible loss but I thank God no one was hurt. And it would have been worse if it had happened after harvest time. How do you suppose it started?"

For a minute he didn't answer. Then he said, "My pipe's gone. I hope I didn't drop it in the barn. I'd been smoking before I went in to do the milking. I thought I put the pipe in my pocket, but it's not there."

She was silent for a time. Then she said softly, "Maybe this is God's way of warning you about the way you live. You smoke and chew tobacco. It's wrong. Maybe God is warning you."

Jonas sprang from bed. "God Almighty, Marcia! Don't I have enough on my mind without your nagging? You knew when you married me that I smoked - and that I don't believe in your God!" He walked to the window and stared into the dark wilderness.

Marcia said softly, "You're right. I made my bed, now I'll lie in it."

Lilla Dale whimpered and Marcia silently turned on her side to nurse the baby. Neither Jonas or Marcia slept that night, but they were silent, each thinking - thinking - and wondering what the future held for their family.

The next day after the load of household goods

was stored at McKees, Samuel and Harmon helped Jonas clean up the remains of the burned buildings. At noon they sat under the scorched maple tree to eat lunch which Fanny had packed.

All morning Jonas had been silent and sullen. Suddenly he exploded. "Marcia thinks I'm being punished by the Almighty because I backslid. That's why my buildings burned! Damn it! And I'm a sinner because I smoke and chew! She keeps at me! She can't understand I don't believe the way I once did. I can see too many faults in religion!"

Harmon and Samuel were silent. Jonas went on. "I don't know how you feel, but think about some of the happenings in the Bible. For instance old Father Abraham and his wife, Sarah. When they went to Egypt for food during a famine, because of his wife's beauty, Abraham passed her off as his sister for he was afraid he might be killed by Pharaoh who had taken Sarah into his household. Her "brother," Abraham, was rewarded with servants and livestock. Seems like deception - lying - was acceptable to God.

"Then, many years later, when Abraham was ninety-nine and Sarah was ninety, the Lord told them they would have a son. Even they thought it was ridiculous, but Sarah bore a son, Isaac. A few years later Abraham was told by God to slay his son and to offer him as a sacrifice. He almost did it, too, but God called to him just in time and Isaac was saved.

"Now, I ask you - what kind of a man would consider slaying his son, and what kind of a God would suggest it? Abraham also had a son, Ishmael, by Sarah's Egyptian maid, Hagar. Because Sarah was jealous of Hagar and Ishmael, Abraham agreed to cast them out, for the Lord had requested that he send them away. So good, kind, old Abraham gave Hagar and his son a supply of bread and water and sent them away. Generous, wasn't he?

"You're probably thinking, 'But that was in Old

Testament days,'" Jonas went on. Yet in the New Testament, Abraham is held up as a God-fearing, righteous man." He paused. "That's only one of many Bible events I cannot accept.

"Another is the Adam and Eve story. Is it justice that all mankind suffer forever because Eve disobeyed, tempted Adam, and they ate the apple? Is that an example of a forgiving God? To punish the whole human race because Mother Eve disobeyed? I suppose that's why my buildings burned - to punish me for my sins. They don't seem as serious to me as the sins of Abraham. And my sister, Melissa - and my father - I suppose they had to die because of some sin they had committed."

Jonas paused, then he apologized. "I'm sorry. This fire's got me all wrought up."

Harmon scratched his head. "It's puzzling. I'll admit I don't understand, but there has to be a power, call it God or whatever you will, that is guiding the universe."

Jonas said, "Our mothers and Marcia believe every word in the Bible. Marcia is a fine woman. I don't deserve her. I make her miserable with my ungovernable temper, and I'm hard on the children." He began to cough.

"Asthma again?" Harmon asked.

Jonas wiped his mouth. "The old Avery curse. Paw said it had been in the family as long as Grandpa Avery could remember. It's worse when I get angry, it seems. Damn this fire! I don't know where to begin."

Harmon got up. "Going to build another log cabin?"

"I'd like to put up a frame house with clapboard siding, but I don't have the time or money." He got up. "I'm going to get Marcia a cast-iron cooking stove. With five young'uns and Maw to look after, it'll be better for her, and the oven will make baking easier. We'll still use the fireplace for heat. Someday we'll get one of those round heating stoves."

Gradually plans materialized over the next weeks and Jonas worked to bring them to fruition. Neighbors and relatives helped with the heavy work, and by November the buildings were completed and the family and animals again were assured of food and shelter for another winter in the Michigan wilderness.

A Plank Road, 1846

Chapter XVI

THE MEETING OF THE CLANS

(1860)

Marcia bustled about as she packed quantities of food in a basket. "Alice," she said, "Would you comb Grandma's hair and get her new black dress?" She turned to Lucy, who sat in her rocker, her hands folded in a resigned manner. "Mother Avery, you're going to look nice in your new dress."

Lucy smiled faintly. "Where is it we're going?" she asked vacantly.

"To the camp meeting at Bell Oak, don't you remember? We're taking our lunch and we'll be gone all day."

"Yes. To the camp meeting." She lapsed again into silence.

Marcia called upstairs. "Boys, wear your best shirts and shoes!"

"Yeah, Ma." They answered in unison.

Ten year old Mary and her five year old sister, Lilla Dale, came in carrying quantities of zinnias, delphiniums and hollyhocks. "Is this enough?" Mary asked.

"That's fine. Take them outside and put them in water in the buckets on the bench. They'll look nice along the edge of the platform. Reverend Williams will appreciate your bringing them. When you're finished, wash your hands. Then, we'll be ready to go."

Lilla Dale stood beside the door. "Pa's already hitching the horses to the surrey," she said.

Ten minutes later the three adults and five children, together with two buckets of flowers and the lunch, all were crowded into the two-seated fringed surrey. "Giddap!" Jonas shouted to the team.

In the years since the early 1840's much of the land in Locke Township had been cleared. Fields of wheat and oat stubble were waiting to be plowed for the planting of winter rye and wheat. Corn ears hung heavy from the stalks giving promise of a bountiful harvest.

Passing through a stretch of dense forest on both sides of the dusty country road, Lilla Dale asked, "Are there bears in there?"

"Bears," Lucy murmured. "Jimmy and Alice are lost and they're in the woods."

Jimmy patted his grandmother's hand. "We're right here, Grandma."

Lilla Dale repeated, "Are there bears in there, Pa?"

"We haven't seen a bear in six, seven years, but I don't think you should go in the woods alone. Go with one of the older children."

Passing the Atkins farms they called and waved to their relatives who were climbing into their buggies in preparation for a day with friends and neighbors at the camp meeting.

Many families at the camp ground, who were not within driving distance of the gathering, lived in tents for the week of daily and evening meetings.

The horses were hitched beneath the trees at the edge of the forest. Adults talked and children raced about greeting school friends. The service was due to start at ten o'clock, and by that time every child was expected to be seated and attentive to the message being delivered by the visiting evangelist.

Marcia, Lucy and Lilla Dale followed Jimmy and Charley who carried the flowers to the platform.

Marcia and Lucy chose seats in the center of the tent beside two women. Marcia sat between a gray-haired woman on her right and Lucy on her left. She spoke to the woman. "I'm Marcia Avery, and this is my husband's mother, Lucy."

The woman held out her hand. "Mrs. Avery!" she

exclaimed. "Ya air Jonas' wife?"

Marcia smiled. "Yes. Do you know him?"

The woman nodded. "Him an' his Paw was two a' the first people we met when we come to Michigan in '36. I'm Mary Colborn." She turned to the dark-eyed woman on her right. "This is my son Amos' wife, Hannah." They shook hands. Mary spoke to Lucy. "Ya air Stephen's wife?" She held out her hand.

"Stephen's gone," Lucy said dully.

"Yes. We heerd. We both air widders."

Marcia said, "I've heard Jonas speak of you. Now that there is a trail between the county line and Bell Oak, perhaps we'll see our neighbors more often."

"How many children does ya have?" Mary asked.

"Five. The oldest is fourteen and the youngest is five."

"I have five, too, only mine's growed up. My youngest, Lucretia, was borned in Michigan in '37. She's twenty-three now, an' married to a neighbor boy." She put her hand on Hannah's arm. "My daughter-in-law's Maw helped me when 'Cretia was borned. There wan't no doctor we could git easy."

Marcia spoke to Hannah. "How many children do you have, Mrs. Colborn?"

"Four. Three girls an' a boy. My oldest girl air twenty-one an' the youngest girl air ten. The boy air eight." She looked at the ground.

Silently Marcia thought Hannah was ill at ease talking to her. "Do you have a neighborhood church?" she asked Mary.

"We goes to the Methodist meetin's at the Parsons settlement, an' sometimes we goes to Byron. My sons ain't much on goin' t' church, but they's good 'bout takin' Hannah an' me." She smiled. "'Course they gits to talk with the men folk, so I thinks they likes goin'."

"Do you live with one of your sons?" Marcia asked.

"I lives with Ben an' his wife, Marias, an'

their leetle boy, Albert. He's four. We lives in the old cabin Robert built in 1836."

The plank benches now were about filled with farmers, their wives and families. Marcia couldn't see Jimmy and Charley. They must be with Jonas. Her girls were seated together at the back.

After the singing of two hymns and a lengthy prayer by the Reverend Williams, the visiting evangelist, Reverend Thompson, was introduced. His topic was "The Second Coming of Christ." He stressed the need for prayer and clean living so that Christians would be prepared when that "glorious day" arrived. He said that because the human body is the temple of the Holy Spirit, people should abstain from anything that might adversely affect bodily health, including tobacco and alcohol. He spoke of the dangers of card-playing and gambling, and concluded by warning that to avoid the eternal fires of Hell, and to be able to earn a place in Heaven, every individual must pray that God would forgive his sins so that he might be saved.

The hymn, "Just As I Am," was sung over and over as Reverend Thompson begged and pleaded that unsaved souls come forward to kneel at the altar "to pray their way through to victory." Half a dozen people went up the straw-covered aisles to kneel before the crude altar. Reverend Thompson continued the slow, mournful hymn-singing until no more sinners came forward.

Marcia, followed by several others in the congregation, went forward at the request of the minister that the "saved members come help pray these souls through to victory."

Voices were raised in prayer, gradually growing louder. Suddenly a young woman who had gone forward, jumped to her feet. Tears streamed down her face as she shouted, "Praise His name! I am saved!" Sobbing, she shook hands joyfully with person after person.

Several others declared they were saved as they

arose from the straw-covered ground. Two, a man and his wife, were unsuccessful in "praying their way through." They arose, dejected, to walk slowly from the tent.

Marcia returned to her seat beside Lucy as the congregation sang the last hymn and the minister pronounced the benediction.

After the service, the women living in tents prepared their noon meal over outdoor campfires. The smell of wood smoke hung over the grounds. Children ran about playing a noisy game of hide-and-seek.

Marcia, Lucy, Mary and Hannah walked slowly toward the surreys where the lunches were waiting. Neighbors stopped to talk. Hannah's two younger children, Lucy and Jim, came to walk with their mother and grandmother.

Shy and sober, with downcast eyes, Lucy and Jim did not respond as Mary said, "These air my grandchildren." Jim looked up, his black eyes coldly appraising the fair-haired stranger.

The Colborn and Avery surreys were close together, so the families talked as they ate. The Avery children invited the young Colborns to sit with them at the side of the group. Reluctantly Jim and Lucy moved beside Alice and Mary.

Alice munched on a ham sandwich. "Do you go to school?" she asked Lucy.

Staring at her outstretched legs the little girl murmured, "Yeah."

Mary asked, "What reading book are you in?"

"The secont."

"You like school?" Charley asked.

Lucy didn't reply, but little Jim's voice exploded in a loud "No!" He jammed half a square of johnny cake into his mouth.

"Why not?"

"'Cause they tease us!" The black eyes flashed.

Silently Lucy ate her johnny cake and cold venison. Occasionally she stole glances at the Avery children. Her blue eyes appeared faded in her dark-skinned face.

"We like school," Alice said, "'specially my sister, Mary, and I do." She grinned impishly at Jimmy and Charley. "My brothers sometimes get in fights with the other boys and the teacher whips them. Then Pa whales them good when they get home, 'cause he says if we get spanked at school, we'll get another one at home."

Jimmy's eyes flashed blue sparks. "You don't have to tell everything you know," he muttered.

"Tattle-tale," Charley chimed in. "Alice is a tattle-tale."

"Children," Marcia said quietly. There was a note of warning in her voice. In a moment she directed a question to Hannah. "You said your other children are grown?"

"Yeah. Betsy and Eliza air married."

The Avery children stared at the Indian woman, intrigued by her coal-black hair and eyes. They wondered why Mr. Colborn chose to marry a squaw.

Mary Colborn said, "Hannah's girl, Eliza, is named for my daughter, Lide. Hannah an' Lide have been friends since 1837. They visit each 'nother 'most every week. My Lide, she been married many years."

A flicker of a smile crossed Hannah's face. "Lide, my good friend," she said.

When the families had finished their lunch, the Avery children went to find friends. Lilla Dale and the Colborn children remained with the women.

"Mother Avery," Marcia said to Lucy, "Why don't you rest in the surrey until time for the next service?"

"Rest. Yes, I'm tired," the senile old woman said softly.

Jonas and Amos strolled into the woods and sat beneath a huge oak. After small talk, Amos said, "Ya has a nice family, Jonas. Ya air lucky ya has two boys. They'll be a big help to ya. I has jest one boy - the leetle one. We waited and waited fer a boy. First one a girl - secont one, a girl - third one, a girl. Then, a boy. But 'tis too late. I air fifty years old now. Purty soon I'll be an ole man. When I need boys, I git girls. Now, too late."

"I hear you own several parcels of land," Jonas said. "You have prospered."

Amos pointed to his wooden leg. "That's held me back er I'd had more land. Two hunnert acres, I've got - my brother Israil's got ninety, an' my leetle brother Ben, he's on the ole place."

"How can you farm two hundred acres alone?"

"Hannah, my wife, she works in the fields, an' so did my oldest girls 'till they got married. Hannah's a good woman, even if she's a squaw. Now, Israil's wife, she wouldn't lift a hand to help outside the house."

He went on, "Then I've got a hired man, my wife's brother. He was jest a boy when we come to Michigan. Him an' Hannah was frum a camp near us. Shobegun, my hired man, is a good worker, an' a good friend. His wife's a squaw named White Fawn, an' she works in the fields too. They has one boy, Joe. He's the same age as my youngest girl, Lucy." Amos smiled. "Shobegun says his last name is Colborn 'cause me an' Ben have been like brothers t' him."

"Was his wife from the Indian camp?"

Amos laughed. "She was a stowaway that hid in my wagon in Howell. I've allus thought that Hannah helped her hide, but it don't matter. 'Twas when the government was drivin' Injuns west to reservations. They was a sorry lookin' bunch, them Injuns. Anyway, when we was 'most home that day, I seen her hidin' n'under a blanket in the back a' the waggin. Wa'nt nothin' t' do but keep her. It's been nice fer Hannah, havin' Fawn here. Her only other friend is my sister, Lide - none a' the other neighbor wimmin, 'cept Maw, has much t' do with Hannah."

"How about your children? They go to school?"

Amos nodded. "They'll need all the book larnin' they kin git. But the other young'uns tease them. They calls 'em half-breeds, an' it makes 'em feel bad." He paused. "Course, they air half-breeds, but take Lucy now. She feels a'body that ain't Injun, a' body that's all white, is better'n her. Jim will be diff'rent. He's got spunk." He scratched his head.

"This hired man of yours and his wife - do they live at the Indian camp?"

"Nope. We built a cabin fer 'em on my land. Shobegun's more of a brother t' me than Israil, an' him an' my brother Ben's been good friends since we met the tribe on the trail 'tween Hannibal's Inn an' Byron when we was comin' in in '36."

Amos went on. "Ya didn't know the Injuns has left the camp?"

"No. I hadn't heard."

"They's so many settlers in our corner of Livingston County, an' in Shiawassee, too, that huntin' ain't good. I got a buck the first a' the week, but sometimes we don't see one fer a month er two. So the Injuns moved out in July an' went north up some'ers near Saginaw. I was sorry they went. They allus was right nice t' my family. 'Course, my brother, Israil, an' his wife, they ain't got no use fer 'em - er fer Hannah an' our young'uns neither."

Jonas changed the subject to politics. "Who do you think will win the election in November? Think Lincoln can beat Douglas?"

"I duno. I'm gonna vote fer Lincoln. He's my kind a' man. He's a common feller an' I think he's got right good sense. Ya think there's trouble comin' with the slave states?"

"I hope not," Jonas replied, "But feelings are running high in both the North and the South. I read in the Free Press that southern leaders are threatening to withdraw their states from the Union if Lincoln wins the election. South Carolina is threatening to secede no matter who wins. Looks like we're a nation divided, as Lincoln says."

"Yeah. I 'spect 'twould come t' war if the South

secedes, don't ya think so?"

Jonas nodded. "There's been bad feelings between the North and South for ten years. The pot's boiling. I'm afraid it's only a matter of time until it boils over." He got up. "I promised my wife I'd go to the service this afternoon, so I guess I'd better get going."

Amos struggled to stand and limped behind Jonas. "'Spect I oughta go too, though 'twon't do me no good. The wimmin in my family air the church ones."

Jonas smiled. "It's the same in my family. Of course, my mother's mind's not good now, but she was once as strict about religion as Paw. You remember him?"

"Yeah. Ya an' him wouldn't drink beer with us in Detroit in '36."

Jonas chuckled. "Paw never changed, but I have. I'd drink beer with you now, Amos."

They sat on the back row of the rough plank seats. The tent was filled and already people were uncomfortably warm. Marcia turned to smile approvingly at Jonas.

After the opening hymn, followed by Scripture reading and prayer by Reverend Williams, the evangelist launched into his sermon. As the temperature inside the tent rose, Reverend Thompson warmed to his subject which centered around the fate of unfortunate souls who died without accepting Christ, or those backsliders, the people who had once accepted Christ but had been unable to follow the strict doctrines of the church. He painted a vivid word picture of the tortures of Hell, and invited the "lost sheep to return to the fold." He exhorted them to repent their sins and to be saved "before it is too late." He pounded the altar rail as his forceful voice boomed out, "My friends, if you reject Christ, you will be eternally lost - eternally lost to burn forever in the indescribable torture of Hell!"

Several agitated people stirred nervously. The

minister's voice suddenly became soft and low. "You know the pain, the unbearable pain and misery of a small burn. You recall the concern of friends and family at your slightest injury." His fist hit the altar rail. "But you will find no friends, no family, to help you in Hell. No one - nothing can help you there. The indescribable torture of Hell - can you imagine the flames licking around you - searing, burning, torturing, but never destroying you for destruction would bring peace. There is no peace in Hell! Only an eternity of torture - eternity my friends."

Reverend Thompson paused, then pleadingly, he continued. "Won't you come to Him now? Come kneel at the altar, confess your sins, renounce your worldly life and beg for forgiveness. While we stand and sing a few stanzas of "Just As I Am," won't you come?"

The congregation stood. The melody of the old hymn filled the tent and echoed from the woods. The same couple who had been unsuccessful in receiving forgiveness in the morning service again went to kneel at the altar. Reverend Thompson held his hand up and the singing stopped. "My friends, some of you are telling yourselves that you're not terrible sinners, that you've never done anything really bad." His voice became low and mournful.

"Last month I held a revival in Jackson. A young man attended. During the altar call one of his friends pleaded with him to give up his sinful ways and to come to God. But he rejected the invitation. That night, on his way home he drank from the bottle he carried in the buggy box. His horse became frightened, ran away, and the buggy overturned throwing the young man against a tree. His neck was broken and his life snuffed out in an instant. He'd made his choice and he went to meet his God, unprepared and unsaved."

The minister struck the altar rail a resounding blow. Several uneasy guilt-ridden people jumped nervously. He shook his clenched fist at the congregation as he shouted, "He will suffer in Hell through eternity! He had his chance and he rejected God!"

The evangelist continued, now in a pleading tone. "Dear friends, you never know when you've had your last chance. Perhaps this may be the final oportunity for someone here today. Won't you come forward as we sing?"

The congregation launched into the second verse of "Just As I Am." Two women went forward, followed by Alice. At the close of the hymn the minister again invited the saved members of the congregation to come to pray with the penitents.

Marcia knelt beside her daughter. With bowed heads they prayed silently, while on either side of them the saved members prayed loudly for salvation and forgiveness for the sinners.

In the heat of the summer afternoon the people perspired as voices grew increasingly louder. Sweat trickled in rivulets down the red, smooth-shaven face of Reverend Thompson. The din of voices continued until suddenly one of the penitents jumped to her feet. Tears streamed down her face as she shouted, "Praise His name! Glory hallelujah! I am saved!" Then, sobbing and shouting, she shook hands with person after person.

"God bless you, sister," Reverend Thompson beamed as he grasped her hand.

The praying continued, growing louder and louder as saved souls pleaded with God to "save these sinners." Silently Alice and Marcia, their heads bowed in prayer, continued their supplications. At last Alice raised her head. A smile lighted her face as she got up.

"You have the victory?" Marcia asked.

"Yes, Ma."

Again the handshaking and joyous shouts rang through the tent to be repeated with greater intensity when the young man and his wife rose from their knees, their faces shining.

The phrases, "Praise His name," and "Praise the

Lord, Brother and Sister Brown," were repeated many times.

At last the people who had gone forward returned to their seats. Reverend Williams, in a brief prayer, thanked God for "these souls who have forsaken the sinful ways of the world," and the benediction was pronounced.

That evening when the children and Lucy were in bed, Jonas and Marcia sat at the table writing in their journals. In part, Marcia wrote: "Today has been a beautiful day. Jonas took us to camp meeting and Alice went forward and was saved. She is the first of our children to dedicate her life to Christian living. I am worried about Jimmy. At fourteen, he should have taken a stand. Is he influenced by Jonas so that he, too, is an unbeliever? I pray this is not true. I keep thinking, 'As the twig is bent, the tree is inclined,' but perhaps he is more bent by Jonas' example than by mine.

I'm praying every day for Jonas. Something will happen so that he accepts Christ. He didn't say anything in front of the children, but I believe he doesn't approve of the frenzied shouting and loud praying that went on today. Though I can't say it aloud, I believe God hears a silent prayer, and that shouting is not necessary. I wonder if all Methodists are as extreme as that evangelist.

I've read about a Baptist minister from York State named William Miller. He stresses the doctrine of the Second Coming and is the man who announced the Second Advent would occur in 1843 or 1844. When the world didn't end as he prophesied, many followers deserted him. I like what I've read about his teachings. He puts emphasis on an extensive missionary program, for he now believes the Second Coming will not take place until all nations have heard the Gospel. I would like to know more about him."

Marcia wrote a few minutes longer before she closed her journal. Jonas still was writing. In part, he wrote:

"We met Amos Colborn and his family at the camp meeting. I like him, but his Indian wife seems cold and quite suspicious of strangers. His ten-year-old daughter, like her mother, is quiet and seems unable to talk with people. She's an unusual appearing child with pale blue eyes, the Indian high cheek bones, coal-black hair and a rather dark complexion. She likely will be a beautiful young woman in a few years - but what man would choose to marry a half-breed? The boy, Jim, could pass for a full blood Indian.

Our Alice was converted today which pleased Marcia. I think the evangelist scared Alice and some of the others "into the fold." I'm glad Marcia isn't one of the shouters. If there is a God, I'm sure that in his perfection, he would not be deaf, but that he would hear and respond to silent prayer.

Poor Maw is growing more senile every day. Her mind is gone, but otherwise she is well except for her blindness. What a dismal way to live - and she may exist this way for years. Marcia is a saint to care for her as she does. Maw's like a sightless infant with an adult body.

All the men I talked with today, Amos Colborn, John Martin, Marcia's brother-in-law, Stephen Scofield, and Marcia's brothers, Harmon and Samuel Atkins, - they all think war between the North and South is not far off. Though I don't like to admit it, I fear they are right. Well - what will be, will be."

Chapter XVII

CIVIL WAR

(1861)

The late February snow drifted lazily through the bare branches of trees lining the road over which children from nearby families walked on their way to the one room log schoolhouse. Six Averys, five Atkins and two Scofields plodded through the snow carrying their lunches. The three families consisting of thirteen children were related. Albert Avery's son, George, was six years old, while Jonas' five ranged in age from Jimmy at fifteen to Lilla Dale, age six. Samuel Atkins' two children, Ada and Wesley, were seven and six, while his brother Harmon had three, namely stepson Israel, aged fifteen, daughter Lucy, who was eleven and seven year old Fanny, who was named for her Grandmother Atkins. Guy and Henry Scofield, aged seventeen and twelve, were the children of Louisa Atkins Scofield, the sister of Marcia, Harmon and Samuel.

Coming from the opposite direction were pupils from the Bell, Rowley, Wright, Cole and Fisher families. In all, a total of fifty students were enrolled at the little Locke School.

The groups met on the schoolground and shouts echoed from the forest as hard-packed snowballs sailed like shots between them. Jimmy scored a hit on the face of Corydon Fisher who was one of the older boys in the school. Tossing his tin lunch pail on the porch, the young man ran after Jimmy pelting him with snowballs as he ran. Catching the younger boy, he threw him to the ground where Jimmy struggled and yelled as Corydon

thoroughly washed his face with handfuls of snow.
"Quit it, Cory!" Jimmy said. "I give up."
The older boy continued rubbing snow into Jimmy's face as though he hadn't heard.
"Cut it out, Cory!" Jimmy yelled. "I've had enough!"
"I'll learn you, you little smart aleck. When I'm through with you, you'll know better'n to fool with me!" Cory muttered.
A ring of pupils circled the two fighting boys. "Give it to him, Jim!" several yelled.
Charley sang,

> "Cory's mad an' I'm glad,
> An' I know what'll please him,
> A bottle of wine to make him shine
> An' Sarah Ann to kiss him!"

Sarah Ann Cole, a pretty, buxom girl of sixteen shouted, "Stop it, Cory! You're hurting him!"
Charley's taunts together with Sarah Ann's pleas served to inflame Cory even more. He beat Jimmy's face, already beet red, with his fists until blood spurted from his nose. "When I'm through with you, you won't look so good to the girls," Cory muttered under his breath.
Charley sprang forward and grabbed the neck of the young man's coat. "Stop it, you big ox!" he shouted, momentarily throwing Cory off balance.
Jimmy sprang to his feet and landed a blow squarely on the chin of the kneeling Cory. He fell backward and Jimmy was on him, fists flailing. Charley, beside him, also was getting in a blow now and then.
The shouts of the pupils echoed through the woods and penetrated the schoolhouse walls. Mr. Woodward, the schoolmaster bolted down the steps and seized Cory and Jimmy by the collars of their coats.
Mary walked beside Charley. "You know what you and Jimmy are gonna get when Pa hears about the fight," she said softly.

"Don't tell him."

"Somebody will."

Inside Mr. Woodward still grasped Cory and Jimmy by their collars. He spoke to them in a low tone. The pupils gathered around the wood-burning stove.

"Jim, clean your face," Mr. Woodward ordered. "And Cory, if you must fight, I'd suggest you pick someone your own size and age."

"Little smart aleck," the young man muttered. "Them Averys and Atkins don't need to go to school. They think they know all there is to know."

The teacher rang the bell. When the rough desks and benches were filled, the students took out their slates upon which assignments would be written. As Mr. Woodward called the role, each pupil responded with "Present." Ten children were absent with whooping cough or measles.

Pupils close to the heating stove perspired, while those near the windows or at the back of the room shivered. The metal on one side of the stove glowed red-hot.

Mr. Woodward frowned as Ada Atkins whispered to her brother, Wesley. "Something wrong, Ada?"

The little girl shook her head.

"Something bothering you, Wesley?"

He shook his head.

"Then neither of you have a reason to talk. Wesley, you've not been in school long, but you're in school to learn, not to talk. And I'd suggest, Ada, that you don't again get your brother into trouble. Each of you go stand facing the corner." Slowly the small children made their way to the front of the room where they stood in opposite corners.

The pupils in the first six grades read from McGuffey's Eclectic Readers. Lilla Dale at age six already was using the second reader and soon would go into the third book. Though all of their children did well in school, Marcia and Jonas realized early in her life that Lilla Dale likely would be the one of their children who became the best educated. She usually was found reading, writing stories on her slate or doing arithmetic.

Her parents were concerned, however, because of her vivid imagination. Scarcely a day passed that she didn't report some imaginary happening which she insisted was true. Though she was punished for "lying," she still persisted in composing "stories."

Lilla Dale recalled when she was small that a former lady teacher had "boarded round" at the Avery home. From that time she had declared she would someday be a teacher.

Boarding round with the families of pupils was the usual practice for rural teachers in the 1800's. Salaries were low, only a few dollars a month for women, while men were paid at a slightly higher rate. School boards preferred men teachers because they were better able, physically, to keep the older boys in line. Some of the young men who attended school in winter were twenty years old, and when disputes arose, as they often did, it took a strong teacher to "trounce" the older boys.

Jimmy stared at his arithmetic book with unseeing eyes. Damn that Cory. There had been bad blood between the two of them since the night of the box social at Uncle Samuel's place. Sarah Ann had previously told him which gaily decorated box contained the lunch she had prepared, because she wanted to eat with him. He'd been so eager to bid on the green and yellow ribbon-trimmed box that Cory had guessed it was Sarah Ann's, so he upped the bid several times, only to be topped by a slightly higher bid from Jimmy. Finally he won the prize and Cory had said in a patronizing way, "Let the boy have it."

Cory had watched them jealously as he and Sarah Ann laughed and devoured their lunch while Cory ate silently with old Grandma Andrews. Jimmy had known there would be more trouble. Cory would catch him off the school ground and he was no match for the six foot man who was five years his senior. Well - he had a temper, and if Cory got him mad enough, he'd fight like a tiger - and right now he was about mad enough. He gingerly touched his aching nose. Maybe it was broken. Sarah Ann caught his eye and smiled coquettishly. He returned the smile as Cory's eyes met his.

Mr. Woodward's sharp voice interrupted his daydream. "Jim, is your arithmetic done?"

"No sir." Cory was grinning.

"Get busy. You're wasting time."

He pretended he was working, but in memory he was back at the box social. After dinner the young people had played games, such as London Bridge, Post Office, The Miller and Forfeits. His Pa called socials "bussing bees," because of the exciting kissing games which the young people indulged in. He remembered kissing Sarah Ann and his heart skipped a beat at the memory.

Cory was still staring at him. Suddenly a frightening thought came to his mind. The adults said war was coming. That would solve everything if Cory went to war. He'd be gone and when he came back things likely would have changed. Maybe then he would be a match for Cory if there still was bad blood between them. But maybe Cory wouldn't come back! Maybe he'd be killed - but then Jimmy would feel that in some way, he'd caused Cory's death. His thoughts were so mixed up. He was miserable. He glanced outside. Snow was piling up on the windowsills and sudden gusts of wind had formed snowbanks at the edge of the schoolground.

Tom McCreary frantically waved two fingers in the air. Finally Mr. Woodward saw him. "No, Tom. You'll have to wait until noon. The little boy put his hand down. The look of distress on his face indicated that the trip to the outside privy was necessary, but Mr. Woodward did not relent.

The teacher looked at the older students as he said, "Eighth grade arithmetic, stand." Jimmy, Cory, Sarah Ann, Guy Scofield, Jane Fisher and

Israel Atkins stood beside their desks. "Pass." They walked to the recitation bench before Mr. Woodward's desk on the raised platform. "Sit."

When they were quiet the teacher said, "I will take your slates, correct the figures and have them back to you by afternoon."

"Mine's not done, sir," Jimmy said.

"Why not? You've been wasting time. Do you know how to work interest problems?"

"Yes sir."

"Complete your work before noon. Cory and Jim, go to the board and calculate the interest on this problem." The teacher read a simple interest problem.

Jimmy figured rapidly, raised his hand, and pointed to his answer of $86.55.

"Correct," the teacher said. "Erase your work."

Cory struggled at the board. Jim threw him a triumphant smirk and returned to the recitation seat. Two at a time the remaining students went to the board to solve problems. Still Cory struggled unsuccessfully.

Mr. Woodward watched. "After three winters you still haven't learned how to work simple interest problems." His sarcastic tone implied his low opinion of Cory's intelligence. "These pupils," he motioned toward the class, "are younger than you, yet they are successful. When will you get this simple work through your head?"

"Never!" the young man shouted as he lumbered awkwardly from the platform, seized his coat and cap and opened the door. "I'm quitting, and I won't be back!" The door slammed behind him.

Jimmy's first reaction was one of relief. No longer would he be annoyed by Cory, and he'd have Sarah Ann to himself. But something had happened. Sarah Ann wouldn't look at him. He remembered that for the past two years she had been considered Cory's girl. Maybe he could talk to her at noon after his arithmetic was finished.

When the cold lunches had been eaten and the

necessary trips made to the outhouses, there was still a few minutes before Mr. Woodward pulled the rope above his desk which rang the bell in the belfry overhead. Sarah Ann was hanging her coat when Jimmy came to stand beside her. "Something's the matter with you. What did I do?" he asked.

"I'm sorry for Cory," she said softly. "He don't learn easy like you do, and Mr. Woodward said things that must 'ave hurt his feelings awful bad."

Jim said slowly, "I don't like Cory, and I'm glad he's gone, but 'twould be bad if you didn't learn easy, 'specially when you're as old as he is."

"Jimmy."

"Yeah."

She lowered her voice to a whisper. "I'm still Cory's girl. I was only teasing him with you. I had to tell you."

For a moment he stared at her in amazement, then anger flared within him. He hissed, "'Everybody to their own fancy,' said the old woman as she kissed her cow!" Turning, he strode to his seat without a backward glance. He wished the bell would ring. He didn't want to talk to anyone.

His cousin Israel Atkins shared a seat with him. "Have a fight with Sarah Ann?" he asked.

"None a' your business!"

"You're touchy as a bear with a sore tail. What'd she say to you?"

"None a' your business! Let me alone! She ain't the only pebble on the beach, or the only fish in the sea!"

"No, I guess not."

At last the bell rang and the room again was quiet.

Two months later on April 12th, 1861, the Civil War started when the Southern Artillery shelled Fort Sumter in the South Carolina harbor. After several days the shattering news reached Locke and Conway Townships in Ingham and Livingston Counties. Even though war had been expected, in every heart there had been a glimmer of hope that in some way it might be avoided. But it had happened. They were at war with their southern brothers.

After several days the initial shock wore off and determination set in. "'Twon't last long," Amos Colborn said to Ben and Shobegun. "Johnny Reb'll find out that when he gits us Northeners het up, we'll fight like a barrel a' wildcats. I figger a few weeks an' 'twill be over."

Ben's voice was low but forceful as he said, "We've gotta save the Union. Them Southern varmints have fired on the stars and stripes."

The men stared silently at one another, their faces sober as Ben continued, "To lift a hand against the flag, why, 'tis 'most like a man's lifting his hand against God." He hesitated, then he said, "I'd go an'list, but I'm forty-one years old an' they want young fellers."

Shobegun nodded, "The guv'ment don't want us."

"Soon now," Amos prophesied, "There'll be thousands a' men in the Army. That means that us fellers they don't want will have t' grow crops t' feed 'em. We gotta all pitch in an' do whatever we kin t' save the Union. We'll work an' git ever' bushel a' grain we kin out a' the land - and' 'tis likely prices'll go up. We'll help the Union win the war, an' we'll put money in our pockets at the same time." He hesitated, thinking aloud. "The War wa'nt a' our makin'. Ain't nothin' wrong in makin' a leetle money while we air helpin' feed our soldiers with the grain we grows."

A few miles to the southwest, Samuel Atkins had just driven into his yard. He unhitched and led his horse to the barn. Returning to the buggy he picked up a newspaper from the seat and went into the house. Mary, eight months pregnant, was ironing and the children were playing school.

"Back already?" she asked. "I told the children you'd likely spend three, four hours in Webberville being as the land's too wet to work."

"Mary."

She looked up, startled at his strange tone of voice. "What is it? Are you sick?"

"Look at this." He held up the State Journal dated April 15, 1861. Two inch headlines screamed, "Lincoln Issues A Call For Troops."

"Yes," Mary said calmly. "The President has to have men if we're to win."

"I'm going, Mary."

She dropped clumsily into a chair. "What are you saying? You don't have to go. You have a family. You're needed here on the farm." Her eyes were wide - frightened.

"I have to go. I've known for months that when war came, I'd have to go. My country needs me."

Ada and Wesley stared at their father. "You're going to be a soldier?" Wesley asked with wonder in his voice.

"Yes, son."

"We won't see you, will we?" Ada asked.

"No. I'll be far away. There won't be fighting around here." He turned to Mary. Tears were streaming down her face.

"I'm sorry," she sobbed. "I'm not brave."

He put his arms around her comforting her as though she were a child. "It will be a few weeks before I go. I'll get the crops in and the work caught up. Then I'll enlist in July or August." He smiled. "And maybe it will be over by then. Everyone thinks the South can't hold out long and that they'll soon be on their knees. Johnny Reb will find he's no match for the Yanks. I'll give 'em three months. You see, Mary, three months will be the middle of July. Maybe it'll be over before I enlist, so let's not fuss."

The children had returned to their Saturday play. Mary picked up her iron and exchanged it for a hot one from the top of the cooking stove as Samuel whispered, "I want to wait 'till you have the baby and I know you're all right before I leave."

And so it went throughout Michigan. Before the end of the summer every neighborhood had several men who had answered the President's call for volunteers. In Locke Township Cory Fisher was among the first to enlist, but not before he and Sarah Ann Cole were married.

By the middle of the summer, people in the North were disappointed that fighting was becoming more intensive. They could see the war stretching on into the future. Johnny Reb in his gray uniform and Billy Yank in blue, fought well, but both remained civilians with the civilian's dislike of military rules and regulations. However, each side fought valiantly for their beliefs. At first the North was fighting to save the Union, and freedom for the slaves became an issue at a later time. The South, with Jefferson Davis as President of the Confederacy, did not have the powerful central government of the North with Lincoln as President. Still, the South was determined to be independent of the North, and on July 21, 1861, Northern troops retreated in disorder after the Battle of Bull Run.

Samuel enlisted from Ingham County on August 15. Thirteen days later on August 28th, he was mustered in for three years at Fort Wayne in Detroit.

As he rode the stage from Webberville to Detroit he had plenty of time for thought. As the six horse team pulled the rumbling, brightly-colored stagecoach over the plank road, Samuel thought of the family he was leaving, perhaps forever. Mary had tried to be brave, but more than once he had seen tears spill from her eyes as she nursed Baby George. The warm tears splashed on the tiny face, sometimes rousing George and causing him to again suck vigorously. Ada and Wesley had cried when he left. Did all of them sense, somehow, that he might not come home to them?

His mother, Fanny, had aged in recent months. Even if he came home, Samuel doubted she would still be there, so fragile she had become. He was glad Harmon and Harriet were with her. Harmon wasn't much of a farmer, but he was a good doctor

- if only he'd forget about birds. He spent hours in bird-watching and in writing about his observations. Harmon said he was a doctor and a naturalist whose hobby was ornithology. Samuel had seen him stop his horse while on the way to visit a sick person so that he could study the appearance and habits of a strange bird, apparently oblivious to the needs of his patient.

There was no doubt that Harmon had a brilliant mind. His articles on birds often appeared in local newspapers and his "Book On Birds," was published by the Michigan Agricultural College at Lansing. Harmon's main thrust was that birds should be protected because they destroyed insects and so were friends of the farmer. But Samuel sympathized with Harmon's patients who complained that "Dr. Atkins will come to visit the sick when there's no new bird to watch."

Still - Harmon was a good doctor. Samuel knew he could meet most medicinal needs through his knowledge of botany. He gathered from the woods and fields the plants and herbs from which he brewed effective potions. For example when he had no quinine and Jonas was down with the ague, Harmon had used white popple bark to make a medicine which checked the chills and fever, and numerous neighbors had also reported that the brew cured them of the "shakes." Harmon had put something together which Jonas said relieved the "Avery curse," the asthmatic cough which ran through the Avery family.

The stage rumbled into Fowlerville, pausing only long enough to change horses, before they again were flying over the plank road. Samuel observed the three young men who were riding with him. They, too, had been silent.

"Going to Detroit?" he asked.

"Yep. T' Fort Wayne. I has 'listed," the black-bearded man volunteered.

"Me, too," the other two added.

"Where you from?" Samuel asked.

"Lansin'," two replied.

"Mason," the third man said.

"I'm from north of Webberville," Samuel said. "I'm going to Fort Wayne, too."

"Ya bin in Detroit?" the man from Mason asked.

Samuel shook his head. "Not since I was five years old when we came to Michigan. You been there?"

"Nope. I was borned near Mason. Guess I've got a lot to learn."

The others nodded. The black-bearded man said, "All a' us has, 'specially 'bout fightin' a war. Them Southern fellers is holdin' out longer than I thought they would."

"Holdin' out?" another man said. "Hell, they's whoopin' us. That's why I signed up." He blew a cloud of smoke from his pipe.

Samuel commented, "We stop overnight in Howell. Tomorrow at this time we should be in Fort Wayne."

Again they lapsed into silence. Samuel considered the possibilities of his male relatives enlisting. His only brother, Harmon, was forty years old and his brother-in-law, Jonas, also was forty - both too old. His sister Louisa Scofield's eldest son, Guy, was seventeen and "rarin' to go." Most likely he'd enlist in spite of his family's objections. Then, there were his other nephews, Jim Avery who was fifteen and Israel, Harmon's stepson, who also was fifteen. Unless the war dragged on, they likely wouldn't go.

Samuel stared out at the passing Livingston County countryside. Many farmers were plowing, preparing the land for the planting of winter wheat and rye in September. Well - he had another job to do - a disagreeable duty that must be fulfilled. If he didn't come back, at least he would have been of some service to his country.

Back in Locke the Avery family members were going about their daily tasks. Marcia had finished bathing her senile mother-in-law, Lucy. Alice washed the dishes as Mary brushed and combed her grandmother's gray hair.

"There, Grandma," Mary said, "you look nice."
For a second a vacant smile tugged at the corners of Lucy's mouth, then she lapsed into her usual docile behavior, rocking slowly and staring straight ahead.

Alice said quietly to her mother, "She'll never be better, will she?"

"Uncle Harmon thinks she'll always be as she is now," Marcia replied.

"Why does God do this to her?" Alice asked. "You said she used to be smart - that she read her Bible and other books and that she always was a good woman."

"We don't know why such things happen to people," Marcia replied. "God must have a purpose. We can be thankful she's quiet. Uncle Harmon says some old people who lose their memory are disagreeable, and even violent."

Mary asked, "Where is Lilla Dale?"

"I sent her to gather eggs. Your Pa and the boys will sell them at the store in Webberville tomorrow on their way to Lansing."

"I wish I could go to Lansing," Alice said wistfully.

Marcia smiled. "Our time is coming. Someday we'll ride the stage and go to Lansing, though it would cost a lot of money." She hesitated. "'Course Jimmy and Charley, being boys, should get to go first. That's why Paw is taking them with him to sell the wheat tomorrow. But he'll bring something to all of us."

"Who will milk the cows while they're gone?" Mary asked.

"Uncle Harmon and Israel." Marcia laughed. "Uncle Harmon will be doing more farm work now that Uncle Samuel has enlisted. I'm sure he doesn't like it, but he and Israel will have to do the work on both their farms. But they'll do our milking for one night, even though Uncle Harmon won't be pleased about it."

Lilla Dale, carrying a pail of brown eggs, burst into the house. "Ma!" she shouted. "There's a bear in the woods behind the barn!"

"Lilla Dale, you're imagining things again. You make up good stories, and maybe someday you'll be a writer, but don't say your stories are true."

"But it's true! A big brown bear walked along the edge of the woods in the hay field!"

Mary snorted. "Lilla Dale, don't lie. We haven't seen a bear since I can remember."

The little girl stamped her foot. "I'm sure I saw a bear! I'm going to tell Pa!"

"He'll spank you for lying," Alice said.

"Then I'll tell Jimmy."

Marcia bent to Lilla Dale's level. "You have to stop telling things that aren't true. Last week you saw a deer in the hog pen, and the week before that it was a tiger in the garden. Lilla Dale, it's a sin to lie."

Tears filled the little girl's eyes. "Well - there wasn't any deer or tiger, but I - I _thought_ there was a bear out by the woods."

Marcia walked to the stove and stirred something in a three-legged black iron kettle. "You'd better think about that story and pray that God will help you not to lie."

Lucy's chair squeaked as she slowly rocked. Her facial expression was serene. Marcia glanced at the old woman as she said, "We have to get our housework all caught up this week, because next week is camp meeting. I want to hear every sermon that Reverend Miller preaches."

"And the week after that we'll be back in school," Alice said.

The following morning Jonas and his boys waved to the family as they headed south atop a large load of wheat. In Webberville Jimmy sold the eggs at the grocery store and divided the money with Charley. Excited and eager for adventure in Lansing, a settlement of four thousand people, the boys hurried back to the wagon.

Charley asked, "Where's the first toll gate?"

"There's five between Webberville and Lansing," Jonas answered. "Going toward the west, there's one near Webberville, another at Podunk, the next is at Red Cedar Bridge near Williamston, another one two miles west of Okemos, and the last one about a mile east of Lansing. Before we had the plank road the mud was terrible deep in the spring. Sometimes we'd have to cut trees and throw logs into the mudholes to get the team and wagon through. Time you got across two, three bad mudholes, you was about tuckered out."

The boys were silent as a bright green stagecoach rumbled past. The driver returned their wave and soon the coach was out of sight.

"I'd like to be a stagecoach driver," Charley said. "I'd like to travel and see the world. I'd like to drive a stagecoach from Lansing to New York City."

Jonas grinned. "You're traveling. You're ten miles from home. Here we are at Podunk." He pulled change for the toll from his pocket.

An elderly man hobbled from the toll house. "Morning, Mr. Gorsline," Jonas said passing the money to the old man.

"Morning, Jonas. Takin' your boys to see the city?"

"Yeah. It's their first trip."

"Things have changed since I settled here abouts back in '36. Wagons and buggies and stagecoaches goin' all the time and, and back then there wa'nt even a good trail."

Jonas nodded. "I remember my brother Albert and I walked from Locke to our first work on the dam in Lansing way back in '43."

David Gorsline nodded. "Times has changed," he muttered again.

As they drove on Jonas called, "See you tomorrow on the way home."

Charley still had his mind on traveling. "I'm not going to be a farmer," he announced. "You work all the time and you don't see anything but the same fields."

Jonas clucked to his team. "What do you want to be?"

"I don't know. I just want to see something besides wilderness and fields and cows and horses. Maybe I'd like to work in a big sawmill. I can't wait until I'm old enough to do something exciting." In a moment he said, "I know! I'd like to be a Pony Express rider! Then I'd ride like the wind across the prairie. With my sacks of mail, I'd arrive in a cloud of dust, jump off my horse and grab the mail sack, throw it over the saddle of a fresh horse and take off for the next swing station fifteen miles away."

Jonas laughed. "You've been reading about the Pony Express."

Charley's eyes shone. "They make lots of money. Why, I could be a Pony Express rider now. There's one named David Jay that's thirteen years old, and another, William F. Cody that's fifteen. You know how much they make?"

"No."

"One hundred to one hundred fifty dollars a month!"

"That's big money," Jonas agreed, "but it's a hard life. Hostile Indians, blazing desert heat and freezing blizzards - a Pony Express rider earns his money. Like you say, some of them are young, but their average age is nineteen."

Charley continued, "Just think, last March they carried President Lincoln's inaugural address from Missouri to California in seven days and seventeen hours! That's almost two thousand miles!"

"The Pony Express will soon be replaced by the new transcontinental telegraph system. They figure Omaha, Nebraska and California will be connected and operating sometime in October."

"This year?"

"That's right."

"Then I guess I'll never be a Pony Express rider," Charley said, "but I'll find something exciting to do."

Jim had been silent. His father asked, "What do you want to do, Jim?"

"Guess I'll be a farmer like you. Long's I can

have books to read, too, I want my own farm."

Jonas puffed on his pipe. "Yeah, Jim. You are like me, from the red hair and blue eyes to the quick temper. But neither of you are much like your mother. The girls are like her, especially Lilla Dale." For a time no one spoke, then Jonas continued. "Your Ma is the finest woman I've ever known, but I've disappointed her." Again they were silent.

At last Charley said, "Do you believe in God and the Bible, Pa?"

Jimmy looked at his father quizzically, waiting for an answer. Finally Jonas said, "You've asked me and I won't lie to you. You're both old enough to think for yourselves. I'm an atheist. I don't believe in God. My mother and father were religious, and I never doubted they were right until I was grown. Then I began to have doubts. But I don't want to influence you. You have to decide for yourselves."

Charley spoke to Jimmy. "Ma would cry if she thought we didn't believe in God. I don't want to make Ma cry. I want to smoke a pipe like you, Pa, but Ma would feel bad."

Jonas smiled. "You have plenty of time for that, and plenty of time to decide what you believe about God. For now, you don't need to talk to Ma about it."

They paid at the toll gate near Okemos. As they left Jimmy asked, "Did Chief Okemos live near here?"

"His camp was just south of here on the Red Cedar River. He died in 1858. He was more than a hundred years old. He fought some fierce battles against the whites."

"Why did he fight us?" Charley asked.

Jimmy said, "'Cause the pioneers were taking the Indians' hunting grounds."

"That's right," Jonas agreed. "The poor old fellow died a beggar, a broken old man. We whites didn't do right by the Indians."

"I feel sorry for him," Jimmy said. "We took

the Indians' land and drove them out." Jonas nodded.

As they approached Lansing, Jonas gestured to the south as he pointed to the Michigan Agricultural College. "That's the M.A.C. where Uncle Harmon spends a lot of time. There's a professor there, a Dr. Cooke who worked with him on the bird book they published."

The boys didn't answer. The road was filled with farmers' wagons and with buggies and surreys driven by well-dressed men and ladies. The boys were silent as they took in the sights of numerous two-storied brick buildings, stores, schools and hotels.

"Over there," Jonas pointed, "is the Boys' Reform School. It's been there about five years. That's where they send bad boys. It's just like a jail."

Charley's eyes were wide. "Do they ever get out?"

"They're released when they're eighteen. Then they have a chance to make a better life for themselves."

"What do they do to get put in there?"

"Stealing, constant fighting - just being troublesome and disobedient."

"Do they flog them?"

"Yes, they do. They have to learn to obey their parents, and parents must obey the laws of the state and nation."

By five that afternoon Jonas had sold his load of wheat. Then the horses were put in the livery stable for the night where they were fed and watered. With the boys, he then made his way to Carley House where they would spend the night.

"Have you been here before, Pa?" Charley asked as they entered the lobby.

Jonas nodded. "I always stay here when I sell my grain."

Caroline, older, but still beautiful, was behind the counter speaking to a guest. A white streak in her auburn hair served to add to her attractiveness. As she reached for a key for the guest, Jonas noticed that she wore one of the fashionable large hoop-skirted dresses with full puffed sleeves. The chocolate-brown color was becoming to her. He would get a dress like that for Marcia, only in a different color. With her fair skin and blonde hair, Marcia looked nice in blue.

"Jonas!" Caroline said holding out her hand. "I've been thinking you'd soon be coming in to sell your grain. And these must be your boys."

Jonas smiled. "Mrs. Albert, my sons, Jim and Charley." The boys shook hands as they murmured, "How-do-you-do."

"But you're almost grown," she said. "I was expecting small boys."

"The years pass," Jonas said. "Seems like it was only last year that I boarded here and worked in the woods. You had just opened Carley House - it was sixteen, no - almost seventeen years ago."

"That's right."

"And how are Jennifer and your husband?"

"Jennifer is fine. I don't hear from Ezra more than two or three times a year. He'll likely be along in a few weeks." She hesitated, then went on. "After you finish supper, why don't you and the boys stop in to visit us?"

"Thank you. We'd like that."

"Now as to a room. I'll give you number sixteen. That has two beds." She reached for the key. "We'll see you after supper."

Inside the room the boys immediately went to the kerosene lamp which set on a high chest. "Light it, Pa," Charley said.

Removing the glass chimney, Jonas struck a match and held it to the wick. After replacing the chimney, a steady light shone, illuminating the corner of the room.

"Gosh!" Jimmy exclaimed. "Ma'd like a lamp like that!"

"Think she'd rather have it than a fancy dress like Mrs. Albert's?"

"Let's get her both of them!" Charley said.

"Well -" Jonas hesitated. "Why not?"

After they had washed and combed their hair, they made their way to the saloon where men were drinking and laughing loudly as they played cards. Jonas and the boys sat at a table near the bar. Jonas ordered beer.

"We didn't know you drink beer," Jimmy said.

"Yeah, I do when I'm away from home so Ma doesn't know. No use to upset her." He wiped his mustache. "I don't see anything wrong with drinking so long as you don't overdo it. 'Course some of these fellows won't quit 'till they're dead drunk. Now those over there," he motioned to a noisy group in the corner, "they're already pretty well under the weather. They'll not stop drinking as long as they can stagger to the bar for another drink. Shakespeare said, 'O God that men should put an enemy in their mouths to steal away their brains.'"

"Do you play cards when you're away from home, too?" Charley asked.

"Why?"

"I just wondered."

"Yes, I play cards when I go to saloons in Howell, Fowlerville, Webberville or Lansing."

Jimmy said, "Do you gamble?"

"Sometimes. But I have sense enough to control my drinking and gambling. I believe everything should be done in moderation." For a few minutes no one spoke, then Jonas said, "When I was about as old as you, Jim, I was in Detroit with my father. We met the Colborns there."

"The man with the Indian wife?" Charley asked.

"Yeah. The whole family, only Amos wasn't married then. My father and I sat at a table in a saloon and we drank tea while the Colborn men had beer. They thought we were sissies, I'm sure. One of them said, 'We thought all men drink beer.'" Jonas laughed. "And I told those grown men that Paw and I didn't do anything to harm our bodies, like smoking or drinking. They must have thought I was a smart aleck young one."

Jim asked, "You like the Colborns, Pa?"

"They're nice fellows. 'Course I'm sorry for Amos' children - half-breeds - no man will want to marry that little girl, unless it's an Indian, and most of them have moved up north."

Jim said, "That little girl, Lucy, that was at camp meeting last year didn't look like an Indian.

"She's a pretty girl, but she's half Indian, and she might have children that look as Indian as her little brother. He could pass for a full-blood."

After supper the Averys knocked on Caroline's door. Jennifer, her auburn hair parted in the center and pulled back to fall in a cascade of curls, invited them inside. "My mother will be right out, Mr. Avery." Though she spoke to Jonas, her eyes rested on Jim who returned her speculative gaze.

"Jennifer," Jonas said, "these are my sons, Jim and Charley."

The boys shook Jennifer's hand.

She laughed. "You're all red-headed, just like Ma and me."

"And Jim and I have tempers to go with it," Jonas chuckled. "Now Charley here, he has red hair, but he's like his Ma. He doesn't fly off the handle and say things he's sorry for later."

Caroline came to stand beside Jennifer. Jim thought Caroline in her brown hoop-skirted dress and Jennifer in green were two of the most beautiful women he'd ever seen.

Jonas studied Jennifer. "You look just as your mother did the first time I saw her," he said.

Caroline added, "Only I was a few years older." She moved toward the door. "It's warm in here," she said. "Suppose we sit on the verandah where we'll get a breeze from the south."

Part of the chairs were occupied, but at the far end of the long verandah they found seats. Jim sat where he could study Jennifer. He was overwhelmed by her flawless smooth skin, expressive brown eyes, dark auburn hair and full red lips. She met his eyes with a steady gaze, smiling. He was speechless. But he must say something. He blundered, "Do you - do you - er - do you go to school?"

Caroline and Jonas were carrying on a conversation. It helped that they weren't listening, but Charley was grinning like a Cheshire cat.

"Yes. I go to a female school." When she smiled a dimple showed in her right cheek. "Do you go to school?"

Jim nodded. "There's near fifty scholars at our school. The older boys go only in winter. This year I'll attend about twelve weeks. Younger children that can't work on the land go five and a half days a week. Do you go to school every day?"

"Most of the time." She twisted an auburn curl that had fallen over her shoulder.

Charley said, "I'll help Pa more this year. We got wheat and rye to get in soon now."

Jennifer said, "I think I'd like living on a farm."

"I'm going to leave soon's I'm old enough," Charley said. "I'd rather work with my brains than with my hands."

Jim laughed. "Huh. You're lazier than a pet coon." In a moment he continued. "I'm going to be a farmer. I like growing crops and raising animals, but I have to have books, too. My uncle, Dr. Harmon Atkins, loans me books. He's a naturalist and a doctor."

"Dr. Atkins is your uncle?" Jennifer asked.

"You know him?"

"We read his essays in the State Journal, and we study his "Book On Birds" at school. I cried when I read his essay about the slaughter of passenger pigeons at Pine Lake last spring. Dr. Atkins said thousands of the birds settled in the spruce trees along Pine Lake where they had built nests. Then hunters came and killed and killed and killed the birds and knocked them from their nests."

Jim nodded. "Uncle Harmon has always worried about the passenger pigeons. He says they'll be extinct some day because people want roast squab and pigeon pie. He says the hunters seem to go crazy. They kill and kill until they can't carry all the birds away and hundreds are left where they were knocked from the trees."

"I'd like to meet Dr. Atkins. Does he live near you?"

"Up the road about a mile. He's my mother's brother. When we were small he used to take us on long walks through the woods. That's how I got interested in nature."

"There are so many nice things to do if you live in the country," Jennifer said enviously. "I think I'll marry a farmer." She looked directly at Jimmy. His face flushed, but he didn't speak.

Jonas entered the conversation. "Life in the city is easier for women, Jennifer. Don't you think so, Caroline?"

"I'd never again want to live on a farm," she said vehemently. "Once was too much!"

Jim bristled. "Our ancestors were farmers," he said defensively, "and we've traced our ancestors back to Edward the First of England. He lived before 1300 A.D."

Jennifer was impressed. "You have an ancestor who was King of England?"

Jim nodded. "'Course he likely wasn't a farmer 'cause he was busy conquering Scotland and making good laws. But our ancestors who came to America in 1635 were farmers in Connecticut."

"How did you trace your family back to the 1300's?" Caroline asked.

Jonas replied, "Our family has always kept records and passed them on to the next generation."

"Pa writes in his journal every day," Charley said, "and so does Ma."

"That's nice," Caroline mused. "I only know what my mother told me about our ancestors. My grandparents in the east likely knew more, but they're dead now."

The evening passed all too rapidly for Jim and Jennifer. Regretfully they said goodnight and the boys went to their room. Jonas strolled toward the saloon for a beer, but promised to join the boys soon.

As they undressed by the light of the kerosene lamp Charley said, "You like Jennifer. I can tell."

"Yeah, I do. I've never seen a prettier girl."

Charley grinned. "She looks different than Sarah Ann. 'Course Sarah Ann's married to Cory now."

"Yeah," Jim replied absently. "I don't think Mrs. Albert likes me."

"Why?"

"I don't know. The way she watches me, I just feel as though she doesn't like me."

"Well - you bragged about our ancestor being a king."

"I shouldn't have done that but I thought she looked down on us 'cause we're farmers. But I'll win her over - and - and - someday I'll marry Jennifer."

Charley stared at his brother in amazement, utterly speechless.

Chapter XVIII

DESPAIR AND ROMANCE

(1862)

The terrible struggle to save the Union continued. For years the slavery issue had nagged at the nation. Families, churches and even entire communities in the North argued the problem. Congregations split, some groups because the minister favored, or condemned slavery.

President Lincoln, at his inauguration, directed his remarks to the rebels: "You have no oath in heaven to destroy the government, while I have the most solemn one to serve, protect and defend it." The South held the view that if a state seceded from the Union, the federal government lost all rights in that state.

In the beginning both sides expected an early victory. But one terrible battle followed another with heavy losses. It was not unusual for the army to lose twenty-five of every one hundred men in a major battle. Now both the North and the South realized the struggle would not end quickly. In the beginning volunteers filled the ranks, but as the war wore on volunteer enlistments decreased and men were drafted. Both sides allowed a draftee to pay a substitute to serve for him. In the North a draftee could pay the government $300 to avoid military service.

After Samuel Atkins went into the army, his family waited impatiently for his infrequent letters. Harmon or Jonas called often at the Webberville post office in the hope there might be a message. In part, one letter Samuel wrote to Harmon said:

A soldier has a hard life. The food is poor, pork, beans and hardtack, mostly. When we are on the march our main food is hardtack and coffee. Our cook has never cooked before and he can spoil good food.

We are paid $11 a month, the same as Johnny Reb. They say we might get a raise to $16 next year. But it's not the money, it's the way we have to live that we deplore the most. Usually we're wet and cold, as well as hungry. Our tents are poor protection against winter weather.

We carry Springfield rifles, the same as Johnny Reb. They have a range of two hundred fifty yards. When we go into battle we know the chance we'll be hit is high so we print our name and address on a handkerchief and pin it to our uniform. The wounded are taken to hospitals, but they are sorry places for there are not enough doctors and nurses. Many men die from infection.

Luck, or perhaps God, has been with me. I haven't been wounded or sick. Many of the men have dysentery and they get weaker and weaker until they are taken to the hospital. Many of them die from infection or disease, probably almost as many as are killed in battle.

We have taken hundreds of Confederate prisoners, just as they have captured hundreds of Union soldiers. Prisons are unclean and cold, they tell me.

I wonder how it all will end. Both sides are paying a terrible price in this war. Grant has more men and supplies than Lee, yet the South continues fighting, refusing to admit defeat. Flour is selling in the South for $300 a barrel. Southern prisoners wear ragged gray uniforms and many have no shoes.

It is a comfort to know Mary and the children are well fed and that you are helping them. I've read the North is prospering. Surely Lee can't hold out much longer. Spring will soon be here. If we survive, at least we'll no longer be cold and wet. Everyone has colds. The coughing is terrible. Many already have died with lung fever - and yet Billy Yank is in better shape than Johnny Reb.

There's a rumor that we'll soon be headed for Williamsburg. If it's possible, I'll write Mary from there. Tell her not to let Ada and Wesley forget me. Baby George is too young to remember, but when this war is over, we'll make up for the lonely months I've been away from my family. Don't tell Mary about the terrible conditions here. Just tell her I'm well and that I'll write soon. But Harmon - just between the two of us - I've painted a rosy picture compared to how both armies are forced to live.

Thank you, Brother, for looking after my family. Give my regards to Maw and all the others.

Your brother,
Samuel

The letter arrived in Webberville in early May of 1862 where Harmon also heard that a traveler from Lansing said it had come over the telegraph lines that a battle was raging in Williamsburg, Virginia, and that casualty lists were long.

Whipping up his horse, Harmon hurried north toward home, his heart heavy with an ominous fear for Samuel's safety. Pulling into the Avery yard, he tied his horse and hurried toward the barn where Jonas and his sons were unhitching their teams for the day.

"Uncle Harmon!" Charley shouted.

When he failed to respond in his usual jovial manner, Jonas paused, his hand on his horse's shoulder. "Something wrong?"

"A letter came from Samuel. He's most likely at Williamsburg and there's a battle there." He hesitated. The sober eyes of Jonas, Jim and Charley focused on him. Finally he said, "I'm going to the County Seat at Mason. They post casualty lists on the court house lawn. I'll leave early tomorrow morning. Israel will do the chores at my place and at Samuel's."

Jonas nodded. "I understand. The boys will help him." He coughed nervously. "Going to tell your Maw and Mary?"

"I don't know. Maw's not well, but -"

Jonas unhitched the tugs from the whiffle tree. "He's likely all right, but you'll feel better when you don't find his name on the list."

The doctor nodded and silently made his way to the buggy.

The next morning Harmon and his mother rode the long miles to the county seat. It was a hard road, up hill and down, around swamps, over corduroy cross ways, through mud and mosquito infested woods to be followed by stretches of deep sand.

"Mosquitoes are early this year," Harmon said. His mother nodded, her gnarled old hands tightly clasped in her lap.

Harmon glanced sidewise at the silent figure beside him. "I shouldn't have told you about Samuel's letter," he said softly. "You're not well enough for this trip."

"I'm all right - just old." She hunched forward and rode on in silence.

There were other vehicles on the road, buggies like their own and springless wagons. Once in a while there was one of the new carriages set high on springs, rocking along the uneven road, its coat of paint so dusty that the curly cues and lines were partly obscured.

The faces of the people were somber as the rigs passed them. Harmon let his horse go at his own gait, fearful of what they might find on the bulletin board at the court house. He greeted the people as they passed him.

Fanny murmured, "They're all like us," as a middle-aged couple, their faces drawn as though they were under great strain acknowledged Harmon's greeting and sped on, their buggy banging over the ruts in the road. "They all have folks at the front." The sunshine was warm but Fanny pulled her shawl together and held it tightly as though it helped her to keep a grip on herself.

In town Harmon hitched his horse to a post in the shade on the north side of the court house. People milled about, some leaned against trees, and some sat on the grass. They were silent, or if someone spoke, it was in a whisper. Harmon helped his mother from the buggy and they slowly made their way to the bulletin board where folks solemnly studied the list of names. His eyes quickly swept the three lists. Samuel's name was not under the heading "Killed." He searched the "Wounded" and "Missing" columns. Drawing a deep breath, he said, "It's not there, Maw."

"Thank God," Fanny breathed.

"There's an empty bench. We'll sit over there." Harmon guided her. They sat and waited.

Young wives, sisters, brothers, mothers, fathers, grandparents - all were there for but one purpose - hoping, hoping the name of their loved one would not appear on the green bulletin board.

Old people, their eyesight dim with age or fear stared vainly at the list of names. After a time a younger person would go to help them search, but even young eyes were dim with anxiety. Its numbing grasp made eyes unseeing and minds fumble with facts too awful to contemplate.

And so folks waited. Listless and weary they sat hunched on benches before nearby stores or beneath shade trees, or on chairs set out for them. Some sprawled on the lawn. There was little talking or walking about - only the all but hopeless waiting for sunset to bring the end of the battle that much closer.

By noon the lists were ominously long. The battleground must be a slaughterhouse. And here they sat, helpless, while their loved one faced enemy muskets and cannon. When would this war end? Would they keep on killing and killing each other until they all were dead while the awful news of it was killing the home folks?

An old couple made their way to the board for the third time since Fanny and Harmon had watched. The man was slender and appeared frail. The wife, big-stomached and pouch-breasted, clung to her husband's arm. They got up close and squinted at the names. Then they turned and walked away. But after they had gone half way across the lawn, they turned and went back. Again they stared at the board before they asked a young woman to look for them. She must have found the name for she cried as she put her arms about the old people. But they stoically stared into the distance, refusing to give in to their grief. They walked away up the street, the old woman still clinging to her husband's arm. They looked no different except that their faces were set in a frozen, impenetrable grimace.

The hearts of the watchers ached for the old couple, but no one approached them. Each person had his own personal anxiety and dread. At the next posting, or the next, the name of their own loved one might appear.

There were groups who cried and clung to one another and wiped away the tears on sodden handkerchiefs. Some, their faces swollen with crying, turned in despair from the bulletin board. Fanny's and Harmon's hearts ached with pity as they watched the grief-stricken all the long afternoon.

Harmon went to the board each time new names were posted. Though he was only forty-one years old, he felt aged. Accustomed as he was to death in his profession as a doctor, this mass of grief and sorrow was overpowering. The air seemed heavy, oppressive. The awful cost to human hearts of this war should be recorded as a warning to the young. But folks would forget after a spell. They'd have to learn the same lessons about war that their fathers and grandfathers had learned. He made his way back to his mother.

"There's no one we know - no neighbor boys," he said softly.

Fanny sighed and lifted her head. "That's good."

Another long wait. The shadows lengthened as the afternoon wore on. Again the man in shirtsleeves came out of the courthouse, and climbing onto a chair he slowly wrote in newly received names. Then he jumped down and hurried inside as though to avoid witnessing the grief that was certain to follow. The crowd pressed forward. Some gave a quick glance and hurried away, thankful and relieved. Others searched the names over and over as though they couldn't believe their good fortune that their loved one's name was missing. Others read with abject silence, or with a sob as they saw the name that put an end to their hopes.

Harmon was one of the last to get close to the board. He planted his feet wide apart and braced himself as his eyes skimmed the names in the "Killed" column. His heart lurched as the ominous words, "Atkins, Samuel Merritt, May 5, 1862, Williamsburg, Virginia" fairly leaped into his consciousness. Like the others, he must read it again. It was true. His brother was dead.

He felt nauseated. He'd have to tell his mother and Mary. He was shaking. He must get hold of himself. He turned and took a deep breath and made his way slowly toward the bench where Fanny waited. Her lined old face was deathly white. She knew. Her eyes met his and he nodded slowly.

He sat beside her and patted her hand. Finally he said, "Come on, Maw, it's time we was starting home."

He helped her into the buggy. She was so weak and feeble. She'd aged today. They started on the long road back to Locke Township. They slumped silently in the buggy seat, and the bay mare plodded on. They would be a long time getting home. They dreaded telling Mary that her husband was dead and that she was a widow with three fatherless children. A screech owl called from a pine overhead. In the distance a whip-poor-will whistled to his mate.

They did not speak, each one deep in thought. In the North and South, over all the land that May evening in 1862 there were many sorrowful hearts like their own.

Three weeks later Jonas picked up a letter in Samuel's handwriting addressed to Mrs. Samuel Atkins. He fingered the thin parchment-like paper. Driving slowly toward home, he wondered how this last message from her husband would affect Mary. She had settled into a stoic acceptance of her widowhood. Mary was not one to weep and complain before others. And Fanny. The old woman was alert mentally, but physically she was failing. Getting old was Hell. His own senile mother, Lucy, once so educated and alert, sat in her rocker day in and day out as she had for years, her hands folded in silent resignation. Marcia and the family did what they could for the old woman, but Jonas wondered if his mother realized they were trying to help her. Marcia insisted on taking Lucy to church each week where she sat quietly like a well-trained child. She was not troublesome, but like an infant, she was entirely dependent on her family.

Suddenly a thought flashed through Jonas' mind. Samuel's letter! Maybe it was all a mistake. Perhaps his name had been included as "Killed," and he was only wounded, or perhaps the whole thing was an error! Hurriedly he dug the letter from his pocket to study the postmark. The date May 9, 1862 was plainly stamped in the circle with Williamsburg, Virginia, above it. It was a slim chance, one he'd not even mention to anyone. No use to get their hopes up.

When he drove in the yard, Marcia and Lilla Dale were feeding the mother hens and their baby chicks. Six little A-shaped coops set between the house and barn. Clucking mother hens inside the coops called the little ones to their dinner of fine cracked corn. Marcia straightened and Lilla Dale skipped toward the buggy.

"There's a letter for Mary from Samuel," Jonas said.

Marcia brushed back a lock of blonde hair, her blue eyes troubled. "Oh! I'm afraid 'twill be like tearing open an old wound for her to read it."

Jonas nodded. "Maybe you should take it to her." He jumped from the buggy and pulled the letter from his pocket.

"I'll go soon's I wash my hands." She went inside the house to return a moment later."

Lilla Dale said, "Can I go, Ma?"

Marcia took the letter and climbed into the buggy. "You stay with Pa and the girls. I don't know how long I'll be gone." She clucked to the horse, "Get up, Prince."

A few minutes later she tied the horse in Mary's yard. The house was quiet, but the doors were open. "Mary!" she called. "Are you here?"

The slender woman came to the door. "Come in," she said. "The baby's sleeping and Ada and Wesley are at Harmon's."

Marcia held out the letter. "Jonas got this at the post office."

As Mary's eyes took in the familiar handwriting, the color left her face. "Samuel," she gasped. "It's from Samuel." She stared at the letter making no move to open it.

After a moment Marcia asked, "Would you like to be alone?"

"Please," she said without looking up. When Marcia was gone, Mary slowly opened the letter. She read:

> My dearest wife and children,
>
> I write to you from the battle field near Williamsburg. I am mortally wounded. When this reaches you, your children will be fatherless. Soon I will go to my final rest.
>
> I have fought well, my darling. I was shot trying to rally our broken forces. I think I could have escaped, but I couldn't run until all hope was gone. Our cause is just. In time God will give us victory.
>
> I must say goodbye to you and our children. You've been a good wife, and now you'll be both mother and father to the children.
>
> It is almost morning. I have spent most of the night writing to you. I'm suffering for a bullet hit me in the chest. I don't think it will be long now.
>
> I've asked a friend to send my gold watch to Wesley. The Rebels didn't take that though they took my horse, saddle and pistols.
>
> Farewell wife and children. We will meet again.
>
> Your loving husband and father,
> Samuel

Mary sat for a long time staring at the familiar

handwriting through tear-filled eyes. She must be brave for the childrens' sake. They missed their father. Ada and Wesley knew he wouldn't be coming home and that he was buried somewhere in Virginia at a place called Williamsburg. She had to keep their lives as pleasant as possible. Samuel's family would help her. His brother, Harmon, and sisters, Louise and Marcia, all were helpful. But they, too, had problems. Marcia had poor Lucy to care for and Harmon and Harriet were looking after the aging Fanny, and Louise and Stephen Scofield were worried about their eighteen year old son, Guy, who had enlisted. The last they heard he was somewhere in Ohio. Why, Guy was just a boy, but she'd read there were thirteen and fourteen year old soldiers. When would the killing end? What was it all about?

Slavery. Secession. Preserve the Union. Just words. Mary had never seen a negro, and neither had most rural Michigan people. Secession. If the South wanted to leave the Union was it worth thousands of lives to force them to remain? Maybe two countries at peace would be better than the two sections fighting one another.

Mary rubbed her forehead. Samuel died to preserve the Union. He believed the cause was worth dying for. She must put these rebellious thoughts from her mind.

Gradually over the next few weeks the Avery and Atkins families accepted Samuel's death. They rolled up their sleeves to produce every possible bushel of grain. The war brought prosperity to Michigan farmers such as they had never known. Bumper crops made it possible for them to send large shipments of grain to the Union armies.

Much to Marcia's disgust there was an enormous increase in the production of hops. A heavy tax on whiskey and a growing taste for lager beer heightened the demand for hops, a major ingredient in the brewing of beer. Jonas, like many farmers, raised hops. Though Marcia objected, he turned a deaf ear to her pleas.

In August the wheat was cradled and flailed and prepared for market. Both Charley and Jim now were doing a man's work. Though Charley was younger, because there was friendly rivalry between them he forced himself to turn out as much work as his sixteen year old brother. Jonas encouraged the rivalry since it resulted in increased productivity.

A man could cradle an acre of wheat in a day. As Jonas and his boys stopped for a drink of water from the jug under a shade tree, Jonas remarked, "Next year we'll buy a reaping machine."

"We'll still have to flail the grain by hand though," Charley objected.

"It won't be many years before there'll be a machine to flail it for us."

Jim replied, "By the time I can buy land, farming will be easy."

Charley retorted, "You can farm, but soon's I'm old enough I'm getting off the farm." He grinned at Jim. "But I can do as much work as you any day."

Jonas removed his tattered straw hat. "The grain's turning out good. We'll likely have more than one load."

"Going to sell it in Williamston or Lansing?" Jim asked.

Charley laughed. "I know what you're thinking, Jim. You're hoping for Lansing so you can see Jennifer!"

Jim's face flushed. "Maybe she's not there. The last letter I had in June she said she'd be going back East early. I wonder why her mother wants her to go away to school."

Jonas shook his head. "I've wondered too. You'd think that being as she's Caroline's only chick, she'd want her at home. She's going to one of those fancy finishing schools, I understand."

Jim was silent for a moment before he said bitterly, "Her mother hopes she'll find some dude in New York. She don't like farmers."

Charley giggled. "You'll win Jennifer's heart

and hand, big brother, in spite of her mother."

Jonas brushed back his perspiration drenched hair and replaced his hat. "She's a nice girl, Jim. Can't say as I blame you for liking her. She's a spittin' image of her mother the first time I saw her back in 1845."

"When are we going to take a load of grain?" Jim asked.

"It's a busy time, and we can't spare more than one away from the farm at a time. We should have a load flailed by next week that you could take, Jim, and the next load Charley could take."

"Gosh!" Charley exclaimed. "I could take a load alone to Lansing?"

Jonas nodded. "The price usually is better there." He grinned. "And Jim can see Jennifer."

A week later at the Lansing elevator, Jim pocketed the money from his father's wheat. After caring for the team at the livery stable, he made his way to Carley House. Caroline, beautiful as ever, was writing in a ledger as he entered the lobby. He was conscious of her nervous start when she saw him.

"'Afternoon, Mrs. Albert." His level gaze met hers. "I'd like a room for the night, please."

Her hands fluttered nervously as she closed the ledger. "Certainly, Jim." Her eyes went to the door. "Are you alone?"

"Yes, mam. I brought a load of wheat to market."

She shoved the register toward him. "Sign, please." She reached for a room key. "You can have number ten," she said. "Supper's at six." She turned abruptly and went toward her living quarters.

In his room, Jim stood for a long time at the window. The woman's behavior puzzled him. He could sense her dislike. What was the matter with him? He watched the people passing on the board walk before Carley House. Some carried packages. It was near the supper hour and they likely were going home.

Suddenly he saw her. Jennifer, auburn hair piled high, in a white hooped skirt and carrying a basket over her arm, went down the steps of Carley House toward a well-tended flower bed. Bending, she cut sprigs of delphinium and cosmos and placed them in the basket.

Walking rapidly through the empty lobby and down the steps, Jim came up behind Jennifer. Boylike, he asked, "Miss, would you recommend Carley House to a stranger?" She turned. Her dark eyes were serious. "Jim!" she exclaimed, holding out her hands. "I've been hoping you'd come before I go back east, but I'd about given up hope. I leave tomorrow."

"I'm glad I'm in time." He looked down at her, still holding both her hands. "It would have been awful if I'd come after you'd gone, 'cause then I wouldn't see you for another year."

She glanced toward Carley House and squeezed his hands. "My mother's watching," she said softly.

He dropped her hands. "Can I see you this evening?"

"I'll manage it. You sit on the verandah after supper and I'll come out when I can."

At the table the conversation was mostly about the progress of the war. Nearly everyone had lost a relative or friend.

"My uncle, Samuel Atkins, was killed in May at Williamsburg," Jim said. "From what I read and from a letter we had from him in February, I guess the men were cold and miserable most of the winter."

"Yeah," an older man went on. "The life of a soldier ain't easy. My boy wrote that men was dying from measles, smallpox, typhoid and lung fever."

There was silence as each person was occupied with his own thoughts and the excellent meal of potatoes, steak, bread, sweet corn and apple pie.

Finally a drummer chuckled. "When I was in Detroit a few days ago I read a letter in the Free Press from a fellow that signed himself "an old soldier." He said in the winter that new soldiers oughta let their beards grow to protect their throat and lungs. And he recommended wearing a soft felt hat with a crown high enough to allow for air over the brain."

The men laughed. One gray-haired farmer said, "I hear that in most campaigns more men die from sickness than by the bullet."

"Yeah," the drummer added. "Last December my youngest brother wrote from Kentucky. He said he'd never heard such coughing as there was in his camp. It was so bad that drill commands couldn't be heard."

Several shook their heads as they visualized the misery and discomfort of the soldiers. Finally the men shoved their chairs back from the table and lighted their pipes. As the elderly farmer blew smoke rings, he muttered, "I wonder how long this danged war will last."

"I think we still got a long row to hoe," the drummer said as he brushed a crumb from his red plaid vest. "Johnny Reb won't give up 'till we beat him plumb into the ground."

"Well, by gum!" the old man said. "Billy Yank's jest the feller that'll do it!"

Soon the men drifted into the bar room and Jim went to the verandah. Picking up a State Journal from a vacant chair, he went to the far end of the long porch where he sat down to wait for Jennifer.

War news filled the paper. He wondered where his eighteen year old cousin, Guy Scofield, might be. Guy's mother was terribly worried about the welfare of her third child, and especially so since the death of her brother, Samuel.

Unlike most of his friends, Jim had no desire to join the army. Many from Locke Township, only a year or two older than he, were gone. He didn't think about it much, but secretly he hoped the war would be over before he reached draft age. Somehow it seemed useless to line up two sides to shoot at one another just to see which side could kill the most men. Maybe he was a coward, but the whole idea of killing and killing seemed senseless.

Important decisions, like preserving the Union and the slavery issue, should be decided through talking, not through killing. But because such opinions were considered unpatriotic, Jim didn't voice his opinions.

He glanced up. Jennifer was threading her way through the groups congregated on the verandah. His heart pounded. She was the most beautiful girl he had ever seen, and one day in the future, she'd be his wife.

He stood as she approached. "Did you think I wasn't coming!" she asked, carefully arranging her full white skirt as she sat on the bench. "Ma found things for me to do."

When she smiled, the dimple in her right cheek enhanced her beauty. "I'd 'ave waited no matter how long your mother kept you busy."

"You're nice." She patted his arm. "Ma said I must finish packing because the stage leaves at ten o'clock tomorrow, and if I left packing 'till morning, I'd forget something."

For a moment Jim was silent, then he asked, "You like school in New York?"

"I guess so." She sighed. "Ma says they'll teach me to be a proper lady."

"You seem a proper lady to me now," Jim replied. "What're they teaching you, how to hold your cup and which fork to use when you eat pie?"

Jennifer giggled. Again the beguiling dimple showed. "Yeah, things like that. And I shouldn't say "yeah," but "yes."

"Here in Michigan we don't judge people by the way they talk, and which fork they use. Someway, it doesn't seem important to us. Many of our neighbors don't use proper English, but they're helpful, friendly people and we like them as well as the educated folks." He paused. "There's a farm family a few miles from us. They can read and write and figger, but they're not well educated. In fact the man of the family is married to an Indian woman."

"Really?"

"She's strange - quiet - but Amos, the husband, says she's a good wife. He has a peg leg and she works in the fields with him."

"Are there children?"

"Yeah. Four, I think, though the two oldest girls are married. Then, there's a girl thirteen, Lucy, and a boy a couple years younger."

"Do the children look Indian?"

"The boy does, but Lucy is a real pretty girl. Her skin and hair are dark, but her eyes are blue like her father's. She used to be terribly shy, but now she talks to me. Pa sent me to their place to buy seed potatoes this spring. Lucy was outside helping her father and we talked a few minutes. She likes farming. 'Course, that's all she knows."

Jennifer swatted a mosquito on her arm. "Ma thinks culture is important. That's the way her mother was brought up in New York, but here in Michigan when Ma came as a young girl, the family had a hard time. They almost starved. There were no books, no concerts, none of the things she'd been taught cultured people enjoy." She lowered her voice so it was almost a whisper. "I think Grandpa Carley was a n'er do well, and I believe deep down, Ma feels the same way about my father."

"Oh? I've never met Mr. Albert."

"No. Hardly anyone in Michigan has. I don't really know my father. He comes about two times a year. He'll soon be along again, but I'll be gone." She paused. "It's a strange way to live, but Ma says she likes it this way. I think she doesn't like men much."

"Hm-m-m. Maybe that's why she doesn't like me."

"My mother's not a friendly person. She keeps things to herself. Nice clothes, money and culture are important to her. She doesn't like Michigan - she'd much rather be in New York, but here she has Carley House and she does well. The rooms most always are filled."

"How do you feel about living in Michigan?"

"I like it better than New York."

"Still think you'd like living on a farm?"

Jennifer turned to look into his eyes. "It's what I've always wanted."

"I wish you could see our farm. Pa's a good farmer. 'Course Charley and I help, and he pays us. Someday I'm going to have my own land."

"What's your mother like?"

"She's tall and thin. She has gold-colored hair that she parts in the middle and pulls back into a wad at the back. Her eyes are blue."

"I mean what's she like? Is she friendly? Does she talk to you about things?"

Jim was silent for a time before he answered. "She's quiet, always busy. She cares for Grandma Avery - she's lost her mind. Ma never complains. I wonder how she does it. She is as near a saint as I ever expect to see."

He went on. "Now take me. I'm like Pa. I lose my temper and yell and throw things. Not Ma. I'd think she'd be boiling inside sometimes."

"Why? 'Cause there's so much work?"

"It's not the work." He hesitated. "I'm not sure she's happy. Ma is religious. She always has been, and the last year or two she's read everything she can find on a religious group called the Seventh-Day Adventists. They believe the true Sabbath is Saturday, and not Sunday. They're very strict about how they live in anything that affects health. No alcohol, tobacco, coffee or tea are allowed, and they won't eat pork because in the Bible, Jesus cast evil spirits out of someone and they went into the hogs, so the Adventists say pork is unclean."

"How about you, Jim? Are you religious?"

"I'm not sure. My father is an atheist."

"Oh? That must be hard for your mother."

Jim nodded. "Pa says Ma's the best woman he's ever known, but he hurts her bad. Ma knows he drinks and gambles when he goes to town and she feels bad about it, but she always says she'll keep praying and some day God will save him."

"Your sisters - are they religious?"

Jim laughed. "Alice, Mary, and even little Lilla Dale are just like Ma. If she becomes a Seventh Day Adventist, they will too. Charley and I are not sure. I guess we've been with Pa too long and we kind of think like he does."

Jennifer brushed back an auburn lock of hair. "Tell me about the farm. I know you raise wheat, but what else do you grow?"

"Oats, barley, rye, corn - and the last couple of years, hops."

"Don't they use hops to make liquor?"

"Yeah. And that's another thing that worries Ma. She's come as near to fighting with Pa about that as anything I can remember. She says it's a sin to make money off a crop that only sends men to Hell. But Pa won't give in. He says the small crop of hops he grows won't make any difference in the drinking, and that it makes him good money." Jim chuckled. "Ma forgets wheat and rye are used to make whiskey as well as flour."

"I wish I could meet your mother," Jennifer said softly, "and your sisters, too."

"Next summer when you're home from New York, you could come to Webberville on the stagecoach. Then I'd meet you and you could spend the day with us. If you took the last coach back in the evening, you'd be home by ten o'clock."

"I'd like that."

"I've been thinking about the things I'd show you at the farm. I have two cows of my own, and I'm saving money to buy a team. It'll be a few years before I can buy land, but that day will come." He paused, then went on, stumbling over his words. "It's - it's what I've always wanted if - if - I can find the right wife to share it with." He grasped her hand. "Will - will you marry me someday?"

She gasped. "Oh, Jim. Yes. Yes."

Suddenly his arms were about her and their lips

met in a lingering kiss. Oblivious to their surroundings, they reveled in each others closeness.

Caroline's icy voice shocked them and brought them to their senses. "Jennifer! Come inside this minute! And you, young man, are like all the others - always looking for an opportunity to take advantage of a young girl. Jim Avery, you're not to see Jennifer again - not ever again!"

He was on his feet. "But Mrs. Albert. We -"

Caroline turned, her skirts swishing. "Hark! There's nothing to talk about! Come Jennifer."

With a shake of her head and a backward look at Jim, Jennifer reluctantly followed her mother into Carley House.

Angrily, Jim stamped inside and through the lobby to the barroom where he ordered his first drink. Three hours later at closing time, the bartender half carried him to his room and dumped him on the bed.

Chapter XIX

DISAGREEMENT AND DISASTER

(1863)

The wheels of war ground on. Across both the North and South, in every neighborhood families mourned the loss of one or more sons. In Locke Township the latest casualty was that of Guy Scofield who had not died in battle but had succumbed to a lingering case of dysentery in an army hospital at Cincinnati, Ohio. His body was one of the few to be shipped home for burial in the Bell Oak Cemetery.

The death of her son, Samuel, and grandson, Guy, had a devasting effect upon the matriarch, Fanny. Frail and physically ill, she sank into depression and lost all desire to live. In spite of the family's efforts to coax her back to a semblance of her former self, she repeatedly turned away with the whispered remark, "Let me rest." Daughter Marcia and daughter-in-laws Harriet and Mary prepared tempting food which Fanny refused. Harmon's numerous herb remedies likewise were refused, always with the plea, "Let me rest." Finally after several weeks during which she grew progressively weaker, Fanny Atkins died quietly. Looking down on her mother's serene face as she lay in the rough coffin, Marcia murmured, "She has her wish. Now she's at rest."

And still the war wore on. Neighbor after neighbor lost sons to the fierce onslaught. Cory Fisher, Charles Rowley, Charles Cole, James Wilder, William Shaw - almost every month news came of a death in Locke Township.

Early in July of 1863 a terrible battle was

fought at Gettysburg. For the first three days of July, the Northern army of 90,000 men met the Southern army of 75,000 in the greatest battle ever fought in the Western Hemisphere.[1] General Lee decided to aim directly at the center of the Union troops. Under General Pickett, the Southern troops, marching in perfect parade formation, swept across an open field near Gettysburg, ignoring the murderous enemy fire. For twenty terrible minutes they held their ground. Then they yielded to superior Northern strength and fell back.

Lee withdrew his battered army to Virginia. Much to President Lincoln's disgust, the Northern General George Meade made little attempt to follow him and the Confederate army escaped. However, Gettysburg was the turning point in the war. Lee had lost more than 20,000 men dead and wounded and never again had the strength to undertake a major offensive.

Jonas, Jim and Charley worked from daylight to dark during the war years to wrest every possible bushel of grain from the land. Prices were good though inflation never reached the level that it had in the South where the Free Press reported that while the six week siege raged for control of Vicksburg, Mississippi, the starving city saw wheat sell for $100 per bushel and rats appeared for sale in food stores.

As Jonas and his boys surveyed their neatly stacked sheaves of wheat, Jim said, "Farming's getting easier. Now we have a reaper and the threshing machine will be here in a few days. I'm glad we don't have to cradle and flail the grain by hand anymore. Now a few men do in hours the work that used to take days."

Charley remarked, "The war brought prosperity to farmers." He stared at the distant horizon. "But

----

1. World Book Encyclopedia

when I leave, I think I'll go north around Saginaw. I'll work there in a lumber mill or in the woods."

Jonas brushed a sweat bee from his beard. "Might's well get the wanderlust out of your blood, Charley. When you plan on going?"

"Maybe this winter. Only Ma won't want me to leave. She'll cry and I can't stand that. And she'll worry that I'm in bad company and that I'm smoking and drinking. I don't know how I'll tell her I'm leaving."

Jonas nodded. "Marcia's whole life is her family and her religion. The girls don't worry her but her men - well - she never gives up hope of converting us."

Jim removed a stem of timothy from between his teeth. "She's making plans with the girls to go to the meetings in Webberville. Even Lilla Dale is writing religious poems now."

"Yeah." Jonas removed his straw hat and ran his hand through the gray streaked red hair. "One of us will drive them to their meetings if we have the hops picked by then."

Three weeks later in the evening while Marcia and Jonas sat at the table writing in their journals, she said, "The meetings start on the Sabbath. Will you or the boys take us?"

Jonas closed his journal with a bang. "Damn it, Marcia! Those meetings last for a week!"

"Sh-h-h. Don't swear."

He lowered his voice so the young people in the loft wouldn't be wakened. "Next week is going to be damned busy. We have the hops to pick and to get to the kiln in Lansing. You know as well as I do that they have to be picked soon's they're ripe or they'll spoil. We need every hand we've got, and you want to take the girls and one of the boys to go hear some crack-pot Seventh Day Adventist preacher!"

"Sh-h-h. Your voice is loud again." She paused, waiting for his eyes to meet hers. At last he looked up and she continued in a low determined tone. "I refuse to let the girls pick hops. If you're going to grow hops to make alcohol to send men to Hell, you'll do it without the girls' help." In a minute she continued. "We'll need one of the boys to drive the surrey each day to the meetings."

Jonas' eyes flashed. "What in hell's got into you? Has that damned Adventist religion made you batty? I can't spare one of the boys! I think you've lost your senses!"

"I don't often cross you, Jonas, but this time I'm standing firm. We're going to the meetings, your mother, the girls and I. If you won't let Jim or Charley drive us, I'll do it myself."

"What ails you Marcia? I've never seen you so obstinate!"

She got up from the table. "God is on my side. He wants us to go to the meetings and He doesn't care if your hops spoil!" She walked into the bedroom with a determined step, her head high and her back straight and rigid.

Jonas followed his wife. "You've never driven the surrey," he argued. "It's harder than driving one horse on the buggy."

She turned to face him, her eyes steely-blue. "I can do it and I _will_ do it - and we'll go to every meeting whether you like it or not. And while we're talking plain-like, I wish you'd consider what you're doing to the boys with your atheistic ideas and the way you live."

Jonas angrily strode to the table and seized Marcia's Bible which he flung across the room. The Bible struck the wall and fell open on the rag-carpet-covered floor. He shouted, "The boys have brains enough to see through this religious sham! They don't have to be told!"

Marcia hastily picked up her Bible. Holding it to her breast, she said, "I hope God can forgive you for the way you live. If you don't repent, you'll go to Hell. I know what happens when you or the boys are in town. I know about the sinful things you do - the drinking, card-playing and gambling - and - and only God knows what else. And I know about some of your business deals. You beat people who are slow at figures. You're dishonest. Jonas, God will punish you. He'll punish you horribly."

Jonas stood at the door silently staring into the darkness. He didn't speak as Marcia continued. "I've known for a long time, but I'd hoped you'd see the light and come back to God - the God you knew when you were young. I only hope it doesn't take a terrible tragedy to open your eyes."

"What do you mean?" His voice was low and controlled.

"This war - our boys might be called and you know what could happen to them." She hesitated. "God moves in mysterious ways -"

"Let's not cross our bridges 'till we get to 'em."

"I won't mention this again, but my mind's made up. I'll drive the surrey to the meetings and I'll keep praying for you and the boys. Please think about what I've said."

Silently he went outside into the night to walk over his land and to think. Cicadas buzzed in the warm August evening air. The low tinkle of the cowbell on Maggie's neck told him the herd was pasturing in the nearby woods. Just over the fence a horse neighed, sensing his presence. The dog, Rover, nuzzled his hand and Jonas bent to pet the faithful animal. Walking slowly with the dog at his heels, he pondered. Financially he had prospered. He had earned every cent by hard work - but Marcia was right - sometimes he had taken advantage of a slow-witted neighbor in business deals.

He hadn't known she knew about the drinking and gambling. And, as usual, she was right about Jim and Charley. They lived as he did when they were away from home. But they'd be all right. All young fellows sow a few wild oats. He'd sowed a few himself. He recalled his first sexual encounter with the maid at the Steamboat Hotel in Detroit, and the one tempestuous experience with Caroline Carley shortly before he and Marcia were married.

That Caroline - she was a strange one. To see her at Carley House anyone would believe she was cold and unresponsive to men. But he knew different though never again, after that January afternoon had she given him the slightest encouragement. She treated him as she did all guests, politely, but with aloofness.

Jim was smitten with Caroline's daughter. Jonas wasn't sure she'd make a good wife for a farmer, but that was Jim's decision. He wondered again about her father and the strange marriage of her parents.

He thought of his senile old mother who obeyed Marcia as though she were a child with no mind or will of her own. How many years had she been like this? Twelve or fourteen?

The air was soft and warm. He sat on the ground and leaned against the trunk of an ancient oak. He thought of his father, Stephen, and remembered that he'd died doing charity work. He'd been a strict father, a deeply religious man and a civic-minded citizen.

Suddenly Jonas was seized with a spell of coughing. His chest felt tight. The hacking cough continued and the wheezing whistling sound of his labored breathing caused Rover to nuzzle his face sympathetically. The cough became more intense until he raised the phlegm which caused the trouble. Sighing, he rested his head against the rough bark. Damned Avery curse - it always plagued him worse after he lost his temper.

What was it Marcia had said? That God might send some horrible tragedy to open his eyes? He stirred uneasily. The universe was so vast, so complicated, yet so orderly. He could understand why people sensed a need for an all-powerful being. It was comforting to them to feel a strong force controlled the universe. This force was what they called God.

Jonas scratched his head. The problem was too great for him to solve. Tomorrow he and the boys would start picking hops. He'd not ask the girls to help with Marcia feeling as she did. Without the girls they'd have to work like blazes to get the crop picked and to the kilns in Lansing before it spoiled. There was no other way - if Marcia was determined to go to those meetings, she'd have to drive the team on the surrey.

The next morning Marcia conducted family devotions as she had every morning since their marriage. Jonas and the boys were restless and eager to get into the field, but out of respect for Marcia, they remained seated until the scripture reading and prayers were completed.

Later as father and sons worked at picking the scaly, cone-like fruit from the twining hop stems, Charley remarked, "Not many farmers around here grow hops, Pa."

"Yeah. Two years ago when Harmon brought me a paper from M.A.C. that explained their experiments at the college, I decided I'd like to try the new crop. It's made us good money. Sometimes, though, I wish I hadn't started it. Your Ma is dead set against the whole thing."

Both boys were silent. At last Jim said, "Don't you think one of us oughta drive them to their meetings?"

Jonas' eyes flashed. "No, damn it! We've got to work from daylight to dark to get the hops picked. You know damn well they spoil fast after they're ripe. One of you will have to take a load to the brewery in Lansing this afternoon, and another load day after tomorrow. If your mother's so set on going to the meetings, she'll have to get there the best way she can!"

After a long silence Jim said, "Last time I was in Webberville the train went through and the grays 'most got away from me."

"There's two trains a day. One at seven in the morning and the other at half past five in the afternoon. There won't be any problem with trains. I'm all for letting her find out that driving a team on a surrey's a man's work. I'll hitch them up for her and then she's on her own." None of them discussed the matter further, though Jonas felt the boys secretly sympathized with their mother.

Two days later in early afternoon, Jim sat atop the wagon box filled with hops. The long slow trip to the Lansing brewery passed quickly as he daydreamed about Jennifer. He hadn't talked with her since the previous summer when Caroline had ordered him never to see her daughter again, but they had written often, long affectionate letters in which they planned for the future together. Tonight after he had delivered the hops to the brewery he'd visit Carley House and together, he and Jennifer would meet Caroline to tell her of their intentions.

After stabling the horses for the night Jim rented a room at Benton House which was located on the northwest corner of Washington Avenue and Main Street. After supper he walked to Carley House.

The old building looked as he remembered it, well kept and tidy with guests rocking on the long verandah. His heart pounded as he walked into the lobby. A man stood behind the counter. He looked up. "You'd like lodging and supper?" he asked.

Jim shook his head. "I'd like to see Miss Albert and her mother if they're here."

The man motioned. "Down the hall, first door on your right." He returned to counting the money.

Jim turned, smoothed his red hair, took a deep breath and walked toward the door of Caroline's living quarters. He hesitated, then squaring his shoulders, he knocked firmly on the oak-paneled door. As it opened he looked past Caroline to Jennifer who sat reading the newspaper before the window.

"Good evening, Mrs. Albert," Jim said. "I'd like to talk with you and Jennifer."

Caroline's face contorted with anger. Red spots

glowed on either cheek. "Jim Avery! You're not welcome here! You must leave immediately!"

Jennifer rushed to her mother's side. "Mother, we have something to say to you. Please come in, Jim." Her eyes were shining.

Caroline gasped and dropped into the nearest chair. "Mother! What's wrong? Are you faint?" Jennifer fanned her mother with the folded newspaper.

"Let me alone!" Caroline demanded. "I told both of you that you were not to see one another!"

"We didn't," Jim explained, "but we wrote letters." He swallowed. "Mrs. Albert, Jennifer and I want your permission to marry."

Caroline's eyes were deep black wells. "That you'll never have," she hissed. "Why can't you go away and leave us alone, Jim Avery? Jennifer's not ready to marry."

Jim nodded. "Neither am I, but we want you to know what our plans are. In a year or two I'll buy my land and then we could be together."

Caroline sat bolt upright. "Do you - do you love this young man, Jennifer?"

"Yes, mother."

Caroline leaned back in the chair with a low moan. "Oh God. My worst fears are coming true."

Jim bristled. "Mrs. Albert, I know I'm no great catch for a girl like Jennifer. I'm a farmer and I don't wear fancy clothes or have fancy manners. But I'll make her happy. I promise."

"Sit down! Both of you sit down!" Caroline ordered. She hesitated before she continued. "I had hoped never to have to say the words I'm about to utter. If only you'd stayed away, Jim." She swallowed. "You and Jennifer can never marry. Never - never - never. Do you understand? You can never marry!"

Jim's troubled eyes bored into Caroline's. Jennifer said, "We'd like your permission, Mother, but whether you give it or not, we'll still marry when we're ready."

"Oh God, I don't know how to tell you," Caroline moaned. "You can never marry because you are brother and sister! Jonas Avery is your real father, Jennifer."

There was absolute silence except for the ticking of the clock as the two young people stared in unbelief at Caroline. Finally Jennifer sobbed, "But - but - I don't understand. You are married to Pa. You have a wedding certificate there in the drawer." She pointed to the centertable.

"Yes. Yes, we're married. But I already was carrying Jonas' baby when I married Ezra."

Jim stood. "Caroline Albert, you're an evil, conniving woman! You'd go to any end to keep me from marrying Jennifer, even to saying we're brother and sister. I don't believe your story!"

"Sit down, Jim. You have to believe. Your father worked as a Lansing lumberman during December of 1843 and January of 1844. He stayed here at Carley House. I was just getting the place organized. Jonas was good company. We talked about books we'd read and he told me he planned to marry your mother in a few months. We never were in love, but one Sunday afternoon our emotions got the better of us. It never happened but once and he left the next day.

"Six weeks later I was convinced I was pregnant. Ezra Albert was a drummer then as he is now, and when he called I maneuvered him into proposing and into immediate marriage. You, Jennifer, were born in October of that year. Marriage to Ezra gave you a name and saved my reputation. He doesn't know and I'll never tell him."

Jennifer stared at the flowered carpeting, tears streaming down her face. For a time no one spoke. Finally she said, "Why didn't you tell me before - before we fell in love?" She wiped her eyes on a lace trimmed handkerchief.

Caroline walked to the window. "I had hoped I'd never have to tell anyone. It's not a pretty story. I'm sorry I've hurt both of you."

Jim stared at Caroline's back. Resentment, anger and unbelief churned within him. His voice was husky as he said, "I'll not believe this until I talk with my father. It's a clever story you've thought up, Mrs. Albert, but -"

Caroline whirled. "Believe it or not, I've told you the truth. Go ask your father. Then you'll understand why I've tried to keep you apart, why I sent Jennifer away to school when I wanted her here. You'll know then -"

Jim didn't reply, but silently he stared at Jennifer, wild thoughts racing through his mind. Was this the end of the dream he'd had since he was fifteen years old, the dream that someday she'd be his wife? His sister! Good God! He was in love with his sister!

He sat beside her and took her hand. "I'm going now. We both need time to think."

She looked up, her eyes red from weeping. "Good-bye, Jim," she whispered. "I'm so sorry."

He squeezed her hand and without a backward look he strode to the door and out into the August evening darkness and across the wooden bridge over the Grand River to Washington Avenue.

Walking north he aimlessly wandered the Lansing streets. Past the Christian Breisch Mill, the first flour mill constructed in Lansing, past the Lansing Brewery where he'd sold the hops a few hours earlier and past the brick mansion of James Turner, known as "Big Chief Jim" Turner on Turner Street. Vaguely Jim recalled stories he'd heard about Jim Turner who had helped build the plank road between Howell and Lansing, and who now was Deputy State Treasurer while he also was involved in building railroad lines from Jackson, through Lansing to Saginaw. Jim walked on oblivious to people on the street. He passed the Capitol, a frame two story building which he and Charley had visited with Jonas a few years after its completion.

After hours of aimless wandering he returned to

the brick-three story Benton House. Depressed, and churning with anger at Caroline and his father, he went to the barroom. Sitting alone at a table, he brooded as he consumed drink after drink. Though he knew he was drunk, the events of the evening remained to haunt him. Relentlessly he drank to drown the memories until finally his mind was blank.

The next day he wakened late. Nausea and a throbbing headache intensified his misery at the recollection of the previous evening. Never before had he been so physically and mentally tortured. Staggering to the wash stand he poured cold water from the pitcher into the bowl and dashed it into his face. He caught a glimpse of himself in the looking glass. God he looked awful. He'd slept in his clothes, and they looked like it.

Making his way to the lobby he was amazed at the time. Twelve o'clock! He should have been home by now. Pa would be furious that he was late. Hell, he didn't care if Pa was furious. Sharp pains shot through his head and he wasn't seeing right. Coffee - maybe that would help.

An hour later he was headed east on Grand River Avenue. He'd be home before supper. When they went to the barn to do the milking, he'd have this thing settled once and for all with his father. He didn't care if Charley knew, but there was no use for Ma and the girls to be upset. Ma had been hurt enough through the years by Pa's mean and ungovernable temper. He and Charley had chuckled the other night when they overheard meek little Ma stand up to him. They were surprised at her spunkiness. Well, if Pa admitted this thing about him and Caroline was true, Jim vowed he'd beat the tar out of the old man and then he'd leave. Damn him!

But - maybe Caroline had made up the story to keep him and Jennifer apart. His mind was confused, but deep down, he knew it was true.

The horses plodded on as Jim brooded. He'd

settle things with Pa, take his money and get out. He'd be damned if he'd even help finish with harvesting the hops and planting the wheat. He'd work somewhere as a hired man. There wasn't anything to plan and save for now, but farming was all he knew, and maybe he could forget the hurt if he buried himself in work. God, he felt awful.

A stiff breeze blew from the east and stirred the 95 degree August air. Soon clouds covered the sun. Jim knew that an east wind often indicates a storm is approaching from the south or southwest. Pa would be furious if rainy weather destroyed the remainder of the hops. 'Twould serve him right.

The storm was coming up fast. In the distance lightning zigzagged toward the ground. Black clouds rolled and tumbled. Jim urged the horses into a trot. If it held off another ten minutes he'd be at Webberville where he could wait out the storm. Suddenly the wind stopped and the air felt oppressive and stifling. The horses' sides were wet with sweat and white lather crept from under the harness straps on their hips. He shouldn't be hurrying them in the heat, but he wanted to reach cover before the storm broke. He pulled off his hat and wiped the sweat from his forehead. He looked back over his shoulder. Heavy black clouds pitched about threateningly. A sharp zigzag of lightning knifed through the still air followed by a deafening clap of thunder. Suddenly the oppressive stillness was shattered by a blast of wind and another flash of lightning and clap of thunder. The horses flinched as though they had been hit.

Jim urged them on as trees along the road swayed wildly and the tops bent toward the northeast. The wind had suddenly swung to the southwest. He didn't like the looks of things.

"Gid-dap! Gid-dap!" he shouted. It was as dark as late evening. The wind howled as it gained momentum. A windmill beside a farmer's house whirled wildly, its tail swinging crazily with the swirling air currents. Slats from the wheel ripped loose and shot over the house to the northeast. A huge branch from a maple tree slammed to the ground less than ten feet from the road.

Suddenly driving rain was added to the sounds of sizzling lightning, ear-splitting thunder and howling wind. The horses were galloping and the wagon rattled over the road. At last they reached the edge of town. Jim drove the team into the livery stable just as hail began to clatter into the wagon box. He stood in the doorway with two farmers and three children who also were caught in the storm. Balls of ice the size of walnuts clattered on the roof and bounced in the street. Occasionally one hit a window. Soon hail was banked along the west side of the general store and saloon. In a few minutes, it stopped, but the downpour of rain continued. Then suddenly, the storm was over. The rain-washed air smelled fresh and clean.

One of the farmers, a giant of a man, remarked to Jim, "Guess it's over. Don't believe I know you, young feller."

"I'm Jim Avery. Live in Locke Township."

"Yeah. I've met your father. I'm Fred Chappel, and these here are my young'uns. Kingston's eight, Freddie is ten and Rose is five. They allus like to come to town with me."

"Where's your place?"

"South and east of town in Livingston, Putnam Township."

The other man, the physical opposite of Fred Chappel, said, "I'm Richard Jacobs. My farm's in Ingham County, White Oak Township. Guess we all come to Webberville to do our trading." The small blue-eyed man stroked his sand-colored beard. "I'd better get goin'. Come in to town to get medicine for our young'un. Little Nettie is mighty sick."

Ten year old Freddie Chappel asked, "What's wrong with her?"

The little man scratched his head. "We don't

rightly know, but she's got a fever and a bad sore throat. She won't eat, and she's so little and sickly. My wife, Eliza, is turrible worried 'bout her. We have other children, but none of 'em have been as sickly as Nettie."

"Your wife's name's Eliza?" Fred Chappel asked. The little man nodded. "My wife's named Eliza, too. It seems there's a powerful lot of Elizas in this part of Michigan. After a moment the big man went on. "Hope the medicine helps your little girl. We most lost Freddie, here, when he was a baby. Had whoopin' cough something fierce, but he finally pulled through, an' look at him now. Looks like he'll be six foot seven like his old dad, don't he?" He patted Freddie's head. "Well, young'uns, jump into the wagon. 'Tis time we headed home. Nice meetin' you, Jim."

"Thanks," Jim replied thinking that the huge man reminded him of a gentle giant.

As he left town and headed north he was appalled to see the Seventh Day Adventist campgrounds in a state of utter confusion. The big tent had been flattened by the storm and people were rushing about in an effort to raise their small tents which were their temporary living quarters. Men were shouting and children crying while women strung lines between trees over which they would dry quilts and clothing that had been soaked in the storm. Several large trees lay uprooted at the edge of the campground.

Jim drove his team near the noisy group. "Anyone hurt?" he shouted.

A man in a black suit and a "backward collar" left the group. "No, praise the Lord. We'll soon be ship-shape again. I'm thankful the service was over so the meeting tent was empty. Those big poles that hold it up could kill anyone if they fell on them."

"How long since the service was over? I think my mother and sisters were here."

The minister pulled a large watch from his pocket. "They all left an hour ago when the storm started coming up."

"Did you notice two women, one of them old, and three girls in a surrey? They would have been driving a dapple gray team."

"They were here. Took them a while to get started, but I finally helped them hook up the team. They were the last ones to leave. Their name was Avery. That your folks?"

Jim nodded. "Hope they're all right." He clucked to the horses.

The minister waved. "They'll likely be home when you get there."

Urging the horses into a trot, Jim somehow felt he must hurry. He wondered at his feeling of premonition. Was it dread at having to confront his father? It wouldn't be long now before he settled things with Jonas once and for all. Damn him.

The horses jogged on. Another two miles and they would be home. There were no other vehicles on the road. They must have all found shelter before the storm. As he passed through a stretch of woods, the horses suddenly pricked up their ears. Jim stared ahead in the half-darkness, trying to see what they were looking at. There was something black beside the road up against a beech tree. Strange moaning sounds came from somewhere ahead.

A surrey! His heart leaped. The family surrey lay on its side and the moaning came from out there in the brush. Stopping the team, he rushed through the broken shoulder-high bushes to the surrey. "Ma!" he shouted. "Ma!" He couldn't see her. He couldn't see any of them.

The moaning stopped. "We're over here."

That was Alice's voice. Plunging toward the sound he saw his sister leaning on one elbow. "Jim," she sobbed. "They're all dead. They don't move!"

He saw them scattered about like broken dolls in unnatural positions. Rushing to his mother, he seized her wrist. "Ma!" he shouted. "Ma wake up!" There was a bleeding gash on her forehead.

"She's dead," Alice sobbed. "They're all dead."

"Her heart's beating!" Jim shouted. He dropped her hand and ran a few feet to grasp his grandmother's wrist. After a long minute he dropped her hand and went to Lilla Dale who was lying face down and moving restlessly. "Lilla Dale, it's Jim! Wake up, little sister." He turned her carefully. She opened her eyes. "Where am I?" She began to cry.

"Just be still. I'll get you home soon. Don't move. You might have broken bones." He looked around. "Where's Mary?" he asked.

Alice was sitting up, her right leg twisted into an unnatural position. "She might be back there closer to the road. She fell out first."

He searched. She was lying motionless near the spot where the surrey first had left the road. Her face lay in a pool of blood. As he turned her she drew a quivering breath, but her eyes remained closed. "She's breathing!" he shouted running back to Alice. He looked at her twisted leg. "It's broken," he said. She nodded.

"I'm going for help. They're all alive, but I'm not sure about Grandma. We'll get Uncle Harmon and be back soon's we can."

Running the team he wheeled into the Avery yard. Charley grinned. "If you knew how mad Pa is you wouldn't be in a hurry to get home."

"Ma and the girls are hurt bad! The surrey tipped over! Get Uncle Harmon and come south to Hayner's woods. Pa and I'll be there!"

Charley stood as though rooted to the spot, his mouth open.

"Shake a leg! Don't you understand? They're all hurt bad! Get Uncle Harmon!"

Without a word, Charley started north on a dead run, and Jim dashed to the barn. Jonas was coming out of the cow stable. When he saw Jim he strode toward him with an angry stride. "Where in hell have you been?" he yelled.

"There's been an accident with the surrey. Ma and the girls are hurt bad, and maybe Grandma's dead. Charley's gone for Uncle Harmon. We gotta get back to 'em!"

Jonas staggered and grasped the fence for support, his eyes wide and staring. Jim looked at him a second, but he offered no words of consolation. Finally he said, "Come on! They're all laying out there on the wet ground! Let's take one of the wide boards from the granary to carry them on." He rushed into the granary. When he came out, Jonas still clung to the fence. Jim glanced at his father as he put the board in the wagon box. He ran into the house and returned with an armful of quilts. And still Jonas stood clinging to the fence.

"Get in!" Jim ordered.

His father obeyed silently. He stared into the bottom of the wagon box with unseeing eyes. Jim whipped up the horses and turned them south.

"I hope you're satisfied, Pa," he said. "You showed Ma it was a man's job to drive the team on a surrey. Only - she may never know it 'cause she's unconscious, and so's Mary. She's bleeding bad. Alice has a broken leg, and Lilla Dale - I don't know how bad she's hurt. Grandma - I think she's dead. Yeah, Pa. You showed Ma all right."

Jim urged the horses on until they reached the overturned surrey. Alice and Lilla Dale shouted when they arrived.

"Hurry!" Alice begged. "Ma and Mary and Grandma haven't moved. Please, please hurry."

Lilla Dale sobbed, "Pa, I hurt."

Ignoring the others Jonas roused himself to go to Marcia. He knelt beside her touching her face tenderly. "Marcia, please forgive me." He bent to kiss her forehead. Looking into the treetops he murmured, "Oh God. What have I done?"

Jim said coldly, "No time now for regret, Pa. Help me get them into the wagon."

Gently they lifted Marcia onto the board and carried her to the wagon, then Mary, still unconscious was moved and placed in the wagon box beside her mother. Both were covered with quilts by the time Harmon and Charley arrived.

Harmon shook his head in disbelief. He held smelling salts under Marcia's and Mary's noses, but the sharp penetrating odor did nothing to rouse them. Both were bleeding from gashes in the head.

Alice and Lilla Dale were loaded while Harmon checked Lucy. "She's dead," he said softly.

Harmon rode with the dead and injured in the wagon and Charley drove his uncle's buggy. Jonas sat with Jim on the wagon seat, his head in his hands.

"What have I done?" he murmured. "Marcia hurt, my mother dead, all my girls hurt - God in heaven, what have I done?"

"You've made good money on the hops," Jim said dryly.

By the time they returned with the injured, Harriet and Mary Atkins were at the house. Gently they carried Marcia and Mary inside and placed them in the big bed. While Alice and Lilla Dale were brought in, Harmon cleaned the gaping wounds in Marcia's forehead and on the top of Mary's head. Then he carefully placed stitches to hold the flesh in place.

Jonas stood silently watching beside the bedroom door. Harriet eyed her brother. He seemed in another world and as incapable of making a decision as an infant. She spoke to him. "We have to let Albert and Mary Ann know Maw is gone. We have to plan for the funeral."

He nodded. "You take care of it." His eyes never left Marcia's still face.

Harriet sighed. "Charley, will you drive over to Uncle Albert's and Aunt Mary Ann's and tell them?" She walked outside with her nephew. "Tell them your Paw is no help. He's too wrapped up in grief. They'll have to come so we can make plans."

"I'll go right away." He started toward the

barn, but turned at the sound of his aunt's voice.

"Could you and Jim make a coffin for Maw?"

"We can do it. Tell Jim to get the boards ready and I'll help when I get back."

"Thanks, Charley, and would you stop and tell Israel and the children I won't be home tonight. He'll look after Mary's children and our little ones. Harmon, Mary and I are needed here."

"I'll tell all of them."

Harriet returned to the house. Her dead mother lay on the table completely covered with a sheet. Harmon worked on Alice's leg. "It's a bad break," he said softly to his wife. "'Tis broken twice. Once in the hip and again below the knee." He went to the kitchen to prepare plaster of paris for a cast. Harriet followed.

"She'll be all right, won't she?"

He shook his head. "I hope so. Sometimes breaks this serious leave the leg short."

"How's Lilla Dale?"

"She got a bad blow on the head, but I don't find any broken bones. She has a headache, but I think she'll be all right."

Jim came into the kitchen. "Uncle Harmon, do you think Ma and Mary will come to? Is there a chance?"

"I don't know, Jim. Sometimes it takes several hours - or even days."

"And - sometimes they die without waking up?" Jim's voice trembled.

Harmon stirred the plaster of paris with a vengeance. "Sometimes."

Jim, his back to the door murmured, "Damn him, damn him. It's all his fault." He turned at the sound of his father's voice.

"No! No, Harmon!" Jonas said dully. "You're wrong! Marcia has to live!" He leaned against the door casing and sobbed like a child.

Harriet led her brother to a chair. "Harmon will do everything he can, then it's in God's hands."

Jim rushed outside the house where he slopped the squealing hogs and milked the long overdue cows. Some, their udders swollen, were leaking tiny streams of milk into the dirt of the barnyard. An hour later he returned to the house.

Jonas, sitting beside the bed, stared at Marcia and his unconscious daughter as though he were in a trance. He seemed oblivious to anything except the two quiet figures on the bed.

Lilla Dale slept beside Alice in the big bed that had been set up in the corner of the dining room. Harriet and Harmon were busy in the kitchen. Jim glanced at the covered body of his grandmother. He must take the lantern and find lumber for her coffin. He stopped beside sixteen year old Alice and said softly, "Does your leg ache bad?"

"Yes."

"I'm sorry. Sis, what happened?"

"Grandma was beside Ma and us girls were in back. It started to storm. The thunder and lightning were awful and the rain poured down. Every time there was a crash of thunder, the horses shied and started to gallop. Ma held them and pulled them back to a trot three or four times. Then the wind got strong and a branch broke and fell on Betsy. She reared and her front feet came down on the other side of the surrey tongue. Dolly got scared then and they both began rearing and plunging. Ma couldn't hold them. No one could have. We were all yelling, "Whoa! Whoa!" But Betsy was wild and Dolly was most as bad. They went off the road and the surrey hit a tree. The horses broke loose. I don't know where they went. Have they come home?"

"No. Then when you hit the tree, Ma and Grandma went out headfirst?"

Alice nodded. "Mary was on the outside and she must have hit a tree too. Lilla Dale was between us. She and I landed on the ground. I guess I was the only one that was conscious all the time."

Jim glanced at his father's back. He whispered, "Has he asked about the team?"

Alice shook her head. "Not a word about anything. What's the matter with him?"

"He blames himself, and damn it, he _is_ to blame. Let him suffer. Both Charley and I offered to drive you to the meetings, but the hops had to be harvested. He couldn't spare one of us."

At one o'clock in the morning Jim and Charley carried the rough pine coffin into the house and set it on chairs beneath the west windows. Alice directed Harriet to a chest in the loft where Marcia had several large pieces of cotton percale. Two hours later Harriet had stitched the pale blue flowered lining in place.

"It's right pretty," Charley said.

"'Tis the last thing I can do for Maw," Harriet replied softly, her eyes on the rigid back of her brother who remained beside the bed.

Alice commented, "Grandma has a blue dress that she always liked. I think she'd like to be buried in it."

When she was dressed the men gently lifted the body of the old woman into the coffin. Afterward Jim looked in on his unconscious mother and sister. There was no change. His father's eyes followed him, but neither of them spoke. Harmon said, "You all may as well rest for a while. I'll stay here in case I'm needed."

Harriet nodded. She put her hand on her brother's shoulder. "Jonas, you'd better get some rest."

He shook his head. "I'll stay here. Marcia might wake up. I want to talk to her."

After a few hours of sleep the household was wakened at five o'clock by the crowing of the Plymouth Rock rooster. When Jim and Charley went outside to do the morning chores, one of the team of dapple gray horses stood by the barnyard gate.

"It's Dolly," Charley said. "Wonder where Betsy

is?"

"The harness is broken. In some way they broke apart. Look! Dolly's legs on the right side are skinned. Betsy must have done that when she jumped over the tongue," Jim said.

As they carried the milk pails to the cow barn, Charley asked fearfully, "You think Ma and Mary will get better?"

Jim shrugged. "They're the same as last night."

"Pa's taking it hard. He's still sitting there."

"Yeah." Jim slapped a black and white cow on the rump. "Get in there!" he shouted driving her through the barn door.

Later they all gathered about the table for breakfast prepared by Harriet and consisting of corn meal mush and milk, bread, fried eggs and ham. Lilla Dale was up, and except for a headache, she seemed to have recovered. Alice bravely endured the pain in her mangled hip and leg as she sat up in bed to eat her breakfast. Jonas reluctantly came to sit with the family at the table in his usual place.

Everyone waited. Marcia always returned thanks. Jonas looked from one to the other. He cleared his throat. "I have something to say." He hesitated. "Marcia and Mary will get well. Last night I promised God if He saved their lives, I'd change my way of living. I feel great peace in my heart. I'm going to stay with Marcia so I can tell her when she wakes up. I'll tell her that her prayers have been answered." He smiled. "I'm saved."

There was dead silence. At last Lilla Dale said, "I'll return thanks for Ma." Everyone bowed their heads as the little girl said, "Dear God, we thank Thee for bringing Pa into the fold. Bless him and Ma and Mary and Alice. Bless this food to our use. Amen."

Shortly after breakfast, family, neighbors and friends began to arrive. After viewing his mother's body Jonas returned to sit with Marcia and Mary. When people began coming in, he quietly closed the door.

Mary Ann and Albert spoke briefly with Harriet about plans for the funeral which would be held that afternoon at the Bell Oak Church with Reverend Thomas Harding officiating. The old lady would be buried beside Stephen in the family cemetery. Jonas chose to stay at the house.

The Bell Oak Church was filled with people who came to pay their last respects to Lucy Avery. Besides relatives and neighbors, people came from as far as the Parsons settlement and from the Livingston and Shiawassee county line. Colborns, Dillinghams, Daileys, Hoyts, Casadys and Sobers all were represented.

And so that hot August afternoon, blind, senile Lucy Avery was buried in the little family burying-ground with her husband Stephen, daughter Melissa and infant grandson on the old Stephen Avery farm which he, Albert and Jonas had carved out of the Michigan wilderness.

When the family returned they found Mary had wakened. Dizzy and nauseated, she complained of a splitting headache. Jonas and Harmon tried vainly to make her comfortable. Over and over they explained about the accident, but a few minutes later she'd again ask what had happened, and why she and her mother were in bed.

Jonas was alarmed. "Her mind's not right," he whispered.

Harmon nodded. "This sometimes happens after a blow to the head. I think her mind will clear in a day or two."

"Thank God. Marcia will wake up soon. I know she will."

"Her mind may be foggy, too," Harmon warned. He checked her pulse. "It's regular and strong," he said.

"She's going to be all right, Harmon. God told me she'd recover."

A few hours later Marcia opened her eyes. She

stared at Jonas. "Who are you?" she asked.

He stroked her forehead above the wound. "I'm Jonas. Marcia, I'm glad you're awake. God told me you'd be all right."

"I don't know you. And who's Marcia?"

He took her hand. "You are Marcia, and I'm your husband. You were in an accident. You're just waking up. Mary, there beside you, was hurt too."

Marcia stared at Mary. "I don't know her. I don't know any of you," she said dully. "I don't know who I am or how I got here."

Jonas patted her hand. "Try to rest now. Harmon said you and Mary might need a few days before you remember things."

"Who's Harmon?"

"Dr. Harmon Atkins, your brother. I'm going to the other room now so you and Mary can rest. I'll be back soon."

He went out and closed the door. With tears streaming down his face, he said, "Alice, your mother doesn't know us. She doesn't remember anything. Oh God, what are we going to do? Is she going to be feeble-minded like Maw? And Mary - her mind's not right either! Is this God's way of punishing me for the way I've lived?" He buried his face in his hands and sobbed softly, his tears glistening in his gray-streaked red beard.

Chapter XX

LIKE FATHER LIKE SON

(1864)

Since April of 1861 the nation had been involved in civil war. Now three and one half years later, no one could predict when the futile struggle would end or how many more lives would be sacrificed before the South was beaten to its knees. The summer of 1864 found both the North and South discouraged and war weary.

Names of places which sounded strange to the ears of northern people were seen in newspapers and repeated in conversation - Chickamauga, Keenesaw Mountain, Murfreesboro, Spotsylvania and Shiloh. During the summer of 1864 the campaign for Atlanta was played out like a chess game. Sherman moved forward trying to trap Johnson, who each time would slip away. The two armies clashed frequently in minor battles. Finally Sherman reached the outskirts of Atlanta where he laid siege to the city. The Confederates evacuated Atlanta on September 1st and Sherman occupied it the next day. It was thought his victory helped Lincoln win reelection.

The wheels of war relentlessly ground on. In the North, wheat and wool production were at an all time high. Factories and farms made widespread use of the new labor-saving machines such as the sewing machine and the reaper. Because of the war, the economy was forced into an early form of mass production. In the meantime, the nation expanded as settlers moved westward.

In the South, Jefferson Davis, President of the Confederacy, lacked Lincoln's mental and physical vigor. He also lacked Lincoln's skill in managing men. The demands of total war strained the economy of the South almost to the breaking point. As the North tightened the blockade, imports dwindled. Southern factories were unable to produce needed resources. People made clothes from curtains and carpets. Inflation raged and weakened the peoples' will to fight, but they stubbornly refused to surrender.

In both the North and South, songs showed the spirit of the people. Northerners hummed "The Battle Hymn Of The Republic," "Tenting On The Old Camp Ground," and "When Johnny Comes Marching Home." In Michigan everyone sang the popular "Michigan, My Michigan" while citizens of the South marched to war to the stirring music of "Dixie" and "The Bonnie Blue Flag."

Finally on November 15 Sherman's troops left Atlanta in flames and his 60,000 men set out for Savannah. As they marched across Georgia virtually unopposed, they destroyed civilian property and laid waste to anything that might help the South to continue fighting.

When the evening chores were done and their baby daughter in bed, Andrew and Lucretia Colborn Dillingham and their hired man, Jim Avery, gathered about the kerosene lamp lighted table to read a newspaper which Andrew had brought from Fowlerville. Silently they read accounts of the rape of Georgia by Sherman and his men. There were stories of stripped houses, barns and fields, of ruined crops and of railroad tracks torn up and the ties burned. Sherman estimated that his men destroyed $100 million worth of property in Georgia. He hoped this horrible destruction would break the will of the South, and thus bring about an end to the war.

Lucretia put the paper down. "I'm sick and tired of reading about killing and burning. Why does the North need to destroy the cities and the farm buildings and crops? They burn everything they can't use. I know the Southern people are the enemy, but I think how we'd feel if our animals were taken and our buildings burned." She sighed. "Will it never end?"

"They can't hold out much longer," Andrew said. "They're beat now but they won't admit it."

"The South reminds me of a chicken with its head cut off," Jim said. "You know how they do - flop and jump and jerk, but it doesn't do any good 'cause they don't have a head to direct them. The South is in its death dance now - jerking and flopping around uselessly with no real head."

"That's a good comparison, Jim," Lucretia laughed. "Sometimes your use of words surprises me."

Jim grinned. "I get that gift from my mother. She writes nice poems - or she used to." He looked away as though to close the subject.

"Maw says your mother's a fine lady. She and Hannah have met her several times at summer camp meetings. My brother, Amos, is a rough sort of man, but he always takes Hannah and Maw to meetings."

"That's right nice of him. My mother and sisters wouldn't have had that accident last year if a man had been driving." Jim's tone of voice revealed his feelings.

"I met your sisters at a social once," Lucretia said. "I remember Alice and Mary. How are they?"

"Mary's all right. Alice walks with a bad limp. Her right leg is shorter than the other one by about an inch. Our cousin, Israel Atkins, is a cobbler at Bell Oak. He's going to build a shoe for her with an inch thick sole and heel. That should help her."

Andrew asked, "How's your mother? We heard she was hurt real bad."

Jim nodded. "At first she couldn't remember anything - not even who she was. But we kept talking to her about things that had happened in the family. One day Alice and I talked about the time when we were small and got lost in the wilderness. A bear killed our dog and there was a storm. I guess we were about three and four years old. We hid all night under the roots of a tree that had blown over."

"Alice and I talked to Ma about it and about how scared we were, and then about Pa finding us. We even talked about how hard he spanked us because we'd disobeyed and had gone alone to the woods.

"All at once Ma said, 'I remember! Charley was just learning to walk and he was scared when your Pa spanked you so hard. He didn't understand - and neither did I - because I was so thankful you were found!'"

"From that time on Ma's memory gradually came back. When I left to come here, she remembered 'most everything. I expect she'll be writing poetry again soon."

"That's a talent," Lucretia said.

"She's always been religious. Some of her poems sound like hymns. My little sister, Lilla Dale writes, too. She's always doing a story or poem."

Lucretia said, "Our school is better than it was when I started. Did you know I was the first white child born in Conway Township? There wasn't any school here then. I hope by the time our Clara's in school, it will be better. We want her to have a good education."

"This part of Livingston must have been pretty wild when you were little."

Lucretia laughed. "When Aunt Hannah's mother helped Ma at the time I was born, there were wolves and bears galore. Now they're all gone and the only Indians left are Aunt Hannah and Shobegun, White Fawn and their son, Joe."

Jim said, "Joe seems like a good sort of fellow."

"He'd rather hunt and fish than to work on the land, but I've seen white men like that," Andrew said. "I think he has his eye on Lucy, Amos' daughter."

"She's about fourteen or fifteen now?"

Lucretia smiled. "Fourteen. Have you seen

her?"

Jim shook his head. "Not for two or three years."

"She's going to be a looker," Andrew grinned. "She's got Amos' blue eyes and Hannah's Indian complexion and hair. She's tall - well, you'll know what I mean when you see her. Now little Jim, he has all the Indian features. He could be quite a help to Amos, but he'd rather traipse around with Joe in the woods."

Lucretia said, "Amos is my brother same as Israil and Ben, but he does things his way. Ma says he changed after he lost his foot. He had always been jealous of Israil, but after he was crippled he seemed driven to out-do Israil in getting more land and making more money. He's succeeded, with the help of Shobegun and Fawn. 'Course he's paid them."

Andrew went on, "Lucretia's mother says Israil's the one that is jealous now, and he has always hated Indians, so he doesn't have anything to do with Amos or his family. Now Ben, the other brother, he grew up with Shobegun. Lucretia's Maw says they're like one big family."

Jim said, "I remember the first time I saw the Colborns. Little Jim said children at school often teased him and Lucy because they were half-breeds."

Lucretia nodded. "Some of the neighbors haven't accepted them even now."

For a time they returned to reading the newspaper. Andrew looked up. "You're good help, Jim, but now that the corn is cut and shocked, I don't have work for you in the winter. Do you plan to go home until farm work starts in the spring?"

"I've thought I might go to Lansing. Maybe I can find some kind of work there."

Lucretia asked, "Aren't you going home for Thanksgiving?"

"Nope." The note of finality in his voice caused Lucretia and Andrew to look at him inquiringly.

After a few moments, she said, "Maw always has the family at her place for a big dinner. Thanksgiving is Thursday. Why don't you stay until the end of the week and spend the day with all of us?"

"'Twould be nice. Thanks." He knew they were wondering why he'd left home, but he wasn't about to discuss the matter with anyone. It was nobody's business but his and Pa's. He'd told Ma and the girls he wanted to "get out of the nest." They hadn't understood, but that was the best excuse he could think of. Pa had given him the money he had coming and he'd even paid him for the two cows he'd raised from calves.

Pa seemed a changed man since he'd got religion. He and Maw and the girls went to the Bell Oak Church, but only because the nearest Seventh Day Adventist meeting house was miles away at Morrice. Poor Alice - she would always be crippled. His mother seemed to have her memory back now.

In a sudden flash Jim's thoughts returned to his discussion with his father about Jennifer and Caroline. It had been less than two weeks ago. He hadn't wanted to leave home until he was sure Ma was all right, so he'd waited to confront his father with his accusations.

He hadn't been very diplomatic. Charley was at Uncle Harmon's and Jim and his father were finishing the milking. Before they left the barn, he had abruptly said, "Pa, I have to ask you something. Are you Jennifer Albert's father?"

Jonas had stood like a statue, his mouth gaping. Finally he wheezed, "Who told you that?" He was seized with a sudden coughing spell.

Ignoring the coughing, Jim continued. "Mrs. Albert said you are Jennifer's father and that is the reason she's tried to keep us apart - because we're half-brother and sister." He waited until Jonas caught his breath. "It's true, isn't it?"

"I - I - I don't know," Jonas said, almost in a whisper. "When is her birthday?"

"October 26."

Jonas leaned against the wall of the barn. "My God. It could be true." Again he was seized with a coughing fit.

"Mrs. Albert is certain. She said she was six weeks pregnant when she made a hurry-up marriage with her husband. At first, when she told me, I was mad enough to kill you, but I've cooled off since the accident. Now that I'm positive about Jennifer, I want to get away from this place - and you! Wouldn't that have been a fine kettle of fish if Jennifer and I had married as we planned? You've ruined both our lives!"

Jonas had covered his face with his hands. "I'm sorry, son." His shoulders shook. "I pray you can forgive me." He wiped his eyes on the back of his hand. "I've sinned and the Bible says the sins of the fathers shall be visited on their children. How true."

They were silent for a time. Then Jonas had asked, "Does Charley know?"

"No. The less said the better. I haven't heard from Jennifer since the night before the accident - that's over a year now."

Jonas shook his head. "I'm sorry. I know you'd hoped to marry Jennifer. Can you forgive me?"

Jim turned his back. "I feel bitter and cheated. I'll never marry. There's not another girl like Jennifer. I can't forgive you." The next day he'd left home.

Vaguely he was aware of hearing Lucretia speak his name. He rubbed his forehead. "Did you say something to me?"

She laughed. "You were off somewhere in another world. I asked what kind of work you'd look for in Lansing."

"Anything I can find. I'd clerk in a store - anything to get me through the winter. Then next spring I'll hire out for the season to a farmer."

Andrew folded his newspaper. "You could work for me. I'll need a man and I'll pay whatever the going rate is."

Jim's face broke into a broad smile. "Thanks, Andrew. I'll plan on it." After a moment he said, "There's a chance I might be drafted."

"We'll cross that bridge when we come to it. The war may be over by then."

Lucretia sighed. "I hope so. What a pity if the men have to go through another winter of sickness and misery and killing and being killed - it's all so useless."

Andrew got up. "Be careful where you say that, Cretia. You might be thought to be a Copperhead."[1]

Two days later Jim joined the Colborns at the old log home for Thanksgiving dinner. Mary, the matriarch of the family, welcomed Jim. He was amazed at her vigor and energy. Poor Grandma Avery would have been about the same age as Mary - perhaps sixty-eight or seventy. Though her hair was white, and most of her front teeth were gone, she stood straight and tall.

Behind Mary were Ben and his wife, Marias, and their little boy, Albert. They lived in the old home with her. Jim watched as she greeted members of her family. Lide and Jack Martin arrived shortly after the Dillinghams. While the men unhitched and stabled the horses, the women and children went inside where the table was set for fourteen people.

Next came Amos, Hannah, Lucy and Jim, soon to be followed by Shobegun, Fawn and Joe. Everyone was talking at once. Jim heard small snatches of conversation from various groups. Amos was saying, "Betsy an' Eliza an' their families air havin' Thanksgivin' with their in-laws. We don't hardly ever see 'em no more. Well - 'tis all right. They got good men."

Ben talked in a low voice to Lucretia. "I knowed Israil's wouldn't come. They're 'shamed a' their

----

1. World Book Encyclopedia

family."

Lucretia nodded. "I got to help Maw, Ben." She hurried to drain a heavy kettle of boiled potatoes. Ben's wife, Marias, took three big roasting chickens from the huge oven of the wood-burning range.

"U-m-m-m. Them chickens look good, Grandma," Lucy said.

Jim's eyes followed the graceful movements of the half-Indian girl. Slender and tall for her age, she appeared older than fourteen. Andrew was right - she would be a "looker" in another year or two. Silently Jim compared Lucy's appearance with that of Hannah and the other squaw, Fawn. Would this pretty girl someday resemble these women? He recalled what his father once had said, "No white man would want to marry a half-breed like Lucy."

Hannah and Fawn wore shapeless dark dresses which served only to emphasize their heavy figures. Their black hair was parted in the middle, braided in two braids and twisted about their heads. Jim could imagine them dressed in deerskin with a braid over each shoulder. The squaws silently carved the chickens and carried them to the table.

Shobegun, Joe, Andrew, Jack and Ben sat out of the way of the bustling women. Jim studied the Indian men. That Joe was almost handsome - straight and tall, he moved silently about the room. He and Lucy would make a handsome couple, yet something about the idea vaguely troubled Jim. He dismissed the thought. It was none of his business who either of them married.

Shobegun and Ben were discussing the price of wheat. "I'm holdin' mine," Ben said. I think 'twill be higher. The South's gonna pay whatever the goin' price is when they gits hungry 'nuff."

Shobegun answered, "We ain't spozed to sell wheat to the South."

Ben laughed. "I won't sell it to the South, but if one of the elevators in Lansing or Howell pays more'n any other place 'round here, they must be gettin' their money back - an' then some. I'll bet it's goin' south."

Nine year old Jim Colborn sat beside his father listening to the mens' conversation. Amos' peg leg was stretched out in front of his chair. The crude prosthesis must be uncomfortable. The stump of the leg rested on a thick pad between two narrow strips of wood which extended up either side of the thigh for about ten inches. The strips of wood and the pad were securely fastened to the round wooden leg which tapered in size from five inches at the knee to about two and one half inches at the bottom. The crude prosthesis was bound to the stump of the leg by three leather straps worn over the thigh and shortened trouser leg.

Jim suddenly was aware that the boy was watching him, his dark eyes sullen. "You've grown since I saw you a few years ago at camp meeting," he remarked.

"Yeah."

"Like school better now than you did then?"

"No! I ain't got no friends!"

Jim nodded. "That must be hard."

Amos patted his son's shoulder. "He helps his old dad real good." A faint smile flickered across the solemn face.

Mary called from beside the table. "Come, everybody. Dinner's ready. Set anywhere."

When the last person was seated, everyone bowed his head as Mary returned thanks. Then platters of chicken, dishes of stuffing, potatoes, gravy, vegetables and plates of bread were passed. Mincemeat and pumpkin pies waited on the kitchen table.

"'Member our first Thanksgivin' in Michigan?" Ben asked.

"I remember," Lide said, "that if Hannah's and Shobegun's Paw hadn't brought us a wild turkey, 'twould have been slim pickin' for us."

Amos laughed. "We didn't know him then, an' he 'most skeered Ma an' me t' death when he come walkin' in 'thout knockin'."

Shobegun grinned. "He knowed ya was skeerd. He tole us Amos was on crutches but he looked ready to fight."

"Yeah, them was the days," Ben said. "Shobegun an' me an' Lide an' Hannah was friends right away."

Hannah smiled briefly. Jim tried to imagine her as she must have looked at Lucy's age. He'd heard she was a beautiful Indian maiden, but you'd never know it now.

"Lide allus my good friend," Hannah said. "She larn me an Shobegun to talk an' t' read. Amos an' me name our Eliza fer her."

Lucy looked up from her plate, her blue eyes troubled. "Ma, you allus had Aunt Lide, but I ain't got no good friend."

"Someday," Ben's wife, Marias, said, "you'll find a good friend. And someday you'll marry."

Joe raised his eyes to Lucy's face but she was staring at Jim who returned her gaze.

"Come, now," Mary said. "Lucy's too young to think 'bout marryin' up. Pass the chicken to Joe, Jack."

"You heard from John lately?" Andrew asked his brother-in-law, Jack Martin.

"We had a letter a couple weeks ago, didn't we Lide?"

"She nodded. "He's somewhere in Georgia. It 'bout worries me sick not knowing how he is. It's hard to raise a boy up to twenty and then to have him go off to war. And now that Susanna's married and gone, Jack and I are all alone just like when we first married. Only now, we're old."

Jack roared, "Who's old? I'm still rearin' to go!"

Lide smiled. "I've noticed you're not rearin' as high as you used to."

After the laughter died down Amos said, "Speakin' a' gettin' letters, Tom Arnold was in the Webberville post office the other day an' he was pickin' up mail for his neighbors. He called to Jesse Webber, the clerk, an' said, 'Any mail fer Mike Howe?' Jesse jest glared at him an' said, disgusted like, 'No mail fer yer cow er anybody's cow!'"

Everyone laughed. Jim noticed that even Hannah and Fawn smiled.

Albert, Ben's and Marias' seven year old son said, "I know a good joke."

"Tell it," Amos urged.

The little boy sat up straight. "A woman asked a boy why his little brother was crying. The boy said, 'Cause he dug a hole an' he wants to bring it into the house.'"

When they were quiet Ben said, "You keep on tellin' stories, Albert, and someday you'll be as good at it as Uncle Amos. He's allus been a crackerjack storyteller."

"Yeah," Albert answered. He turned to his cousin, Jim. "Tell them the one about the shoe with letters on it."

The sullen little boy shook his head. "I don't wanna."

"Aw, come on son," Amos urged.

Reluctantly the boy began, his voice low. "One boy said to the other, 'What's them letters that's on yer shoe?' The other boy wasn't very smart, but he said 'TGIF.' 'What's that mean?' the first boy said. The dumb boy said, 'Toes go in first.'"

Ben shouted, "That's real good, Jim!" The others at the table clapped their hands.

The feasting and talking continued. Jim noticed that Shobegun's wife, Fawn, seldom spoke. He'd never been acquainted with any Indian women, but he decided from observing Hannah and Fawn that they didn't enter into conversation as white women do. Joe, too, was less talkative than his father who seemed entirely at ease. But maybe Joe didn't talk much because he was preoccupied with thoughts of Lucy. Jim was aware of the young man's frequent glances at the girl, just as he, himself, was aware that her eyes often wandered in his direction. Pshaw! 'Twas likely a coincidence. After all, she sat directly opposite him.

While the women were cutting the pies and refilling coffee cups, Jim spoke to Lucy. "Are you going to school?"

Her dark skin flushed a dusky red. "Yes," she murmured softly.

"Yer darn tootin', she's goin' t' school," Amos said. "My young'uns air gonna git all the education they kin. Wisht I'd had more myself. People says a girl don't need all that education 'cause they'll only git married an' keep house." He stopped a moment. "I've seen yer Maw, Jim. She's an educated lady."

Jim nodded. "She's better educated than I am. My youngest sister, Lilla Dale, says she's going to college someday. 'Twouldn't surprise me if she did, too. She wants to be a teacher, but you don't have to go to college to be a teacher."

"An education is good," Mary commented as she passed a pumpkin pie to Jim, "but there air some things ya can't larn in school. Now Hannah an' Fawn have larned me so much. They've larned me 'bout yarbs that kin be used for medicine an' cookin'. An' you should see the way they kin dye cloth. They gits lovely yellow colors using dye made from peach tree leaves, an' they gits a purty rich brown frum butternut shucks an' bark. Now ya don't larn that in school."

"That's true," Jim agreed.

Mary continued. "Lucy air lucky. She'll have both book larnin' an' the things her maw an' Fawn have larned her."

"You're right, Maw," Lucretia said. "We've all learned from them, and Fawn, coming to us from a far-away tribe knew things that Hannah's tribe hadn't known."

Amos guffawed. "Speakin' of Fawn comin' t' us. I kin see her yet - lookin' all skeerd like she thought I'd hit er when I lifted up the blanket an' found er hidin' in the waggin box. I 'spect Hannah hid er that day in Howell when they was drivin' them Injuns west." Amos shook his head. "'Most makes me sick when I think 'bout it. I've never said it before, but I'm glad Fawn hid in my waggin that day."

Shobegun nodded. The two squaws did not lift their eyes from their plates as they consumed huge slabs of mincemeat pie.

Jim studied Amos. He was a rough, explosive man, but a kindly spirit showed beneath the rough exterior. And he apparently loved Hannah. A proverb from Shakespeare flashed through his mind. "Love looks not with the eyes but with the heart."

Chapter XXI

THE LIGHT THROUGH THE TREES

(1865)

Jim settled in his new quarters in Lansing at the Capitol City Boarding House on Washington Avenue. He surveyed the meagerly furnished room. It contained a bed, a chest with a looking glass above it, a wash stand, a straight chair, a small table on which a kerosene lamp set and, behind the door, a row of hooks where he would hang his clothes. It was comfortable. He walked to the single narrow window.

Below was one of the streets where he'd walked the night Caroline Albert had told him that he and Jennifer were half-brother and sister. He couldn't think of that night without a resurgence of the old hurt, and the familiar resentment he continued to feel toward his father.

Forcefully he put the thoughts from his mind. There was no use to think about it - 'twas like crying over spilt milk. There was, however, one more thing he would do before he put an end to it. He'd go see Jennifer, tell her he was glad he'd known her and ask if they could keep in touch by an occasional letter. After all, they were brother and sister.

He pulled a watch from his vest pocket. Half past five. He'd go tonight after supper. He might's well get it over with and off his mind. Replacing the watch in his pocket, he thoughtfully fingered the heavy gold chain draped across his vest. Tomorrow he would start work at Knight's Department Store as a clerk, sweeper, or whatever work Mr. Knight might have for him. He had been fortunate in getting work, but with the Christmas season just ahead, Mr. Knight said he could use a young man who "could figger and make change and who was polite to customers." And, if he proved to be a satisfactory employee, Mr. Knight had said he would keep him on.

At seven o'clock Jim set out for Carley House. Deep in thought, he was vaguely aware of people on the walk and of horses clopping their way along the brick pavement of Michigan Street. As he crossed the river and neared Carley House, he drew a deep breath and squared his shoulders.

A strange new sign hung on the old post. They'd changed the name to The Wayside Inn. Pushing open the door, Jim went to the desk. The clerk adjusted his green eyeshade and looked up.

"You'd like a room?" he asked.

"No. I'd like to talk with Miss Jennifer Albert. Is she here?"

The young man shook his head. "She's moved."

"Moved? Where to? Did she go back to New York?"

The man shifted his quid of tobacco and aimed a direct hit at a brass spittoon in the corner. He wiped his mouth on the back of his hand. "I don't know where she is. They left here in October when we took the place over."

"Mrs. Albert sold Carley House?"

"That she did. She sold it to my father."

"And you don't know where they went?"

"Nope. I heard Mrs. Albert say something about "going back east." I don't think she liked Michigan. They left the day after we signed the papers. When Paw paid her off, she said, 'At last I can get out of this state after thirty years of misery. Now I can take my daughter back east where folk are civilized!'"

Jim was silent, but the clerk continued. "Miss Jennifer said, 'Ma, I like Michigan. I was born here, remember?' And her mother said, 'How could I forget?' Well, they left the next day and we ain't heard from 'em since."

Jim turned. "Thanks for the information." He

walked swiftly to the door and out into the dark December evening, his mind confused and muddled. The matter was out of his hands. Jennifer was gone without a word to him. Deep down, he knew it was better this way, but he would have liked to know where she was and that things were well with her.

Strolling slowly back towards the boarding house, deep in thought, he suddenly realized it was snowing. He liked snow. As children, he and Charley always looked forward to winter. He recalled the snowball fights at school with Cory Fisher who was a grown man when he was still a child. Cory had won every fight they had and his superior strength also had won the admiration and the heart of Sarah Ann Cole. Cory was dead - one of Locke Township's first Civil War casualties, and his wife, Sarah Ann, was left a widow with a child who was now four years old. Jim had seen her often before he left home, and as a man he wondered what he'd once found attractive about Sarah Ann. The thought struck him that perhaps the day would come when he'd wonder why he'd been so drawn to Jennifer. But that wasn't likely for he'd probably never see her again. Right now it seemed she'd always be his ideal woman, in appearance, disposition and intelligence. If things had been different they could have had a beautiful life together. But that was over. He'd never marry.

Damn his father! Years ago he'd ruined Jim's life before he was even born. But on the other hand there would have been no Jennifer if his father and Caroline hadn't been sexually attracted. The world was a better place for Jennifer's having been born, even if he could never have her. His thoughts were so confused with resentment toward his father and feelings of unrequited love that he was not thinking sanely.

Stamping the fluffy snow from his feet, Jim entered the Capitol City Boarding House and went directly to the barroom. After several drinks his tortured mind forgot the hurt for a few hours.

Soon his life fell into a routine. Ten hours of work six days a week at the Knight store kept him occupied so there was little time to think of personal problems. Evenings and Sundays, however, were lonely times. Most evenings were spent in the barroom drinking and playing cards with boarding house acquaintances.

One evening each week Jim visited "Miss Millie's Place" for a "social evening." Though it was no secret around Lansing that this place was a house of "ill repute," Miss Millie, thus far, had cleverly escaped arrest. Her method was so simple that it succeeded. In order to become a member of Miss Millie's social club, a gentleman must be recommended by "a member in good standing," which translated to a man who visited on a weekly basis. Miss Millie then instructed her husband to quietly investigate the applicant's work and daily habits to make certain he was not employed by the tiny Lansing police department, or actively connected with one of the churches of the area. After he was cleared, he became a member in good standing with the privilege of visiting as often as he wished, of course for a substantial fee.

The ten attractive girls who lived at Miss Millie's were instructed to entertain lonely club members in the large, tastefully furnished living room. Dainty sandwiches, cake and coffee were spread on a lace covered table and members were encouraged to mingle with the young ladies.

No more than two couples at a time were permitted to slip through the curtains at the back of the living room to the private bedrooms of the girls. Should a curious unknown man wander in, he was invited to view the seemingly innocent social gathering of perhaps fifteen or twenty people. Then, politely, Miss Millie informed him that her private club was open to members only, and she inquired whether the gentleman wished to apply for membership.

However, while Miss Millie, charming, beautiful, blonde and immaculately groomed, entertained the chance visitor for a few minutes, a hidden observer quietly alerted the couples behind the curtains so that in the event the man was a policeman who demanded that he search the back rooms, everything was in order.

So, though Jim had few unoccupied hours, he was not content. Drinking only dulled his senses, and though he won often at cards, he was interested only in winning enough money to pay his "membership fee" at Miss Millie's.

But the sexual experiences at the club lacked something. The girls were beautiful and eager to please, and he'd tried all of them, but deep down he felt there should be something more, something that was lacking in his weekly encounters. He felt if there was love between a couple, only then would the sexual experience be satisfying.

So day after day and week after week his monotonous life wore on. The Christmas and New Years Holidays were lonely times. He'd written his family but made no explanation as to the reason for his long absence. He hoped they would believe he couldn't leave his work. Deep down, Jim knew he was homesick. City life bored him. More than ever he was convinced that farming was the work he wanted to do. Then one evening when he returned to the boarding house, Charley was waiting. He tried to hide the tears that welled up as his brother greeted him.

"It's good to see you!" Jim exclaimed. "What are you doing here?"

Charley, his blue eyes twinkling, grinned from ear to ear as he slapped Jim on the shoulder. "There's not much doing at home. Just thought I'd visit you and try to find work at one of the sawmills."

As they ate a hearty dinner at the large boarding house table, Charley and Jim listened to the conversation which centered on the war.

"It's been 'most a year since the Railsplitter put Grant in command of the Union armies," a grizzled older man commented. "I thought he'd end it before this."

"Yeah, Grant's a butcher, but as tough as he is, the South is fighting for its life. It'll take more than that cigar chomping butcher to finish them off," a black bearded man replied.

"The Railsplitter's more popular now than he was a year ago. He defeated McClellan by an electoral vote of 212 to 21. The Union's behind him. I think they'll wind it up soon after he's inaugurated in March. Then we can get back to living without the war hanging over our heads."

A neatly dressed man of about thirty-five said, "The war's made good times in the North. Factories booming, mills goin' full tilt, farmers getting high prices - the war's been good for us here. I kind of hate to see it end."

There was dead silence around the table with only the sound of silverware clicking against plates. Jim's face was fire red. Suddenly he exploded. "Damn it! You're profiting from the blood of thousands of men who've died! Your customers are making big money so they buy your furniture! And you pocket your earnings and hope the killing goes on! I'll warrant you've not lost a close relative or friend or you'd feel different!"

Jim's attack on the man opened the flood gates of pent up emotions. A moment later angry shouts were hurled at the furniture merchant from several directions. "Selfish cur!" "Unfeeling bastard!" "Murderer!" "People like you keep the war going!" "You'd be a punk stick to lean on in a time of trouble!" "War monger!" "Pampered dandies like you ain't got no feelins!" "Muttonhead!" "Ignoramus!" "Dirty skunk!"

Suddenly Jim Brady, owner of the boarding house, appeared in the door. "What's all the ruckus about?" he yelled.

Again the shouting started coupled with fingers leveled at the merchant. Hurriedly he shoved his chair away from the table and stalked out of the room. Looking back over his shoulder he shouted

Abraham Lincoln and Sojourner Truth

The State Capitol at Lansing, 1847

to the owner, "Figger up what I owe you. I'm leavin'!"

"Good riddance," Jim muttered.

"Yeah. He bit off more'n he can chew with them remarks."

"Always was a conceited bugger."

"He oughta be tarred and feathered an' rode out of town on a rail!" The man lowered his voice. "My boy died at Gettysburg."

The remark sobered the men about the table, and once more the room became quiet as each one silently pondered the disastrous results of the long struggle on his family or that of friends.

Later when the brothers were together in Jim's room Charley said, "You stirred up a storm with your attack on that fellow."

"He deserved it. It didn't take long for him to decide which way the wind blew from."

Charley grinned. "I can see that you're as hot-headed as ever - just like Pa used to be."

"I guess so - though I'm sorry to admit it."

"Why? Pa's a good man. And since he got religion he doesn't fly off the handle like he used to. What happened between you and Pa?"

Jim hung his coat behind the door. "I don't want to talk about it."

Charley continued probing. "It had something to do with you and Jennifer breaking up. What happened? Did she give you the mitten?"

"She moved away. Carley House has been sold. I don't know where she went." Jim sat on the edge of the bed. "I'll probably never see her again. I guess it's just as well."

"Why? Since you were fourteen you've planned to marry her."

"Charley, stop it before I lose my temper! It's over and I don't want to talk about it."

"All right. All right. But I'd still like to know what happened between you and Pa."

"It's none a' your damn business!" They were silent for a few minutes, then Jim said softly, "How's Ma?"

"Her memory's all right again. She writes in her diary every afternoon - she's written some good poems. She misses you, and she's as puzzled as the rest of us as to why you left."

"Yeah. I expect she is."

Charley tipped back in the straight chair and balanced it on the two back legs. He took a pouch of tobacco and a pipe from his pocket.

"You smoking?" Jim asked.

An impish grin spread across Charley's face. "I will be soon. When Ma found out I was going to Lansing to look for work she was upset. She said, 'Both of my boys will be in that sinful city.' Then when she kissed me goodbye she whispered, 'Promise me you won't smoke or drink.' I promised."

"You did? You lied to her?"

Again the impish grin spread across the freckled face. He struck a match and puffed until the tobacco caught. Slowly he blew a cloud of smoke. "What she doesn't know won't hurt her. I don't want her to worry. I can't stand to see her cry and she would if she knew, so I figure what's the harm in a little white lie if it makes her happy."

"H-m-m. Maybe you're right. How are the girls?" Jim took his pipe from his pocket, filled the bowl from a tobacco pouch and lighted up.

"Alice is getting along real well with the built-up shoe. Israel did a fine job. He's quite a cobbler. 'Course the shoe looks different, but Alice walks better. She's got a beau. Fellow named George Harper. Ma and Pa like him."

"Farmer?"

"Yeah. He's from Shiawassee County - somewhere between Morrice and Bancroft. He's a Seventh Day Adventist."

"That figgers. Are Mary and Lilla Dale all right?"

Charley nodded. "I hope I can find work. If I do I probably won't go home much."

Jim laughed. "You're leaving the nest too?"

Charley scratched his head thoughtfully. "It's too damn religious around there for me. Pa's always quoting the Bible, and believe me, he knows it, chapter and verse. Says he ought to know it, he was brought up on it. Then he backslid before he married Ma. He's a different man than we knew as young'uns. Ma says it proves that if you bring a child up in the way he should go, when he is old he will not depart from it. She means you and me, too."

"Are you an atheist, Charley?"

"Yeah." He grinned. "I'm named for the Methodist hymn writer, Charles Wesley, but I don't believe angels are sitting up there in Heaven on little pink clouds twanging away on their harps, do you?"

Jim laughed. "I'm not sure what I believe. Maybe there's a God - then again, maybe there's not." He got up. "Let's go to the barroom."

Charley placed his pipe in the ash tray on the chest. "That's enough for now," he muttered.

"Feel sick?"

"A little."

"You'll get used to it. I did. Ever try snuff?"

"No."

"I like it. Want some?"

Charley shook his head. "Not 'till my stomach settles down."

Jim chuckled. "You're not used to the way city people live. You're like a young robin learning to fly. You don't quite know how to do it. Stay with me, little brother, and I'll educate you."

Charley smiled a sickly grin. "I'll bet you will - and -" he swallowed, "I'm ready to learn - only not too many more lessons tonight, please."

"I'll get you into my social club. That'll make you a man of the world. Sit down a few minutes. You look kind a' green around the gills."

Charley dropped into the chair. "What's - what's the social club?"

"A place to meet women. Ever been with a

girl?"

Charley shook his head. "Not the way you mean. I've played around a little under the blanket on sleighrides with some of the girls, but that's all."

"Miss Millie's girls will teach you all you need to know in a hurry. There's ten girls at the club. I've had all of them."

"You have? How was it?"

Jim scratched his head. "Well - they're pretty, but they are empty-headed. They only know one thing - how to pleasure a man. 'Course that's what they're hired for. They're not paid to give customers educated conversation."

Charley stood up. "If you don't mind, I think I won't go to the barroom tonight. Even those girls don't interest me right now. My stomach's rolling and that bed looks good. Tomorrow I've got to get out and find work."

As the days passed, Jim was more content with his work at Knight's store. He and Charley spent evenings and Sundays together. The younger boy had found employment at the sawmill where Jonas worked before he and Marcia were married.

After a month at the mill Charley reported enthusiastically, "I'm going to be a millwright! Mr. Jones has let me help make repairs on the machinery. I want to design and build mills. With all the lumber in Michigan and Canada, sawmills will be big business for a long time."

"Really think you'd like it?" Jim asked.

Charley's eyes had a far away look. "Yeah. The fast moving water of the millrace has great power. It's exciting to see it drive the huge mill wheel. Then when something goes wrong and I can repair the machinery, I feel good - like I'd done something worthwhile. And I've got ideas for better mills. Mr. Jones says they'll be building mills wherever there are big stands of timber and good sized rivers."

Jim got up. "Well, it's everybody to his own fancy. For me, it's always been farming. Being outdoors, watching nature, predicting the weather, growing crops - that's what I like. By the way - has Pa stopped growing hops?"

Charley laughed. "He wouldn't touch 'em now with a ten foot pole. He says that it was the work of the devil that made him grow hops, and that Ma wouldn't have had the accident if he hadn't been so darn busy harvesting the goldarned crop. But Ma says 'twas God's hand pushing him, and that without the accident Pa wouldn't have been converted. She said, 'Jonas, you have to take the bitter with the sweet in this world. Life is a long bittersweet trail.'"

"How many times have we heard her say that? But it's true."

"You knew they found the gray that disappeared after the accident?"

"No. Where?"

"We think she must have run dragging the surrey tongue. Probably she was wild like runaway horses are. Anyway she got hung up between two trees and she died there. Starved, I guess. A farmer several miles west of us found her in his swamp two years after the accident."

The winter months passed. By the first of April Jim was planning to leave Lansing. But it was a wet, rainy spring and little farming could be done until the rains stopped, so he continued working at the store.

The State Journal predicted an early end to the war. On April 2 Confederate troops gave up Petersburg and Richmond. Then on April 9, 1865, word came over the wires that Lee had surrendered to Grant at the Appomattox Court House in Virginia.

People in the North were jubilant. The fighting was over, the South was conquered and soon their loved ones in the army would return. Victory celebrations were held in every community.

Then on April 14, a new disaster struck the country. President Lincoln was assassinated. Jim and Charley poured over copies of the April 16

Free Press and State Journal. The Free Press reported,

> The astounding intelligence conveyed through our telegraphic dispatches this Saturday morning of the assassination of President Lincoln and Secretary Seward, fell like a thunderbolt among our citizens. The calamity appeared too horrible to be real. Few could believe until the official dispatches were read that so great a disaster had fallen upon us . . . The city wore a funeral aspect. The black solemn garb of mourning draped almost every building.[1]

Charley looked up from the paper. "Remember last fall how the Free Press called Lincoln the most miserable civil, military and financial failure the world had ever seen? And they said his reelection would bring untold misery to every family in the land?"

"I remember. But now that he's dead, he's praised for his goodness and selflessness. I read where the Free Press says, 'A blow has been aimed at the principles of popular self-government.'"

"I wonder if Secretary of State Seward will live?" Charley said.

"The doctors think he will pull through."

The brothers became silent, listening, as the voice of a newspaper hawker drifted in from the street. "Read all about it! President's assassin killed! Come get your paper!"

Jim jumped up and ran outside. The hawker was at the center of an eager group, all clamoring to

---

1. "Detroit Magazine" from The Detroit Free Press, 5/3/1981.

buy. The faces of Lansing's citizens showed the strain and grief of the past hours. A few women with drawn faces, their bustles causing an unnatural bulge beneath their capes, eagerly sought the latest news. Miss Millie's Social Club was dark. A woman, tightly grasping her newspaper and wiping her eyes, hurried into a nearby house.

When Jim finally got a paper he returned to the boarding house where he read aloud to Charley:

> On Saturday evening, April 14, President Lincoln attended a performance of "Our American Cousin" at Ford's Theater in Washington. John Wilkes Booth, an actor, had been sympathetic with the Southern cause in the war. He had learned that Lincoln was to attend the performance.
>
> A few minutes after 10 p.m. Booth entered the President's private box from behind. A shot rang out which hit Mr. Lincoln in the head. Then the actor leaped to the stage below shouting, "Sic semper tyrannis!" Translated, this means, "Thus always to tyrants."
>
> In the leap to the stage, however, Booth broke his leg, but with the accomplice who had shot Secretary of State Seward, both men escaped through a back door, mounted their horses and fled to Virginia.
>
> Booth was hunted down and shot dead in a barn in Bowling Green, Virginia for the terrible crime he had committed.
>
> Mrs. Mary Todd Lincoln, the President's wife, is in deep sorrow. The assassination of her husband has left her in a state of shock.

The brothers read numerous articles about the

tragedy in the black-bordered newspaper.

A few days later Jim returned to the farm of Andrew and Lucretia Colborn Dillingham where he would work for the season. For days wherever two or more people gathered, the conversation was of the assassination and of the end of the war.

Over supper one night in early June, Jim and the Dillinghams lingered and talked while Clara played with her dog on the floor. "Thank God it's over," Lucretia breathed. "For more than four years we've lived with the killing."

Jim stared outside into the gray twilight. "I'll wager the results of this war will haunt the country for years to come. One million killed or wounded, and actual deaths from battle and disease total more than half a million. And to top it off, there's the financial cost to both sides."

"I don't think we can reckon the costs in dollars," Lucretia commented. "Most of the fighting was done in the South. Think how they must feel - their towns and cities and their beautiful big homes and farms all ruined or burned."

Andrew nodded. "Their railroads are shattered and things are in a state of collapse. We Northerners don't know anything about the suffering they've been through. And it's still not over for them. There's the reconstruction time to get through."

"I'm glad the negroes are free," Lucretia said softly.

Jim nodded. "They're free, but they need direction. They're not used to making decisions about their lives. They have always been told what to do - now they're adrift like a ship without a rudder. Looks to me like it'll be years before the South is on an even keel."

Lucretia patted Clara's head. "I've read they hate us. 'Twill be a long time before that hate is gone. The Southerners are the only Americans ever to be defeated in a war, the State Journal says. They're bitter. I guess they want an eye for an eye and a tooth for a tooth to even the score."

Andrew rubbed his forehead. "There are plenty of Northerners who are bitter too. There's hate on both sides, and they both want to get even. 'Twill take many years before the North and South are united in the way Lincoln wanted. I doubt if President Johnson is a big enough man to do the job."

Lucretia sighed. "If only Lincoln could have lived to carry out his plans -"

Chapter XXII

SOCIAL ACTIVITIES

(1871)

Clara and Ida Dillingham sat on the bottom step of their frame home. "When's it coming?" Ida asked impatiently.

"Listen. I can hear it. It's just leaving Casadys. 'Twill be here soon." Clara laughed. "Why are you in such a hurry? Last year you were too scared to watch."

"It makes an awful loud noise. There it goes! Ain't that loud?"

Clara nodded. "They blow the whistle when they leave a place so the next people will know the threshing machine's on the way."

"Pa and Jim know. They been at Casadys helpin', an' they helped Uncle Amos and Uncle Ben."

Lucretia came to the door. She brushed back a damp lock of hair from her perspiring forehead. "Clara, will you go to the garden and cut a head of cabbage? The threshers will be here for dinner. I'd hoped they wouldn't get here 'till afternoon."

Clara brushed a fly away from her face. "Then they'll be here for dinner and supper."

"Looks that way. I've got pies and cakes baked, but there'll be lots to do. Threshers have awful appetites, and I don't want them to go away hungry and then say Lucretia Dillingham sets a skimpy table."

"Goody! We'll have lots of things to eat!" Ida exclaimed.

"Here's the butcher knife. Cut a cabbage that's popped open. They spoil first. And hurry back.

There's work for all of us."

"Lucy's coming, and Aunt Marias and Grandma, ain't they? They'll help." Ida followed her sister as they started toward the garden.

"We'll get along fine," Lucretia said turning back to the kitchen. "Many hands make light work."

Threshing was a mid-summer event. With the McCormick reaping machine to cut the grain, and the puffing steam engine to provide power to run the separator which threshed it, farmers families felt they were living in a new age. When they recalled the days of cradling, binding and flailing their grain by hand, they marveled at the changes modern machinery had made in their lives.

Lucretia hurriedly set the table for nine men. The frame house was uncomfortably hot. Heat from the wood burning kitchen range increased the inside temperature by many degrees. She brushed back the unruly lock of brown hair. The threshing machine must be getting close to the county line by the sound of the puffing engine.

Ben's wife, Marias, called from the door, "Need some help?"

"Oh, Marias - and Lucy, too. I was hoping you'd come. Things will be ready now that I have help. Lucy, would you finish setting the table? And, Marias, if you'd slice the bread - 'twon't cut too good. It's only been out of the oven a few minutes."

Lucy hesitated before the cupboard. "Aunt Cretia, are you having coffee?"

"No. 'Tis too hot. Put tumblers on for cold tea." Lucretia paused to look at her niece. "I declare, Lucy, I don't know how you do it. You look cool as a cucumber in that flowered dress. The blue just matches the blue in your eyes. Marias, wouldn't we like to be young and beautiful again like Lucy?"

The girl's dusky face flushed at the compliment. Silently she placed the tumblers on the table. Marias giggled. "I swan, if I didn't know she was as good as engaged to Joe, I'd think she was settin' her cap for Jim Avery."

Lucy whirled to face her aunt. "I ain't settin' my cap for nobody - least of all for Jim Avery! An' I ain't engaged to Joe!"

Lucretia shoved more wood into the firebox of the range. The potatoes bubbled and boiled as the heat increased. "Come now, Lucy. Don't be so touchy. Jim would be quite a catch for any girl."

Lucy's eyes flashed. "Any girl? How about a half Indian girl? Nobody lets me forget I'm a half-breed!"

Lucretia put her arm about Lucy's shoulders. "I wouldn't hurt you for the world. Marias and I were just teasing. You can hold your own with any girl in Conway, and I haven't seen another as pretty as you. Have you, Marias?"

"No, I haven't. And Lucy's a hard worker. She knows how to keep house and she'll work in the fields. She'd make any man a good wife."

Lucy looked down as she muttered, "Not Jim Avery with his educated talk and his books -"

"Maybe if you wasn't so uppity he'd ask you to go to dances at the Independence Hall in Fowlerville," Marias suggested.

Lucretia peeped in the oven. The pan of baked beans was nearly done, and the ham was coming along nicely. "Andrew took me to Independence Hall soon after we were married. Dancing to fiddle music was nice. Everyone was laughing and having a great time until one fellow got drunk and started a fight. When they got rowdy, we left. Andrew says things get pretty wild there sometimes. Anyway I'm glad I went." She unconsciously brushed back the unruly lock of hair. "You're how old now, Lucy, about twenty?" the girl nodded. "You ought to get out more. Maybe Joe would take you."

Lucy stared outside where Clara and Ida were running toward the house. "Joe never wants to do things like that. He just stays home with

Shobegun and Fawn or he hunts and fishes. That's all he wants to do. Pa says he's lazy. He ain't coming to help with the threshing. He's fishing. Sometimes I think Pa's right, he's just a lazy Indian."

"Well - someday the right man will come along for you," Marias said.

"I ain't in no hurry," Lucy commented.

Ida shouted from the porch, "The threshing machine's 'most here!"

"I hear it." She took the head of cabbage from Clara. "Would you chop a big dishful of this and put sugar and vinegar over it, Lucy?" The tall graceful girl went to the kitchen.

"We have to fill the washtubs with water so the men can wash," Lucretia said. "I 'most forgot."

Hurrying outside the women pulled a bench beneath a large tree near the open well. Marias brought tubs from the shed and Lucretia drew pail after pail of water.

By this time the puffing engine pulled the separator into the yard and past the house on the way to the barn. Ida and Clara watched from the porch, their eyes wide. Bill Roberts, owner of the threshing rig grinned as he blew the whistle, a long, sharp, screeching blast. Ida ran into the house and Clara covered her ears.

Part of the threshing procession was the water wagon, a round horse drawn wooden tank which carried water for the steam engine. Water was pumped from the nearby creek through a large hose to the water wagon. Three men came with the rig, the owner driving the engine, a straw stacker and the driver of the water wagon.

The separator was placed between two stacks of grain. The long curved pipe which blew out the threshed straw extended toward the barn where the new straw stack would stand. The separator was connected to the steam engine by a foot wide revolving belt which drove the separator. Bill Roberts and the two men from his crew quickly set up the machines.

While Andrew hurried to the house, Amos, Ben, Shobegun and Jeremiah Casady watched the proceedings. In a minute Andrew returned as Bill Roberts jumped from the steam engine.

"Dinner's ready!" Andrew shouted. "We might's well eat before we start."

Laughing and joking the men made their way to the water-filled wash tubs under the oak tree. After throwing sweat-stained tattered straw hats on the ground, they brushed chaff and dust from their overalls, then rolling up shirt sleeves, they dove into the water. After rubbing homemade soap on their wet hands and faces, they cupped their hands and threw water into their dust and perspiration-streaked faces, snorting as they cleared chaff from their nostrils. Drying themselves and their beards on the cream colored unbleached linen towel, they tossed it to the next man in line. Then, standing to one side, they brushed their hair back with still damp hands.

Clara and Ida sat on the steps silently watching. Both girls were shy and quiet around strangers.

"Why ain't ya helpin' yer Maw, Clara?" Amos asked as his peg leg clumped up the steps.

"She told us we could watch the men wash," Clara replied.

Amos bent to chuck both girls under the chin. "Yeah. Play while ya kin. When you're growed up there's nothin' but work." He clumped into the house followed by the strawstacker.

Inside the men were seating themselves at the table as the women carried in huge dishes of food. Conversation was loud and jovial. When the men were seated the women began passing the heaping dishes of food. The children had come inside and stood next to the door, watching and hoping there would be food left for them and the women.

Jeremiah Casady stroked his beard as he waited for the first dish to reach him at the far end of the table. "The way you fellers are divin' in,

Lucretia'll think you ain't et fer a week."

"You'll eat your share," Amos replied. "Fer a little man ya've got a heck of an appetite."

"'Cause I'm small I have to take two steps to you big fellers one. So I have to eat twice as much to keep goin'."

The men chuckled. "Good thinkin', Jeremiah," Andrew said.

"Wheat an' rye's turnin' out good this year," Bill Roberts commented, "but prices ain't too good."

"Yeah, them war prices spoiled us," Amos added, "an' the Southerners ain't got no money t' buy what they need."

"They ain't forgot the lickin' they took. They hate us. They wouldn't buy from us less'n they was starvin'," the strawstacker commented.

"Johnson was a poor stick as president," Ben remarked. "He was a scalawag."

"Johnson had a hard row to hoe," Andrew said. "He wanted to carry out Lincoln's ideas of kind treatment for the beaten Southern states, but Congress felt the South had to be punished and they passed harsh laws over Johnson's veto. I'm glad he wasn't impeached."

"He just got out of it by the skin of his teeth," Bill Roberts said. "The Senate only failed by one vote to impeach him. All that wranglin' that went on didn't help the country to forget the war."

"They passed the 13th and 14th amendments freeing the rest of the slaves and making them citizens," Ben remarked, his eyes on Jim Avery across the table from him. "You're mighty quiet, Jim. You allus has ideas 'bout the guv'ment."

Jim's eyes were on Lucy's retreating figure as she returned to the kitchen. "Huh?" he replied. "Guess I wasn't listening." Suddenly he was aware of Shobegun's piercing stare.

Ben laughed. "I seen you watching Lucy. She's a looker, ain't she? But she's spoke for. We've all knowed fer a long time she'd marry up with Joe someday."

Lucy flounced into the dining room, her skirts swishing. She slammed a dish of boiled potatoes down on the table. "I ain't marryin' nobody! I'm tired of hearin' folks say I'm spoke for! I ain't!" Her dusky skin was flushed with emotion. She went on, "an' - an' - my name's Lucia!"

Her father grinned. "Now, now don't get riled, Lucy - er, Lucia. Ben was only jokin'."

She turned on her heel. "I don't like his jokes!" She went to the kitchen where pots and pans clattered for the remainder of the meal.

Amos shook his head. "I declare, that young'un has got a temper."

"You oughtn tease her, Ben," Marias said softly.

Ben chuckled. "I like to see her eyes flash. She's got spunk, that one. The feller that gets her will have his hands full."

After the men topped off the meal with huge pieces of apple pie, they returned to the barn. Then the women and children cleared the dirty dishes, reset the table and sat down to eat.

"Here's Grandma!" Clara shouted as Mary Colborn slowly made her way up the steps leaning on her cane.

Lucretia jumped up. "You didn't need to come, Maw."

The toothless old face broke into a smile. "I kin still wash dishes, Cretia. It's gettin' so I ain't much good what with my rheumatiz, but I wants to do what I kin."

Lucretia set another place for her mother. "Now, let's take our time eating, and catch our breath 'fore we tackle the mess in the kitchen."

"Aunt Cretia," Lucy began. "I forgot to tell you Ma said she couldn't come to help today. She's plowin' the oat stubble where Pa'll plant rye this fall."

"Your Maw is a worker, Lucy," Ben's wife said. "I don't know another woman that works in the fields like she does."

Mary's old eyes had a distant look. "Hannah's been a good wife to Amos. I can't say it often 'nuff. An' she's savin'. Some women throws out more with a teaspoon than their men kin bring in with a scoop shovel, but not Hannah. She's a real helpmate to Amos." The old eyes softened as she looked at her granddaughter. "Lucy, you are like her. Ya ain't skeerd of work, an' though ya like purty things, ya ain't wasteful. Ya'll make some man a good woman."

Lucy dropped her fork on her plate. "Why," she demanded, "are all of you tryin' to get me married off?"

"That's what women's fer," Mary answered. "To make a good home, have babies an' help their husbands git ahead. There's no other life fer a woman."

Lucy poured another glass of tea. "Well - I ain't seen no man 'round here I'd want to marry," she said dryly.

"Ma," Clara said, "Can we watch the threshin' now?"

"Yeah. But keep out of the mens' way," Lucretia answered. When the girls were gone, she asked, "Where's Albert and Jim? I thought they'd be here."

Lucy sniffed. "My brother Jim's lazy. He's gone fishin' with Joe. I can't stand lazy people."

Ben's wife nodded. "Albert's with them, too. 'Course there's nothin' wrong with fishin', but they ought 'n do it when there's work to be done. I ain't sure it's good for them boys to be with Joe. They're pickin' up his ways."

Mary leaned on her cane and struggled to her feet, her back bent forward. "We ain't all alike in what we likes. 'Tis ever'body to his own fancy." She slowly made her way to the kitchen.

The hum of the separator intrigued Clara and Ida who sat watching beneath the big oak. Amos, rapidly chewing tobacco and with dust and chaff flying about him, clumped about as he tended the bagger, while Ben carried the grain to the granary inside the barn. The strawstacker, his shirt sleeves buttoned at the wrist, overall legs tied at the bottom, a large red bandanna about his neck and across his nose, and with straw hat pulled low, labored to place the threshed straw in a symmetrical stack which would withstand the weather.

Clara said, "I wouldn't want that man's job. The straw falls on him and it's awful dusty. Look at his beard - it's full of dust and chaff."

"Yeah," Ida commented. "And it's hot walking around in the soft straw."

"Pa says strawstackers are paid real good 'cause the work's so dirty."

While the men worked and sweated in the dust, chaff and grime, the women were busy in the kitchen. When the dinner dishes were done, preparations were started for the evening meal.

Lucy took the water bucket and started toward the well. She stopped at the bottom of the steps, hesitating. Jim Avery was pulling up a bucket of water. She considered returning to the house to avoid him, but it was too late.

He came toward her. "I'll pull up the bucket for you."

"I kin do it," she said looking at the ground, but she released the bucket when he grasped the bail.

"I don't see you often," Jim remarked as he pulled up the filled pail. "What do you like to do?"

"I work in the house and the fields. There's always work on a farm."

"What do you do to have a good time?"

Her face flushed. "I go to church with Ma and Grandma Colborn."

"Is that all?"

"There ain't nothin' else to do 'round here."

"I have a horse and buggy now. Will you go with me to the dance at Independence Hall in Fowlerville on Saturday night?"

She hesitated. Then she said softly, "I don't know how to dance."

"It's easy. I'll teach you. Lucy, I'd be proud to take you to the dance. Will you go?" Silently she nodded without looking up.

"Good!" Jim handed her the bucket. "I'll come along about half-past six." He grinned. "We'll have a high old time. Tell your Pa and Ma I'll take good care of you." He looked toward the barn. "I've got to get back to pitching bundles. I'm glad you're going," he said softly.

"Me too," Lucy murmured. Walking to the house there was a happy spring to her step. Her common sense said that Jim only wanted a girl to take to the dance, and that any attractive young woman would do, but deep down she hoped he'd like her well enough to invite her again - and again - to socials, sleigh rides and parties. She had envied the young people of the community their social life, but none of the young men asked to escort her. She knew they considered themselves above her, an Indian half-breed.

When she was home that afternoon Lucy cut out a dress from the lovely rose-colored silk material which her parents had given her the previous Christmas. She had been taught by Hannah and her Grandmother Colborn, so Lucy was an adept seamstress. By looking at a picture in the State Journal she skillfully cut the material in the style of the 1870's with a long slightly flared skirt. A ruffled overskirt in the back swept to the floor ending in a short eighteen inch train.

As she worked, Lucy was aware of her mother's questioning glances, but she didn't explain. Sixteen year old Jim came in and tossed a string of bluegills into the sink.

"Fish for supper, Ma," he said.

Hannah set about scaling and cleaning the fish. Her shapeless body had a weary droop to the shoulders. Silently she removed the heads and scaled each fish before dipping it into a kettle of water.

"What you doin', Lucy?" Jim asked.
"Makin' a dress."
"Why? Where ya goin'?"
"To the big dance at the Independence Hall in Fowlerville." She didn't look up.
"Who's takin' ya?"
"Jim Avery."
There was dead silence. Hannah paused, knife in hand, to stare at her daughter. Young Jim said, "Pa an' Joe won't like it."
Lucy tossed her head. "I don't care. I'm going."
When Amos clumped in after eating supper at the Dillinghams, he was bursting with news. "I'm gonna sell some a' our land," he announced. "Young Jim Avery talked to me about buying eighty acres, an' I tole him I'd sell."
Hannah leaned against the cupboard. "You not sell our land," she said dully.
"Yeah, Hannah. You an' me air gettin' old. We can't work so hard anymore. An' Lucy, I don't want her spoilin' her looks with hard farm work." He spoke to his son, "An' you, Jim - you don't like farmin'. You'd rather fish or hunt with Joe. So I tole Jim Avery he could have the north eighty. He's got 'most 'nuff money an' we'd take a mortgage on the farm. We'll close the deal in a few days."
Silently Lucy continued sewing on her dress. Jim, his piercing black eyes on his father, was speechless. Hannah shuffled to the kitchen range where she stood staring at the greasy fish frying pan.
Amos laughed. "What's wrong? I thought you'd be glad we didn't have to work so hard no more. I'm ready now to take it a little easy. Old Israil can't never have as much land free and clear as I've got. I've showed him up - with your help, Hannah - an' that's what I set out t' do back in 1838."
In a moment he went on. "Ya ain't said nothin', Lucy. What do ya think?"

"'Tis all right with me." She held her needle to the light of the window as she threaded it.

"Pa," Jim began. "Lucy's goin' to the dance in Fowlerville with Jim Avery next Saturday night."

"Oh? Think ya oughta? I ain't sure that's a good thing. Somebody's likely t' say somethin' t' hurt yer feelings."

Lucy continued sewing without looking up. "My feelings have been hurt so many times I can stand it once more. I'm young, Pa, and nobody else asks me to go with them. Jim has asked, an' I'm goin'."

"Well -" Amos scratched his head. "I hope ya knows what yer doin'."

Three days later at half-past six in the evening Jim tied his sorrel horse to the hitching rail and went to the Colborns' door.

"Come in!" young Jim shouted. "Lucy's 'most ready."

Inside the old log cabin which had had many additions over the years, Jim waited. Hannah was nowhere to be seen, and it was likely Amos was at the barn. Suddenly he was aware of the half Indian boy's piercing stare. "Something wrong?" he asked.

The boy shook his head. "Nope. I was lookin' at your fancy suit."

Jim glanced down at his black, high-vested woolen suit. He ran his finger around the inside of the stiff, celluloid shirt collar which was fastened with a gold collar button over which a black cravat was tied. He grinned. "I call this my monkey suit. I wore it every day when I worked in the store in Lansing."

Lucy silently entered the room from a side bedroom and stood waiting. Jim started when he saw her in the stylish rose-colored ruffled silk dress. Her black hair was parted in the center in the style of the 1870's and pulled back into a tight knot at the back of her head.

"Evening, Lucy," he said. "You walk so quietly, I didn't know you were there."

Young Jim laughed. "That's the Injun way a' walkin'. Sneak up on 'em, ya know."

Without replying Jim held the door for Lucy. "Shall we go?"

Her ruffled train swept the floor. Carefully she gathered it over her left forearm and preceded him down the steps.

"That's a pretty dress," he said softly. "You look real nice." He helped her into the shiny black buggy. Her eyes were deep blue and her high cheekbones showed a rosy blush through the dusky skin. Darn, she was beautiful. Untying his horse, Jim climbed into the buggy. "You go to town often?" he asked.

"Once or twice a year." In a moment she added, "I don't get out much."

"Then I'll see you have a fine time tonight. A pretty girl like you should have lots of beaux."

"I don't." She stared into the bottom of the buggy. "You know why."

Jim clucked to his horse. "All I got to say is any man should be proud to be seen with you."

She changed the subject. "How's your sisters?"

"They're fine. Mary was married two years ago to Chauncy Faulkner. They live north of Bell Oak. Alice is keeping company with a farmer near Bancroft. Lilla Dale went to school last summer at the University of Michigan in Ann Arbor, and she's teaching at the Bell Oak School. She's doing real good, I hear."

"And Charley. Where is he?"

"He's up north near Saginaw and Bay City. He sets up mills in the lumber country. He's a millwright."

"Then he travels?"

"Yeah. I had a letter from him a few days ago. He says they have bad forest fires almost every year in lumber country. The woods are burned but people, too, are killed. Charley said if a strong wind is blowing there's not much people can do but to run. He told of a fire near Saginaw that trapped the farmers. He didn't know how many people were killed, but he said they found charred bodies and some others that were still alive but half cooked with their ears and noses burned off, and their eyes most burned out of their sockets. He said it was a horrible thing to see."

"That would be awful."

"And Charley said the roads were lined with dead horses, cattle, sheep, pigs and chickens."

"I wouldn't want to live there. I think my mother's people went somewhere near Saginaw when they left here."

"Do you hear from any of them?"

"No." She paused. "They can't read or write. Maybe they're all dead now."

The horse's feet stirred up little puffs of dust in the dry sandy road. After a time Jim said, "I've known who you were since we were children, but we've never said a dozen words to one another before tonight."

Lucy didn't reply. Finally Jim said, "Tell me about yourself. What do you really like to do?"

"I like being outside on the farm. And I like walking in the woods, and I sew. I made this dress."

"You did? You're a real seamstress."

"Pa and Ma got me a Singer Sewing Machine two years ago. It's the nicest gift I've ever had. I like working the treadle with my feet and seeing the needle go up and down and make even little stitches."

"Your Pa and Ma must think you're pretty special. My sisters don't have a sewing machine."

In a moment Lucy said, "If we lived closer, they could use mine."

He nodded. "Did your Pa tell you he's going to sell me eighty acres?"

"Yeah. There ain't no house or barn on it."

"I'll live with Dillinghams and work for my room and board. Someday soon I'll build a barn, and then in a year or two I'll put up a frame house - just a small one. A single man doesn't need much room."

A cottontail rabbit bounded across the road in front of the horse. Lucy said, "I'm glad you're buying our land."

"Thanks." He glanced at the sky. "A mackeral sky never lets the world go dry. It probably will rain tomorrow."

"My father and Uncle Shobegun can tell what the weather's going to be by looking at the clouds, too. They say a ring around the moon means rain. And Pa says his leg, the stump, hurts worse before a storm. S'poze they really can tell them things by the weather?"

"I don't know. The old timers think they can."

They rode in silence for a time. Then Lucy said, "Grandma Colborn says your Pa goes to church now with your sisters and Ma."

"He was converted after the buggy accident. He's changed. He used to be like I am now - he had a bad temper."

She turned to look at Jim, observing his neatly trimmed red beard and the intensely blue eyes. "I've never seen you lose your temper."

"You've not been around me much. All the Avery men have a mean streak, they tell me." He laughed. "It goes with the red hair."

"I think everybody gets mad - some just keep quiet, but they're mad. Like my mother - she doesn't talk much, but we all know when she's mad. Now me, I'm like Pa - always jawing about something."

"I could tell the other day when the threshers were at Dillinghams that you were put out with Ben."

"Uncle Ben teases me about Joe. I'm tired of it - they all keep talkin' about Joe and me marryin'. Well - we ain't. I'll be an old maid first!"

Jim laughed. "I can't see you as an old maid - not a pretty girl like you."

She didn't answer for a moment, then she said softly, "Pretty don't mean much 'round here if you're Indian - Injun - they call Jim an' me - half-breeds."

"It's hard, I'm sure, but you have your family. They love you."

"Yeah." She stared into the forest at the side of the road. As they neared Fowlerville Lucy said, "I'm scared. There'll be so many people and I don't know how to dance."

"Don't tell anyone and they won't know. I'll help you."

Many horses were tied to the hitching posts along the street before Independence Hall. Ladies in sweeping skirts leaned on the arms of their dark-suited escorts as they ascended the steps ahead of Jim and Lucy. From inside the sounds of fast fiddle music could be heard through the open windows.

The ballroom was hot and crowded. Ladies, who were dancing, fanned themselves dantily with flowered folding fans which were on sale near the door. Jim paused. "Pick out a fan you like," he suggested.

Lucy's eyes slid over the selection. "This one," she said choosing a farm scene of a neat white house and a red barn with animals in the nearby pasture. He paid the man behind the counter who, Jim noticed, was keenly aware of Lucy's striking beauty.

Handing her the fan, he whispered, "We'll watch here at the side for a few minutes. When you're ready we'll get out on the dance floor."

"Thank you for the fan," she murmured as they slid into a pair of vacant chairs and watched several sets as the fiddles sawed out "Turkey In The Straw," "Yankee Doodle" and "Home Sweet Home." Lucy gently waved her fan as she studied the couples on the dance floor. She was glad they all were strangers - all but Jim, and he had been nice. She felt comfortable and protected with him.

"Want to try it?" he whispered. She nodded. "Just follow me. I'll lead, and it's so crowded on the floor if you miss a step they'll think I stepped on your foot."

Lucy laughed. He'd never heard her laugh before he suddenly realized. Poor girl, she hadn't known what it was to have a good time.

She gathered her short train over her forearm and they edged onto the dance floor to the relatively slow music of "Home Sweet Home." Expertly Jim guided her through the simple steps. "You're doing fine," he whispered, aware of the admiring glances of the men as they glided past. There was no doubt about it; she was the most beautiful lady at the ball.

Suddenly a commotion broke out in the adjoining barroom. People stopped dancing to watch. "Who is it?" the man behind Jim asked a friend.

"Joe Davis - he's drunk again. They oughta keep the troublemakers out of here. A feller'd like to bring his lady friend to the dance on Saturday night without havin' her see a drunken brawl."

"Throw 'em out!" a man's voice shouted. Other voices joined in. "Throw 'em out! Throw 'em out!"

The bartender, a mountain of a man, seized the two staggering young men by their coat collars, one in each hand, and marched them unceremoniously to the outside door which he kicked open. Giving them a vigorous shove down the steps, he returned to the barroom without a word or a backward look. The people cheered and applauded and again the fiddles called the dancers to the floor.

At ten o'clock after they had finished a late supper in the floral-carpeted dining room, Lucy said, "Shouldn't we start home?"

"Your Pa and Ma will worry?" Jim asked.

She nodded. "I didn't know we'd be so late. 'Twill be half-past eleven before we get home."

It was a rare late August evening. Stars twinkled in the velvety dark blue sky. Cicadas buzzed in the trees. Fireflies glowed like sparks in the darkness. Dogs, disturbed by the passing buggy, barked a warning to intruders. A cow lowed and the lonesome sound carried on the still air.

They had ridden in silence for some time. Jim slapped the reins against the sorrel's sides. "Giddap!" he said. "Prince's not in any hurry tonight." Lucy didn't reply.

After a time Jim said, "My mother or Lilla Dale could write a poem about a night like this that would sound like a song."

"They're educated ladies." There was a note of envy in Lucy's voice. "It would be nice to know things like why lightning bugs can make light and little locusts can buzz so loud, and how plants grow, and what makes stars twinkle - and - so many things. Do you know things like that?"

"Some of them, and the ones I wonder about the most, I hunt up the answers in books. I wonder about astronomy. What's out there where the stars are? Are there other worlds with people on them? Nobody knows. It's like life after death. My father now has faith there's a God, and a Heaven and Hell."

"Don't you? I do. I'm a strong Methodist."

"I'm not sure. Charley's an atheist. I sort of waver like a reed in the wind. Sometimes I believe, but I doubt a lot, too. All of my family, but Charley and me, are strict Seventh Day Adventists."

"I don't know much about them."

"They believe in the Second Coming. They believe Jesus Christ may return to the earth at any time. They think the human body is the temple of the Holy Spirit, so they are careful not to do anything that they believe is harmful to the body. They don't use alcohol, tobacco, coffee or tea. They refuse to eat pork or any food that contains lard - not even pie crust. Ma makes pie crust using butter."

"Hm-m-m. They do have different ideas."

"They're good people, but I'm not sure about their doctrine. They're not an old denomination like the Methodist religion. I think they organized in 1863."

"I've heard they don't keep Sunday."

"That's right. They observe the Sabbath on Saturday. From sundown Friday night until sundown Saturday evening is their Sabbath. My parents and sisters don't do a tap of work during that time."

"How about milking and feeding the animals and getting meals?"

"I mean, they only do what is necessary. The animals are cared for but food for the family is mostly prepared on Friday before sundown."

"'Twould be a strange way to live. Where do they get their ideas?"

"From the Bible. They can show you chapter and verse for every one of their beliefs." He was silent a moment before he added, "And they may be right."

Lucy replied emphatically, "They can't be! All these years the Methodists can't have been wrong. I could never be a Seventh Day Adventist."

Jim laughed. "You're a real dyed-in-the-wool Methodist. At least you're not like me, wavering, undecided about which way to go."

When they pulled into the Colborn yard Jim noticed the lamp was turned low on the table. As he helped Lucy from the buggy she said, "I had a good time, Jim. Even the dancing was nice."

He squeezed her hand as she stepped down. "I'm glad we went, too." He took her to the door and goodnights were said.

Driving the short distance to the Dillingham home, Jim pondered. It would be easy to become deeply interested in Lucy Colborn, but it wouldn't be wise. Their backgrounds were too different. Though she was beautiful, spirited and hard working, they did not have many common interests. She was not well educated and she was half Indian. They'd be friends and he'd take her to an occasional social or dance, but he'd not get deeply involved. Maybe he could help her meet a young man who could overlook her background. He liked her, but he'd not go beyond that point. He sighed. In no way did she compare to his ideal woman, Jennifer. In no way, that was, except for her beauty.

A Rail Fence

Chapter XXIII

THE ATTRACTION OF OPPOSITES

(1872)

The late July sun beat down on the sweat-stained backs of Jim Avery and his neighbors as they labored to raise the barn on his land. Children lounged beneath the trees watching the fifteen or more men as they sawed and hammered on the framework of the building. "Heave-oh-hee!" rang out as the men pulled the ropes in unison that raised an end of the framework to an upright position. They repeated the operation several times, and when the standing sections were securely fastened together, the skeleton of the building was in place.

All day the banging of the hammers cut through the sultry air. Dinner was served on the lawn by Hannah and Lucy at their home with the help of neighbor women who brought food. Families who contributed labor and food besides the Colborns were the Casadys, Brimleys, Dailys, Dillinghams, Sobers, Parsons, Benjamins and Fullers. By late afternoon most of the exterior of the building was complete except for finishing touches.

Work bees were common in rural Michigan in the latter part of the 19th century. Farmers and their wives enjoyed a day with their neighbors. Barn raisings and threshing were two of the most common bees, and though the work was hard, no one expected pay. A heartfelt "thanks," and the knowledge that the favor would be returned whenever a neighbor needed help was all that was expected.

As the last of the rigs pulled away in the late

afternoon, Jim and Amos surveyed the new building. "'Tis a fine strong barn," Amos said approvingly. "'Twill last ya many years."

Jim nodded. "I'm going to start building a small house. I'd like to live on my land as soon as I can." He paused. "'Course I've got part of the fall plowing done, but I'd like to get a little house up before winter."

Amos aimed at a burdock plant and let fly with a stream of tobacco juice. He wiped his mouth with the back of his hand. "Thinkin' a' gettin' hitched?" he asked.

Jim laughed, "No." He turned suddenly at a sound behimd him. "I didn't hear you, Joe. Haven't seen you all day."

"I don't like all them people yellin' an' hammerin'." The Indian stared at Jim, his eyes piercing and unfriendly. Though the words were not spoken, Jim knew Joe disliked him because he frequently escorted Lucy to community social affairs. Joe turned suddenly and made his way towards his parents cabin.

"He's an odd duck," Jim commented.

"He's neither fish nor fowl," Amos replied. He's a full-blood Injun that's growed up with whites. My boy Jim's a little like Joe - he don't jest know which way t' go. Though he likes Injun ways, he knows he's gotta work fer a livin'. Joe ain't found that out yet."

Jim said, "Lucy's more white than Indian."

"Yeah. But the Injun blood's there. 'Tis too late now, an' Hannah's been a good wife, but I feel bad fer the young'uns. My oldest girls got out into a part of Michigan where nobody knows 'bout their Maw. But it has been bad fer the youngest two. 'Course I know nothin' will come of it, but I've meant t' thank ya fer takin' Lucy places."

Jim smiled. "She's the prettiest girl in Conway." He glanced around. "Do you think over there near the corner would be a good place to build my house?"

Amos studied the land. "'Tis nice an' level. 'Twould be a good spot. Close 'nuff t' the barn, but not too close. When ya air ready, I'll help an' I'm sure Ben an' Shobegun will too."

"Thanks. I've got good neighbors." He turned. "I have to get back to help Andrew with the chores."

A few days later Jim's uncle, Dr. Harmon Atkins stopped at the Dillinghams on his way home from a call at Charles Sobers where Isabelle was ill with lung fever. Lucretia shifted baby Tommy to her left arm as she held the screen door open.

"Come in, Doctor. You've come to see Jim?"

Harmon removed his hat. "Yes, mam. I have a letter for him."

"He's working with Andrew on the back forty, and they won't be up until suppertime. I'll give him the letter."

Harmon produced a letter from his inside coat pocket. "I think it might be important. It's postmarked New York."

Lucretia took the envelope. "Will you sit down?"

"No, thank you. It's time I'm getting back to Bell Oak." He hesitated. "The Sobers said Jim had a barn raising a few days ago, and that he's building a house soon."

"That's right."

"He doesn't stop to see Jonas and Marcia very often. I wonder if you know why."

Tommy whimpered and his mother patted him on the back. She shook her head. "He's busy, what with working here and trying to get things done at his place. He talks often about his mother and Lilla Dale."

"But not about Jonas?"

"He doesn't say much about his father."

Dr. Atkins turned. "Tell him his folks miss him, and to stop and see them."

Lucretia relayed the message as she handed the letter to Jim. He started as he glanced at the neat, even handwriting.

"Someone you know?" Lucretia inquired.

"Er - I don't think so." He went outside and threw himself down beneath the old oak tree near the well. His heart was pounding furiously.

Rapidly tearing open the envelope, Jim turned to the signature. "Your friend, Jennifer."

"Good God!" he muttered to himself as he skimmed the beautifully written pages. "How in Hell could she?"

Leaning against the warm trunk of the old tree, he slowly reread the letter.

> Dear Jim,
>
> I've meant to write you for a long time, but my life is busy. You must have wondered why my mother and I left Lansing so suddenly. The chance to sell the hotel for a profit seemed the best way for us to get out of a difficult situation. If we had remained in Lansing it would have been harder for Mother, for you, and for me. A clean break was best for all of us.
>
> Life has been good to us here. I am married to a fine man, a lawyer, and we have two beautiful children, a little red-haired girl named Anne (who looks like me) and a black-eyed year old boy named Arthur (he is named for his father). Mother lives with us and we're happy to have her. She adores the babies.
>
> I hope things have gone well with you. I'll always think fondly of you, and I'm glad we met.
>
> Perhaps you realize I've written this letter in such a way that should others see it no one but you will recognize underlying facts we both know to be true. It's better this way for all concerned.

I hope you, too, are married and that you have a long and happy life. Goodbye, Jim.

Your friend,
Jennifer

Jim replaced the letter in the envelope. There was not even a return address. He'd thought he was over Jennifer, but suddenly he felt ill. Ambivalent feelings struggled within him. Anger at his father and Caroline who had started the chain of events, anger at Jennifer who had so quickly forgotten their young love, and disgust with himself that he could be so upset by the thought of Jennifer's marriage to another man. After all - he never could have married her - not his half-sister.

Clara called from the door. "Supper's ready, Jim!"

He rubbed his forehead. "Don't wait for me. I'm not hungry." He leaned his head against the tree and closed his eyes, his mind in turmoil. In a few minutes he read the letter again. When he finished, he muttered, "Damn her, I'll forget her as she forgot me."

Pulling a match from his pocket he struck it on the sole of his shoe and held the flame to the edge of the letter, watching as the last message he'd ever have from Jennifer was consumed. The paper blackened. He saw the words, "Your friend, Jennifer."

It was over. Taking his pipe from his pocket he mechanically filled and lighted it but his stomach rebelled at the first puff. "Hell," he thought, "I'm acting like a boy getting over his first attack of puppy love." He tapped the tobacco from his pipe on the root of the oak.

When Andrew came outside, Jim got up and they walked toward the barn to do the evening chores.

"Feelin' better?" Andrew asked.

"Yeah. Got a touch of something, I guess."

"Bad news in your letter?"

"Er - no. Just a few lines from an old - er - friend."

During the next few days Jim did some serious thinking. He was twenty-six years old. He had his farm, though it wasn't paid for. Amos had taken a mortgage on the land and Jim had held back enough money to build a small house and to buy a team, two cows and a sow. He'd start small, but with any luck he'd be out of debt in a few years. Both Amos and Andrew had promised he might use their tools until he was financially on his feet.

"You'll get along fine," Andrew said. "There's just one thing you need."

"What's that?" Jim puffed on his pipe.

"A wife. Someone to keep house for you."

Jim was silent as he blew a series of smoke rings. "Yeah. Got any ideas?"

"Lucy."

"I've thought about it. But - she has a sharp tongue - and I have a hell of a temper. I'm afraid the sparks would fly if we were married." He hesitated.

Andrew watched him. "You're thinking of the children you'd have. They'd only be a quarter Indian. That's not enough to hardly show. And Lucy doesn't look Indian at all. She's different looking, but that only makes her more beautiful."

Jim was silent, staring out across the fields. Finally Andrew said, "You like her. I've seen the two of you together at socials."

"Yeah, I like her. But maybe it wouldn't work."

The following Sunday Jim invited Lucy to go for a buggy ride. He had carefully laid his plans. He would ask her to marry him, and if she accepted he'd speak to Amos. Then they would call on Jonas and Marcia and break the news to them. His father wouldn't approve, but let him squirm. Served him right.

The day was a beautiful one. Jim was vitally aware of the brilliant blue sky dotted with fluffy white clouds. As he helped Lucy into the buggy he remarked, "This is the kind of day poets write about. Nature is beautiful whether it's summer or winter, wet or dry."

"I don't think 'tis beautiful when it rains on your cut grain, or when it don't rain and your crops dry up."

Jim laughed. "Practical Lucy. If Nature doesn't cooperate with the farmer to grow crops to make money, it's - it's ugly. Is that what you think?"

"I guess so. The land and crops are why farmers work, ain't it?" He nodded. "Then when the weather spoils the crops, 'tis not beautiful."

Jim clucked to the sorrel, his eyes on the bittersweet vines that climbed over tree trunks and fences. "Michigan's bittersweet soon will be turning bright red and orange. My mother loves bittersweet. She gathers armsful in October and uses it for winter bouquets."

"I never heard of a bittersweet bouquet. Aunt Lide tells about coming to Michigan in November in 1836 and she said the woods was orange with bittersweet then. I've never paid much attention to it."

"Ma puts bittersweet with cattails and dried weeds. Looks real pretty."

Lucy was silent, thinking. Jim continued. "Ma says life is a bittersweet trail."

"Oh? What's she mean?"

"That from the time you're born until you die, bad things and good things happen to you and that you have to take the bitter with the sweet - so - we walk a bittersweet trail."

"A bittersweet trail. They're pretty words."

Jim turned to look her full in the face. "And you're a pretty lady."

Her dusky dark face flushed. She twisted her handkerchief. "Nobody - nobody ever called me a lady 'afore."

The sorrel trotted on over the wooded road near Dansby Lake. Jim twisted the reins about the whip socket at the right of the buggy box. Impulsively he took Lucy's hands in his. "I'm sorry you've been hurt so many times. You are a lady. That's the way I think of you. Lucy, look at me." He lifted her chin. Her blue eyes were brimming with tears. Softly he whispered, "Will you marry me?"

She covered her face with her hands and sobbed without answering. Puzzled, Jim asked, "What's wrong? I'd hoped you liked me enough to be my wife."

She wiped her eyes. "I ain't good enough for you. Your family wouldn't like me."

"You'd be marrying me - not my family. Lucy, I love you."

After another flood of tears she said, "I'd be a good wife to you, Jim. I'd work hard for you like Maw has for Paw."

"Dammit!" Jim dropped her hands and seized the reins. "I want you to be my wife - not my slave!"

She blew her nose. "Good wives work to help their husbands make money."

"My wife's not going to spoil her looks working in the fields. My wife will do the housework and raise our children!" He hesitated a moment. "What do you say - will you marry me soon?"

She grasped his arm. "Yes - yes." Again the tears came. "This is the happiest day of my life."

Jim laughed. "With all the tears, I'd never guessed it." He took her in his arms. At first she resisted, but in a few moments she relaxed and put up her lips to be kissed. Shortly, however, she pulled away.

"You have to ask Paw," Lucy said softly.

"I'll do it today. And if he and your mother agree, can we be married this fall?"

"Your - our house ain't built."

"It will be. The lumber's ready. We only need a small house to start."

They rode in silence for several minutes. Then, she said haltingly, "Can - can we be married by the Methodist preacher? I wouldn't feel married if 'twas anyone else."

Jim laughed. "It's all right with me."

"I thought maybe you'd want a Seventh Day Adventist preacher."

He shook his head. "I'll admit I lean toward the Adventist way of thinking - mainly because of my mother - but I'm not set in my ways. I won't try to change your belief, Lucy."

"If - if we have children, I'd want them to be Methodists. Would you care?"

"We'll let them know about both religions - and about the Catholic and Jewish way, too. Then when they're old enough they can decide for themselves."

Again there was a long silence. Finally Jim commented, "You're mighty quiet."

"I'm - I'm scared."

"Things will work out fine. I'll talk to your Paw right away. Then when we know, we'll make our plans." He brushed her cheek with a light kiss.

Half an hour later Jim tied the sorrel at the Colborn hitching post. As Lucy made her way to the house, Jim strode to the barn where he could hear hammering.

Amos looked up as Jim entered the cow barn. "Gol-darned cows," he muttered. "They jumped into the manger and tore off the top boards. Don't know what in blazes ails the ornery critters."

Jim didn't answer but stood leaning against the wall of the barn. Amos hammered in the last nail and limped toward Jim, concern showing on his grisly bearded face. "Somethin' wrong?"

"Lucy and I want to get married."

Amos tossed the hammer onto the stone wall of the barn. "Be ya sure?"

"We've talked about it."

"Ya know 'bout Lucy. Don't it make no difference to ya?"

"No."

"When ya marry up, 'tis fer a long time. Folks 'round here marry up fer keeps."

"I know. It will be for keeps."

Amos rubbed his gray-bearded cheek. "There'll be days when you'll wonder why ya married her. I know -"

"People are accepting Lucy better than they did four, five years ago."

"Yeah. It's helped that you didn't mind about Hannah. Maybe sometime they'll forgit an' like Lucy fer herself."

"I'll wager ten years from now nobody will give it a thought."

Amos picked up his hammer. "When ya gonna start yer house?"

"Right away. We want to be married this fall - about the first of October, if that's all right with Lucy."

"We've got work to do. We'll round up a few neighbors an' we'll have that pile a' lumber a' yourn into a nice li'l house in no time."

"Thanks, Amos."

"An' we'll have a big party fer ya after the weddin'. I want t' give ya two a real send off."

"I'm lucky to have you for a father-in-law. I'll pay you the rest of the money for the farm soon's I can."

"I ain't worryin'."

"Shouldn't we talk to Lucy's mother about our plans?"

"Naw. I'll tell 'er. She'll go 'long with whatever we have in mind to do. She's smart an' she has idees, but she don't tell ya what she's thinkin'. I quit tryin' t' figger it out long ago."

The following month was a busy one. Jim and Lucy built their small frame house a short distance north of the barn. "Someday we'll have a big house over there." Jim pointed to the northwest. "Then we'll use our little house for a granary."

"I like this house," Lucy said. "It's clean and new and I'll sew curtains and braid rugs. I'll never want a bigger house."

"It's big enough now," Jim said glancing around the large room that would serve as kitchen, dining and living rooms, "but we only have one bedroom. When we have two, three children, we'll want more room."

"Maybe. Like Paw says, we'll cross that bridge when we come to it."

The fourth Sunday in September Jim and Lucy drove to the Avery farm. There had been an early frost and Jonas was in the field cutting corn. Jim saw him from a distance as they passed on the road, but he made no comment to Lucy. After tying the sorrel to the familiar hitching post, they went to the door.

"Anybody home?" Jim shouted.

Marcia, recognizing his voice, came running. "Jim!" she exclaimed throwing her arms about his neck before she held him at arm's length to study his face. "You look good!"

"So do you, Ma. You're as pretty as ever!" He turned to Lucy who was staring at the floor. "Ma, you remember Lucy Colborn?"

"Why - yes. How do you do?" The women shook hands.

"Ma," Jim began. "We're getting married October 9th, and we want all of you to come to the wedding."

Marcia dropped into the nearest rocker, her face somber. "Married? So soon? Why - why -" She didn't finish.

Jim laughed. "It's not so sudden. We have our house built, and you knew I'd bought the farm. We decided a few weeks ago we'd be married this fall."

"Well -" Marcia's blue eyes were serious. "'Tis a big step - marriage. There's always ups and downs - but I hope the path of life is smooth for you."

"Yeah, Ma. The old bittersweet trail."

Marcia smiled. "You're laughing at me. But it's true, children. You have to learn to take the bitter with the sweet." She glanced at Lucy who still stood just inside the door. "Have a chair, child. But you're not a child now. You're a young woman about to become the wife of my son."

"Thanks, Mrs. Avery." Lucy sat upright in the nearest straight chair.

"Where's Lilla Dale?" Jim asked.

"She's over at her school. She works there every Sunday. And Pa is cutting corn. You'll see him before you leave?"

"Yeah. Heard from Charley?"

"We had a letter last week. They've been having terrible forest fires near Saginaw again. He says it happens every year. It's bad enough that the woods are burned, but there are always people and animals killed too."

Jim agreed. "It's bad, but hardly a drop in the bucket to the disaster of the Chicago fire last October."

Marcia nodded. "And to think that whole terrible fire was started when Mrs. O'Leary's cow kicked over the lantern in the barn."

"How many people died in the Chicago fire?" Lucy asked.

"At least three hundred," Marcia replied. "And thousands were homeless. They say the wind was strong and it fanned the flames for twenty-four hours. There wasn't much left of Chicago when it was over."

In a moment Marcia continued. "Charley said he's planning on going to Canada in a few months. They need millwrights there, and he'll make more money. I don't like him to be around those sinful lumber camps."

"He's a big boy, Ma. And you know what you've always said. 'Train a child up in the way he should go, and when he is old he will not depart from it.'"

Marcia smiled. "I've tried. As it says in Psalms, 'I will instruct thee and teach thee in the way which thou shalt go.'"

Jim walked to the door. "I'm going to the field

to talk with Pa. I won't be gone long, but you and Lucy can get acquainted."

Self-consciously Lucy looked at the floor as she twisted her handkerchief. Marcia asked, "How is your Grandmother Colborn?"

"She's got rheumatiz real bad. She can't hardly walk without her cane. She's real old. It makes me feel bad. Grandma's a good woman."

"So you'll be married October 9th?" Marcia said.

"The Methodist preacher will marry us and Pa and Ma are planning a nice party for us afterward." She paused. "You and Mr. Avery and Lilla Dale will come, won't you?"

"Is it on our Sabbath - on Saturday?"

"No. Jim thought of that. It's on Thursday."

"I'd like to come if Jonas would."

"And Jim's sisters, Alice and Mary, you think they'd come with their families?"

"Mary lives near Newberg in Shiawassee County. I don't know if they can come. She has a baby, Hubert, almost a year old."

"I've never seen Alice since the buggy accident."

Marcia smiled. "She gets along fine with the shoe her cousin made for her." In a moment she asked, "What do you like to do, Lucy?"

"I like to sew. I'm making my wedding dress."

"You are? I've been wondering where you got that lovely wine-colored dress you're wearing. It's beautiful. Do you like to read?"

"When there's time. Seems like there ain't never been enough time for me to read much."

"That's too bad. You should make time to read. It exercises the mind just like walking exercises the body."

"Yeah. I guess so."

"Jonas, Lilla Dale and I have been reading that awful Charles Darwin's new book, "The Descent of Man." Has Jim read it?"

"I don't know. What's it about?"

"Darwin believes that man came from the same

group of animals as the apes."

"You mean 'way back a long time ago we was apes?"

"That's what Darwin says."

Lucy shook her head. "That's not what the Bible says. I don't read much but I know the Bible says the first man was Adam and his wife was Eve. We never come from no apes!"

Marcia smiled. "I agree. Darwin's been writing for several years. We also have his first book, "The Origin Of Species." There's been many angry discussions about his belief. I believe he is the Devil personified and that his idea of the origin of man is Satan's plot to destroy our morals."

Lucy shook her head. "How could anyone believe we came from apes? We were made by God! In Genesis it says that man was made in the image of God."

Marcia nodded. "'Tis a terrible thing to put such ideas out to confuse people." She listened. "I hear Jonas and Jim coming."

As soon as the men entered, the atmosphere changed. Lucy sensed a chill in the air. Both men appeared grim and unsmiling.

Marcia said, "Jonas, you remember Lucy Colborn?"

He nodded. "How do you do?"

Marcia continued. "Lucy and I have been getting acquainted. We've had a nice visit."

Jonas dropped into a chair. "Did you talk about mixing the races?"

Marcia's pale face flushed. "Well, no."

Jim shouted, "Go on, Pa! Get it off your chest! After you've made everyone miserable, you'll feel highly religious! Ha! Is that your idea of a Christian?"

Lucy stared at the two men, puzzled. Were they referring to her?

"Well - go on!" Jim shouted. "You've started it - now finish it!"

Jonas had a violent coughing spell. After a minute or two, he caught his breath. "Serves you right," Jim muttered, "Maybe God is giving you a bit of Hell on earth in your asthma, or whatever it is. You've got no business throwing stones at someone for something in their past that they had nothing to do with. Not with what I know about your past life. Now go ahead and say what you came in for!"

Marcia got up. "Now Jonas, don't say something you'll regret."

He was seized with another coughing spell. Finally he said hoarsely, "I'll say only what I have to, according to the Scriptures." He looked directly at Lucy. "Jim says you two are planning on marrying."

Her voice was almost inaudible. "Yes."

"Do you believe in the Bible?"

"Yes."

"The Bible says God created separate races and that the races were meant to be separate from one another. Negroes and whites should not marry. Orientals and whites shouldn't marry, and Indians and whites shouldn't marry."

Lucy stared at Jonas, her eyes wide. Jim came to stand beside her, his hand resting on her shoulder. "You've had your say, Pa, but it's not going to change anything. The wedding will be October 9th. I'd like to have my family there, if you'd care to come. Let's go, Lucy."

Marcia put out her hand to Lucy. "I'm sorry," she whispered. "It will work out, with God's help - it will work out." She kissed her future daughter-in-law lightly on the cheek.

Through tear-filled eyes Lucy saw Marcia's blurred face. "Thank you, mother," she whispered.

As they left the yard and drove onto the dusty country road, Jim muttered, "The old bittersweet trail -"

Chapter XXIV

PNEUMONIA, THE DREADED ILLNESS

(1875)

Jim hunched his shoulders and pulled his collar high against the late March rain. He urged the team on. It would be good to get inside at the Wayside Inn. He wondered why he wanted to go there where there were so many memories. Well - it was the nearest inn to downtown Lansing and they had a livery stable for his horses. 'Twas as good a place as any.

He daydreamed as the team splashed through puddles from a week's steady rain. He'd been foolish to start out this morning, but for an hour or two the sky had cleared and the sun had shone faintly. Soon, however, the cold rain returned. The Red Cedar River at Williamston had overflowed its banks and the water and ice floes swirled only a few inches below the wooden bridge.

"Giddap!" Jim shouted to his team as he slapped their sides with the reins. He'd get to Lansing, buy the rocker for Lucy and some candy for Charley, then he'd stay over night and start home in the morning. On the way back he'd stop at M.A.C. to get a few bushel of an improved seed corn the agricultural college had developed. Uncle Harmon had influence at the college. Without his help, he wouldn't have stood a chance of getting any of the new seed.

His thoughts returned to his little son. Charley was starting to talk. Strange how much he resembled the Averys. There wasn't a sign of the Indian heritage in his appearance. Everyone remarked, almost in surprise Jim thought, that

Charley was a beautiful baby. Another year or two and they could go to the barn and fields together, and sometimes they'd go to town, too. Charley'd like that for he always squealed with delight when they rode in the buggy or cutter.

There were few rigs on the road. The rain would turn to sleet if the temperature fell a few degrees. Miserable and cold, Jim decided he'd buy Lucy's rocker before he put the team in the stable. Then he'd stay inside and dry out. Maybe tomorrow the rain would have stopped.

As he crossed the Grand River on Michigan Avenue he was astonished to see the water only a short distance below the level of the street. Huge pieces of ice floated beneath the bridge. There was no cause for worry, though, because in 1873 and 1874 the city had built five iron span bridges across the Grand River that would withstand any amount of rushing water.

An hour later his purchases were made and Jim was at the Wayside Inn. He felt like Santa Claus. Lucy didn't know he planned to buy her a rocking chair, but she'd enjoy rocking Charley. 'Twould be nice for both of them. And the little boy would like the top Jim had bought for him, and the candy, too. With a sudden pang, he realized he was homesick for his family.

Jim stood before the fireplace in the barroom. The heat felt good. He hung his wet coat over a chair and pulled it before the fire to dry.

A man came in from the kitchen. "Did you want something?" he asked as he tied on a white apron.

"A bit of whiskey might warm me up," Jim replied. "Miserable day."

"Yeah. Help yourself to the sandwiches." He motioned toward a filled plate on the bar.

Jim sat by the fireplace with his drink and a sandwich. "Not many people around today," he remarked wolfing down half of a sandwich.

"Nope. They'll start comin' in about four this afternoon if the rain stops. I'm goin' back to the kitchen. If you need anything, jest holler."

Jim pulled a book from his pocket and sat with his back to the fire. For two hours he lost himself in Mark Twain's "The Innocents Abroad." He chuckled over the stories, character sketches and satirical comments of the author as he related his travel experiences.

Jim closed his book. Like his grandfather, Stephen Avery, Jim knew he had "itchy feet." He craved new experiences and being able to see new places. But Lucy would never leave the land where she was born. He sighed. Might as well give up that dream. He'd live and die on the old Amos Colborn farm. He went to his room to wash up for supper.

Outside the rain continued beating against the windows in torrents. He wondered what Lucy and Charley were doing. Lucy's brother, Jim, would milk the cows and feed the hogs and sheep. They were all right at home. Tomorrow he'd be back with them.

After supper was served to Jim and three other guests, he returned to the bar for a smoke and a drink. Somehow he didn't feel like socializing so he returned to his room where he read by lamplight until eleven o'clock.

All night long the rain beat against his window. Finally about six in the morning the rain tapered off to a heavy mist. By seven thirty when he had finished breakfast the sun was breaking through the clouds in the east.

As he paid his bill at the desk the clerk commented, "The river's over its banks and rushing like blazes. Twouldn't surprise me to see the bridges go."

Jim laughed. "I know - April fool! You didn't catch me." He pocketed his change.

"I ain't foolin'. Go see for yourself."

Jim went out the back way, harnessed and hitched his team and drove onto Grand Avenue. People on both sides lined the banks, all looking south toward the new Mineral Wells bridge. He stopped the horses to watch. The ice-filled river rose and churned. The usually calm stream was now a raging torrent.

As he watched, the center span of the bridge upstream caved slowly, like a man who has been shot but doesn't fully realize what has happened to him. A terrific roar and a wide geyser of spume drifted above the river. Then the bridge sank to bob up downstream.

A great cry went up from the spectators which could be heard above the disastrous crash.

"It can't be," Jim muttered aloud. "I'm dreaming. No flood waters could smash those iron spans." But the Mineral Wells bridge was there to the south bobbing along among the ice floes on its way to the Michigan Avenue span. That would go next.

Like a drunken monster the Mineral Wells bridge lurched and tumbled squarely under the Michigan Avenue span, its upper steel work scraping and grinding the span above. The tumbling structure lurched on its mad way toward North Lansing. Then Jim saw why the Michigan Avenue bridge still stood. It had no central pier.

The people now were running north in an effort to keep up with the riling water and the rampaging bridge. Jim turned his team and followed the others who were whipping their horses and sending them in a mad dash north along Grand Avenue as excited pedestrians scattered. The Shiawassee Street bridge was directly in the path of the runaway span.

Shortly the Mineral Wells bridge smashed against the central pier of the Shiawassee Street structure. For a split second they clung like fighters in a death clinch. Then, together they went tumbling straight down the river toward the Saginaw Street iron bridge. It never had a chance.

Now three bridges were wildly lunging down the course of the Grand River toward the millrace at North Lansing - a chilling, yet a thrilling sight. For fifteen minutes the wreckage of the three bridges pounded at the Franklin Street span. Then finally it toppled to join the wreckage of its sister bridges and the rubble of four bridges roared past the millrace toward the Seymour Street bridge less than two blocks away. It died a quick death.

Bewildered residents of the Delta Mills Community a few miles downstream gaped at the mass of wreckage, wooden beams and iron which piled up along their shores, or of that still sliding through the boiling water and grinding ice.

Jim felt dazed. He had never imagined such destruction could result from the usually calm Grand River. The people spoke softly, as though they were in the presence of death, as they were, for on that day, April 1, 1875, five of their beautiful new bridges had been carried to their death.[1]

Six weeks after the disastrous flood in Lansing, Lucy hummed "Rock Of Ages" as she went about her housework. Her paring knife slid through a potato, then before dropping it into a kettle of water, she cut a thick slice from the raw vegetable and offered it to twenty-two month old Charley. He shoved her hand away.

"Good," she coaxed. "Good potato. 'Twill make you grow."

Charley shook his head so vigorously his red curls danced. "No!" He toddled to the window. "Pa?" he said pointing toward the barn.

"Pretty soon. Pa's plowing."

Charley suddenly was seized with a violent spell of coughing. After a minute Lucy went to the cupboard where she removed the cork from a bottle and poured a spoonful of liquid. She held the spoon out to Charley. "Open," she ordered.

----

1. Darling, Bert, City In the Forest. Stratford House, 1950.

"No!"

"Open. 'Tis honey medicine. 'Twill stop your cough."

"No!"

"Uncle Harmon says it's good for a cough and so does Great-grandma Colborn. Come now, Charley. Open up."

He shook his head and ran to sit in a corner behind the kitchen range. The hacking cough continued. Lucy poured the honey and vinegar back into the bottle and returned to peeling potatoes. Something was wrong with Charley. Usually he was good natured, unless he was crossed, when he showed the well-known Avery temper. But the last day or two he'd coughed more than usual, and he wasn't eating right. The cough was different from the one she'd grown accustomed to - the one Jim called "the Avery curse." Maybe Charley was coming down with something. Both measles and whooping cough had been going around Conway Township.

When she looked behind the kitchen range the baby was sleeping. An hour later Jim came in for dinner. Tossing his battered hat onto a hook beside the door, he asked, "Where's Charley?"

"Sleeping. He hasn't been like himself this morning. His cough is worse and he's cross and ornery. Maybe he's teething."

"He'll likely be better when he wakes up."

Lucy poured the coffee and they sat down to eat. "How long before you'll have the corn ground plowed," she asked.

"Another three, four days. But I think it's going to rain. That'll hold me up." He looked toward the west. "I kind of like rainy days."

"In planting time?"

"Any time. Gives me a chance to catch up on my reading. I have two new books I haven't opened."

Lucy laid her fork on the plate with a clatter. "You and your books! They're more important to you than the crops!"

Jim's blue eyes flashed. "You'd be better off

if you spent some time reading!"

"You're ashamed a' me 'cause I ain't educated!"

Jim drew a deep breath. "No, I'm not ashamed of you. I'm proud of you. But you'd be happier if you thought of something besides Charley, and housework and farming."

Lucy tossed her head. "Them's the things I like to think about. An' I wish you'd quit jawing at me about reading -"

Charley whined, a weary, tired sound. Lucy peeped behind the kitchen range. Suddenly she froze, trying in vain to speak. At last she croaked, "Jim - Jim - Charley's - Charley's -"

Jim jumped up so suddenly his chair tipped and hit the floor with a bang. Reaching behind the range he seized the baby and cradled him in his arms. The little body was jerking with violent convulsions as it twisted and turned and the muscles of the tiny face, arms and legs twitched. Suddenly the whole body stiffened and became rigid.

Lucy screamed, "He's dying!"

"Fill the wash tub with cool water!" Jim ordered as he began to undress the rigid little body. "Hurry!"

Lucy ran to the shed for the tub. Two minutes later Jim gently lowered the unconscious baby into the cool water. Suddenly the rigidity left the body but the arms and legs still twitched violently.

Lucy, wringing her hands, was crying as she moaned over and over, "He's dying. He's dying. He's dying."

All at once the twitching stopped and Charley's blue eyes opened wide. "Pa," he said.

"Yeah, Charley. Pa and Ma are here." He spoke to Lucy. "Get his nightdress."

The baby yelled, "No! No bed!"

While they dried him and got him into his nightgown, the baby complained loudly. Finally he settled down in Lucy's arms in the rocking chair. She hummed as she rocked and soon he again was sleeping.

Jim sat at the table with a medical book. "Convulsions," he said. "Here it is." In a moment he added, "We did the right thing. It says 'immerse the body in cool water.'"

Lucy laid her hand on the baby's forehead. "He's burning up with fever."

"That happens, it says here, with convulsions."

"But what's he got?"

"I don't know. I'm going for Uncle Harmon."

Ten minutes later he whipped up the sorrel horse and drove toward the south. Lucy threw a quilt about the sleeping baby and hurried the short distance to her parents' home. Her mother was alone. Hurriedly she explained to Hannah what had happened. The Indian woman seized her shawl and started for the door.

"Ma," Lucy exclaimed. "Don't leave me! He might have another spell!"

"You go home. Wait for doctor. I get Fawn and come to your house." Then she was gone.

Carrying her feverish, sleeping child, Lucy prayed silently for the baby's recovery. Shortly after she was home Hannah and Fawn arrived carrying a handful of willow switches.

From the rocking chair Lucy asked, "What you doin'?"

"Make Indian medicine for Charley," Hannah replied as she and Fawn broke the willow twigs into short lengths, covered them with water and placed them on the stove to steep. The two women hovered over the steaming kettle, silently stirring and poking to hurry the cooking process.

Charley opened his eyes. Quickly Lucy unbuttoned her dress and gave him her breast to nurse. He sucked feebly a few times before he again fell asleep. She meditated. He was a beautiful baby. The moment Jim saw him after he was born, he'd exclaimed, "Another Charley Avery! He looks just like Charley!" And from that moment they had called him "Charley."

As she rocked the sick child Lucy was conscious

of a familiar dull ache in one of her back teeth. She'd heard women say you lose a tooth for every baby you have. One of these days she'd have to have that tooth pulled. Well - she wouldn't have another baby as long as she nursed Charley because you didn't get in the family way when you were nursing a child. Of course she wanted more children, but not too soon.

Hannah brought a spoon and a little of the liquid from the steeped willow twigs to Lucy. "Give to baby. Good for fever," she said.

"I wish Jim would come with the doctor," Lucy said as she shifted Charley to a sitting position. He opened his eyes and began to cough, a harsh, dry, hacking cough which caused the tiny face to contort with pain. "It hurts him bad," Lucy commented. "And his nose is running. Maybe it's just catarrh." She wiped his nose gently.

When the baby was quiet they tried to get him to swallow a few spoonfuls of the willow liquid, but he turned his head away and clamped his lips shut.

"It's no use," Lucy said.

"Doctor here," Fawn announced as Jim and his uncle pulled into the yard.

Harmon, with his black bag in hand, came inside while Jim tied the horses. "What have we here?" he asked pulling a chair beside Lucy's.

"He's awful sick, Uncle Harmon. Tell us what to do," Lucy begged.

Harmon grasped the little wrist, his eyes on the second hand of his watch. "Uh-huh. His heart's beating fast, but that goes with the high fever. Has he had more convulsions?"

"No."

"How long's he had the cough and runny nose?"

"A few days. But he won't eat."

"See that rash up there near his hair?"

"Yeah."

"Let's see his chest." They uncovered the sleeping baby. "Uh-huh," the doctor repeated. "He's got measles. See the fine rash on his chest?"

Jim came in. "The baby's got measles," Lucy announced. "I guess we got worried for nothing."

"Measles aren't anything to fool with," Harmon said. "Get him into the bedroom and keep the shades down. Light's bad for the eyes. Keep him warm so he breaks out good. His throat is sore so he won't eat much, but try to get him to drink cool water. If he goes into convulsions again, put him in lukewarm water like you did before."

The Indian women stood silently in the background. "Then he'll be all right?" Jim asked.

"Usually they are, but sometimes children develop other problems with measles."

"Like what?"

"Weak eyes or earaches and occasionally pneumonia - lung fever. But that doesn't happen often. I'll stop by in a day or two. He should be over the worst of it by then."

Lucy said, "He's slept 'most all day. That ain't like him."

"That's from the fever." Harmon grinned at Jim. "You named him right. I remember when your brother, Charley, looked just like this little feller - he's a nice baby." His eyes went to the silent Indian women at the far end of the room. "Your Ma and aunt going to help you, Lucy?"

"Yeah." She brushed back a damp curl from the baby's forehead. "We'd better get him into the bedroom."

Through the next several days they hovered over the sick little boy coaxing him to eat and drink. The racking cough and the high fever were taking their toll in rapidly weakening the baby's resistance. Each time he came Harmon looked more grave. Finally he reluctantly said, "It's lung fever."

Lucy covered her eyes and sobbed. Jim said softly, "Is there any hope?"

Harmon absently rubbed his neatly trimmed gray beard. "While there's life, there's hope. Keep onion poultices and mustard plasters on his chest, but watch you don't blister the skin."

"We've done that," Jim said tersely.

"I've something here that I use for croup. It's alum and sugar. It might help him breathe easier." Removing a jar from his black bag, he poured some of the powder into an envelope. "Lucy, stir a teaspoonful of this in a little warm water and we'll try to get it down him."

But in spite of Harmon's efforts and the Indian folk remedies of Hannah, White Fawn and Great-grandmother Mary, Little Charley continued to lose ground in his battle for life. The desperately ill child clung to Lucy and was quiet only when she rocked him. Her heart ached as she looked down into the wan, drawn face of her first born. Neighbors and friends took turns staying round the clock with Jim and Lucy.

Then one day shortly after noon as Ben's wife washed dishes and Lucy hovered over Charley, Jonas and Marcia arrived. After Jonas tied his horse he hurried to the barn where Jim was feeding the livestock. Surprised at the unexpected visit, Jim waited for his father to speak.

"Afternoon, son." Jonas' eyes were sad.

"Afternoon."

"We had to come. Harmon told us about little Charley."

Jim nodded, staring at the barn floor.

"Ma and I have prayed for him, and for you and Lucy."

"It's not done much good so far."

"I know how you feel, but don't turn against God the way I did when I was young." Jonas hesitated. "You know about my sister, Melissa?"

"I know she died young."

"Eighteen years old. A beautiful girl. She had consumption for years, but she ended her life with a butcher knife that I left beside her bed."

"I never knew that."

"Only my family knew. Your Ma doesn't know it - we weren't married then." They were quiet for a time before Jonas continued. "I was young - hot-headed and rebellious. I felt God was unjust to allow such a thing to happen. I brooded, and eventually decided there was no God. As you know, I was an atheist for years."

"Yeah."

"But I was wrong. I repented and now I know God lives. But I did things for years that hurt people." He put his hand on Jim's shoulder. "I'm sorry son, about - about Jennifer. I swear I never knew until you told me."

"That's over. She's married to a lawyer in New York. Got a couple children. She's out of our lives for good."

"I'm glad to hear it. Now I want to make my peace with you. Can you forgive me for the hurt I've caused you and Lucy? Surely God has forgiven Amos Colborn for marrying an Indian woman even though they produced a family that's of mixed races."

"Lucy's a good wife and mother. I don't know what it'll do to her if Charley dies."

"She'll pull through. She has faith in God."

"Yes. Likely more than I do."

Jonas put his arm about his son's shoulder. "Are things right between us again? Do you forgive me for the hurt I've caused you?"

"Yes, Pa." Tearfully they embraced.

"I feel better," Jonas said blowing his nose on his red bandanna.

They started toward the house. Suddenly the door burst open and Ben's wife, Marias, ran toward them, her skirts flapping about her ankles. "Hurry, Jim!" she shouted. "Little Charley -"

Jim sprinted up the steps into the house closely followed by his father. They found Lucy, dry-eyed, holding her dead baby. She looked up, her eyes vacant. "He's gone, Jim. Our baby's gone."

He nodded. "I'll take him."

"No! I want to hold him. I want to hold him as long as I can." She cuddled the little body.

"Poor baby. He's been so sick."

Marcia sat beside her daughter-in-law. "He's at rest now. He's not suffering and gasping for every breath. He's with God."

Lucy did not answer but continued rocking the little body, oblivious to everyone around her.

Marcia spoke to Jim. "Jonas and I will make the coffin. We'll fix it pretty. He'll have a nice soft place to rest. We're so sorry, son." Tears spilled down her cheeks.

Jim nodded. "Yes, Ma."

Jonas motioned to Jim. "Try to get the baby away from her," he whispered.

"I will when I can. I understand how she feels. She can't give him up."

"We'll be back, Lucy," Marcia said as she put on her bonnet. The bereaved woman did not look up. Marcia turned to Jim. "We'll bring the little coffin tomorrow as soon as it's finished." They closed the door softly on the grieving parents and their dead baby.

Chapter XXV

MEMORIALS AND MARITAL FRICTION

(1886 - 1894)

Lucy, carrying baby Gertrude, wandered with Hannah through the fields to the little family cemetery a short distance from the tumble down log cabin built by Robert and Israil Colborn in 1836. Behind them trailed Lucy and Jim's children, all born since 1876. Linneus, age ten, Otis nine, Edna five and Lucia three, all carried armloads of wild flowers. White lillies, adder's tongues, wild geranium and blue and white violets had been picked by the children to be placed on the graves of relatives. Each year at the end of May, Lucy, Hannah and the children made the pilgrimage to the cemetery.

Lucy said, as she had each year since the children could remember, "It's fittin' that we remember our dead relatives. If soldiers' graves are decorated on Decoration Day, why shouldn't we remember our family who wasn't soldiers?"

When they arrived at the tiny burying ground Lucy said, "We have six graves here. "We'll start with Great-grandmother Mary Colborn. Linn, read what it says on her marker."

Linn was a short pudgy child with a dark complexion and gray-blue eyes. He stood before the wooden marker and read, "Mary Colborn, born August 4, 1796; died May 17, 1877, age 81 years. Wife of Robert Colborn."

Lucy handed the baby to Hannah. "Scatter your flowers over Great-grandmother's grave, Linn." They stood quietly until he was finished. Lucy said softly, "She was a great lady, wasn't she

Ma?"

Hannah nodded. "Mrs. Colborn - nice lady."

Lucy continued. "And notice the date your Great-grandfather, Robert Colborn, died. 1837. Ma, you said he had only been in Michigan a few months when he was killed, didn't you?"

"Yeah. Tree fall on Robert Colborn. He die."

"Ote, put your adder's tongue flowers on Great-grandfather's grave." The child stepped forward. Though he was a year younger than Linn, he was taller. His dark skin and black eyes were a striking contrast to the fair skin and gray-blue eyes of his sisters, Edna, Lutie and Gertie.

When Ote was finished, he stepped back. "Ma," Lucy said, "Do you remember anything about Great-grandfather?"

"Robert Colborn help my family. Bring us food when smallpox sickness come."

The little group moved on to Israil Colborn's grave. "Edna, this man was your uncle. None of us knew him very well. He was my father's brother. He died in 1882. Put your flowers on his grave." The attractive little girl spread wild geraniums over Israil's grave.

They moved to a marker that bore the name Benjamin Colborn. Lucy said, "Uncle Ben has been dead only two years. Like Uncle Israil, he died from a heart attack. He was fifty-nine years old. Aunt Marias, his wife, is Albert's mother. Some of you remember Uncle Ben. Lutie, scatter your violets on his grave." The tiny girl did as her mother asked.

"Linn," Lucy said. "Do you remember my Pa?"

"A little. He had a peg leg."

"That's right. He died six years ago. He had brain fever and he was sixty-five years old."

Hannah passed the baby back to Lucy and took a bouquet of wild geraniums from beneath her shawl. She straightened, studied the grave and said, "My good husband, Amos." She slowly scattered her flowers.

They moved on to Baby Charley's grave. Lucy

stared silently at the ground. "Your little brother is buried here. He had red hair like your Pa. He died from measles and pneumonia." Lucy took a bouquet of white violets from a large pocket in her apron. Silently she scattered the dainty flowers over the grave. "You don't know it, Charley, but your brothers and sisters have come to visit you," she whispered.

The children stood respectfully, waiting for the ceremony to be concluded. Their mother said, "'Most all of the old ones are gone - all but Aunt Lide, Aunt Lucretia and Grandma Hannah. Remember this is where our relatives are buried. You can go now."

Linn and Ote let out a whoop and dashed off through the trees. Lucy muttered, "They sound like wild Indians."

Thrashing through the woods the boys yelled with relief at being released from their mother's yearly ceremony. Finally they slowed to a walk.

"We didn't hardly know them old people," Otis said.

"We remember Grandpa Amos. He clumped when he walked on his peg leg," Linn said. "And we remember Uncle Ben."

"Hey look!" Otis cried. "The old Indian burying ground!"

"Yeah. Looks like somebody put a fence 'round it once. It's 'bout all rotted now."

"Pa says when Grandpa Jonas Avery was a boy there was Indian tribes 'round here. Mebbe this was their cemetery."

Linn studied the slight mounds. "Spoze there's Indians' bones in there?"

"Mebbe."

"Hey! Let's get shovels and dig 'em up!"

"Yeah."

Ten minutes later the boys were cutting through the sod above the largest mound. The soil was sandy and the digging was easy. Otis stopped to swat a mosquito. Somewhat reluctantly he returned to the digging.

"Come on! You're slowing up!" Linn shouted.

"I'm - I'm scared," Otis panted. "Mebbe we hadn't oughta be diggin' up dead people."

"Scaredy cat. They're jest Indians." Suddenly Linn's shovel struck something. He stooped to brush the damp sand away. Otis hung over his shoulder.

"What is it? What is it?" the younger boy breathed.

Something white was showing through the sand. Linn burrowed with his hands and pulled out a human skull. "Jumpin' Jupiter!" he exclaimed. "There _are_ Indians in there!" He dropped the skull. "Help me cover it up."

Otis' black eyes were huge against his tannish-white face. "I'm too scared. Let's go."

"Come on! Help me cover it up! Then we'll go."

Quickly they replaced the loose soil. As they were smoothing it over Otis muttered, "They'll haunt us. All them dead Indians will haunt us."

"There ain't no ghosts. Nobody'll know we dug 'em up."

"Listen," Otis whispered. "I hear something."

Linn laughed. "It's jest Ma an' Grandma an' the girls goin' to the house. We better get 'way from here."

But it was too late. Edna shouted, "There's Ote and Linn!"

Lucy stopped, staring through the trees. "You boys wait right there!" she commanded. A minute or two later the two women and the little girls stood beside the Indian burying ground. Aghast, Lucy said, "You've been diggin' in the buryin' ground."

Frightened, they didn't reply.

"Answer me! You've been diggin'!"

"No, Ma," Linn said.

"We ain't, Ma," Ote muttered.

Lucy was furious and verbal. Hannah was furious, but silent. "That's an awful thing to do!" Lucy shouted. "Disturbin' the dead! What got into you? And on top of everything else, you lied! God will punish you! Mebbe them dead Indians will haunt you!" She handed Baby Gertrude to Hannah. and picked up a stout three-foot-long stick from the ground.

"Bend over, Linn." Her voice was low but determined.

The boy obeyed. Wielding the stick, Lucy vented her displeasure on her son's buttocks. Whack! Whack! Whack!

Linn refused to cry. He clamped his lips shut and stared at his bare sandy feet. Finally it was over.

"You're next, Ote. Bend over." The stick slammed against the younger boy's bottom.

"Ow! Ow! Ouch! It hurts! Ma it hurts! Ow! Ow!" Ote yelled with each whack of the stick.

Frightened, Lutie clung to her grandmother's skirts. Finally Lucy tossed the stick away. "Let this be a lesson to you. Don't never dig in this buryin' ground again! And whenever I catch you in a lie, you'll get whaled! Just remember!"

"Can we go?" Linn asked.

"Yes. Get out of my sight! Such young'uns! Ma, what do you suppose ails 'em?"

Hannah shook her head as Lucy again took the baby who had been awakened by the uproar. "Ain't she sweet, Ma?" Lucy was smiling as she gazed into the face of her two month old daughter. "They're nice when they're little, 'fore they get big enough to be ornery." She glanced at her mother. "You all right, Ma?" Hannah nodded. "You're holdin' your side."

The old lady gasped. "'Twas long walk. I go home."

"Edna, you and Lute walk home with Grandma."

When they were gone Lucy, carrying Gertrude, hurried home. She nursed the baby before putting her down for her morning nap.

She glanced at the clock. Half-past ten. She stuffed wood into the kitchen range and stirred up a molasses cake. Seemed like she was never done with cooking and baking. Her garden was planted but nothing was big enough to eat yet, though lettuce and radishes were coming along.

Shoving a large pan of molasses cake into the oven, she went to the shed for potatoes. They'd have boiled potatoes, fried eggs, bread and molasses cake for dinner. As she turned a shadow fell across the doorway. "Jim?" she asked.

A strange ragged man with a bundle on a stick over his shoulder blocked the doorway. "Mam," he said, "would you give me a bite to eat?"

Lucy squared her shoulders. A hobo, a lazy, good-for-nothing hobo. "I don't have dinner ready," she said shortly. "If you want to go to the field behind the barn, my husband might have something for you to do. Then I'd give you dinner."

"Mam, I ain't able to work."

"You're able to walk all over creation."

"But I can't work. I'm sick."

"You look all right to me. If you ain't able to work, you can move on. I don't feed men too lazy to work for a livin'." She brushed past him, went into the house and shut the door. She watched as he went south past the Brimley place.

A few minutes later Edna and Lute burst into the house. "Ma!" Edna shouted, "Grandma's sick! She's layin' on her bed and she won't talk!"

Lucy siezed Gertrude and as she ran down the steps she called, "Get Pa! Tell him to come to Grandma's."

They found the old Indian woman dead on her bed, the apparent victim of a heart attack. The next day she was buried in the family cemetery beside Amos.

That night when the children were in bed, Jim and Lucy talked. "You think the young'uns know about Ma and me?" she asked.

"I doubt it. There's no need for them to know. No one mentions it anymore."

Lucy sighed. "I'll never tell 'em. I ain't proud of it." In a minute she continued. "Ma was upset when Linn and Ote dug in the old burying ground. She had a pain in her side. You think that brought on the spell?"

"Indians have strange ideas about disturbing the dead. Were some of her relatives buried there?"

"I don't know. She never told me nothin' - only that it was an Indian burying ground."

"We can't do anything about it," Jim answered. "It's no use to upset the boys by accusing them of bringing on the attack."

"I told them Indian spirits would haunt 'em."

Jim laughed. "That's punishment enough - along with the whaling you gave them. The buggers, they deserved it. And lying, too. I won't stand for young'uns lying."

****

The years passed. By the early 1890's two more children were born to Jim and Lucy. Max arrived in 1888 and Marcia in 1893. A new, large white frame house now stood on the corner of the county line road and the narrow road to the south. A Methodist church had been built across the road where Lucy and the girls attended regularly. Lucy was disappointed that Jim and their two older boys refused to go to church with her. The last time she had urged him to set an example for the boys, he'd exploded in rage.

"Nag! Nag!" he'd shouted. "You go to your church, but let me alone! The boys can go or not, just as they damn please!"

"I know," she retorted. "You lean toward the crazy Seventh Day Adventist way! I see you doin' less and less work on Saturday and leaving big jobs for Sunday. You do it to bother me! Next you'll stop eatin' pork! Well, when you do, you'll go hungry!"

His tone moderated. "I've been thinking about it. The Bible says swine are unclean. We shouldn't eat or drink things that harm our body."

"Humph!"

"And I may as well tell you. I'm going to start sending money to the Adventist Church at Newberg where Pa and Ma go since they've moved."

"What? Are you out of your mind? We can't afford to send them money!"

"Since Pa and Ma have moved to Shiawassee County near Lilla Dale and her husband, they've told me about the good their church does. They're starting missions in foreign countries."

"Humph!"

"You give to the Methodist church and I don't stop you. I'm sending five dollars a month to Pa and Ma's church."

"You're crazy! I always knew it! You waste our money on books we don't need - and - and - that - that - old dust catcher you bought! Spendin' money we was goin' to use to buy more land for an organ! An organ nobody can play! You're plumb crazy, Jim Avery. Any fast talking city slicker can get your money away from you! Every time I look at that organ I feel like blowin' up. You wasted our money and now you want to send sixty dollars a year to the Adventists!"

Jim's voice dropped. "I'd hoped the young'uns would learn to play the organ. They need music."

"There's music 'cross the road at the church."

Jim sighed. "You'll never understand there's more in life than grubbing the land to make more money to buy more land. Linn, Ote and Edna are about grown. It's too late to do much for them, but the younger ones need a chance to know about some of the finer things in life. I thought they might learn to play the organ by ear."

After openly declaring his beliefs Jim practiced the Seventh Day Adventist creed. He refused to do any farm work on Saturday, other than caring for the animals. He became disagreeable if Lucy did her weekly cleaning and baking on Saturday. He tithed religiously, sending money monthly to his church. The abrasive friction between husband and wife over the religious issue resulted in a tense family atmosphere.

Though Linn and Ote witnessed their parents' religious problems, they remained uncommitted and secretly longed for the day when they were able to go out into the world.

For several years Jim had spoken often of his admiration for men who were homesteading government land in the West. After the Dakota Territory became the states of North and South Dakota, the 39th and 40th states in 1889, adventurous families set out to make new homes. The Indian wars were over and the era of bonanza wheat farming had continued for several years. Population increased rapidly after statehood.

Sitting around the dining room table one winter night after the younger children were in bed, Jim dreamed aloud to his sons. "I've always wanted to see the West. Uncle Sam will give anyone land - good land - in North Dakota, just for living on it for five years."

Lucy, clasping Baby Marcia to her breast, rocked furiously. "I ain't goin'."

Jim ignored his wife's outburst. "'Twould be a chance to see the country and to get one hundred sixty acres of good land for nothing."

"Who'd do the work here?" Linn asked.

"Two of us could go in November when the fall work's done and the other could stay here to keep up the chores and cut wood for Ma and the young'uns. Then in early May, we'd be back to get the crops in here."

"Sounds good to me," Ote said enthusiastically. "I'd like to try it. 'Twould give me a chance to get a start."

"You have to be a United States citizen, which you are, and you have to be twenty-one, which you're not. But I could homestead the land in my name, and I'd see you got it cheap." He stared at the organ in the corner. "I'd like to get away and see something different."

"Humph!" Lucy snorted.

"What do you think, Linn?"

"I don't want to be a farmer. If you go, take Ote."

Jim got up. "'Tis an idea. We'll think about it."

Two days later Jim and his boys drove the team and wagon to Webberville to get a supply of cornmeal and flour made from their home grown grains. Ote looked at his brother questioningly. "You're mighty dressed up just to go to town."

"I might go on to Lansing."

"What you got in mind, son?" Jim asked.

"Nothing special." He grinned. "I'm like you. I want a change." He hesitated. "I didn't say anything to Ma. I knew she wouldn't like it. I'll be back in a day or two."

Jim clucked to his horses. "'Twill do you good to see something different."

"Pa," Ote began. "I've been thinking about your homesteading plan. I'd like to try it."

Jim smiled. "So would I. Let's not say much to Ma now. There'll be time enough when our plans are made. Let's aim for this fall, though."

The rest of the way to Webberville Jim and Ote discussed the anticipated adventure. Linn listened but did not enter the discussion. He left them at the mill.

As they unloaded the grain at the elevator Jim recognized an elderly man in the wagon behind them. His thoughts flew back to the day years before when his mother and sisters had been in the buggy accident. That now feeble old man had been in the livery barn with him during the cyclone. What was his name? Then it came to him. Chappel.

He walked back to the old man. "Are you Fred Chappel?" he asked. The old gentleman cupped his ear with his hand. "Are you Fred Chappel?" Jim shouted.

The old fellow shook his head. A large man of near forty came from inside the mill. He looked exactly as the older man had when Jim first saw him. He smiled.

"Pa don't hear. Yes, he's Fred Chappel, and so

am I."

"You were a little guy thirty years ago when I saw you with your father and sister. There was another man caught in the storm that day. I think his name was Jacobs."

"You got a good memory, mister. What's your name?"

"Jim Avery."

The younger man nodded. He studied Jim's face. "Now I remember. Richard Jacobs was there and he was worried about Nettie."

"Who?"

"Nettie, his daughter. She was sickly when she was little, but she's healthy now. She's my wife." He lowered his voice. "She's in the family way."

"Your first young'un?"

The big man beamed. "Yeah. Nettie's real happy 'bout it. I hope she don't have trouble. She's a tiny little lady."

The men stopped their conversation to watch a young man and his lady friend pedal by on a tandem bicycle. The woman wore a mutton sleeve, waist fitting black blouse with a long full black skirt that covered her high button shoes. A ribbon bedecked her hat which was pinned to her high pompadour-styled hair. The man wore a striped blue jacket and tight fitting trousers. Over his shoes, white spats were buttoned, and on his head a flat straw sailor was anchored to his lapel with a black cord. His dark handle-bar mustache was waxed and trained into an upward coil.

"Looks like fun," Ote commented. "That old high wheeler of yours, Pa, is hard to ride. Whenever I hit a rock it throws me forward and the little back wheel comes up and clips me in the back of the head."

Jim laughed. "I've had many a bump from that little wheel." He turned back to the younger Chappel. "Your sister was with you that day in the livery barn. She's grown by now."

"Yes. She's married to George Judson. Her name

is Rose. Rose Judson."

"The years make changes," Jim said. "I have seven children. The oldest is seventeen and the youngest is thirteen months old."

"It's nice seeing you again. "I hope we meet before another thirty years go by. I'd be 'most as old as Pa by then."

On the way home Jim said, "I'm going to stop over at a German family's place. I hear they have a Jersey cow for sale." He grinned. "Your Ma'd be glad to see me bringing home a cow instead of 'books or somethin' foolish,' as she says."

"Is this place far out of our way?"

"A couple of miles. They live on the road a mile east of ours, and about three miles south. We'll cut across east on the road that passes the Sixteen school."

"What's their name?"

"Klein. Charley Klein's the father. I've never met him. Guess they must do their trading in Fowlerville."

They rounded a curve and turned south for a short distance. A few tombstones on a little knoll to the left likely was the family burying ground.

"This is the place," Jim said pointing to a small wood-colored house on the hill to the right. "Jeremiah Casady said 'twas the first place past the curve."

"They have a nice barn," Ote commented. "Looks new."

The team leaned into their harnesses as they pulled the wagon up the steep hill to the house. Jim knocked. A tall, big boned woman came to the door. A tiny dark-eyed girl clung to the woman's skirt.

"I'm Jim Avery, Mrs. Klein. I heard your husband has a Jersey cow for sale."

The woman nodded. "Yah. Ve has. Charley iss in barn." She motioned. The little girl peeped through her fingers at Jim.

"What's your name?" Jim asked.

The child hid behind her mother. "Her name iss Clara. She iss five. She iss the baby."

Jim nodded. "I'll go to the barn now." He tipped his hat and returned to the wagon while Ote tied the horses to the hitching post.

A few rods to the south the barn doors stood open. Two young men were cleaning the stables. Forkfuls of manure flew from a door on either end to a high pile of manure in front of each door. Cows stood in the barnyard contentedly chewing their cuds.

The blue eyed young man in the cowbarn paused as Jim and Ote approached. "We heard you have a Jersey cow for sale," Jim began.

"That's right. Pa!" he shouted.

A short heavy set man came from the alley before the cow's manger. He walked with a slight limp. Yah?" he asked.

"We're the Averys. We came to see the cow you have for sale."

"Yah." He limped into the barnyard. "There." He pointed to a fat tan-colored cow in the corner of the barnyard. "Theodore, bring her in. We milk her for the man. She good cow. We show him how much milk she give."

While the young man milked, his father called to the boy in the horse barn. "Dan, go to house and get cup. I like Mr. Avery taste Jersey milk."

"Why are you selling her?" Jim asked.

"Ve need new house. Old house too little for eight childs, my sick ma an' me and Layah."

"Eleven of you live there?"

"Yah. Need new house. Need money. Ve sell few cows."

A short time later the deal was made, the cow was tied behind the wagon and by half-past four the Averys were headed home. A short distance up the road they met a group of five children returning from school. "They must be the Kleins," Ote said.

Jim stopped the team. "They got Molly!" a small boy shouted.

"I bought your cow. What's your name?"

"George. George Klein." The gray-eyed child had a shy appealing smile.

"Are these your brothers and sisters?"

The tallest boy who looked to be about sixteen replied, "We're all Kleins. I'm Charles, Will is fourteen, Lydia is twelve, Sarah is ten and George here, is eight."

Jim stroked his beard. "I've got an eight year old girl. Her name's Gertrude," he said smiling at George. "When's your birthday?"

The child stared down at his heavy felt shoes. "January 9th," he said.

"Gertie is a little younger. Her birthday is March 24th." He clucked to the team. "Nice talking to you Kleins."

As they moved on Ote said with a grin. "They're Dutchy - the mother and father sound like they're right out of the old country. Wonder what happened to Charley's foot?"

"Jeremiah Casady said he cut part of it off getting lumber out for the barn. But they're workers. Those German people all are."

They rode in silence for a time, then Ote said, "We've got our work cut out for us if we homestead in Dakota. Ma won't want us to go."

Jim stroked his beard absently. "I'm nigh to fifty years old. Your Ma and I don't see eye to eye. She's content to stay home. I like the farm, but there's other things than work in life."

The horses plodded on and the Jersey cow tied behind the wagon meekly followed. Finally Jim continued. "Linn's got itchy feet. 'Twouldn't surprise me if he enlists in the army."

"He's mentioned it a few times."

"Course 'twill be hard for your Ma with the baby and all - but I'll be back next May."

"Sure, Pa. And Ma's so wrapped up in Baby Marcia, she'll hardly miss us."

"Lucy always loves her children best when they're babies." Jim's eyes twinkled. "They're easier to handle before they have minds of their own." He paused. "Maybe that's not it - she's never got over your brother Charley's death, and maybe she's afraid something will happen to each baby as it comes along. Eight young'uns, we've had - Hm-m-m-m." He was silent for a time, then he said, "Like I said, I'll soon be fifty years old. If I'm going to see anything outside Michigan in my lifetime, I'd better do it soon. Brother Charley travels all over Canada putting in mills. He's always had the Avery itchy feet. I have a touch of the same disease. Ote, we'll go this fall."

Chapter XXVI

THE END OF THE TRAIL

(1895)

Lucy vigorously stirred the kettle of steaming cornmeal mush on the kitchen range. Seven year old Max leaned against the table and whined, "I don't like old mush."

"Me neither," Gertrude said.

"You'll eat it if you're hungry." Lucy turned to Edna. "Set the table and put on bread and applesauce. We're all tired of it, but 'twill fill us up." Edna, tall and graceful at fourteen, gave promise of her mature beauty. Lucy saw in the child her own once beautiful face and figure. Now she was shapeless from childbearing and fat from the monotonous diet of pork and beef, bread, cornmeal mush and potatoes.

"Lute, slice the bread," Lucy ordered, "while I get Marcia. Poor baby, she ain't feelin' good."

"Maybe she's teething," twelve year old Lute suggested. The wails of the youngest Avery child echoed through the big farmhouse.

Max pouted, "I wish she'd shut up. I'm sick a' her yellin'."

Gertrude retorted, "We're sick a' your whinin', too."

"Yeah," Lute and Edna answered as one. Edna continued, "She's not two yet and you whine more than she does."

Max stamped his right foot on the bare wooden floor. "I'm sick! I've got the wheezes!"

"We know," Lute replied wearily. "So do I and so does Marcia."

Lucy carried her auburn-haired baby to the

rocking chair beside the dining room window. "Girls, put supper on the table while I rock her. She's feverish." The child coughed violently. Lucy settled her large body in the rocker Jim had bought in Lansing many years before when Baby Charley was small. The old chair had rocked all eight of the Avery children. It squeaked as she moved to cuddle her youngest child.

"Max, carry in two or three chunks of wood from the porch. Edna'll throw it in the heater for you." She sighed. "Anyway, your Pa cut wood for us." She glanced outside at the snowy winter twilight. Late February. Would this winter never end? Resentment constantly seethed within her. What right did Jim have to go gallivanting off to Dakota leaving her with the children and responsibility of the farm? Suppose something happened to him? How would she manage? Linn was in the army, and Ote was with Jim in Dakota - she was alone with the children and the farm animals.

"Ma! You gonna eat?" Lute called.

Lucy roused herself. "Yeah. Baby's sleeping again." She carried Marcia back to the bedroom and returned to the head of the table. After murmuring a few words of grace she silently poured milk on her mush.

"What you s'poze Pa and Ote are doin'?" Gertrude asked.

Lucy stared into her bowl. Edna answered. "They're living in their little sod shanty, Pa said in his letter. I wonder what they find to do when they have one of them Dakota blizzards?"

"Just stay in the shanty, I guess." Gertrude replied.

"Pa said in his letter they go with the team and sleigh to the coal mine to buy coal," Lute said through a mouthful of applesauce. "What was the name of the town they go to?"

"Minot!" Max yelled.

"Hush," Lucy ordered. "You'll wake Marcia."

"I don't care! I don't like her!"

"Shame on you. And you'd better care. If you

wake her with your yellin', I'll tan your breeches."

Glumly the boy spooned applesauce into his mouth. In a moment he muttered, "My throat hurts." No one responded.

Lucy stared outside into the falling snow, oblivious to the smug smiles of her daughters who seldom missed an opportunity to tantalize Max. There had been only one letter from Jim and Ote. Ote, like his Grandmother Marcia Avery, had taken to writing poetry. Only he didn't write religious poems, he wrote of life in Dakota. 'Twould be nice to get more letters, but 'twas so far and none of them got to town often.

As though aware of her mother's thoughts, Edna said, "Ma, when is it there'll be someone to bring our mail to us?"

"Next year. 1896."

"Will we have to pay?" Gertrude asked.

"Just for the stamp. The government will pay men to bring mail to the farms."

"Will Pa go back to Dakota this fall?" Lute asked.

"Humph! Heaven knows how many years he'll go traipsin' off leavin' us here alone! A fine Christian he is, desertin' his family this way!"

Edna changed the subject. "It's nice Linn likes the army. I 'spect he'll stay in after his time is up. He wants to see the world."

"The Averys is all alike," Lucy retorted. "They're never content - always got to wander 'round from place to place. I'm s'prized your father hasn't gone before." Lucy got up.

"Edna, you and me has to go do the chores. I declare, I'm tired a' milkin', feedin' animals an' cleanin' stables - but it has to be done. Lute, you and Gertie do the dishes, an' - an' Max, you behave!"

As they bundled up Lucy said, "If Marcia wakes up, leave the dishes and one of you girls rock her. I hope she feels better tomorrow. She didn't eat a thing this afternoon. Her throat is awful red inside, and she's coughed all day."

"Maybe it's just the wheezes again," Gertrude said.

Lucy and Edna, with milk pails over their arms, walked through the blowing snow to the barn. An hour later the cows and horses were watered and fed, the hogs slopped, and the two cows milked. Returning to the house they carried near full milk pails. The sound of Marcia's crying reached them as they went up the steps into the house.

In spite of her size, Lucy moved quickly to take the baby from Lute. Cradling the child in her arms she sank into the rocker without removing her coat.

"She's coughed and sneezed all the time you were gone," Lute said. "And she's got red spots all over her face."

Lucy carried the child to the kerosene lamp on the table. Her heart lurched as she stared into Marcia's mottled little face. Suddenly the baby was seized with a fit of coughing and the strain caused the rash to stand out in a frightening manner. "Ma, rock," the child gasped. Clasping Marcia to her breast, Lucy dropped into the rocker. Softly she sang:

"Rock-a-bye baby in the tree tops
When the wind blows, the cradle will rock,
When the bough breaks, the cradle will fall,
Down will come rock-a-bye, baby and all."

From a chair near the stove Max said, "That's a funny song. Babies don't have cradles in trees."

"Bird babies do," Gertrude said.

"Indian papooses' cradles sometimes hang on tree branches," Lute said. "I seen pictures."

Max snorted. "You're making up lies, ain't she Ma?"

Lucy didn't answer.

"Ma!" the boy yelled. "Did Indians hang their babies in trees?"

"I don't know. Edna, would you skim the cream

from the morning's milk and fill the pans again with fresh milk? We'll have to churn butter in a day or two."

Max muttered, "I ain't gonna churn."

Gertrude retorted, "You never do."

"I don't feel good," Max whined. "My throat hurts and I feel sick an' - an' -" he shivered, "I'm cold."

"You'll live," Lute replied.

After a sleepless night, at six o'clock in the morning, Lucy and Edna made their way to the barn. The snow creaked under their feet. "I don't know what to do," Lucy confided to Edna. "Something bad is wrong with Marcia."

"Maybe it's measles."

"There ain't been any measles around this winter. She's all broke out. Her chest is covered with a red rash. She has an awful fever." She paused. "Max is getting the same thing."

"After breakfast I could go for the doctor," Edna said.

Lucy was silent. Her thoughts went back to little Charley. Maybe if - maybe - Marcia looked just like Charley had - beautiful, blue-eyed, auburn-haired. Surely God wouldn't take two of her babies.

Edna opened the barn door. "Think I ought to go for the doctor?"

"It's awful cold. Could you manage Prince on the cutter?"

"I can do it, Ma."

"All right." She sighed. "Two of them sick. Drat your father! He ought to be here helpin' us 'stead a' rammin' round out there in that God-forsaken country!"

After breakfast Lucy sent Lute and Gertrude to the rural Gallagher school a short distance west of their home. Her time was occupied between caring for Marcia and Max, but her thoughts constantly returned to little Charley, her first born. If he'd lived he'd have been twenty-two years old. Dr. Atkins, Jim's uncle, had been the only doctor in the area. Now Uncle Harmon had been dead almost ten years. The new Doctor Randall in Webberville was young. He was the only doctor nearby.

Marcia wailed and Lucy rocked faster. Max, his face flushed and mottled, whined, "Ma, I wish I was a baby so you'd rock me."

Lucy swallowed. "Come here. My lap's big enough for my two littlest babies." She cuddled a child with each arm. "Ain't you glad you've got a big Ma?"

The children didn't answer but each snuggled close to their mother's ample bosom.

Edna was back by noon. "The doctor will come soon," she said. "He says there's a lot of scarlet fever goin' 'round." The girl looked at Max on his mother's lap and grinned. "We always knew you was a baby," she teased.

Lucy bristled. "Leave him alone! He's sick!"

As if to prove the point, Max coughed and wheezed for several minutes. His sister ignored the demonstration as she put on her old clothes and went to the barn to unhitch the horse from the cutter. Then she fed and watered the cattle and horses and cleaned the stables. By the time she finished Dr. Randall was tying his horse at the hitching post.

Inside the house Lucy took the doctor's coat and they went to the bedroom. Opening his black sachel he removed the stethoscope and held it in his hands to warm it. Lucy stood between Marcia's crib and the big bed where Max wheezed and coughed. "The baby's been ailing for two days, but Max started feelin' bad last night," she said.

The tall young doctor approached Marcia's crib with the stethoscope. The little girl screamed, which brought on a coughing spell followed by labored breathing. Lucy spoke in a soothing manner. "Don't cry, Baby. The doctor will help you. Ma will stay here with you."

Finally Marcia allowed the stethoscope to be placed on her chest and back. "Hm-m-m," Dr. Randall murmured. "Her lungs are congested."

Lucy commented, "She always wheezes and coughs, but it's worse now."

"Open your mouth," the doctor said softly to the child. She obeyed. "Uh-huh. Now I'm going to put this thermometer in your mouth. It won't hurt."

Marcia watched the doctor, her blue eyes wide and frightened. "Leave it in your mouth a minute or two," he said smiling at the child. He walked over to peer down at Max. "How do you feel? Where do you hurt?"

Max whined, "My throat hurts. My head aches and I'm awful hot."

"Cough much?"

"Yeah. I always cough. I got the wheezes."

Dr. Randall removed the thermometer from Marcia's mouth and went to the window. He shook his head. "Watch her," he warned. "There's danger of convulsions - and pneumonia."

Lucy gasped. Little Charley had been like this. "What - what have they got?"

"Looks like scarlet fever. I'll check Max's temperature."

In a moment he said, "His temperature is high. It's scarlet fever, all right. Keep them warm. I'll leave some medicine. You could stew some willow bark and let them drink the water. Might help them sleep and lower the fever." The doctor paused. "Where's your husband? I'd like to talk to him."

Lucy stared across the road at a huge snowbank. "He's in Dakota," she said dully.

"Dakota?"

"He's homesteadin'."

There was a long pause. "Oh. Well - I'll get the medicine for you. The boy, being older, likely will get better in a few days. Scarlet fever is harder on younger children. I'll stop in a day or two to see how they are. Better keep the other children away from these two, and boil their handkerchiefs and bedding when you wash your clothes."

After the doctor was gone Lucy pulled the rocking chair into the bedroom.

"Us girls will help take care of them," Edna said softly.

"No. When Lute and Gertie come home from school all of you must stay out of the bedroom."

Edna's voice was low. "You think we'll all get it?"

Lucy's face was drawn. "I pray you won't."

"The doctor put a red quarantine sign on the side door, Ma."

"I know. None of us can go anywhere - but we don't want to - and none of the neighbors can come in. I'm afraid there's some bad days 'head a' us."

Edna went to stand with her back to the stove. The wind moaned down the chimney. "I'm strong, Ma. I won't get it." In a minute she added wistfully, "I wish Pa was here."

Lucy didn't answer. She was peering down at Marcia who was babbling in delirium. "No - no - go 'way."

Lucy bent to rub the baby's hot forehead. "Ma's here. The doctor's gone." She carefully tucked the quilt under Marcia's chin."

Max whined. "I don't feel good."

"Edna'll make you some milk toast."

"I ain't hungry. Stay here, Ma."

For several days Lucy remained with the children. When they were quiet she dozed in her chair. Neighbors came to the door with soup for the sick children and hot food for the rest of the family. Invariably tears filled Lucy's eyes as she thanked the Casadys, Brimleys, Nicholsons and her relatives the Colborn cousins for their thoughfulness. The neighborhood men took turns doing the milking and feeding the animals.

Dr. Randall had stopped to check on the children. He seemed satisfied with Max's improvement, but Marcia was losing ground. As he prepared to leave, the doctor said, "Put mustard plaster on her chest but watch you don't blister her. The fever's still at 103 degrees. It's lasting too long." He paused. "She has pneumonia, I'm afraid."

"Oh, God, no!" Lucy cried, wringing her hands. "Can't you do something?"

Marcia's deep tearing cough rang through the house. Gloomily the three girls sat listening at the kitchen table, tears streaming down their faces.

Dr. Randall took Lucy's hand. "Mrs. Avery, I'm doing everything I know," he said helplessly. "She's in God's hands." He turned. "I'll be back tomorrow." He closed the door against the cold northwest wind.

All that night Lucy walked the floor, from bedroom to kitchen to bedroom. She was unable to rest, even when Marcia was quiet. In spite of occasional spells of wheezing and coughing, Max slept. Accustomed to Marcia's feeble crying and her racking cough, he was undisturbed.

At breakfast the next morning Gertrude said hopefully, "Maybe the rest of us won't get it."

Lucy, deep in thought, didn't reply. Most of the time she seemed aware only of her sick children and of their calls for her. In spite of her size, she got up quickly at Max's shout.

Edna smiled. "He's better. He'll 'bout run Ma ragged."

"I wish we could all go to school, "Lute complained. "There's nothing to do."

About eleven o'clock the rhythmic jingle of sleigh bells brought the girls to the kitchen window. A cutter containing a well bundled couple turned into the yard.

"Grandma and Grandpa Avery!" Gertrude shouted as Lute rushed to call her mother. Edna was at the door before the cutter stopped.

Jonas, his white beard blowing over his shoulder, tied the bay mare to the hitching post. The jingling sleigh bells on the horse quieted to a tinkle. The old man helped Marcia from the cutter.

Edna shouted from the doorway. "You can't come in! We're quarantined!"

Without missing a step the old couple continued toward the house. "'Twill take more than a red sign on the door to keep us out!" Jonas shouted. He held his wife's arm as they came up the icy steps.

Inside, the grandparents embraced each of the girls. Lucy, her face drawn, sobbed as her mother-in-law kissed her. "I'm so glad you came. We don't know what to do. Marcia - our - little Marcia has double pneumonia. I'm afraid we're going to lose her."

Tall and white-haired, Grandmother Marcia removed her black bonnet and long coat. She said softly, "We came as soon as we heard. You shouldn't be alone at a time like this."

Jonas muttered, "Jim should be here with you. I don't know what's wrong with him."

"Now that we're here," Marcia said, "we'll care for the children. You look worn out." She went to the bedroom followed by Lucy and Jonas.

Max shouted a greeting from the darkened bedroom. "I'm better! My rash is gone but my skin's peelin' off."

Jonas chuckled. "That's scarlet fever for you." He made his way to the baby's crib where Lucy and his wife stood.

"She's - she doesn't know us," Marcia whispered. The sound of the little girl's irregular, labored breathing tore at their hearts.

"If we could only _do_ something." Lucy whispered. "She's been burning up with fever for days. She don't call for me anymore." She wiped her eyes on her apron.

Max said softly, "Is she gonna die?"

His grandmother replied, "We'll pray for her, and if it's God's will, she'll get better."

Max slid down in bed and silently covered his

head with the wedding-ring quilt. Jonas, Marcia and Lucy knelt beside the little crib. For fifteen minutes they prayed for the baby's recovery. When they rose from their knees, Marcia said, "Lucy, we'll stay with the children. You go out in the other room."

Jonas added, "I'll put my horse in the barn. We'll stay here as long as you need us." As he turned away he muttered, "Drat Jim. He should be here."

Lucy wiped her eyes. "I've been bitter and mad all winter 'cause he's left us alone. Maybe God is punishing me."

"We understand your feelings," Marcia said. "Jim's not done right by you."

Later that afternoon Dr. Randall could give them no encouragement about the baby. "She's sinking," he said. Slowly he added, "She's a beautiful child - but sometimes when young children have a high fever for many days, if they recover - they are feeble-minded." Lucy turned away without speaking.

Max had not spoken for hours. He refused to talk and insisted on hiding beneath the covers. In the kitchen Dr. Randall said to Lucy, "You'd better put the boy on the couch in the dining room. 'Tisn't good for him to see his little sister - like this."

The atmosphere in the home was heavy with gloom and the dread of what lay ahead. Neighbors and relatives stopped to inquire, to bring food and to volunteer help. Lucy's cousins, Albert Colborn and Tommy Dillingham, neighbors John Casady, George Harris, the Brimleys, Hempsteads and Snapps, all called. Lucy was overwhelmed by their kindness.

The hours passed slowly, minute by minute, as Jonas and Marcia sat and prayed over their dying granddaughter. Lucy dozed, exhausted, her head on her arms on the kitchen table until 3 a.m. She was wakened by Marcia's hand on her shoulder.

"Come," the older woman said softly. "She's

going very soon."

Lucy tried to swallow the lump in her throat. She followed her mother-in-law to the baby's crib. They were there only a minute when the rasping, rattling breathing paused, then stopped.

Lucy seized the body of her youngest child and clasped it to her breast. "Ma's baby," she sobbed. "Why has God taken you away? My oldest and youngest babies - gone." She suddenly seemed aware of Jonas' and Marcia's presence. "Leave me with her. I want to rock her one last time."

Marcia brushed Lucy's cheek with a kiss. "Yes, dear. We understand." She sighed. "Life is a bittersweet trail from beginning to end." They went out leaving Lucy to mourn over her dead baby.

After an hour she came from the bedroom and silently went to the couch where Max slept. She uncovered his face and stroked his forehead until he opened his eyes. "What - what's the matter?" he asked.

"Our baby's gone to heaven, Maxie. You're the man of the house. Your father and brothers ain't here. You're the man of the house."

Max choked back a sob. "I don't want to be a man. I - I - I just want to be your little boy. I don't want to be a man!"

Neither of them spoke for a time. Finally Max said, "Will God do something bad to me because I didn't like Marcia? I wanted to be your baby, but you held her all the time." He was seized with a sudden spell of wheezing.

"God won't punish a little boy for the way he feels. Now you're my baby <u>and</u> the man of the house." He dove beneath the covers where he remained until morning.

Immediately after the little girl's death Jonas went to Jim's shop where he fashioned a tiny coffin from oak boards. After the family ate a small breakfast, Marcia and Edna lined the coffin with a length of pale yellow material which Lucy had saved for something special.

As she bathed and dressed her child a last time, Lucy's face was set in a frozen, mask-like expression. She seemed oblivious to anything but her dead baby. Finally the tiny body was dressed in last summer's light green dress, and the auburn curls brushed before she was placed in the little coffin.

Jonas, Marcia, Lucy, Edna, Lute and Gertrude gathered around the baby's body. Only Max was absent, his head buried beneath the quilts.

Marcia went to him and tried to pull the covers away from his face. "Come, Maxie, Grandma wants you to tell the baby goodbye," she whispered.

"No!" he shouted. "Let me alone! I don't want to see her!"

Jonas whispered, "Let him be." He paused. "I'll sit with him while the rest of you go to the cemetery," he said softly.

By two o'clock the yard was filled with cutters and sleighs of relatives, neighbors and friends who would accompany the tiny child to her final resting place in the old family cemetery. Because of the danger of contagion, no service was held in the home, though Lucy's minister, Reverend Josiah Williams, accompanied them to the cemetery where he conducted a brief graveside service. As he uttered the familiar words, "Ashes to ashes, and dust to dust," a gust of wind hurled icy pellets into their faces.

Sad, miserable and cold, the family returned home. No one talked, each one occupied with his or her own thoughts.

When the children were in bed that evening, Marcia said, "Lucy, will you write Jim and Otis?"

"I guess so."

Jonas remarked, "They won't get it for weeks, maybe not until Jim goes into Minot to start home in April."

"Don't matter," Lucy said dully. "He can't do anything." She hesitated. "I'll write Linn, too."

Marcia brushed back a wisp of white hair. "'Tis

hard now, but it's good you're busy. And you have the girls and Max."

After a long pause Lucy said, "My men folks all leave me - Jim - my two boys -" Tears stood in her eyes.

"'Tis the Avery disposition, Lucy," Jonas replied. "We're all alike."

Marcia said, "'Tis only the men. Our girls aren't affected." Changing the subject, she said, "Lucy did you know Lilla Dale has had a childrens' book published? It's called, 'Making Home Happy,' and she's working on a second one that she'll call 'Making Home Peaceful.'"

Lucy didn't answer, but Marcia continued, "She's a good school teacher. Looks like she loves being with other folks' children because she doesn't have any of her own."

Deep in thought, Lucy made no response. Finally she said, "The Averys all talk about the men having itchy feet. They have more than itchy feet. They have bad lungs. Two of my babies died because of it. And Father Avery, your sister Melissa - consumption took her. My Maxie, he has the wheezes, and so does Lute. I think Gertie may get it too, the way she coughs sometimes. And Father Avery, you have it too. Jim calls it the 'Avery curse.'"

Jonas nodded. "We all carry it in our blood and pass it on to our children."

For two weeks Jonas and Marcia remained with Lucy until Dr. Randall said the danger of the three girls contracting scarlet fever had passed. Marcia and Lucy washed and boiled the sheets, towels and clothing that had been used by the sick children during their illness.

As they prepared to leave for home in Newberg, Lucy said, "It was good of you to stay with us while I buried my baby. 'Tain't likely I'll have another." Her hand rested on Maxie's shoulder. "This is my baby now, and the only man in the house."

Max stamped his foot. "I ain't no man, Ma! I

don't never want to get big!"

Jonas studied the angry little face. "Why not?"

"'Cause big folks have too many things to worry 'em. Their young'uns die, er they ain't got no money, er they have to work hard -"

"Max," his grandmother said, "You can't stay a baby. It's God's way that children grow up and learn to face life, even if it is a long, long, bittersweet trail."

Jonas smiled. "I wonder how many times you've used that expression - the bittersweet trail?"

"You're laughing at me - but it says it all." She kissed Lucy. "We'll pray for you and hope the time will pass quickly until Jim is home again." Standing with her arm about Lucy's shoulder she added, "You're a good mother to the children, dear, and you've been a good wife to Jim."

"Thank you, Mother Avery." Tears streamed down her face.

Jonas cleared his throat. "I want to say I agree with Marcia. Jim is lucky to have a wife like you. I've changed my mind - I was wrong. We're both glad you are his wife."

"It means so much that you've told me," Lucy sobbed.

The old couple went to the cutter and Jonas placed a heated soapstone on the floor for Marcia to rest her feet upon. He spread a wool blanket across their laps and clucked to the bay mare. As she broke into a trot, the sleigh bells jingled merrily. They waved and Lucy and Max watched until they were out of sight. He whined, "Rock me, Ma."

They settled into the old rocker in front of the dining room window. "Sing, Ma," he begged.

"I can't sing. There's a lump in my throat."

"You wish I was Marcia."

"I wish I had both of you."

Max sat upright on Lucy's ample lap. "I don't! I'm glad she's gone!"

"Sh-h-h. Don't say such things. It's a sin to

feel that way about your sister."

He jumped down, yelling, "I don't care! I'm glad she's dead!"

Lucy's eyes filled with tears. What was she going to do with Max?

A week later he returned to school. The big farmhouse was quiet and lonely when all the children were at school. Lucy tried to keep busy with barn chores and housework. She read some of Jim's books, but astronomy and the Seventh Day Adventist material didn't hold her interest. She pondered over her marriage. She and Jim had had so many disagreements - in fact, there were few things they agreed about. They both had tempers which flared easily. Had she driven him away by her tirades when he planned to go to Dakota? He'd said, "At least, 'twill be peaceful there."

And she didn't have much patience with the girls. As soon as they were old enough, they'd get married and leave, too. Max was the only one that really wanted to stay with her - and something was wrong that he should be so jealous of poor little dead Marcia. She'd try to give him all the love he thought he'd been denied. She would make it up to him.

Lucy wiped her eyes on her apron. She and Jim were a team pulling in opposite directions - they were pulling against one another. Was it her fault? She was an uneducated half-breed Indian. Jim had been attracted to her beauty - but that was gone now. He should have married an educated lady. But - it was too late for that - they were married for life, and they'd have to make the best of it.

The days passed slowly. Lucy mourned for Marcia, but when Max was with her she lavished him with attention. One evening Gertrude said angrily, "I'm here too, Ma, but you only like Max!"

"Hark!" Lucy exclaimed. "Max is sick. Surely you ain't jealous a' your sick brother." The boy smirked as he looked at his sister. He wheezed loudly.

On a rainy day near the end of April Jim Colborn's rig stopped in the drive. Someone was with him. Jim! Jim was home! In spite of her size, Lucy dashed down the steps through the rain toward the buggy.

As Jim and Lucy rushed to embrace, her brother called, "See what I brought you from town?"

Jim's only suit was wrinkled from the long train journey and his gray streaked hair and beard needed trimming, but his blue eyes sparkled as he looked at his wife. "I'm glad to be home," he said simply. After seizing his grip from the buggy box while he thanked his brother-in-law for the ride home, Lucy and Jim hurried into the house. Inside the door, they embraced again.

"The young'uns at school?" Jim inquired.

Lucy nodded. "Max is wheezin' bad, but he went this morning."

Jim glanced around. "Where's Marcia? Sleeping?"

Lucy gasped. "You - you don't know?"

Jim's eyes were wide with concern. "Know what?"

"About -" Lucy choked back a sob. "About Marcia? Didn't you get my letter?"

"I had one early in February. That's all. Lucy! What's happened?"

"Marcia's dead."

The carved mantel clock ticked loudly in the sudden silence. Speechless, Jim dropped into the old rocker. Lucy stared outside at the rain. She swallowed. "Marcia and Max had scarlet fever. She got pneumonia, just like Charley."

Jim buried his head in his hands. "Oh God. The Avery curse again - little Marcia - my mother's namesake -"

They grieved silently. After a time he said, "You faced it alone. I should have been here."

She nodded. "I was mad and bitter 'cause you was gone. Sometimes I wonder if God punished me for my bad feelings by taking our baby - and - and - you know Max never did like Marcia. He - he says he's glad she's dead." She wiped her eyes on her handkerchief. "I don't know what to do. He's my baby now."

"He's 'most eight years old. Did you bury Marcia beside little Charley?"

"Yeah. Your Ma and Pa was with us. We talked about the Durfee Cemetery, but I wanted her beside Charley and my Ma and Pa."

"You did right." After a time he repeated, "I should have been here."

"How's Ote?" Lucy asked. "Ain't he comin' home?"

"He's going to put out as much spring wheat as he can. Then next winter he'll get a job clerking in a store in town. He don't want to spend another winter on the land. It's a desolate place in winter. I don't think we'll see him in Michigan much anymore."

Lucy rubbed her forehead. "Our big boys are gone."

"How are the girls?" Jim asked.

"All right. I - I have to know, Jim. Are you going back to Dakota this fall?"

"Well," he paused, "I had planned to. But, my place is here."

A faint smile crossed her face. "I ain't been easy to live with. I'll try to watch what I say. Did I drive you away with my sharp tongue?"

"We both have our faults. We don't like the same things. Our tempers flare. Let's both try to make our home a better place for the children."

For three weeks Jim plowed and worked his land. The oats were planted and part of the corn ground was plowed. Lucy and the girls gardened. By night everyone was exhausted. Jim religiously kept Saturday, his Sabbath, and to Lucy, it seemed, he saved disagreeable jobs until Sunday.

Over Sunday dinner Lucy brought up the subject. "Reverend Williams preached a good sermon today, but the church windows was open and you was spreading manure in the field 'cross the road.

Nobody could keep their mind on the sermon 'cause of the stink."

Jim grinned. "Should 'ave closed the windows."

"You didn't have to spread manure so close to the church! You've got the whole field!"

"I'll spread manure on my land any place and any time I want! No Methodist preacher can tell me where and when to work!"

Max jumped up from the table. "Stop yellin' at Ma! We didn't have nobody to yell at us when you was gone!" He ran to lean against his mother.

Jim's eyes blazed. "Young fellow, you need to be straightened out! You're not going to talk to me like you do to your mother!" He got up and seized the boy's arm. "Another outburst like that and I'll whip you! Understand?"

Max pulled away and seized his mother's arm. Lucy got up to face her husband. "Let him alone! The child is sick!" Max immediately began wheezing and coughing.

The three girls stared silently at their plates as the argument continued.

Jim shouted, "You're making a baby of him. A sniveling, whining, eight year old baby!"

Lucy went to the kitchen followed by Max. Glancing over her shoulder she said, "I ain't gonna fight with you."

Silently Jim and the girls finished dinner.

That evening as they sat alone on the front porch in the dusk Jim said, "I've been thinking. Looks like we're back to our old ways."

Lucy didn't answer, but he continued, "We can't change. Maybe we don't want to. It's like the leopard can't change his spots." He hesitated. "I remember 'way back when you were a young girl. Ben teased you one day when we were threshing at Dillinghams. You put him in his place in a hurry. I liked your spunk. You're still the same - and so am I." He laughed. "I guess we deserve one another."

She put her hand on his arm. "I know I'm touchy, but it bothers me when you pitch onto Max.

He's our littlest one."

"But you're spoiling him. Can't you see it?"

"I'm giving him the love he missed when he was little and Marcia was born. He was shoved away, he thinks. I'm trying to make it up to him."

Jim was silent. Finally he said, "Ma is right. Life's a bittersweet trail." He took Lucy's hand. "But, in spite of our differences, we'll walk that long trail to the end together, won't we?"

She squeezed his hand and smiled. "Yeah, together."

*****

EPILOGUE

In early July of 1925 Lucy Avery suffered a massive stroke. Her daughters, Lute Harris and Gertrude Klein cared for her in the family home for several weeks. During this time Jim became ill with pneumonia.

On August 16th at 11:45 p.m., Lucy Avery died. Though Jim was desperately ill he sensed that his wife had died for as Gertrude sat by his side he gasped, "Ma's gone." Gertrude nodded.

He was silent a moment before he whispered, "Now I can go too." He turned to the wall and died a few minutes later.

Lucy and Jim Avery were buried from their home in a double funeral ceremony on August 20th, 1925. They had their wish for they had walked life's bittersweet trail together to the end.

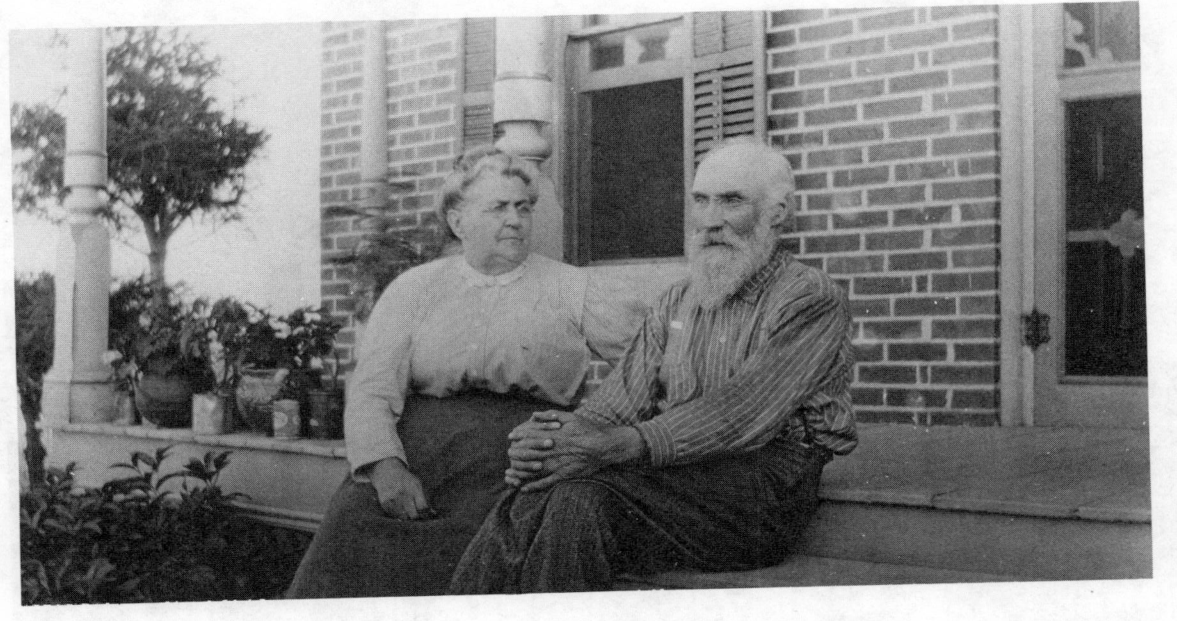

Jim and Lucy Avery in their Later Years

MICHIGAN
REGISTERED
HISTORIC SITE
GREAT FIRE OF 1881
Small fires were burning in the forests of the Thumb, tinder-dry after a long, hot summer, when a gale swept in from the southwest on Sept. 5, 1881. Fanned into an inferno, the fires raged for three days. A million acres were devastated in Sanilac and Huron counties alone. At least 125 persons died, and thousands more were left destitute. The new American Red Cross won support for its prompt aid to the fire victims. This was the first disaster relief furnished by this great organization.

Great Fire of 1881 Marker

BIBLIOGRAPHY

Adams, Roy W. _Peg Leg_. Sherman Printing Company, 1950.

Boening, Mary Lockwood. _Webberville, Yesterday and Today_. Rudnicki Publications, 1970.

Ceasar, Ford Stevens. _Bicentennial History of Ingham County_. 1976.

Coffin and Cohen. _Folklore in America_. Doubleday & Company, 1966.

Cook, Darius B. _Six Months Among Indians_. Published by the Niles Mirror, 1899.

Crittenden, A. Riley. _History of Howell_. Tidings Print, 1911.

Croy, Homer. _Wheels West_. Hastings House Publishers, 1955.

Darling, Birt. _The City in the Forest_. Stratford House, 1950.

Davis, Maggie. _The Far Side of Home_. Macmillan Company, 1963.

Detroit Bicentennial Commission. _Detroit, 1701-1976_.

Detroit Free Press, July 13, 1980. "Sunday Magazine."

Detroit Free Press, May 3, 1981. "Sunday Magazine."

The Detroit News, July 4, 1976. "A Bicentennial Keepsake."

Dickinson, Lulu. A Table in the Wilderness. William B. Eerdmans Publishing Company, 1959.

Dunbar. Michigan. William B. Eerdmans, 1965.

Everts and Abbot. History of Livingston County, Michigan. 1880. A Reproduction, J.B. Lippencott & Co., 1974.

Fasquelle, Ethel Rowan. When Michigan was Young. William B. Eerdmans Publishing Company, 1950.

Hagman, Harlan L. Bright Michigan Morning. Green Oak Press, 1981.

Historical Society of Greater Lansing and Livingston County. Historical Society Topographical Map of the Counties of Ingham and Livingston. 1959, Geil, Harley and Siverd, 1859.

Illinois State Journal. "Souvenir Album of Abraham Lincoln Portraits." Feb. 11, 1959.

Illinois State Journal. "First Draft of Lincoln's Inaugural Address." Feb. 11, 1959.

Kirtland, Caroline. A New Home. G.P. Putnam's Sons, 1953.

May and Brinks. A Michigan Reader, A.D. to 1865. William B. Eerdmans, 1974.

Needham, Walter. A Book of Country Things. The Stephen Green Press, 1965.

Warner and Vanderhill. A Michigan Reader - 1865 to the Present. William B. Eerdmans, 1974.

White, John I. American Vignettes. Travel Vision, 1976.

ABOUT THE AUTHOR

Bernice M. Chappel was born on a farm near Fowlerville, Michigan, on June 4, 1910, where she lived until she graduated from High School in 1927. She attended Eastern Michigan University and University of Michigan where she earned Bachelor of Science and Master's degrees. She served in the public schools of her home state for twenty-nine years, first as a classroom teacher and later as a school social worker.

She has had several adult and juvenile books published. They include:

IN THE PALM OF THE MITTEN
a sequel to BITTERSWEET TRAIL.

LISTENING AND LEARNING
a book designed to develop
listening skills in children.

A TIME FOR LEARNING
a self-instructional handbook
for parents and teachers.

HARVEY HOPPER
a series of three juvenile books.

RUDOLPH, THE ROOSTER
a juvenile book.

Since her retirement, Bernice M. Chappel has visited nearly every country in North and Central America, several in South America, most of the Asian countries, including Siberia, and a few European countries. She remains an inveterate traveler with a passion for remote places and peoples.

Great Lakes Books
P.O. Box 164
Brighton, MI 48116

___Autographed

Books by Bernice M. Chappel

BITTERSWEET TRAIL
___ Hardcover $15.95
___ Paperback $9.95

IN THE PALM OF THE MITTEN
___ Paperback $7.95

(Please add $1.00 per copy to cover postage and handling.)

Please send me ___ copies of ____ and
___ copies of ____
I am enclosing check or money order for $________________

Mr./Mrs./Miss ____
Address ____
City ______________________________ State _______________ Zip ____________

Please Cut Along Dotted Line

Great Lakes Books
P.O. Box 164
Brighton, MI 48116

___Autographed

Books by Bernice M. Chappel

BITTERSWEET TRAIL
___ Hardcover $15.95
___ Paperback $9.95

IN THE PALM OF THE MITTEN
___ Paperback $7.95

(Please add $1.00 per copy to cover postage and handling.)

Please send me ___ copies of ____ and
___ copies of ____
I am enclosing check or money order for $________________

Mr./Mrs./Miss ____
Address ____
City ______________________________ State _______________ Zip ____________

Great Lakes Books
P.O. Box 164
Brighton, MI 48116

___Autographed

Books by Bernice M. Chappel

BITTERSWEET TRAIL
___ Hardcover $15.95
___ Paperback $9.95

IN THE PALM OF THE MITTEN
___ Paperback $7.95

(Please add $1.00 per copy to cover postage and handling.)

Please send me ___ copies of ________________________________ and
___ copies of ________________________________
I am enclosing check or money order for $______________

Mr./Mrs./Miss ________________________________
Address ________________________________
City ______________________ State ____________ Zip __________

Please Cut Along Dotted Line

Great Lakes Books
P.O. Box 164
Brighton, MI 48116

___Autographed

Books by Bernice M. Chappel

BITTERSWEET TRAIL
___ Hardcover $15.95
___ Paperback $9.95

IN THE PALM OF THE MITTEN
___ Paperback $7.95

(Please add $1.00 per copy to cover postage and handling.)

Please send me ___ copies of ________________________________ and
___ copies of ________________________________
I am enclosing check or money order for $______________

Mr./Mrs./Miss ________________________________
Address ________________________________
City ______________________ State ____________ Zip __________